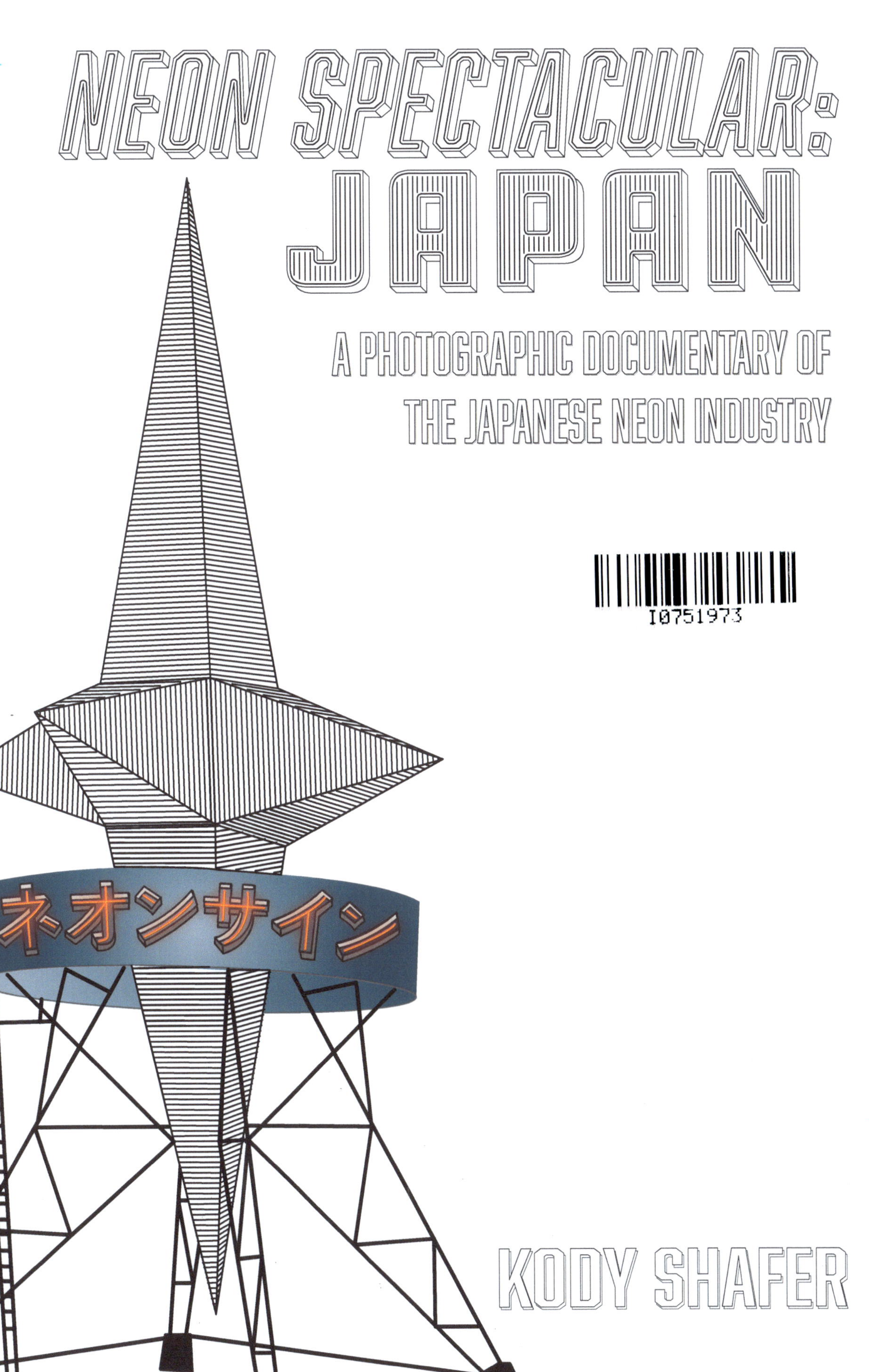
NEON SPECTACULAR:
JAPAN
A PHOTOGRAPHIC DOCUMENTARY OF
THE JAPANESE NEON INDUSTRY
I0751973
ネオンサイン
KODY SHAFER

ISBN: 978-0-578-68997-5

Authored & Published by: Kody Shafer

Contact: neonspectacularjapan@gmail.com

Cover design by Kody Shafer

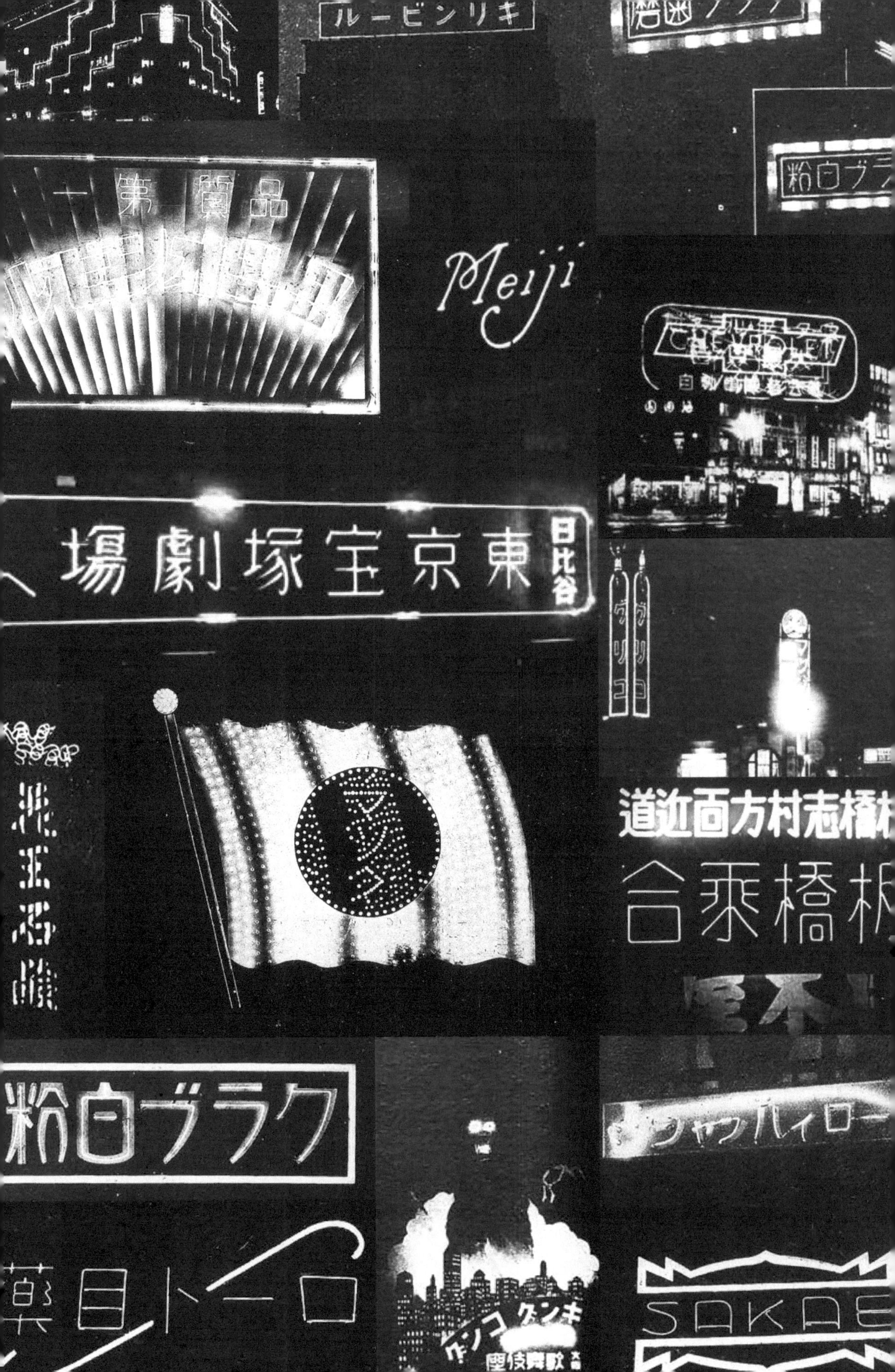

キリンビール
品質第一
Meiji
日比谷
東京宝塚劇場へ
グリコ
グリコ
橋志村方面近道
橋乗合
クラブ白粉
クラブ白粉
ロート目薬
キングコング
歌舞伎座
SAKAE

About the Author

Kody Shafer (b.1994) grew up in Ridgefield, Connecticut. He attended the University of New Mexico, receiving a Bachelors of Business Administration in 2016. During his time in university, he began working at Absolutely Neon, a boutique neon shop along Route 66 in Albuquerque.

After graduating university, he returned to the East Coast to continue working in the neon trade. He began work at the neon shop within Brooklyn Glass, and soon led projects and installations around New York City.

In September 2018, Kody moved to Osaka, Japan to rejoice with his girlfriend from university, whom he has since married. With the intention to learn about the Japanese neon industry, Kody began working at Yoshi's Neon Studio. He worked there until December 2019, when he began working on the Neon Spectacular: Japan project.

After completing this book, Kody plans to return to the United States to continue working in neon design and production.

Contents

Acknowledgments

I couldn't have taken on this project without the kindness and patience of Mr. Yoshihito Yasutomi of Yoshi's Neon Studio. He worked with me as I slowly learned Japanese, and was flexible with my language school schedule. Yoshi-san taught me invaluable lessons that led me to an understanding of the Japanese neon industry.

In addition, I would like to acknowledge the All Japan Neon-sign Association. They were kind enough to allow me access to much of the information in this book.

Also, many thanks to Mr. Yoshiaki Tsukawaki of Asahi Denso Co,.Ltd for his kindness in providing many images used in this project.

Thank you to my great family, in the United States and in Japan. My parents, step-parents, brothers and sisters, Aunt Lisa and Uncle Ricky. Especially my wife, Yui, and her family that always make me feel at home.

A special thanks to Waku Fukui, and his family, for their kindness and support.

Thanks to Robert Randazzo, a great mentor and friend of mine, for his continuous support.

Finally, thank you to everyone who supported the first edition of this book through crowd-funding, especially my good friends. It is because of you that I could take the time to focus on creation of this project.

Preface

This book is intended to document the history and techniques of the Japanese neon industry. A brief understanding of the country's culture, past, and geography provides a foundation for this information. Wartime, recession, and politics put the industry on a roller-coaster of booms and busts. Due to the faith of the people involved, tradition has carried on, allowing the progression of neon spectaculars for nearly a century.

Controversy is expected when discussing history and international relations. I did my best to not go into specifics regarding wars and battles, as the details are not directly relevant to neon and outdoor advertising.

Much of the information in this book has been translated from Japanese books and articles, so it's possible that some information has been taken out of context or mistranslated. I did my best not to make claims that are unverifiable. Many of the stories are from professionals within the industry, but have most likely been subjected to the "telephone game" over many decades.

Whether you're a neon fan or professional, the technical section can be informative. You don't need to comprehend it to understand the meat of this book. In my opinion, the best way to experience this book is to let the photographs guide you, looking back to the text for the details and stories.

Introduction

Neon lights, a key medium for outdoor advertising, has been used since the early 1900s. The bright red glow helped to coin the term "red light district", and has proved to be an invaluable tool for a slew of businesses. Unlike other advertising methods, neon works as a subliminal magnet that lures patrons inside, and has evolved into many other applications over the decades.

As stated by Wolfgang Schivelbush, "Electric lighting transforms the Parisian Boulevard in to open spaces of intimacy…The artificial illumination drew attention to the way music halls, theaters, restaurants, hotels, and department stores". Lighting up the evening streets with colorful signs has a psychological effect on urbanites, it subconsciously moves people around, encouraging socialization, ultimately relieving people of their daily stresses.

Early outdoor advertisers such as Douglas Leigh understood that the bright, colorful light of neon attracted people's attention "like moths to a flame". Leigh is credited as the master of "Neon Spectaculars". He describes them as "oversized advertising displays with neon or lamps in unusual animations". He transformed New York City's Times Square using flamboyant and outlandish designs such as pouring coffee pots and waterfalls. In Leigh's time, it could be argued that the United States was at the top of the neon advertising industry.

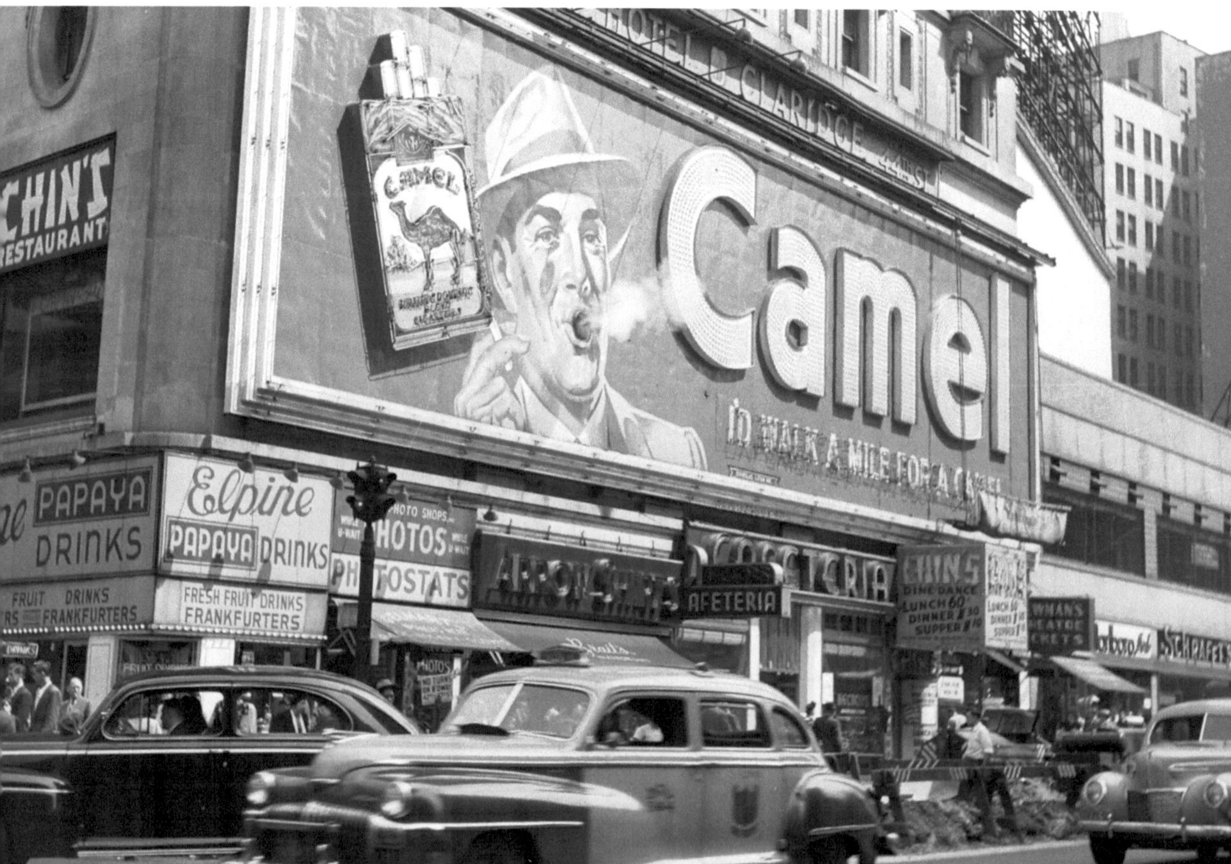

"I'D WALK A MILE FOR A CAMEL", TIMES SQUARE, NEW YORK CITY, 1948

A few decades later, after the recovery from World War II, Japan swiftly worked itself to economic prosperity. As illuminated signs were reconstructed, Japan quickly took the craft to the next level, jumping to a more advanced point than before the war. Soon Japan was known as the world's mecca for neon signage. Whether promoting a beer company, bank, or restaurant, huge neon signs could be seen in abundance along highways, skyscrapers, and train tracks.

Over the years, Japan developed their own production methods, materials, and designs. Stories are told of companies working around the clock, with neon benders working in shifts to meet the large demand. It was not unusual for orders of thousands of neon tubes to be fulfilled in a month's time.

The era of neon spectaculars is now fading away as LED boards take their place. Advertisers find it more convenient to rent a 30 second time slot than make a 10-year commitment for a neon sign. In addition, typhoons seem to get stronger every year, putting older signs into states of disrepair. This has had a dramatic effect on the neon industry Japan once knew, and has driven many companies out of business. Tools and supplies for making neon have gotten harder to find and the number of working neon benders has dwindled. Japan is changing, just like the rest of the world.

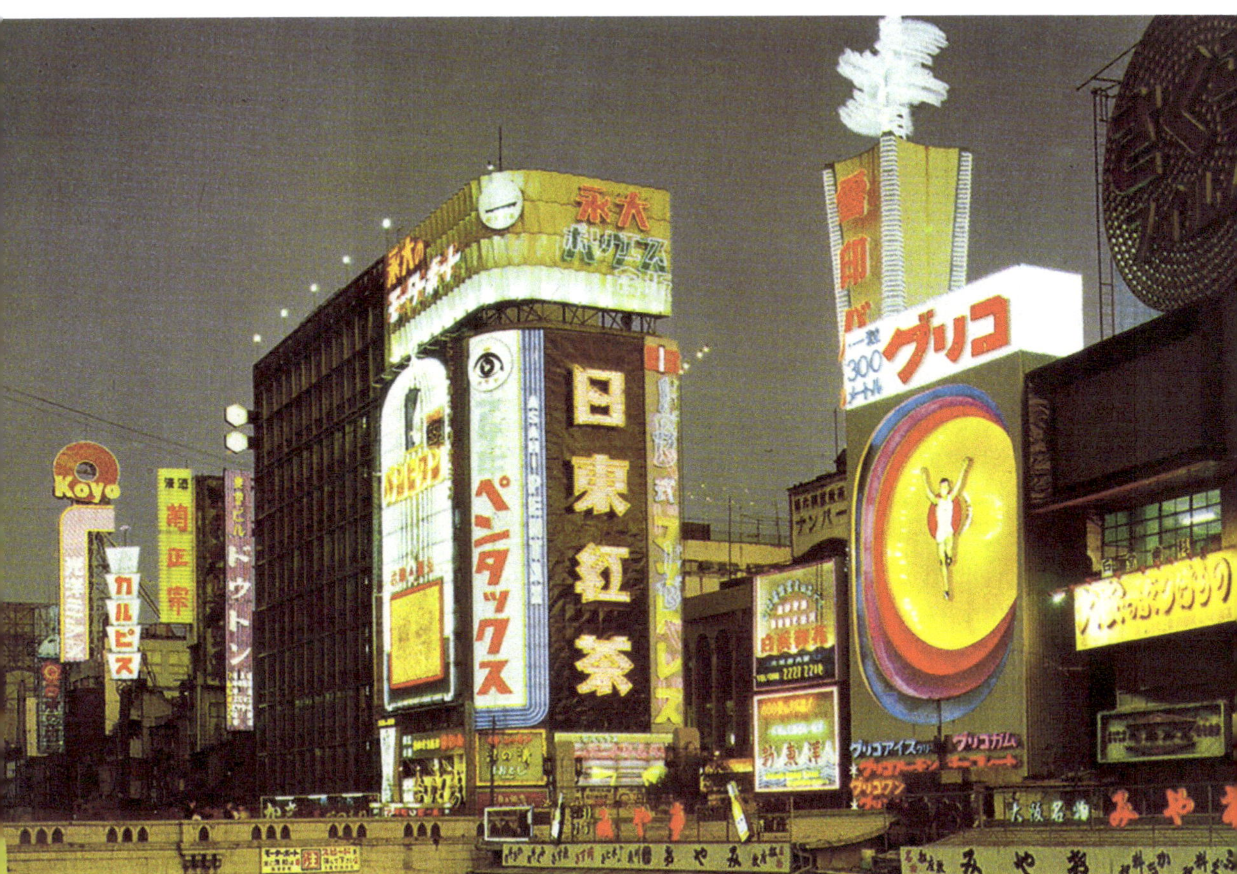

NEON SIGNBOARDS ALONG THE DOTONBORI CANAL, OSAKA, JAPAN, 1964

The Beginning of Neon

What is known as "neon" is a colloquial term for luminous gas discharge tubes, used for commercial lighting, art, and other various applications. The discovery of discharge tubes dates back to 1675, when French astronomer Jean Picard would transport his barometer at night from his observatory. He noticed a glow of light when the barometer shook, the effect of ionizing mercury vapor in a low pressure environment.

A handful of scientists and engineers continued to study the phenomenon of creating light via gas discharge throughout the 19th century. Discoveries of the noble gases, development of vacuum technology, and the findings of magnetic induction were key contributions to the creation of neon lighting.

A number of discharge tubes preceded what we know as the neon tube today. For example, Moore Lamps were known to be some of the first commercially viable discharge tubes, and were installed around the Northeastern United States at the beginning of the 20th century. It is rumored that the first neon sign in America was made for the Ingersoll Watch Company in New York around 1909. The sign was supposedly built as a collaboration between Daniel McFarlan Moore and the Westinghouse Company, and the neon gas was said to be obtained from a professor in Berlin. The Moore Lamp was soon succeeded by the Claude Tube because of increased efficiency and reliability.

By the late 1920s, neon spread around the globe, eventually taking over as the dominant commercial light source. As means of communication were slower, neon makers around the world developed their own techniques, methods, and tools for creating neon signs. A big industry sprung up around neon sign making, with companies such as General Electric and Corning involved with the mass production of neon tube stock. Hundreds of companies specialized in making parts for neon signs such as transformers, porcelain components, wiring, electrodes, and more.

The Pioneers

Michael Faraday (1791-1867)

Faraday is known as one of the most influential scientists in history. He is best known for his work regarding electricity and magnetism, as his research created a foundation for electromagnetic technology. His breakthrough occurred when he wrapped two insulated coils of wire around an iron ring, and found that upon passing a current through one coil, a momentary current was induced in the other coil, a phenomenon known as mutual induction.

His research founded concepts that paved the road towards the development of the electric motor, generator, and high-voltage transformers.

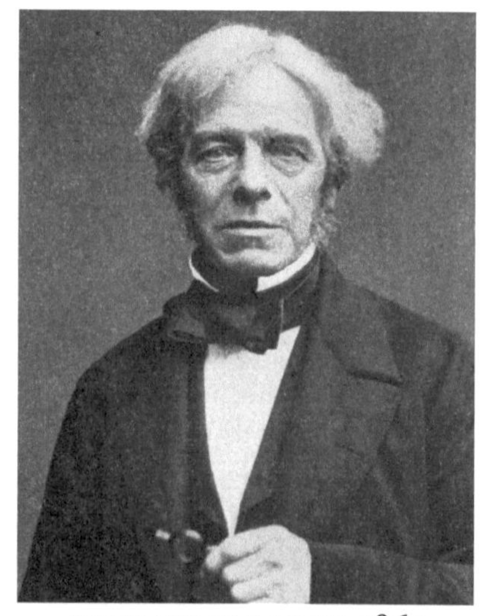

MICHAEL FARADAY, 1861

Heinrich Geissler (1814-1879)

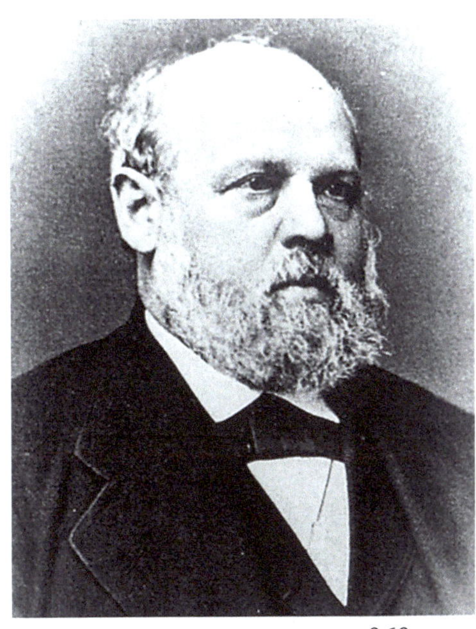

HEINRICH GEISSLER, ~1868

Born in Germany, Geissler was a highly skilled glassblower by trade, as he was forced to work in his family's glass shop from the age of five. Geissler is known as one of the main pioneers in the creation of a practical discharge lamp. He experiments included attaching electrodes to both ends of a glass tube, reducing the internal pressure to a partial vacuum, and applying high voltage. He would vary the types of gases and pressures, and would send his tubes to researchers such as Faraday and Crookes for experimentation, which led to a handful of scientific discoveries.

In addition, Geissler invented a hand-crank mercury pump, which removed the air from glass tubes, producing a superior vacuum. The mercury pump was an indispensable device for vacuum tube production.

Geissler tubes were also used for entertainment throughout the 1800s and eventually evolved into novelty lighting after the turn of the century. Although these tubes were not a huge commercial success, Geissler's work developed into the foundation of the amplifying vacuum tube, used for long distance radio and television communications.

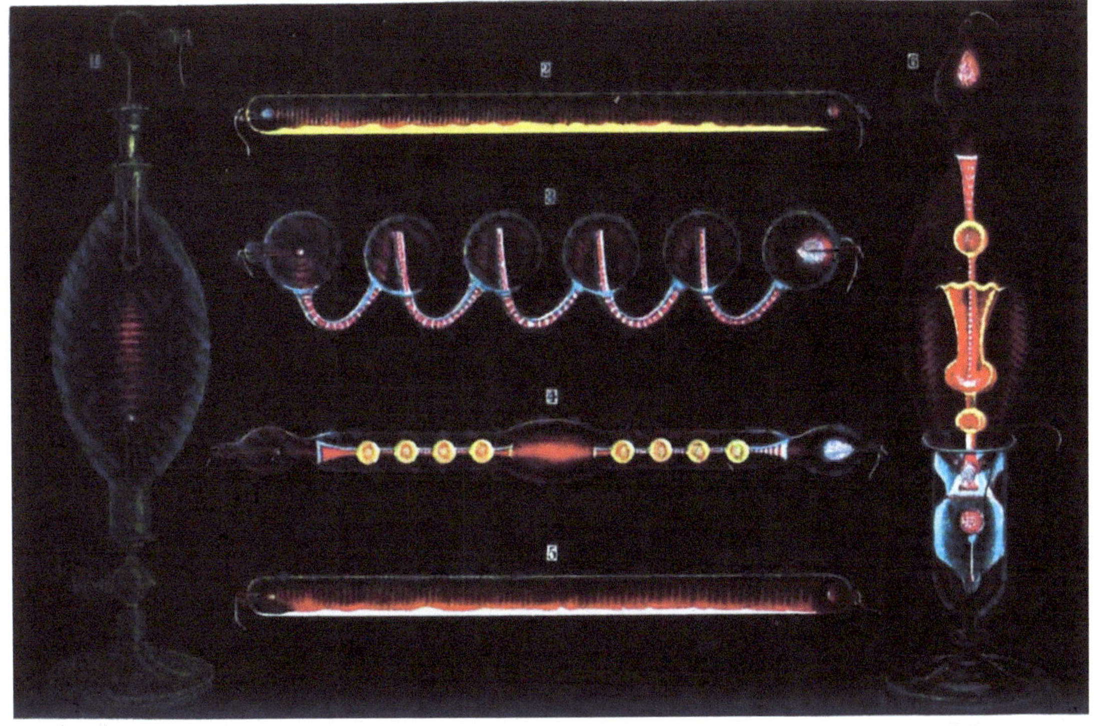

COLOR DRAWINGS OF GEISSLER TUBES, LIT BY AN INDUCTION COIL, 1869

William Crookes (1832-1919)

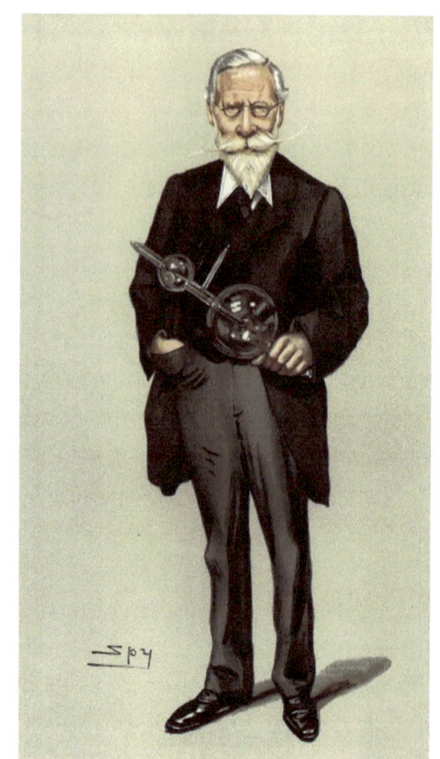

WILLIAM CROOKES, 1902

Working off of the Geissler Tube, Crookes pioneered the construction and use of vacuum tubes for the study of physical phenomena. His work in this field led to many discoveries that challenged past theories of chemistry and physics. He was one of the first scientists to study and speak of the fourth state of matter, plasma.

The first practical use for the Crookes Tube was discovered around the beginning of the 20th century, as it was discovered that x-rays were generated while applying about 5000 volts to the tube. The tube was then mass-produced for x-ray use for about 20 years until it was superseded by a hot-cathode x-ray tube. Crookes had a handful of other discoveries and inventions, including the 100% ultraviolet blocking sunglass lens, and lenses to protect the eyes of glass-workers.

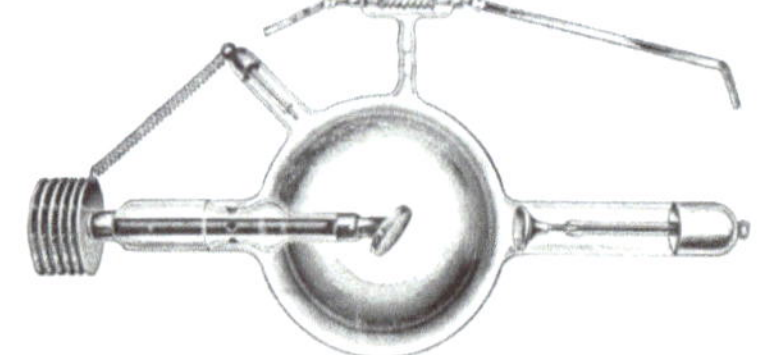

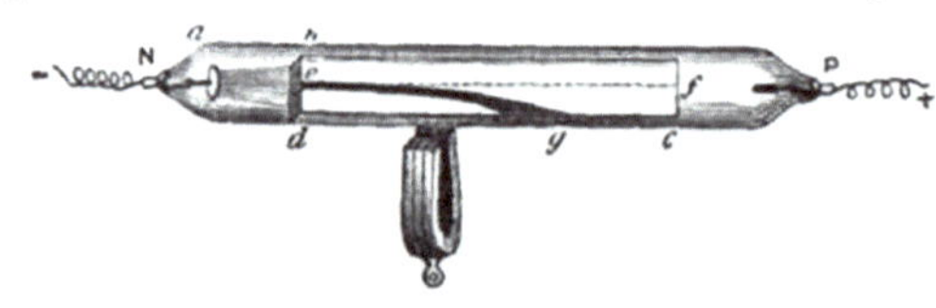

CROOKES X-RAY TUBE AND MAGNETIC DEFLECTION TUBE

William Ramsay (1852-1916)

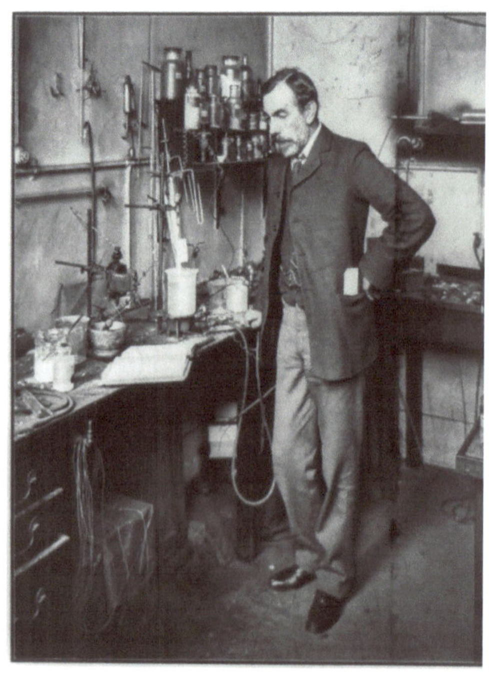

RAMSAY IN HIS LABORATORY, 1904

A Scottish chemist who received the Noble Award in 1904, Ramsay played a main role in the discovery of most of the noble gases in the atmosphere following William Crookes. He first characterized argon, naming it after the Greek word for "lazy". Then with the help of Morris W. Travers, they discovered neon, krypton, and xenon while distilling liquid air.

The discovery of these inert gases was a crucial finding that has contributed a great deal to science and industry. Argon, an inert and heavy gas, has a great number of applications. Uses for argon include medical implements, welding, lighting, and product packaging.

Daniel McFarlan Moore (1869-1936)

With the experience of working under Thomas Edison at the United Edison Manufacturing Company, Moore had the opportunity to experiment creating light from glow discharges. He eventually left the company to start his own business, where he manufactured the Moore lamp.

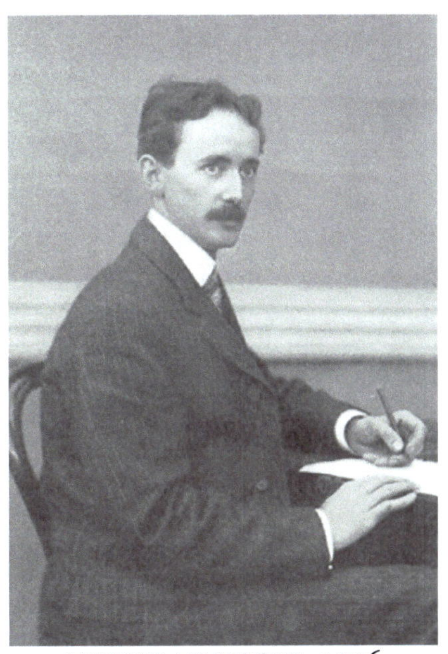

MCFARLAN MOORE, 1906

At first, the Moore lamp used nitrogen or carbon dioxide inside the tube, which gave off a white light. The Moore lamp used high voltage electricity, and yielded about 10 lumens per watt. Moore's lamp was the predecessor to the Claude's invention. It was the first commercially viable discharge lamp, and was used in multiple applications around New York and New Jersey.

On June 15, 1936, at the age of 67, Moore was shot to death on the lawn of his home in East Orange, New Jersey, by an unemployed inventor who became enraged after finding that an invention he filed for was already the subject of a patent granted to Moore.

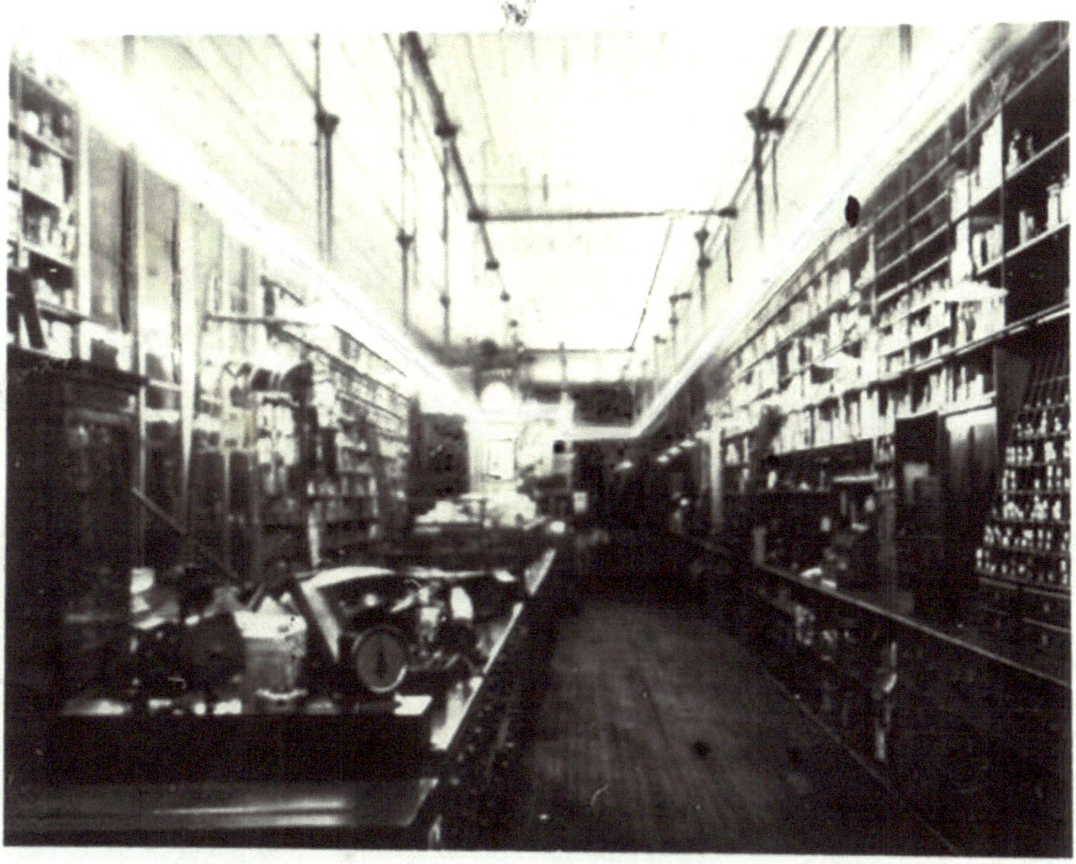

HARDWARE STORE USING MOORE LAMPS IN NEWARK, NEW JERSEY, 1904

George Claude. (1870-1960)

Claude's introduction to neon occurred while conducting experiments to produce high-quality oxygen for hospitals and industrial uses. The by-product of his expiriment included a variety of inert gases, including neon. Claude noticed that a neon gas-filled tube, ionized with high voltage electricity, produces a bright red glow. He then succeeded in making a blue glow using argon gas and mercury vapor.

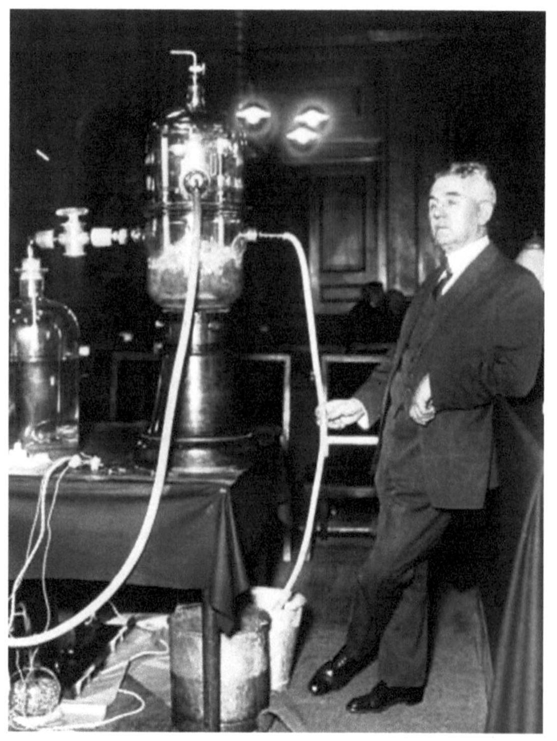

GEORGE CLAUDE CONDUCTING A DEMONSTRATION ON OCEAN THERMAL ENERGY CONVERSION

By 1910, The Claude Neon Company was born in Paris. The development of Claude's tubes continued as he moved into the US market. He filed multiple patents on the system to purify neon gas effectively, the design of an effective cold cathode electrode, and an adjustable neon transformer. Claude provided licenses to neon shops around the world, operating as a franchise system, until the key patents expired in 1932. As of 1927, 611 of about 750 neon signs in New York were produced by The Claude Neon Company.

Claude left a bad impression on the world, as he was extremely litigious. He was quick to file legal action against those who came anywhere close to using his patented technology. During the occupation of France during World War II, Claude supported the German collaboration, and was eventually arrested for his participation with the Axis Powers. He was sentenced to life imprisonment, though was released in 1950.

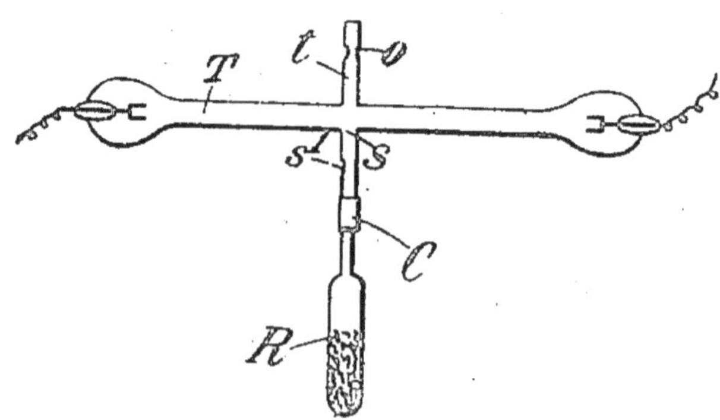

CLAUDE'S PATENT FOR VACUUM DISCHARGE TUBES FOR LIGHTING PURPOSES WAS GRANTED IN 1915 (US1131910)

The Physics of Neon Lights

Light

The light of a neon tube is produced by a process called ionization. It's the same reaction that takes place during a lightning strike. When a sufficient electrical charge excites molecules of gas, it sparks a chain reaction of electron rearrangement. Once ionized, particles assume a negative or positive charge, and speed toward the oppositely charged electrode. The particles collide with other molecules, causing the release of electrons. The output of the loss of an electron from a molecule is in the form of light. This reaction transitions the noble gas into the fourth state of matter, known as plasma. This reaction continues to occur as long as the conditions permit. Once the power is turned off, recombination occurs, transitioning the plasma back into a gaseous state.

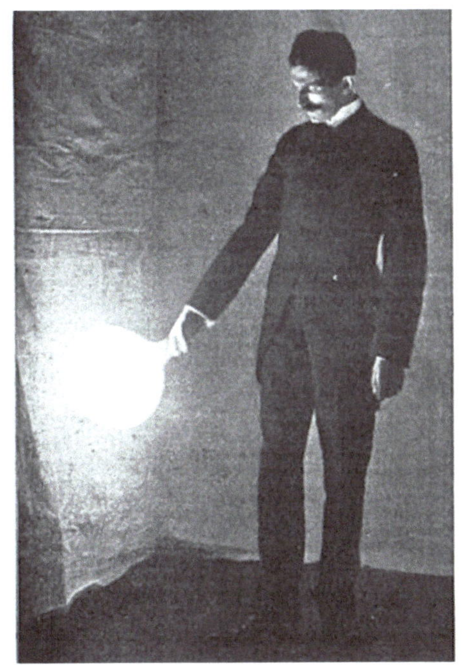

NIKOLA TESLA LIGHTING A BULB BY HIGH-FREQUENCY TRANSMISSION

A tube's brightness depends on the electrical current being supplied by the transformer, the gas in use, and diameter of the tube. An increased current will speed up electron flow, creating a brighter glow. Small diameter tubes provide more resistance for electron flow, which also creates a greater light output. Outdoor signs in cold climates typically use a greater operating current transformer (60mA), as argon+mercury tubes tend to run dim in low temperatures. Neon gas shines bright regardless of temperature, so an increased operating current isn't necessary.

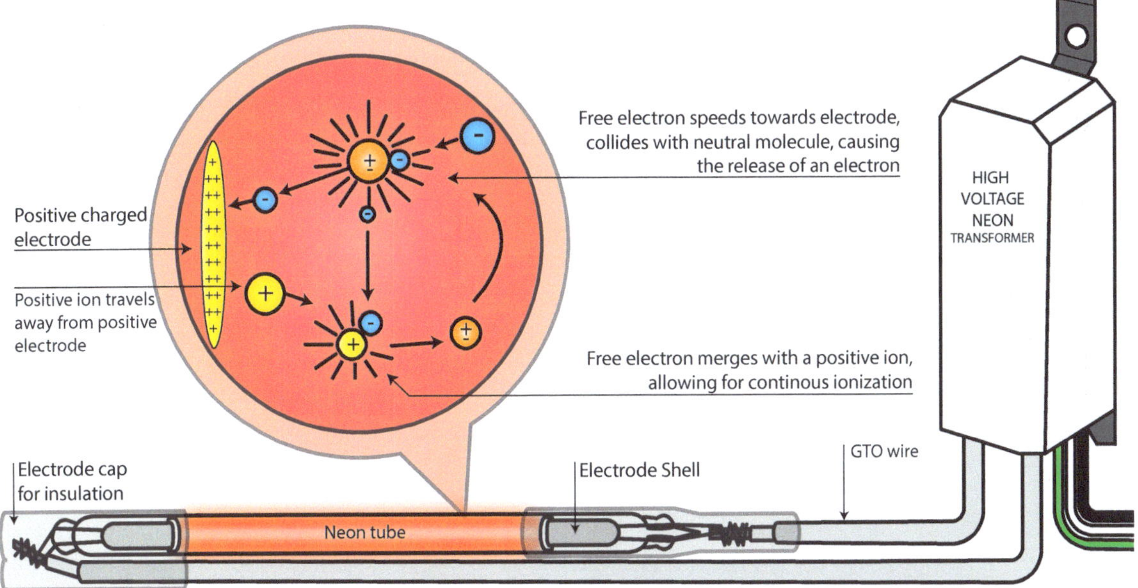

Electricity

High voltage electricity starts the process of ionization within the tube. The amount of voltage required is based on the inside diameter, total length of tubing in the circuit, and the gas used. Smaller diameter and longer tubes require more voltage, as there is more resistance to electron flow. In addition, neon gas requires higher voltage compared to argon+mercury tubes.

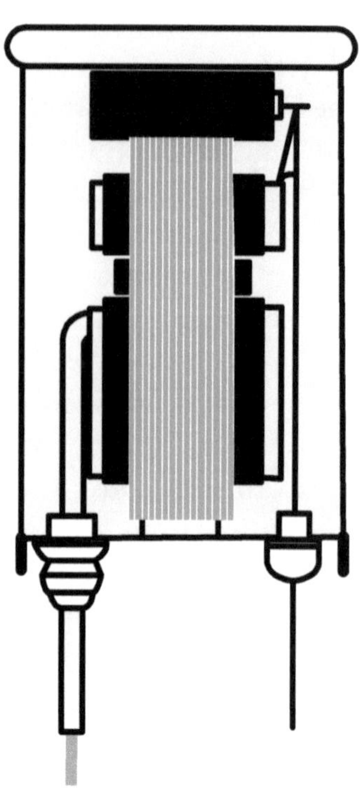

X-RAY OF A CONVENTIONAL NEON TRANSFORMER

Neon transformers are used to supply adequate voltage to light a tube. They operate on the principles discovered by Michael Faraday. Conventional transformers consist of wound copper wire in stages. They are known to be very reliable, but are heavy and bulky. Electronic transformers are a somewhat recent innovation, and are much lighter and more compact. They operate using a series of components, including rectifiers, transistors, and inverters to create a high frequency charge. Neon transformers are typically rated from 1,000-15,000 volts, and a current rating of 15 milliampere to 60 milliampere.

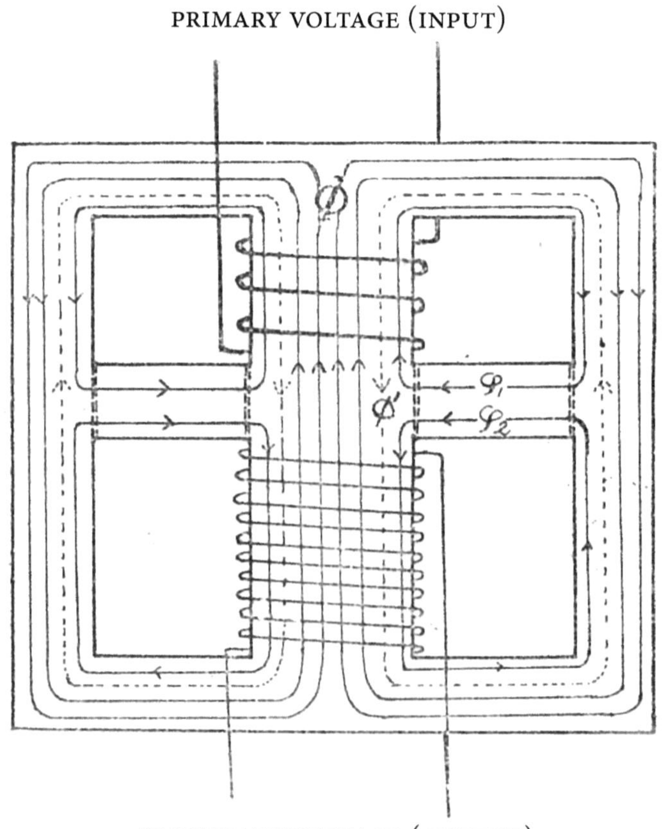

Color

Color is strategically used on advertisements to evoke feelings about products and brands. Red hues tend to elicit excitement and action, popular among alcohol and entertainment companies. Whites and blues represent tranquility and comfort, and are frequently used among baby products, health services, and medicines. It was important to develop the wide range of colors for neon tubes to maximize their efficiency for advertising.

The combination of gas, glass, and fluorescent coatings contribute to create the dozens of colors used in neon lighting. Gas discharges emit various wavelengths, the light from the discharge then filters through the glass, and the ultraviolet radiation excites the colored phosphor coating.

Glass

Neon tubing comes in a variety of colors and sizes. Tubes generally range from five to thirty millimeters in diameter, and typically measure about 1500mm in length (about five feet). Today's standard neon tube is clear, lead-free glass.

Glass tubing made from colored glass is known as "classic glass". These colors include ruby red, novial gold, citrus orange, cobalt blue, emerald green, and a few others. The colored glass acts as a filter to change the color of the light discharge. Colored glass tubing made up the original spectrum of neon colors before phosphor technology was introduced. Classic glass is considerably more expensive than standard glass.

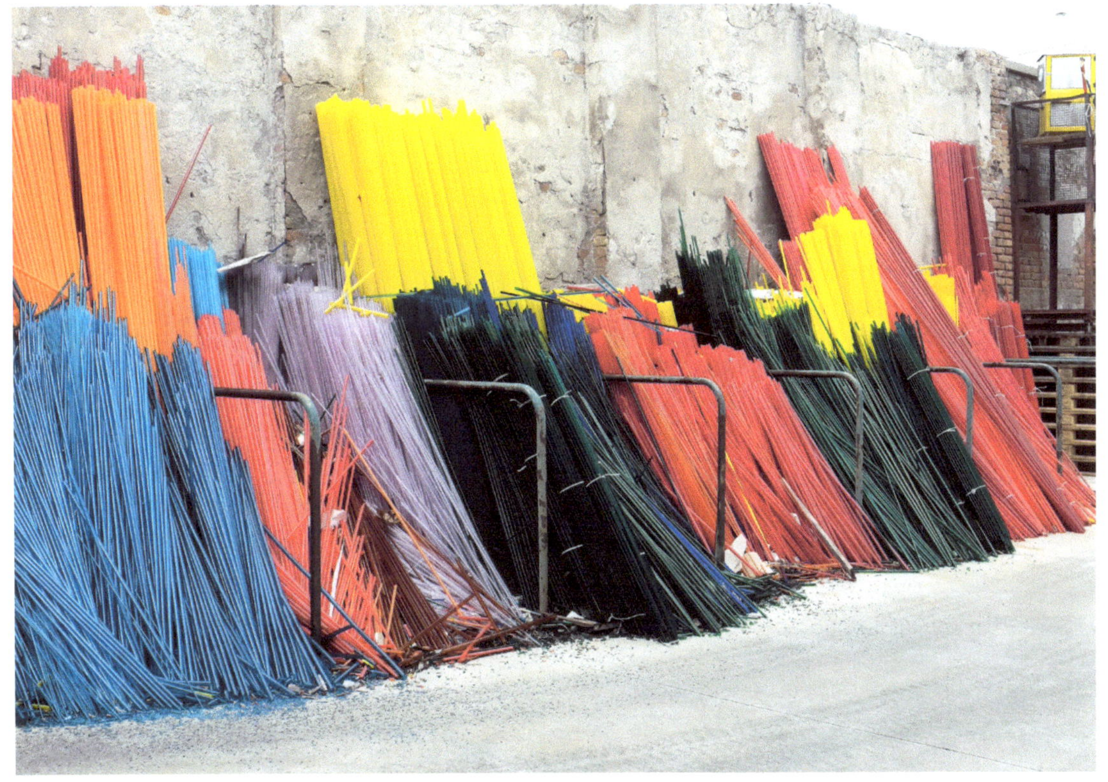

SCRAP CLASSIC GLASS TUBES AT A PRODUCTION FURNACE IN MURANO, ITALY

Gas

Each gas generates a unique color depending on its atomic structure. For example, neon gas gives off the signature bright red glow. Argon gas gives off a faint purple glow. When mercury is added, usually with argon, bright blue light and intense ultraviolet rays are produced (UV radiation is then filtered out by the glass). Neon and argon+mercury are the most common gases found in commercial neon signs. Other noble gases, such as helium, krypton, and xenon are sometimes used in artwork or industrial applications.

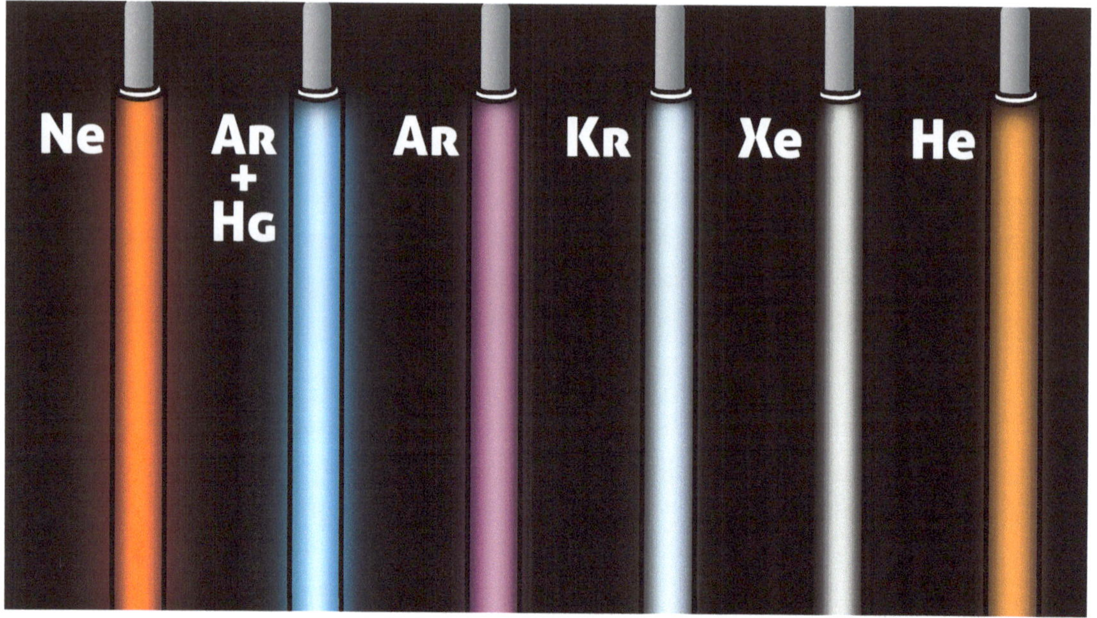

COLOR SPECTRUM OF SELECT GAS DISCHARGES

Fluorescent Phosphors

Some neon tubes have an inner coating of phosphor powder. The neon industry used developments in phosphor technologies from the fluorescent lighting and television tube industry, greatly increasing the available color range. Phosphor coatings allow for colors such as whites, greens, blues, and yellows. Typically, argon+mercury is used for phosphor coated tube, as the mercury vapor discharge produces ultraviolet radiation, which converts to visible light by the fluorescent coating.

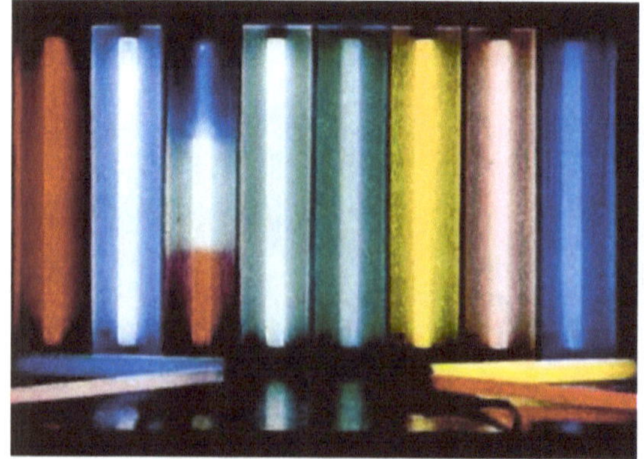

FLUORESCENT TUBE LAMPS AT THE WESTINGHOUSE LAMP DIVISION, 1944

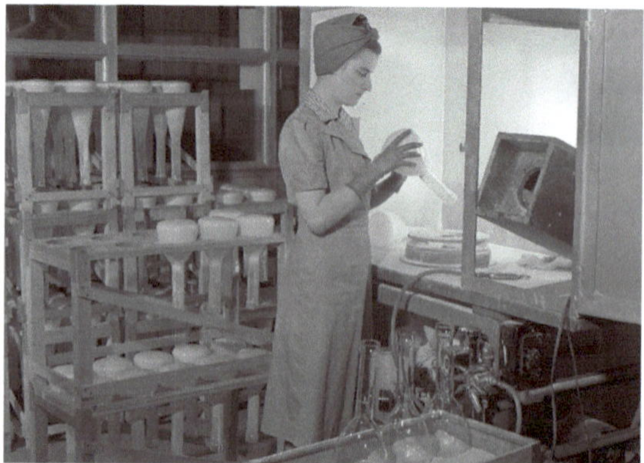

CATHODE RAY TUBES BEING COATED FOR RADIO NAVIGATION SYSTEMS

The Process

Preparation

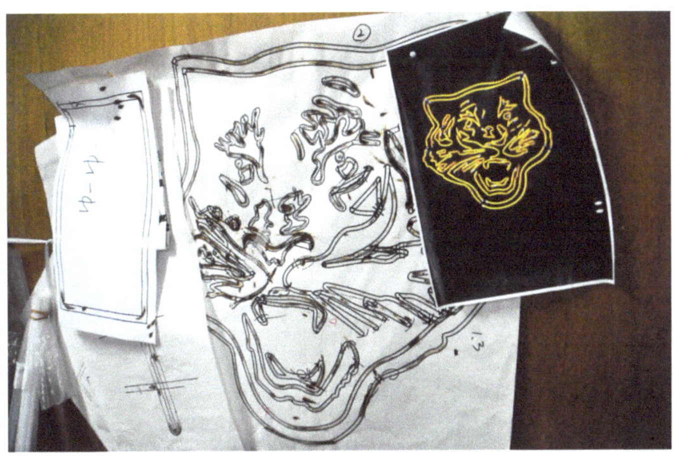

BENDING PATTERNS GET CHARRED BY HOT GLASS

The first step to producing a neon sign after the design is creation of a bending layout. The layouts are usually reversed horizontally to keep the neon in the correct orientation. Layouts are typically created using a computer program or drawn by hand. When remaking a broken tube, the glass can be pieced together, and traced directly onto paper.

Many neon makers claim that the layout is the most important step of the process, as layouts that are hard to follow often affect the quality of the finished product. Details such as tube diameter, color, electrode type, and other notes are written down on the layout for the neon bender to reference. The glass bender should collect the materials prior to starting to avoid interruptions.

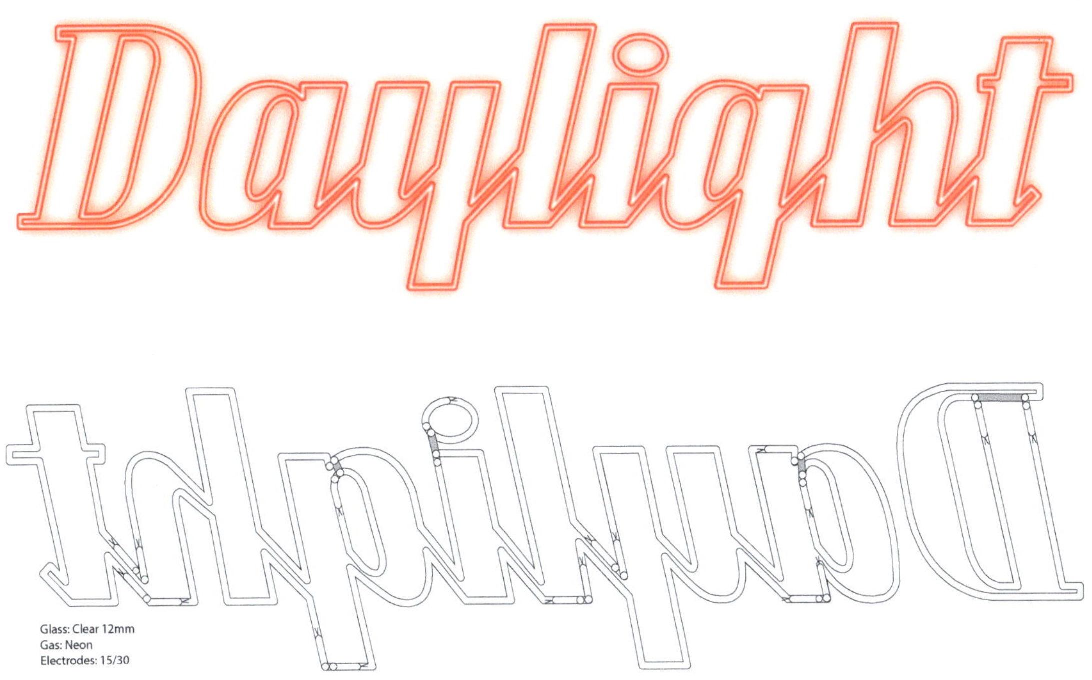

A NEON SIGN RENDERING AND A BENDING LAYOUT

Bending Glass

The neon bender marks the tube with a pencil or soapstone in direct reference to the layout. They proceed to heat the tube in sections, according to the markings. A series of torches are used based on the type of bend being performed. One must figure out the best order to make bends in avoidance of bending oneself "into a corner". The glass can be worked once it reaches the adequate temperature, which varies for each type of glass. Once the tube is bent, the glass is laid on top of the layout, using a layer of transparent metal screen or mica to prevent the hot glass from burning the paper. The bender must do their best to stay within the lines of the layout, while making strong bends.

STEP 1: HEAT THE GLASS TO A WORKABLE TEMPERATURE

STEP 2: BEND THE GLASS

STEP 3: REMOVE THE GLASS FROM THE FIRE AND BLOW OUT THE BEND

STEP 4: PUT GLASS ON THE LAYOUT AND QUICKLY ADJUST

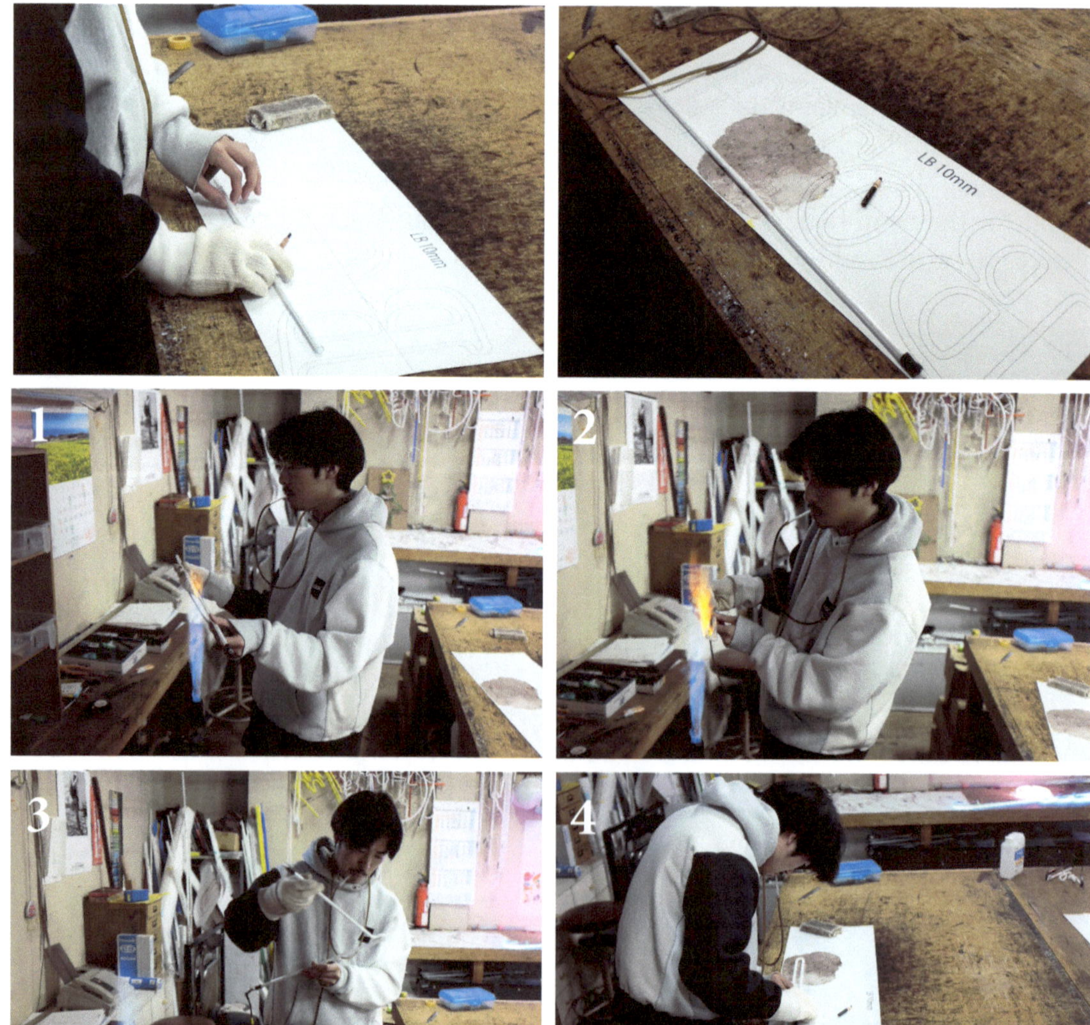

WAKU FUKUI BENDING GLASS

Glass tubes can be cut by scoring the surface with the edge of a file. Sections of glass can be welded together. Small bends tend to cave in while bending, therefor benders usually utilize a blow-hose. This allows the bender to inflate the tube after making a bend or splice, pushing out any collapsed bends while the glass is still hot and formable. The goal is to keep the wall thickness and diameter uniform.

Glass is a temperamental medium. Neon bending requires years of experience to work efficiently. Muscle memory and a feeling for the glass can only be developed by practicing. Neon tubes that are poorly made are highly susceptible to breakage. Ill-preformed welds often contain holes, making it impossible to pump a successful tube.

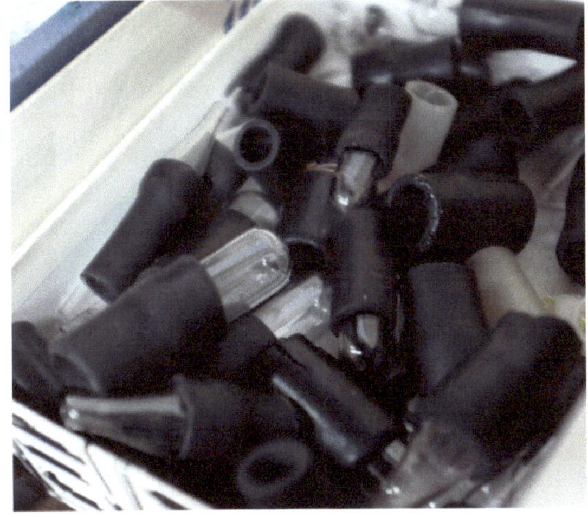

PLUGS MUST BE USED WITH BLOW-HOSE

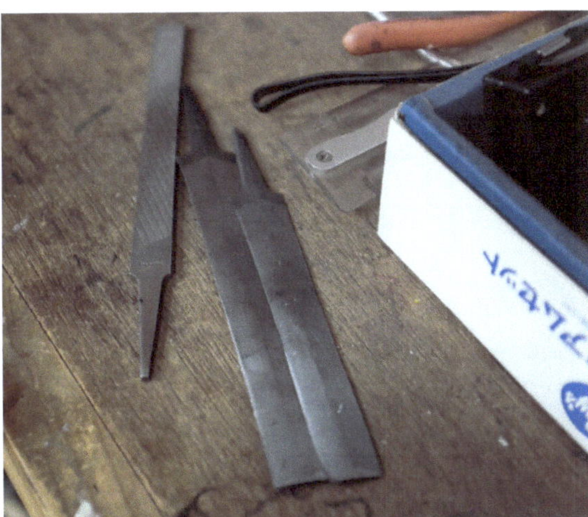

FILES FOR CUTTING GLASS

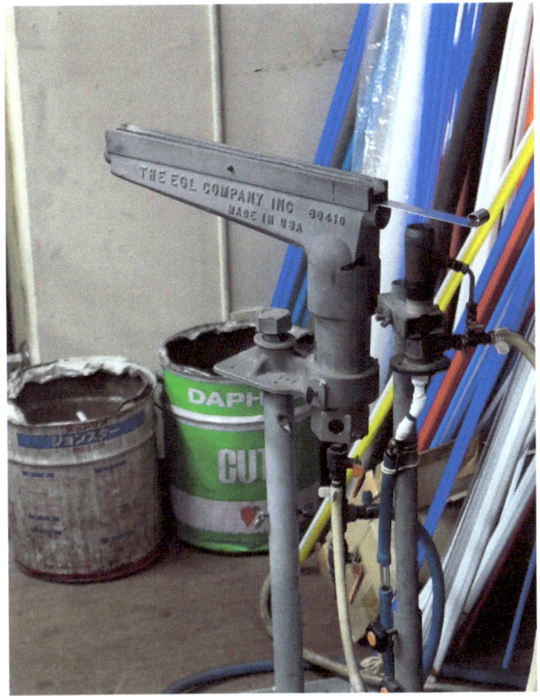

RIBBON BURNER: MOSTLY USED FOR LARGE SWEEPING BENDS

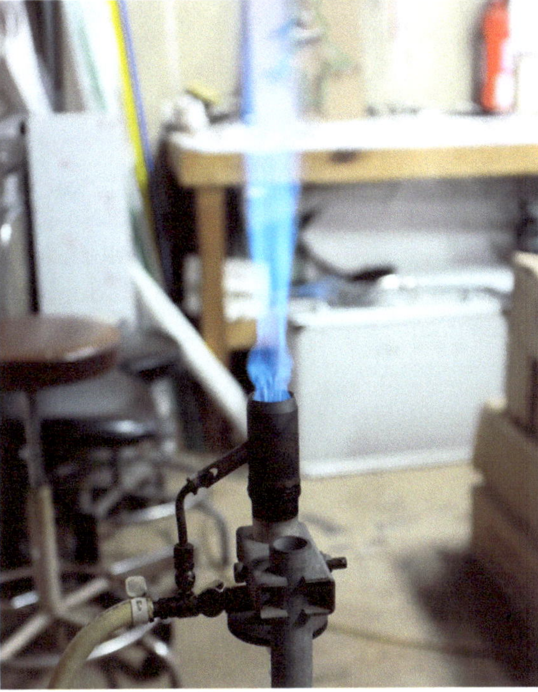

CANNON FIRE: MOSTLY USED FOR SMALLER BENDS AND WELDS

Electrodes and Tubulation

After bending is complete, electrodes are welded on to each end of the tube. A neon electrode is a metal shell within a glass tube, with wires sealed through the glass. The electrodes act as a terminal for the current that runs through the tube. In addition, the electrodes help to absorb any impurities inside of the tube after processing.

After attaching the electrodes, the tube is given a brief inspection for cracks or holes, and is then placed aside for processing. If the tube is an argon+mercury tube, a mercury trap is added to the tubulation. A mercury trap is a glass bubble that keeps the mercury separated from the tube during processing.

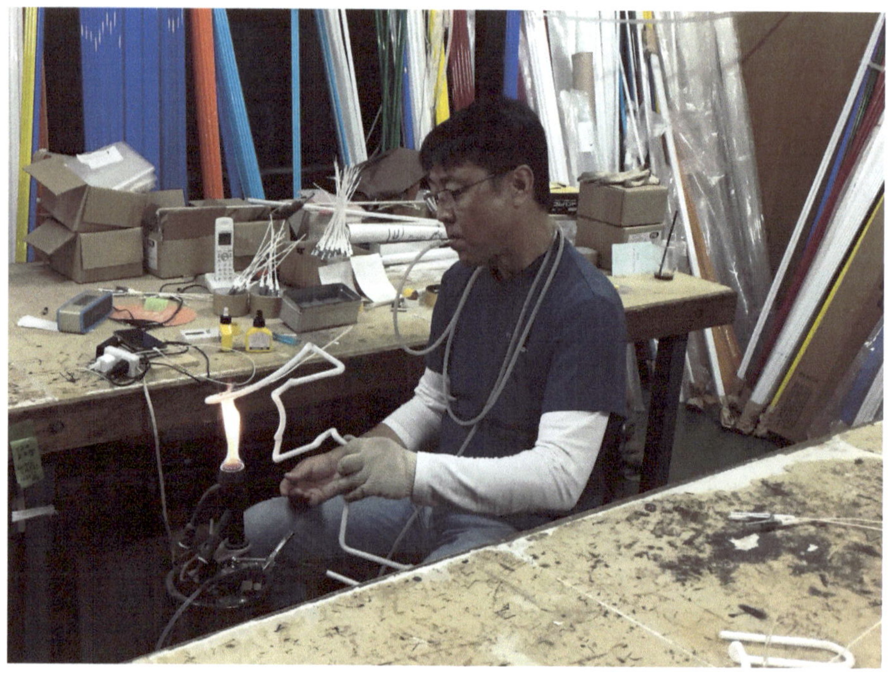

YOSHI-SAN ADDING ELECTRODES TO A NEON TUBE

Tubulation is the term for a small tube that acts as a passageway between the neon unit and the processing manifold. Some electrodes come pre-tubulated, a time-saving convenience for neon makers. If electrodes are not tubulated, the bender must manually add tubulation to the tube by blowing a hole in the glass, and welding it on.

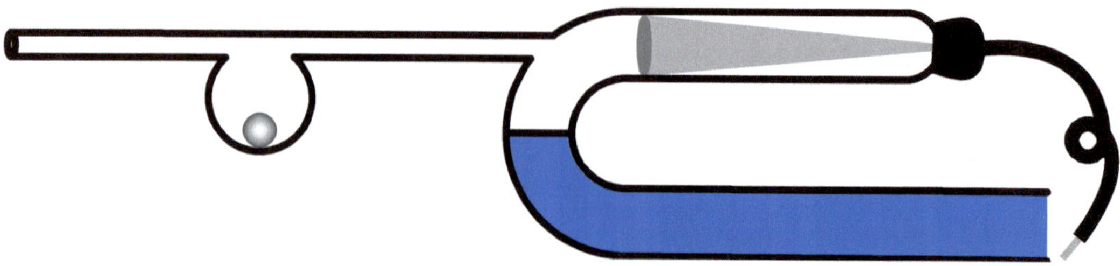

TUBULATION WITH A MERCURY TRAP WELDED TO A NEON TUBE'S ELECTRODE

Steps to Processing

First, the tube is hooked up to the vacuum manifold via tubulation. High voltage leads from the bombarding transformer are clipped onto the electrode wires. The operator will open the main stopcock to evacuate the air inside of the tube, bringing the pressure down to about 2mmHg. (760mmHg is atmospheric pressure).

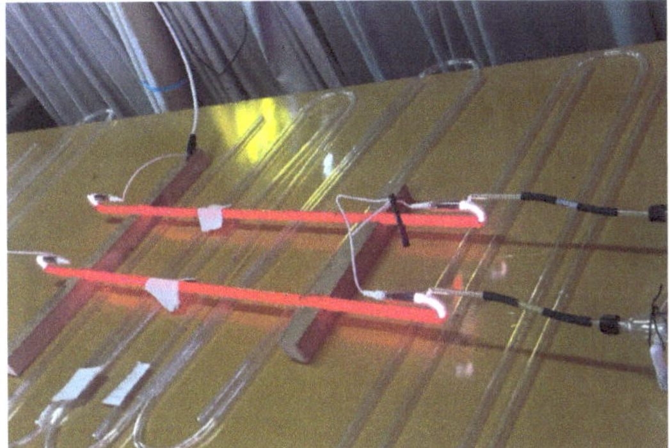

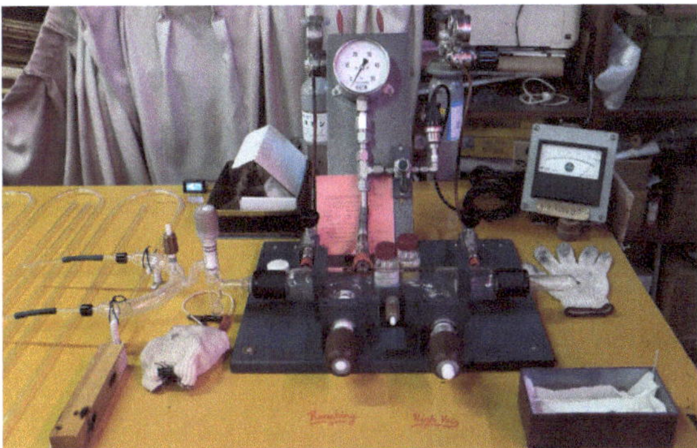

TWO TUBES HOOKED UP TO THE MANIFOLD USING VACUUM HOSE FOR THE CONNECTION

The operator then turns on the bombarding transformer, sending an electrical arc through the tube. This heats the tube, causing a rise in air pressure. The air is routinely evacuated to maintain a somewhat constant pressure. The goal of bombardment is to bring the tube up to 250° Celsius, and to activate the electrodes by getting them red-hot. After the heating is complete, the main stopcock is opened for the final evacuation.

The operator must monitor vacuum levels, temperature, and condition of the tube during this delicate process. A tube can be easily ruined if the operator is not mindful. If the tube is not processing normally, the operator will troubleshoot by reading the gauges and inspecting the tube for cracks or holes.

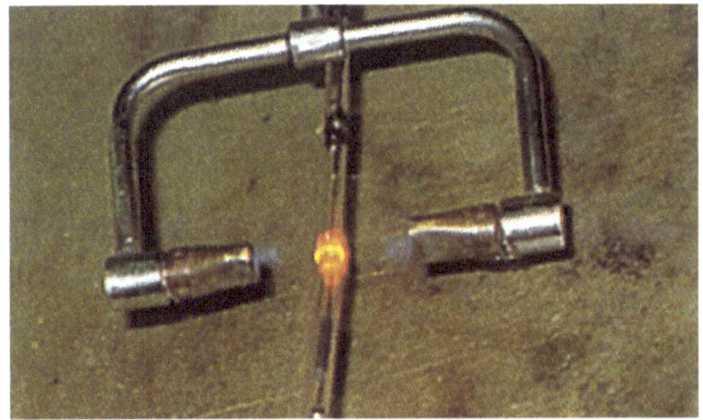

After high vacuum is achieved and the tube has cooled considerably, the operator closes the main stopcock, and administers the inert gas of choice (neon, argon, etc.). A quick flash from the bombarding transformer will show the color of the gas, to hint of the condition of the tube. The tube is then pulled off the manifold by heating up the tubulation with the tipping torch, sealing it off with the mercury trap still attached.

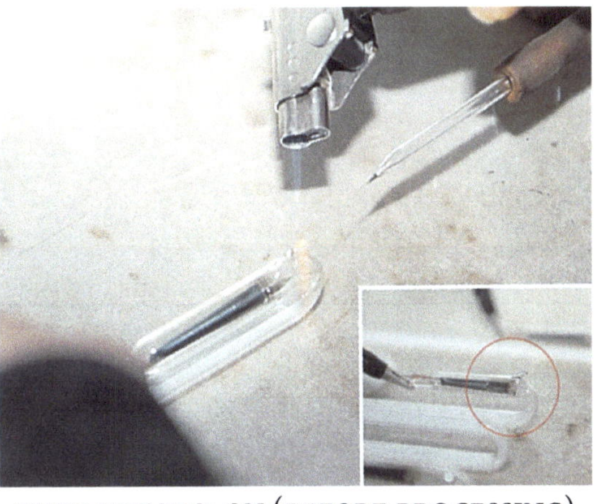

TUBE WELDED ON (BEFORE PROCESSING) AND SEALED OFF OF THE MANIFOLD

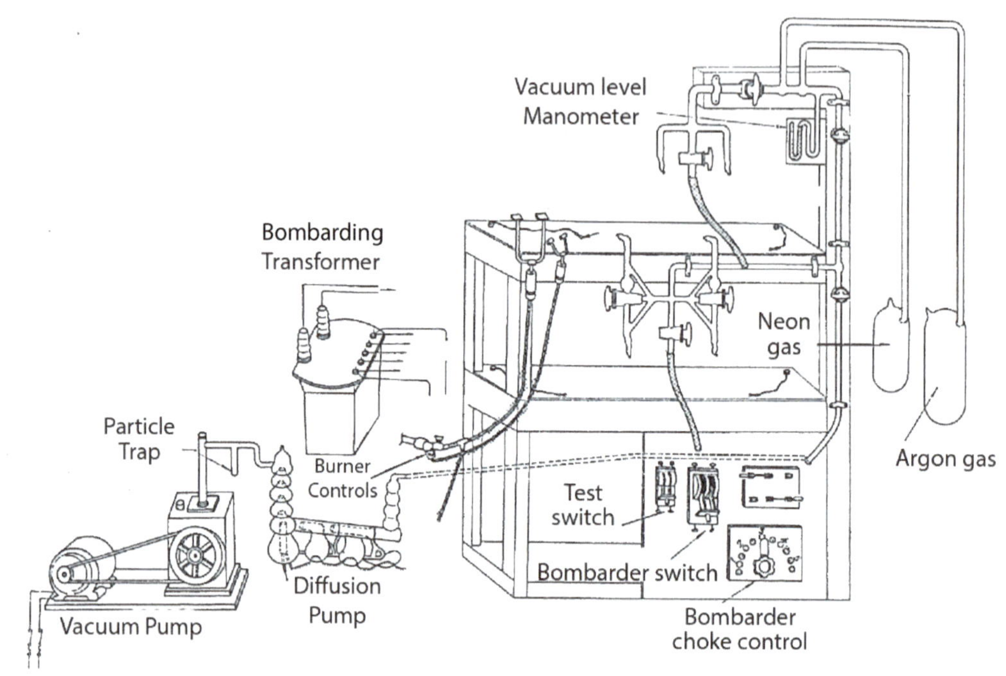

PUMPING STATION DIAGRAM

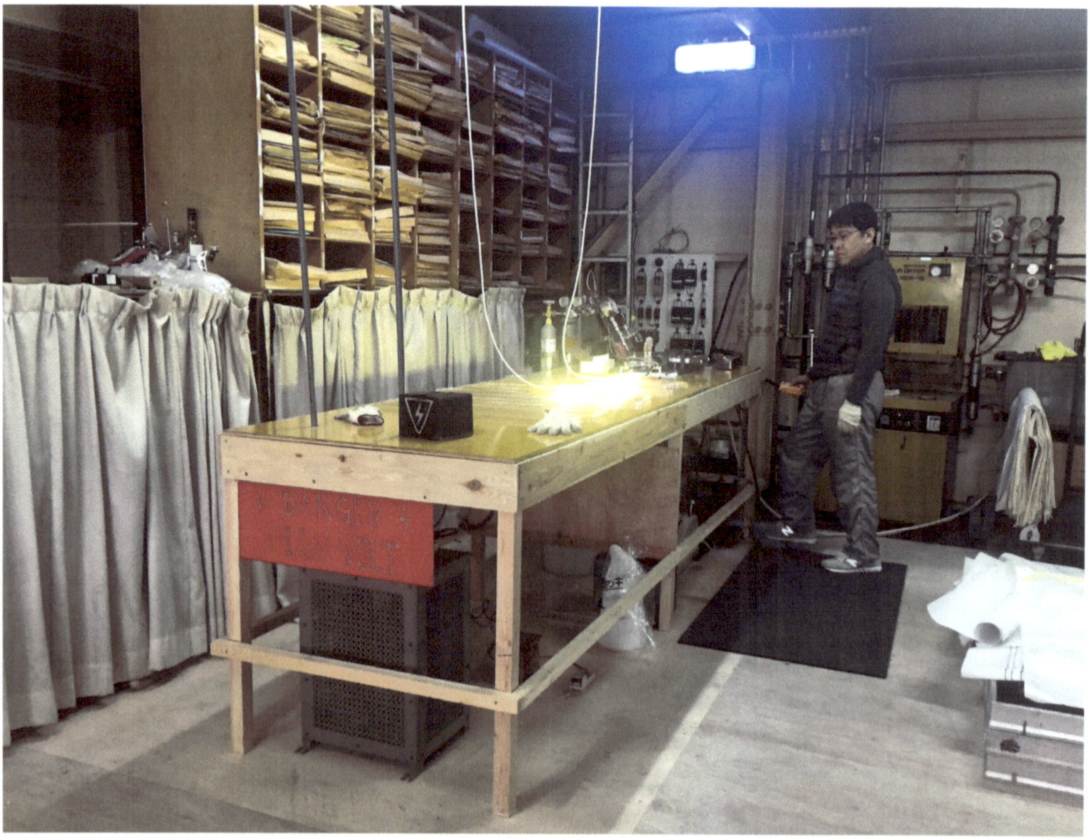

BOMBARDMENT AIDS THE RELEASE OF FOREIGN PARTICLES/IMPURITIES, AS THEY CAUSE PREMATURE FAILURES, OVERHEATING TUBES, AND STAINING.

Aging

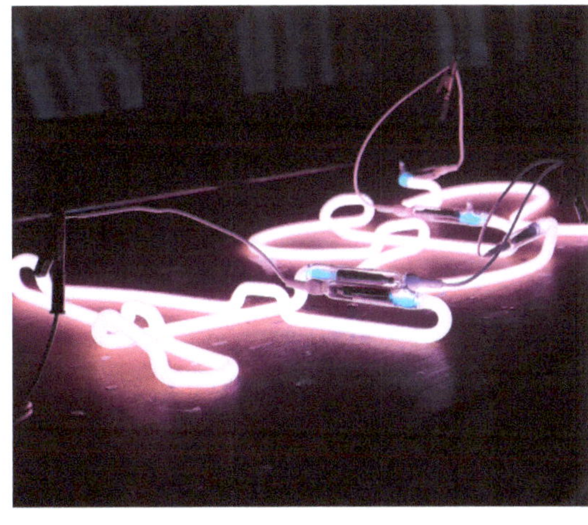

After being sealed off from the manifold, the tube is transferred to the aging table. The tube will be lit for several hours, and passively monitored for discoloration, stains, and high temperature. Hairline cracks or pinholes that went undetected during pumping will often show themselves by changing the color of the gas to a dull peachy color.

If the tube is an argon+mercury tube, and seems to have no issues, the mercury will be dumped into the tube from the trap and rolled around to meet each electrode. The mercury trap will then be sealed off using the tipping torch. The tube is then further aged and brought up to full brightness. Argon+mercury tubes should not be reworked or repaired, as heating up mercury gives off a toxic vapor.

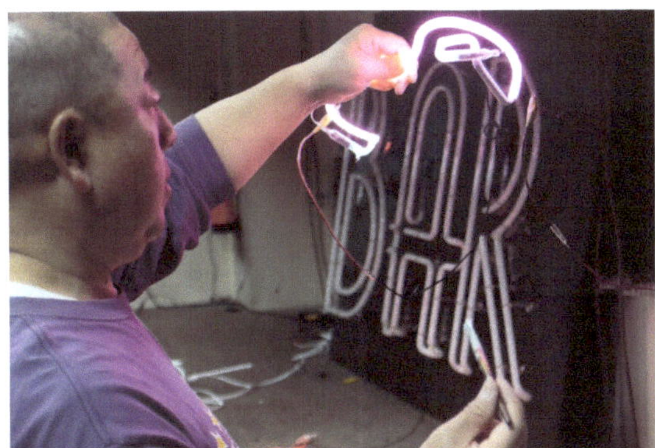

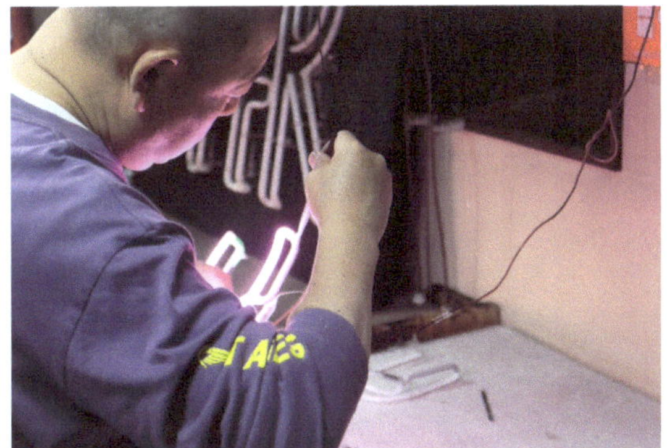

AFTER AGING IS COMPLETE, AN OPAQUE LIGHT BLOCKING PAINT IS APPLIED TO CROSS SECTIONS AND ELECTRODES IN ACCORDING TO THE DESIGN.

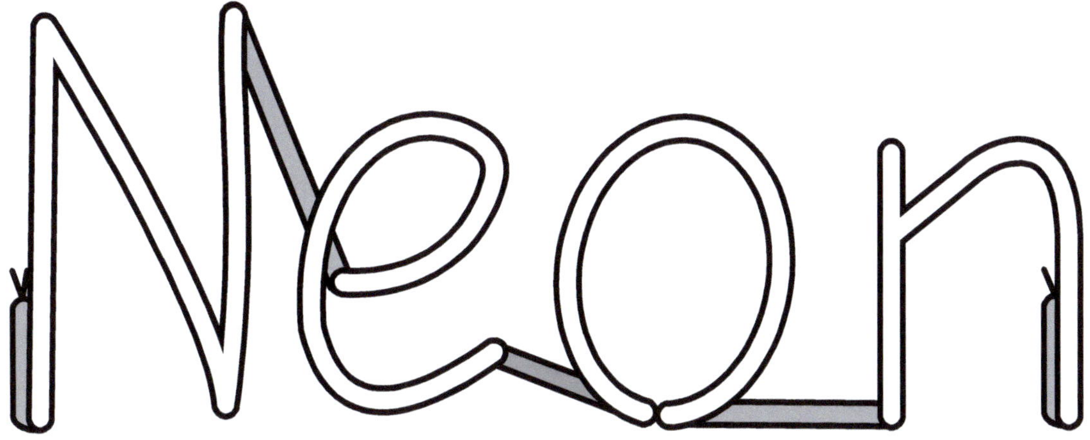

CONNECTIONS BETWEEN LETTERS ARE "BLOCKED OUT" FOR LEGIBILITY

About Japan

Japan is home to about 125 million residents. Most of the population lives in close proximity to the big cities. Tokyo, Japan's biggest city, has the most populated metropolitan area in the world with about 38 million people. Compare this to the most populous city in the United States, New York City, with a metropolitan area population of 20 million people.

Japan's landmass is slightly smaller than the state of California. It is made up of thousands of islands, and sits off the coast of Eastern Asia. It is particularly vulnerable to seasonal typhoons that develop over the Pacific Ocean. In addition, several continental and oceanic plates meet beneath Japan, making it vulnerable to frequent seismic activity.

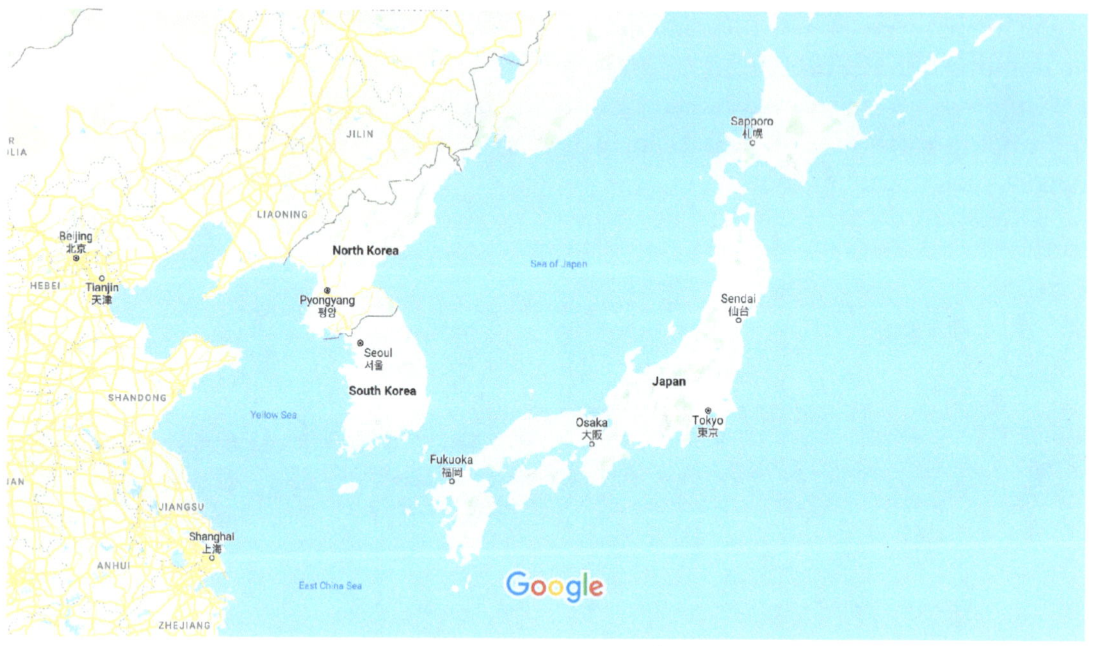

Map data ©2020 Google, SK telecom 200 km

Despite being a small country, Japan currently has the 3rd largest economy by GDP. They've excelled in the production of automobiles, electronics, and optical instruments, which helped to revive the country after their defeat in World War II. Japan now faces economic challenges due to their aging workforce, low birth rates, and increased competition among other developing counties in Asia.

Japan is known to be a late adopter, taking foreign concepts and making significant improvements on them. For example, the network of convenience stores throughout the country provide a vast inventory of products, an large array of services, and are usually open 24 hours every day of the year. Department stores, home improvement warehouses, and shopping malls are other examples of excellent shopping experiences in comparison to other developed nations.

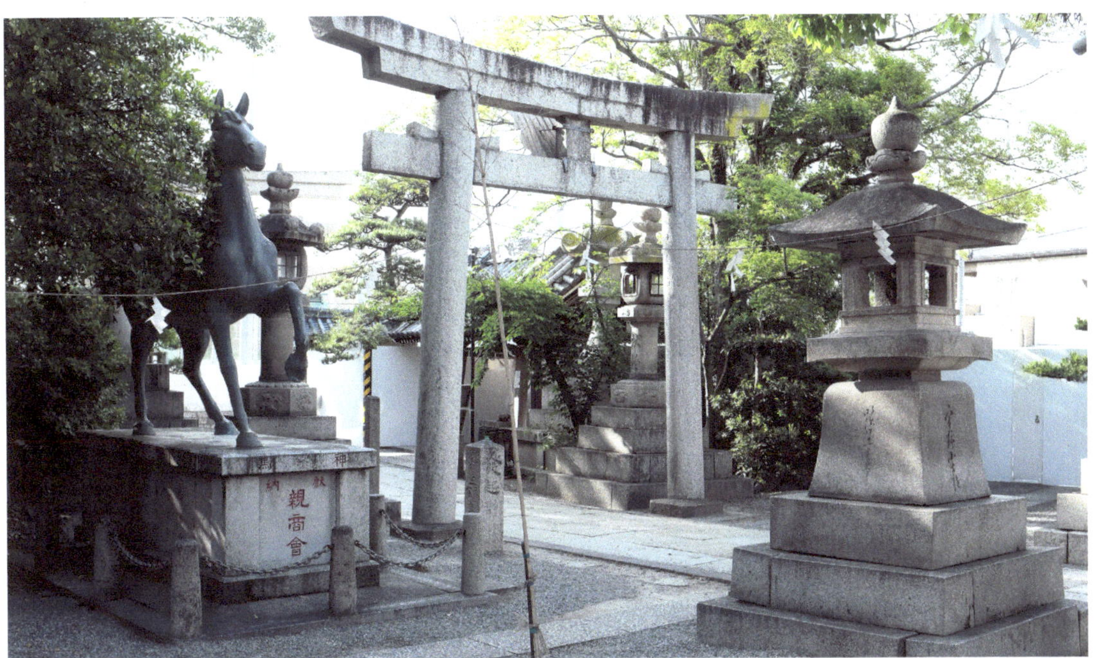

KISHIKI-JINJA SHRINE, KISHIWADA, OSAKA

Japan is a homogeneous society in both racial and cultural aspects. Buddhism is the main religion. Temples and shrines can found throughout cities, towns, and mountains. In modern times, Japan has become foreigner-friendly for tourism and international business, although immigration is difficult. This is in effort to preserve the rich historical culture developed through thousands of years.

While there are always exceptions, the people of Japan value cleanliness and consideration towards others. Companies often host cleaning days, where employees pick up litter off of the streets. . It is common courtesy to refrain from speaking on the phone while riding the train. In addition, rush-hour train platforms are often quieter than a library. There are expectations to display good manners and to abide by the unwritten rules of society.

The Japanese language uses 3 alphabets. The base alphabet is Hiragana, used for native words. Katakana, a separate alphabet, is used for foreign words, although it has the same pronunciations as Hiragana. For example, sushi is a native word, therefor it's written in Hiragana. "Su-pa", the word for super market, is a non-native word derived from English, therefor it's written in Katakana. The Japanese language also uses Kanji, the Chinese character system. Kanji replaces some hiragana characters in writing native words. It is a complicated alphabet, with over 2000 characters in common use.

HELLO: KONICHIWA - こにちわ (HIRAGANA)
WATER: MIZU - みず (HIRAGANA) - 水 (KANJI)
CONVENIENCE STORE: KONBINI - コンビニ (KATAKANA)
AMERICA: アメリカ (KATAKANA)

The Story

Japan is an ancient country that dates back to prehistoric times. Cultural rituals and crafts have been passed down through generations, preserving the styles exhibited in carpentry, pottery, calligraphy, and other crafts. The Japanese calendar uses the traditional era system known as "nengō". This system came from China over 1000 years ago. The modern eras typically coincide with the ruling period of the emperor. For example, The Reiwa era began in 2019, so 2020 is called Reiwa 2nd year.

For most of the Edo era (1603-1868), Japanese people were prohibited from traveling overseas, facing the punishment of death. International trade was prohibited for the most part. Warriors, farmers, artisans, and merchants made up the classes of society. During this time, Japan developed basic infrastructure, cities, schools, and marketplaces throughout the country.

Meiji Era (1868-1912)

The Meiji Era was a revolutionary time in Japan. Following the arrival of Matthew Perry in 1854, leaders understood that they must industrialize and modernize Japan. If they didn't act, they risked invasion by the industrialized nations. Influenced by western ideas and practices, scientific research and technology advanced in effort to catch up with the rest of the world. This influence also affected the philosophical, political, and legal structure of the country. The changes to Japan were profound, and paved the road to the state of the country today.

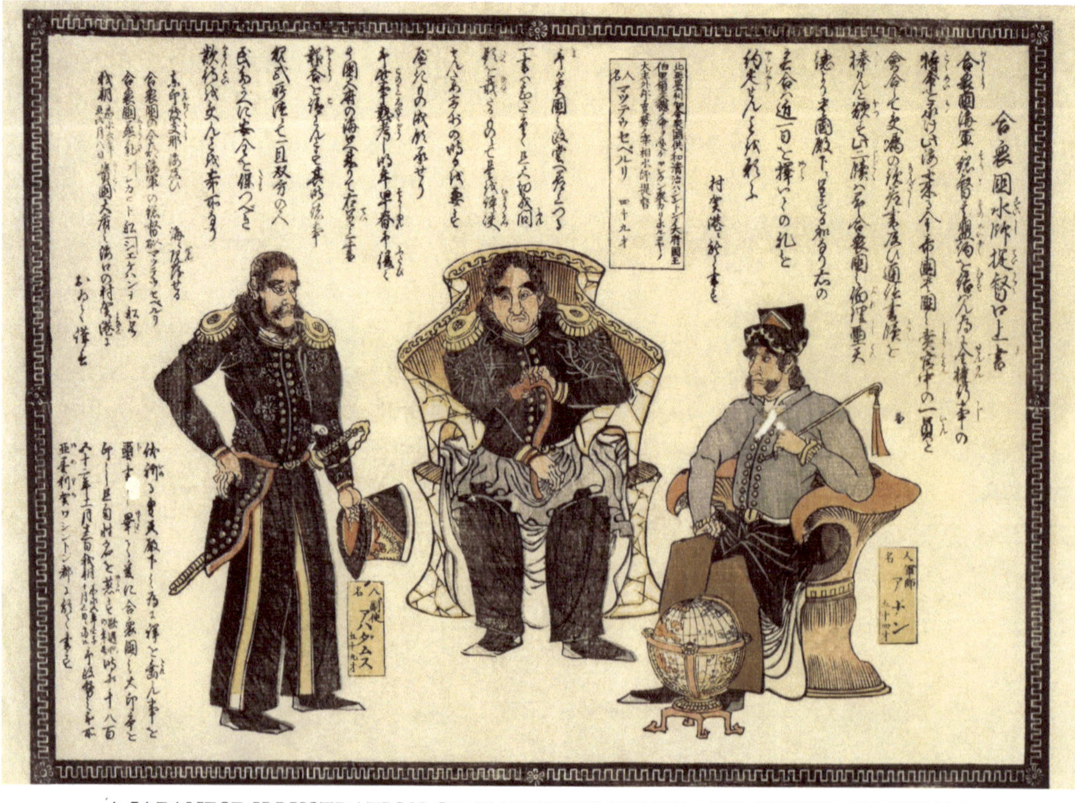

A JAPANESE ILLUSTRATION OF MATTHEW PERRY AND OTHER OFFICIALS

“The Japanese are an exceedingly industrious and ingenious people, and in certain manufactures are surpassed by no nation.”

“They are exceedingly quick in observing any improvement brought in among them by foreigners, soon make themselves masters of it, and copy it with great skill and exactness.”

-MATTHEW PERRY, 1854

Centralized education became an important tool for shaping the people of Japan. Nationalism began to rise as the government tried to garner public support to modernize. With insufficient natural resources, Japan emulated the imperialistic ways of the west to obtain needed materials. Between 1894 and 1910, Japan forcefully acquired Taiwan, Korea, and Manchuria.

Japanese engineers began to study vacuum technology. Light bulbs were developed and used mainly for military ships and bulletin boards. Illuminated signs were limited to lanterns made of oil paper stretched over a bamboo frame, an aesthetic that is still mimicked by traditional shops. Lantern makers would draw characters on the surface of the paper, creating an illuminated silhouette. Although the oil paper could withstand the elements, they still left shop owners to feel uneasy in the event of strong winds.

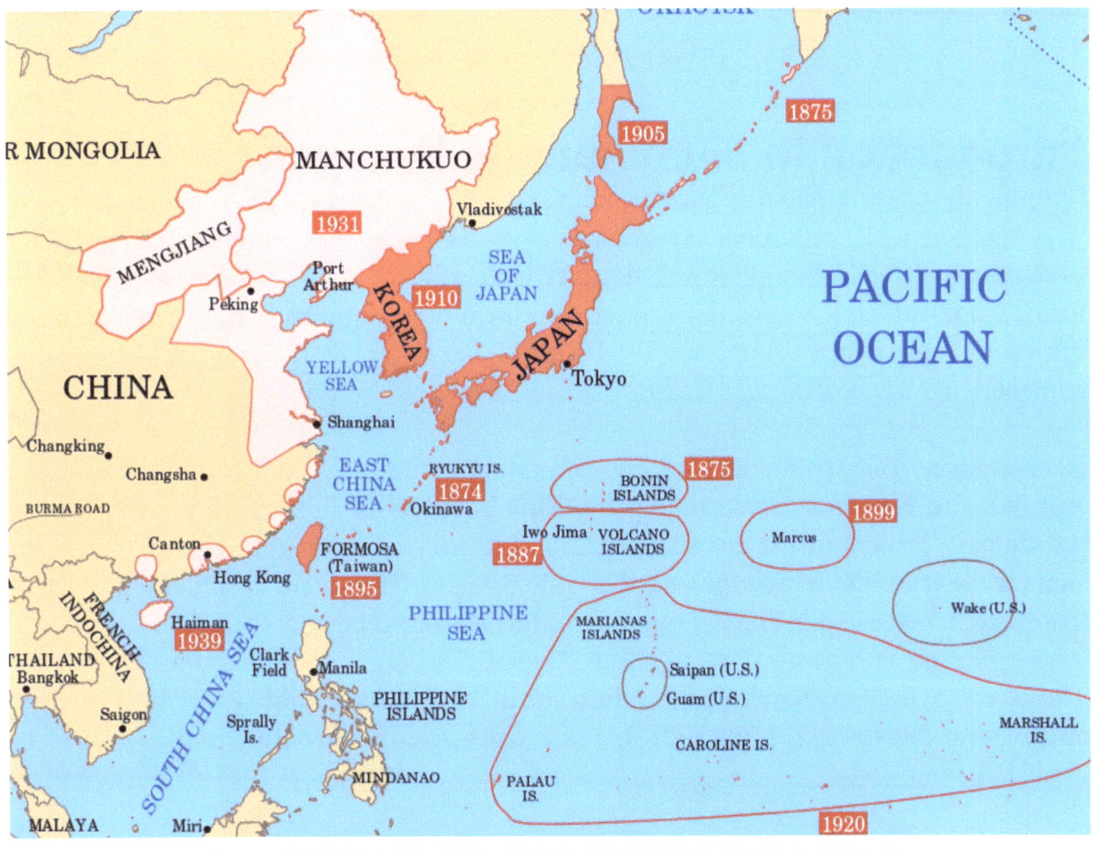

TERRITORIES ANNEXED BY JAPAN BEFORE WORLD WAR II

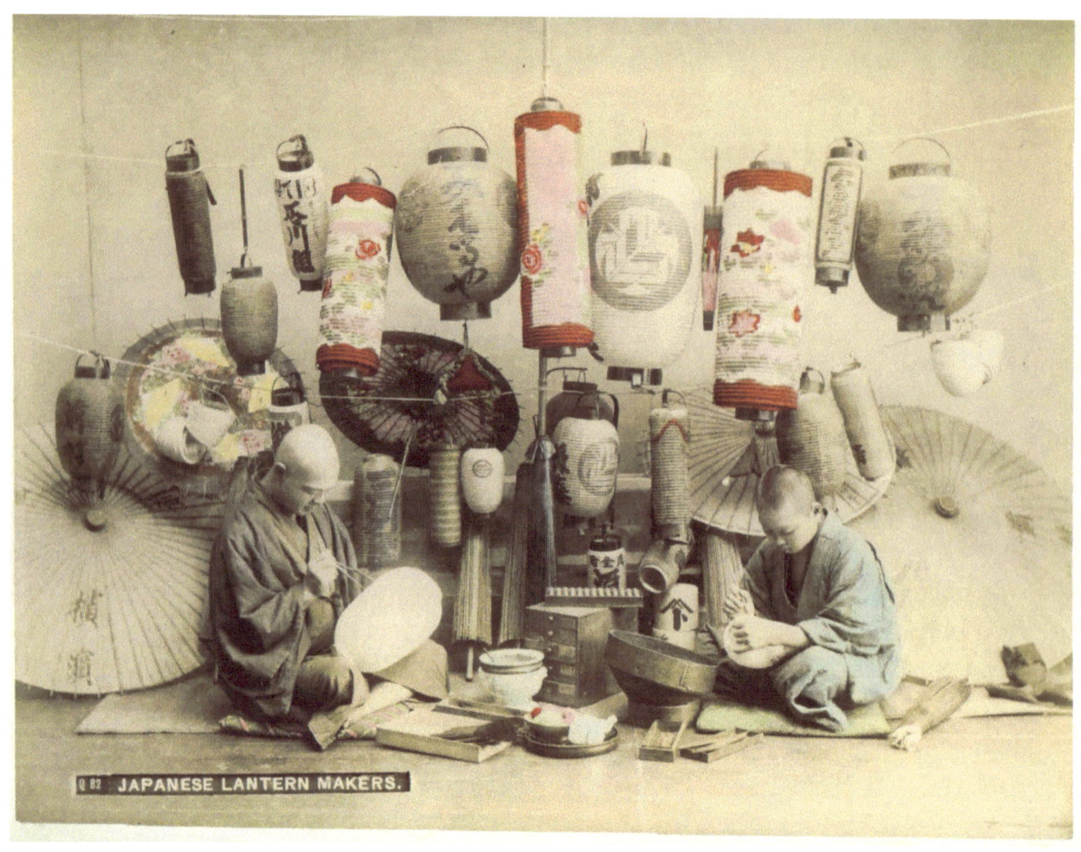

TRADITIONAL JAPANESE LANTERN MAKERS

Introduction to Illuminations in Japan

Illuminations and signboards have been a part of Japan's cityscapes for centuries. Streets were once lit with traditional oil lanterns made of paper and bamboo. As electricity became widely available, illuminated advertising advanced into a safer, more reliable form. The streets slowly became brighter with incandescent bulbs. It wasn't much longer until neon lights began to appear. By 1918, just 8 years after George Claude's product was launched in Paris, a neon sign was glowing in Ginza.

Neon signs spread rapidly around big cities during the early 20th century. Paris, Los Angeles, and New York were among the early adopters of this revolutionary lighting technology. Traders in the electrical lighting industry of Japan started to notice neon signs while traveling to Europe and the United States. They were eventually imported, inspected, reverse engineered, and mass produced around Japan.

The neon sign industry tends to follow the trend of the economy. Politics, war, bureaucracy, and natural disasters keep the industry in a feast or famine routine, but has failed to abolish it completely.

Gas lanterns

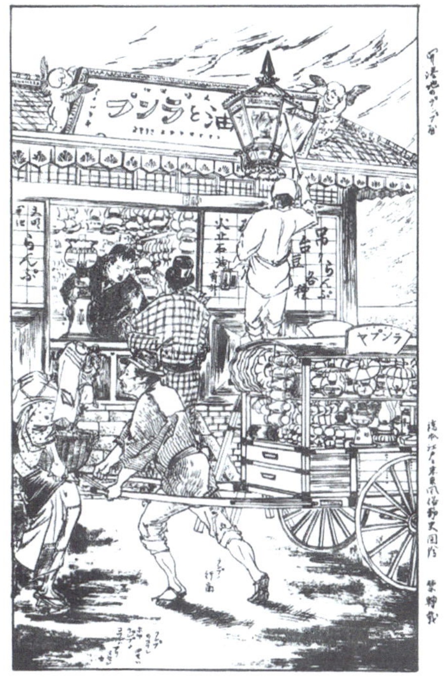

LAMP PEDDLERS

It wasn't until 1872 that the first gas-lit street lamps appeared in Japan. Gas was better than oil because it had a controlled flame and a brighter light. The destruction resulting from the Great Ginza Fire of 1872 gave city officials the opportunity to rebuild. They installed a network of gas lights around the district, which slowly spread around the city of Tokyo. Gas lights would soon be found in theaters, allowing performances to take place later in the evening, and eventually freed shops, restaurants and homes from the darkness of night.

Before gas lamps, people mainly burned candles, wood, and animal grease for light. Some cities burned oil to light their streets, though personal lanterns were more usual. Going out at night was considered dangerous, as passing faces were indistinguishable soon after the sun went down.

In 1877, A ground-breaking illuminated gas sign was installed outside of the Gas Hall of the First National Industrial Expo in Ueno, Tokyo. A Chrysanthemum flower-shaped gas burner was ignited during sunset. It attracted a lot of attention and became featured in famous paintings. The Tokyo Gas Company promoted itself with the gas burner sign, though it swiftly fell out of use after the introduction of electricity.

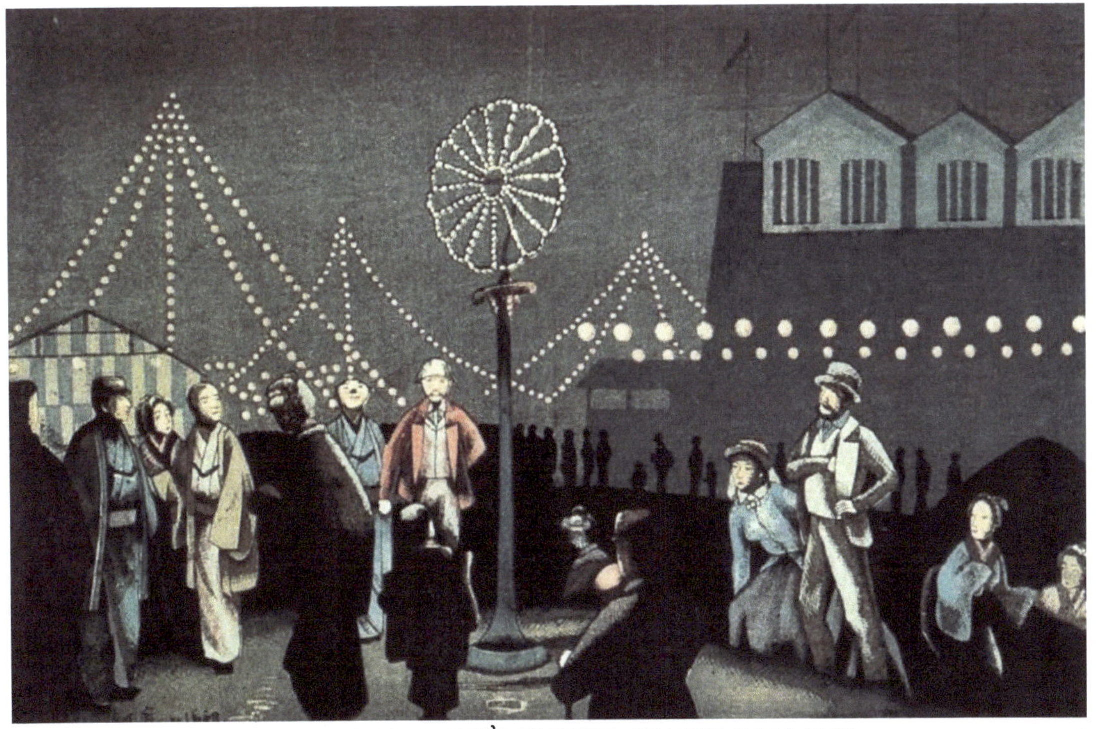

TOKYO GAS COMPANY'S FLOWER-SHAPED GAS LAMP

Electricity

The first display of electricity in Japan was in 1878, when an arc lamp was switched on at the opening banquet of the Tokyo Central Telegraph Station's main office. This was a turning point for Japan, as many places in Europe and America were still without electricity at this point. The first use of incandescent light in Japan was on June 25, 1884. This took place at the commencement ceremony of the railroad line running from Ueno to Takasaki. Twenty-four incandescent bulbs and one arc light welcomed the Japanese emperor and empress for their appearance.

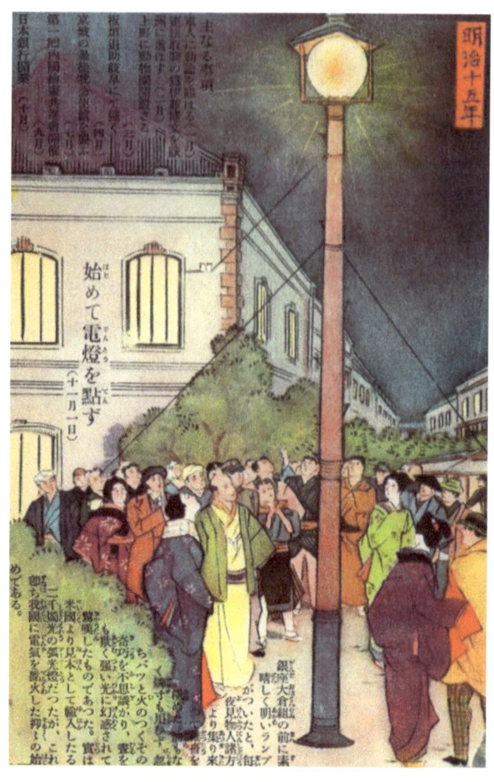

RIGHT: JAPAN'S FIRST ELECTRIC POWER COMPANY "TOKYO ELECTRIC LIGHT" IGNITES AN ARC LAMP IN FRONT OF OKURAGUMI FOR ADVERTISING

By 1887, The Tokyo Electric Light Company completed the first power generation plant for consumer use. They installed a 25kW Edison direct-current generator and supplied power using a low-voltage direct-current distribution system. They upgraded systems in 1895 to generators from Germany's AEG. At the same time, Osaka Electric Lamp imported generators from General Electric in America. The AEG generators produced electricity at the European standard of 50Hz (cycles per second). The General Electric generators used the American standard of 60Hz. This split Japan's power grid in half between east and west, as it remains today.

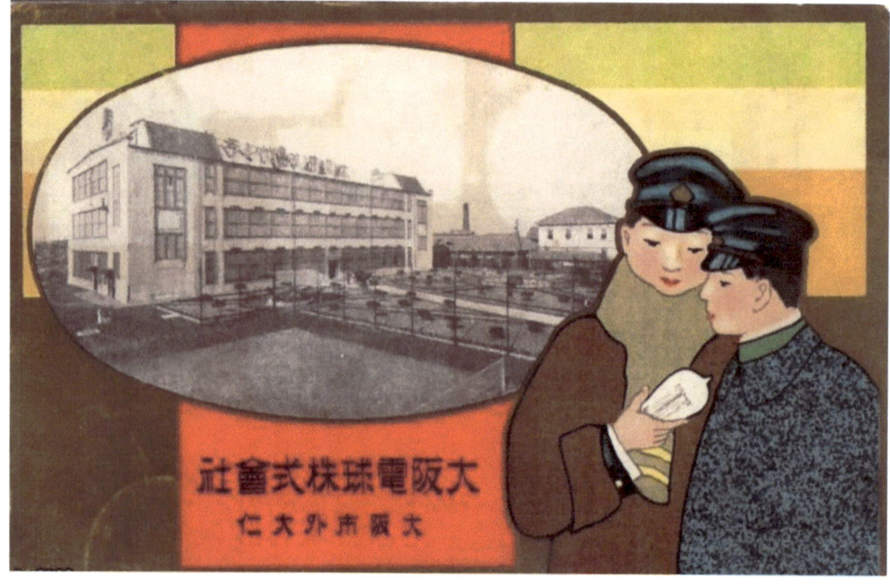

ADVERTISEMENT FOR OSAKA ELECTRIC LAMP

Electric Light Illuminations

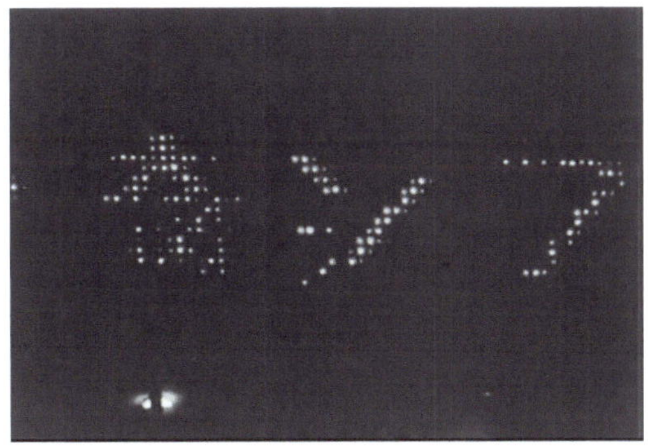

AN EARLY LIGHT BULB SIGN

Early electric signs were comprised of a series of light bulbs installed within letter shaped grooves on wooden boards. Electric signs were much brighter, convenient, and safer than the gas lamps. They could be turned on and off with a switch, and were not as vulnerable to wind and rain. Special effects such as colors were achieved by dipping the bulbs in translucent varnish. Flashers were subsequently used to make the bulbs blink in exiting patterns, a revolutionary sight at the time.

One of the first large-scale electric signs in Japan was debuted at the 5th Osaka Industrial Expo in 1903. "Industrial Expo" was written in light bulbs, and strung across a wire mesh above the crowd. At the time, the most remarkable feature of the sign was its animation. One character at a time would light up, slowly spelling out the name. In addition to the sign, many prominent buildings in Japan were illuminated with incandescent bulbs during the Industrial Expo. The tower of Morinaga chocolates and the Murai Tobacco Tower became famous attractions as the crowds flocked towards the light.

The Tokyo Industrial Exposition in 1907 used approximately 3,500 light bulbs to illuminate the building's exterior along the roof. The scene reflecting in the Shinobazu Pond had a mesmerizing effect on people. Since then, illumination became a standard part of the expositions, thus allowing events to carry on through the evening. This was the turning point when electric lighting took over due to the employment of hydroelectric power generation. The achievement of long-distance power transmission and the further development of light bulbs made electric light widespread across Japan.

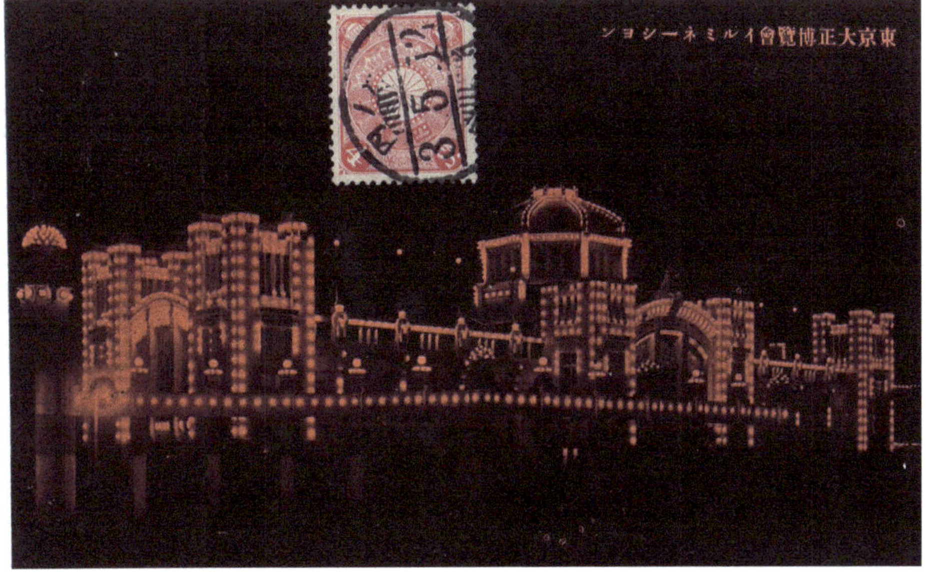

ILLUMINATION AT THE TOKYO INDUSTRIAL EXPOSITION, 1907

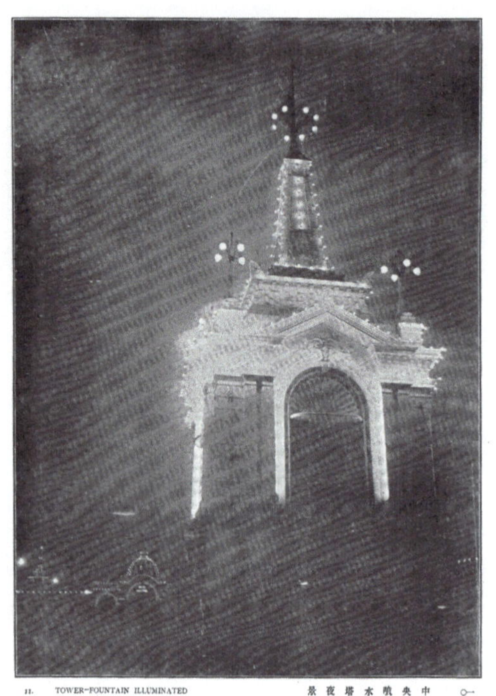

TOWER-FOUNTAIN
OSAKA INDUSTRIAL EXPOSITION, 1903

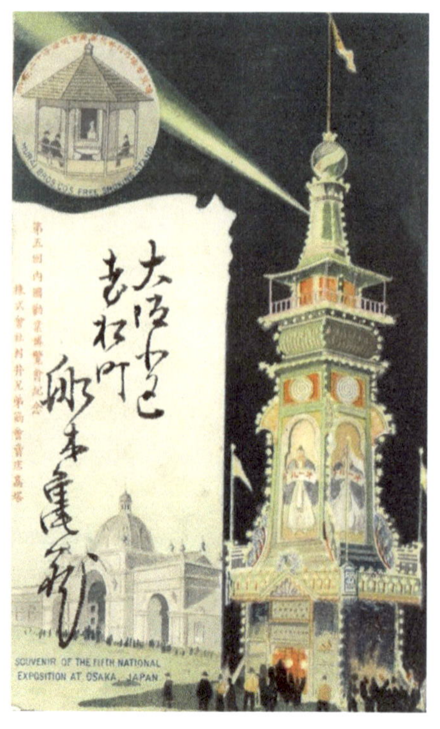

MURAI TOBACCO TOWER
OSAKA, 1903

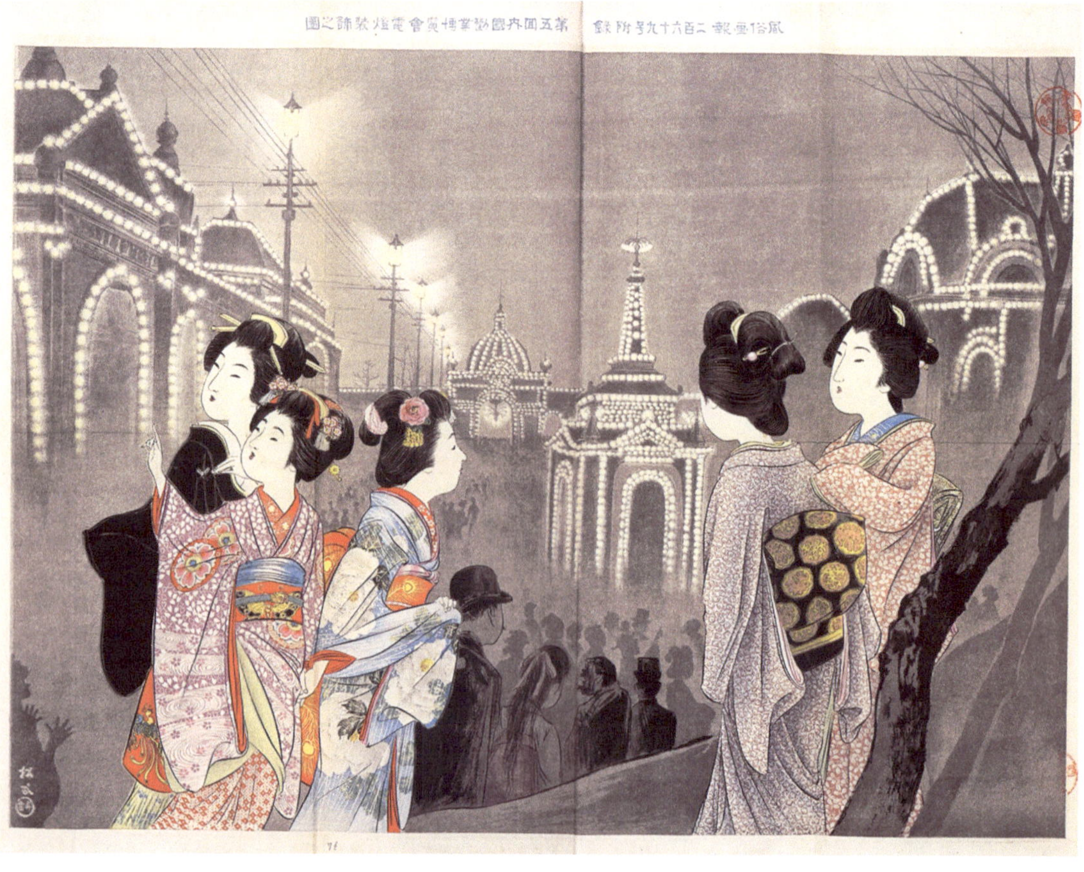

風俗畫報二百六十九号附録 第五回内國勧業博覧會電燈装飾之圖

SPECTATORS AT THE OSAKA INDUSTRIAL EXPOSITION, 1903

Taisho Era (1912-1926)

A short and turbulent era, Taisho played a crucial role in shaping modern Japan. Nationalism and imperialism continued to grow as Japan joined the Allied Powers in WWI. Japan declared war on Germany in effort to take over German leased territories in China and along the Pacific Coast. This expansion provided Japan with resources they lacked and diversified their economy as they provided war materials for the European allies. This promoted Japan's economic status, sparking further development of the country. Large advertising towers were soon constructed in big cities for brands like Lion Toothpaste and Jintan Foods.

Tsutenkaku Tower

The Tsutenkaku Tower was one of the tallest structures in Asia during the time of its construction in 1912. It originally stood 210 feet tall, and was connected to an amusement park via cable car. The amusement park was named Luna Park, modeled after the original Luna Park in New York City's Coney Island. Tsutenkaku translates to "tower reaching heaven", and was a marvel of Osaka until 1943, when a fire damaged the structure. The metal tower was then salvaged for the war effort.

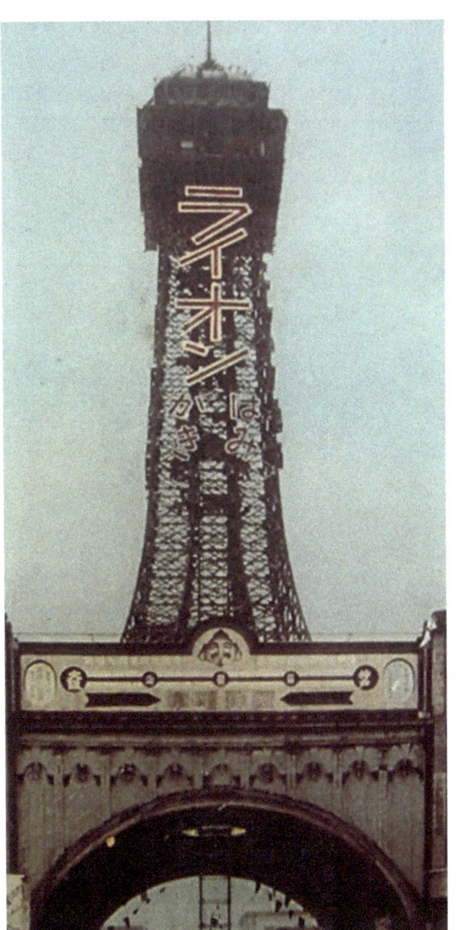

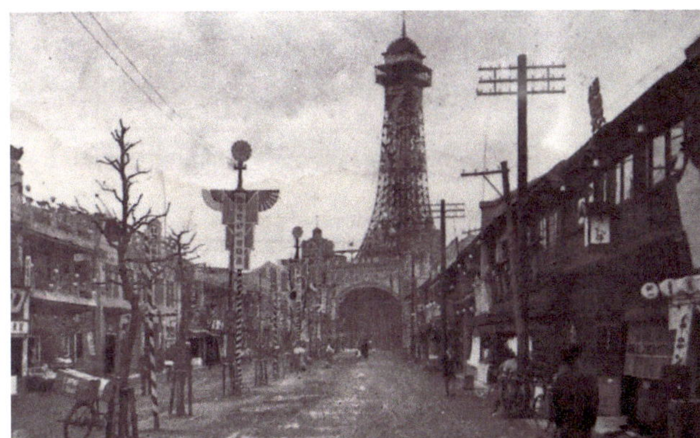

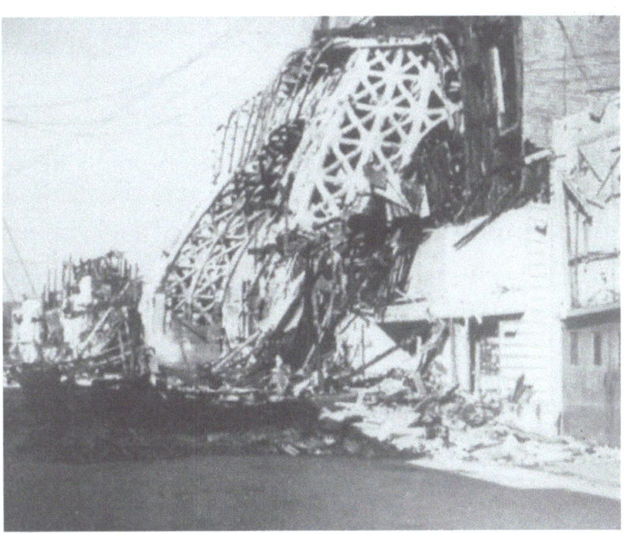

THE ORIGINAL TSUTENKAKU TOWER IN OSAKA

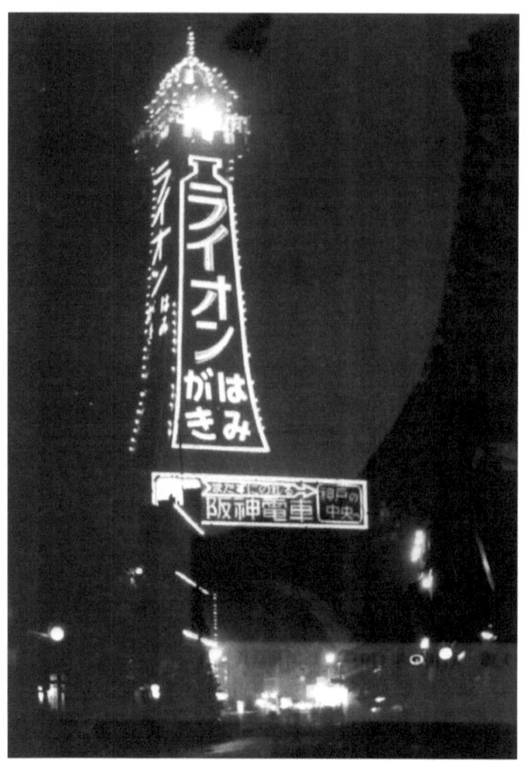

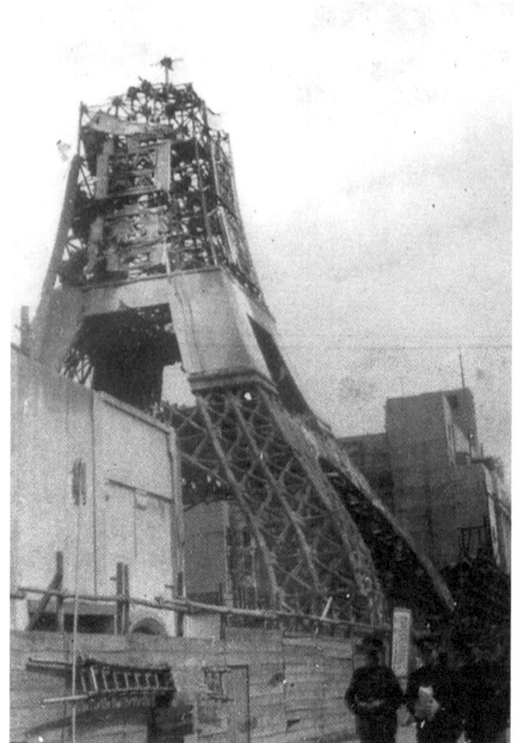

TSUTENKAKU BEFORE AND AFTER THE FIRE

The Beginning of Neon in Japan

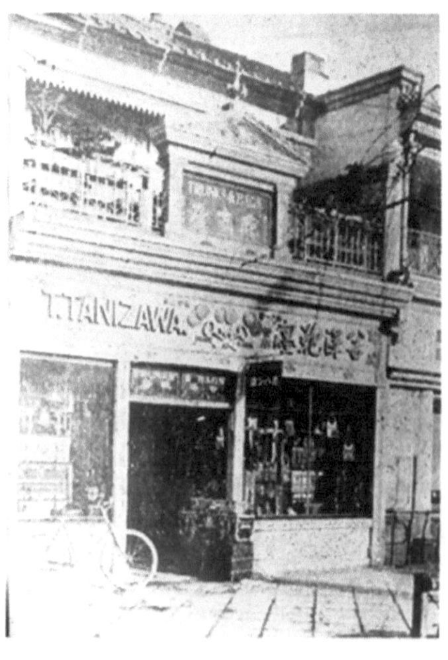

In 1918, three clear tubes filled with neon gas shined a bright red light over the entrance of the Tanizawa bag store in Ginza, Tokyo. This was the first known installation of neon tubes in Japan. The tubes were imported from the United States, and are suspected to have been Moore Lamps filled with neon gas. They were unconventionally wide tubes as they were reportedly 30mm in diameter.

This new lighting method sparked the interest of many electric lighting product traders. Japanese businessmen traveled to Europe and the United States to inspect commercial lighting of department stores and shops. The street views of New York and Paris inspired the race to bring neon signs to Japan.

By 1921, a neon sign spelling “NEON” was brought back from the United States by Mr. Koji Kosone. He lit the display at the Hiroshimaya Hotel in Yokohama in an effort to promote the new product. At this time, the Tokyo Electronic Company, predecessor to Toshiba, began to research neon sign and transformer manufacturing.

The fragility of neon tubes presented a challenge for importers. In addition, sea freight was costly and slow. Japanese technicians would continue to travel to the United States and Europe to study neon light making. Due to the hyper-competitive industry, neon makers were extremely esoteric, making it difficult for the technicians to learn the trade. The Japanese companies knew that they would have to produce neon domestically if they wanted to be successful.

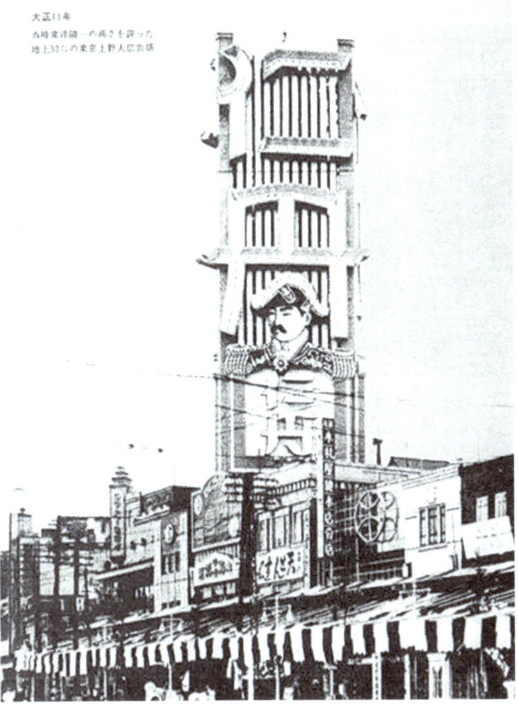

JINTAN TOWER IN UENO, TOKYO

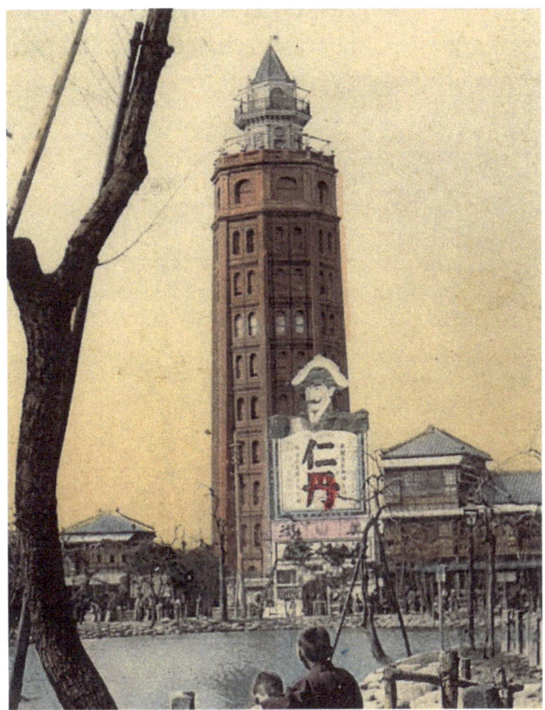

RYŌUNKAKU TOWER IN ASAKUSA, TOKYO

The Great Kantō Earthquake

On September 1st, 1923, The Kanto region of Japan experienced a large earthquake. The 7.9 magnitude earthquake devastated parts of Tokyo, Yokohama, and other surrounding regions, which resulted in approximately 142,800 casualties. Homes, factories, and other large buildings were completely leveled. Tokyo, the largest city and financial epicenter of Japan suffered a major setback. The focus temporarily shifted to reconstruction of the hard hit regions.

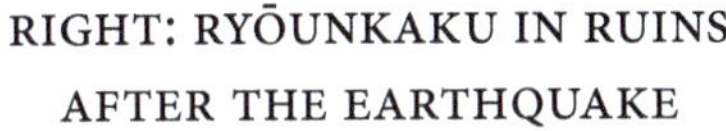

RIGHT: RYŌUNKAKU IN RUINS
AFTER THE EARTHQUAKE

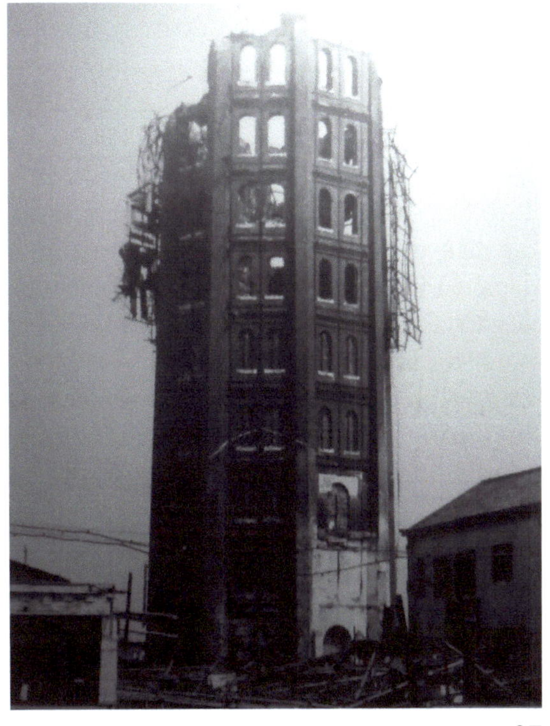

Shirokiya Department Store

The first full-fledged neon sign in Japan was imported from France by Tokyo Electric. The vertical sign read "Shirokiya" and was installed in 1925 at Osaka's Shirokiya Department Store. The sign glowed red, and supposedly flickered like a flame. This was concerning for Osaka Prefectural authorities, and was ordered to be removed after one month. As neon was still in its infancy, there were fears that this sign would start a fire. After removal, the sign was moved to the front window of Tokyo's Shirokiya store in 1926. This display garnered much attention for Tokyo Electric. Soon after, they started to successfully repair other various damaged imported neon signs. The Shirokiya sign was presumably destroyed a few years later when an incandescent bulb on a Christmas tree started a major fire in the department store on December 16, 1932.

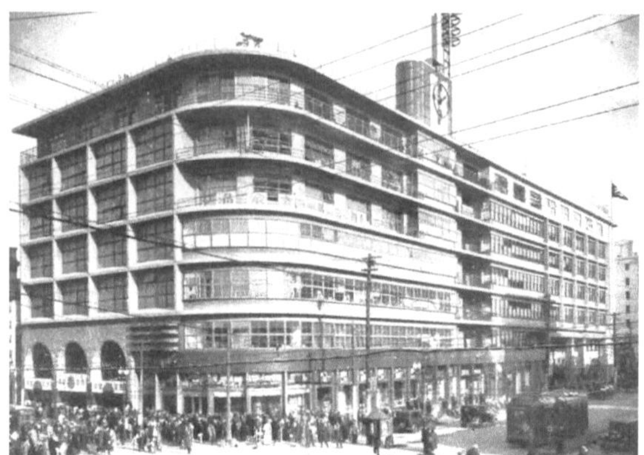

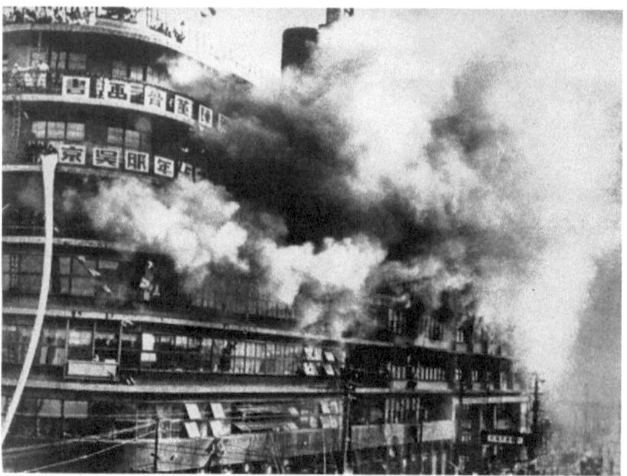

BEFORE AND DURING THE SHIROKIYA DEPARTMENT STORE FIRE IN TOKYO

Domestic Neon

It was only eight years after the first neon import to Japan that domestic neon companies were able to produce and repair neon signs. The first domestic sign decorated the entrance of the Summer Cool-down Festival in Hibiya Park, Tokyo in July 1926. Developed by Imamura, Tachibana, Seki, and Ishigami of Tokyo Electric, the sign used 11 meters of 9mm tubing, and depicted boys and girls blowing soap bubbles face to face. A number of other neon signs were produced around this time such as the Matsuda Lamp Sign, Kao Soaps, and the Ginza Palace. These early signs set a precedent for the coming neon spectaculars of Japan.

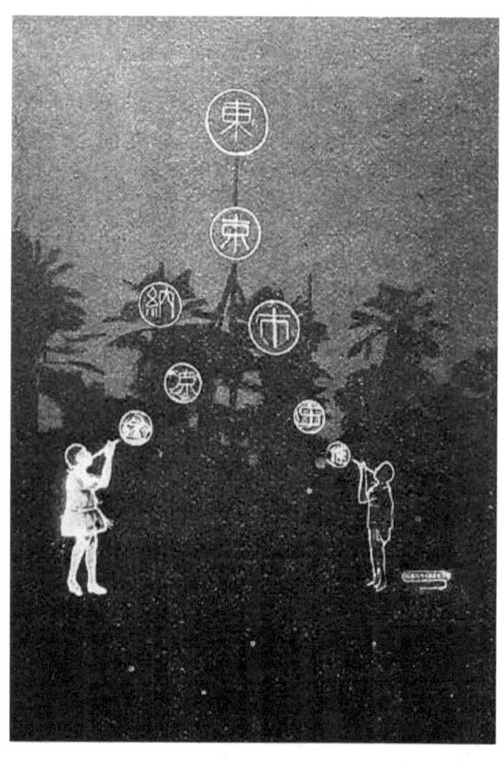

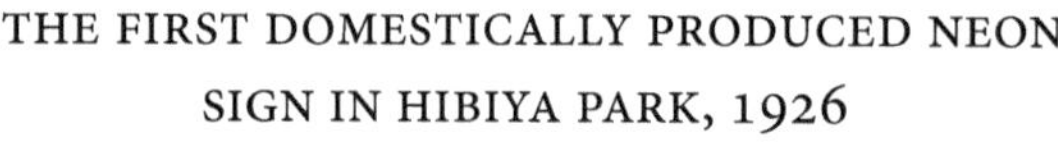

THE FIRST DOMESTICALLY PRODUCED NEON SIGN IN HIBIYA PARK, 1926

Showa Era (1926-1989)

The Showa Era kicked off with a financial crisis, directly following the post-World War I business boom. The bust brought down the prime minister, and led to the formation of the zaibatsu (family monopolies). Many companies were heavily invested in increased production capacities, which turned out to be a bubble. Although the bust was a setback to Japan's economy, the country continued to move forward into a progressive era.

Neon suddenly took over streets of the big cities. Used in conjunction with flashing incandescent bulbs, the glamour of the neon glow in the night sky captured the hearts of urbanites. Advertisers raced to make contracts for signs. Some of the first companies to jump on board were the food and beverage businesses. Asahi beer, Meiji Chocolates, and Glico foods were some of the early adopters of this new advertising medium.

The development of neon signs in Japan was accompanied by a handful of difficulties. Perhaps it had to do with the high profile character of neon itself. The industry endured a series of setbacks and challenges including patent disputes, bans, unreasonable taxation, and strict regulations. Nonetheless, the industry prospered and was successful in covering the country for almost a century. Shortly into the beginning of the Showa Era, the industry went in to its first heyday.

THE FIRST GLICO NEON SIGNBOARD IN OSAKA'S DOTONBORI, 1937

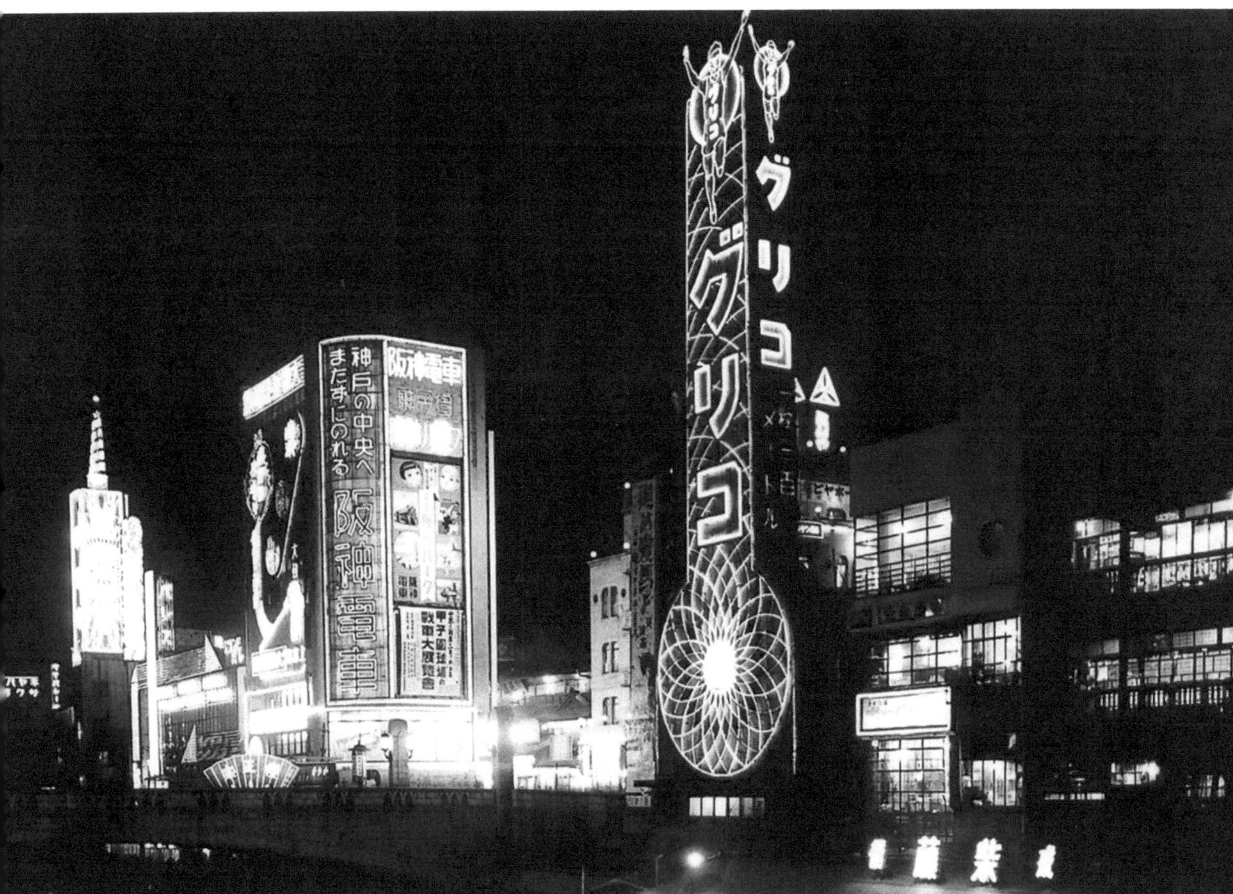

The First Heyday

The pre-war neon heyday started around 1930. It revolved largely around bars, clubs and cafes. Until then, these establishments relied on lamp lighting for illumination. The vividness of the neon colors enhanced the atmosphere, the key to attracting patrons. Neon signs for liquor, beer, and food manufacturers became popular shortly afterwards. Neon is known to be contagious, as it quickly multiplies once it appears in an area. Soon neon signs were adopted as a primary advertising media by a wide range of companies such as department stores, electric railways, general stores, pharmaceutical companies and more.

Though neon gained immense popularity, there was still a demand for other illuminated signs. Electric companies would offer incentives for using their electric bulbs. TEPCO, the Tokyo Electric Light Company, offered a 5 yen subsidy for every light bulb used in a sign. Indirect lighting also became popular as it was used for store lighting. Many electric signs used an incandescent light source in combination with painted translucent glass plate. Milk glass, a translucent white glass, soon replaced a lot of the painted glass plates, and was often used in architectural lighting.

EARLY 1930S - NEON SIGNS AROUND JAPAN

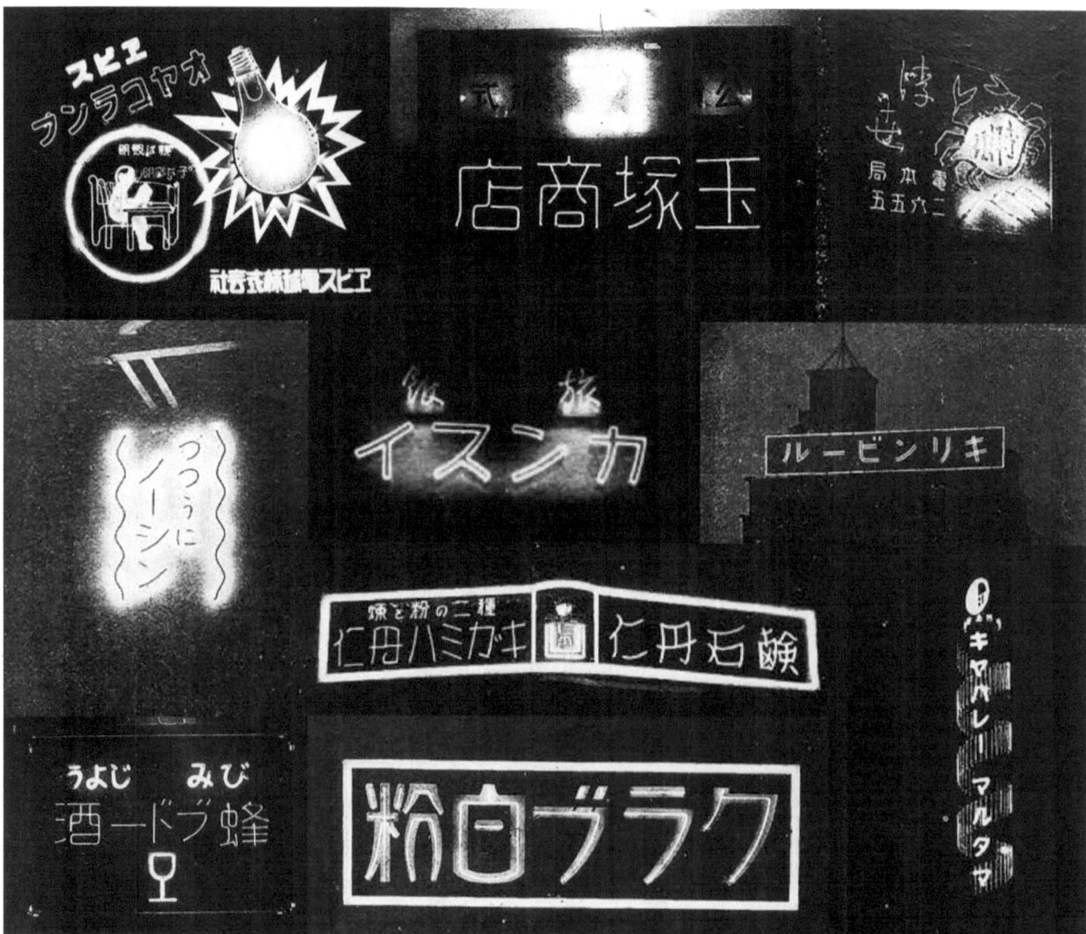

JAPANESE WRITING USED TO BE READ FROM RIGHT TO LEFT PRIOR TO WORLD WAR II (AS SEEN IN THESE SIGNS)

Early Neon Companies

The success of the industry is due to the early effort of the pioneers, from technicians to material suppliers, that worked to import neon technology to Japan. Domestic neon companies generally started by sending technicians to the United States in the late 1920s. They quickly learned that information on neon manufacturing was hard to come by because of the competitive nature of the industry.

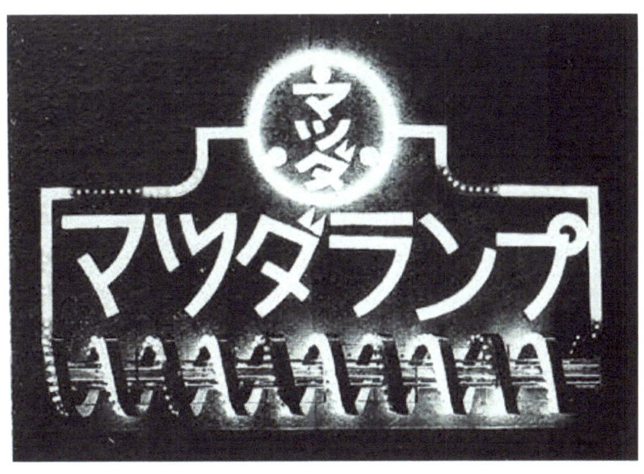

ADVERTISEMENT OF MATSUDA LAMP COMPANY, A DIVISION OF TOKYO ELECTRIC

Established in 1890, the Hakunetsu-sha Company originally specialized in manufacturing light bulbs that used bamboo filaments. They were soon beat by foreign competitors that had better quality and less expensive products. In 1905, the company was renamed Tokyo Electric, and began to collaborate with General Electric. Tokyo Electric began to study neon in the early 1920s, and eventually produced neon signs. Tokyo Electric made many of the early neon signs in Japan. Tokyo Electric is a predecessor to Toshiba, a world renowned electronics company.

Tokyo Neon was one of the first to incorporate as a company specialized in neon manufacturing. This was a reorganization of Mr. Hirobe's Nippon Vacuum Tube Works (N.V.V.) that was previously founded in 1923. Mr. Hirobe dispatched a technician to the United States in 1927 to research manufacturing techniques. The technician returned to Japan six months later with various materials that would be studied for replication. Shortly afterwards, Tokyo Neon started to manufacture neon signs.

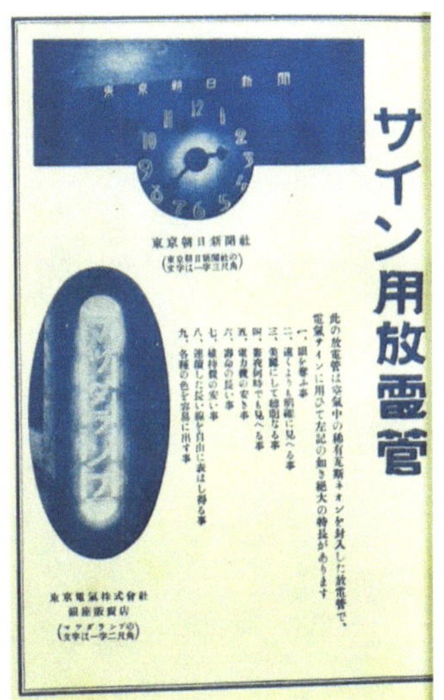

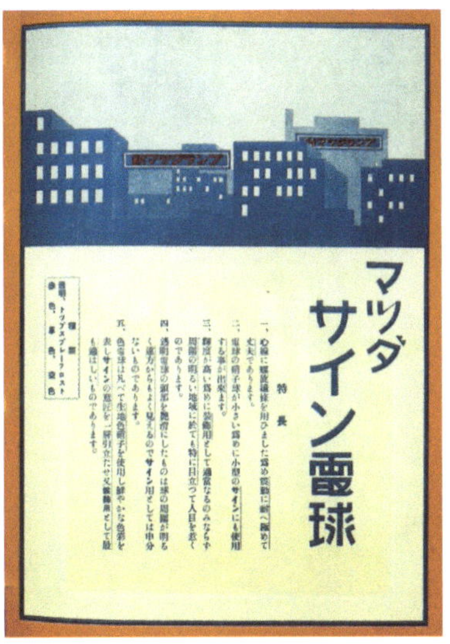

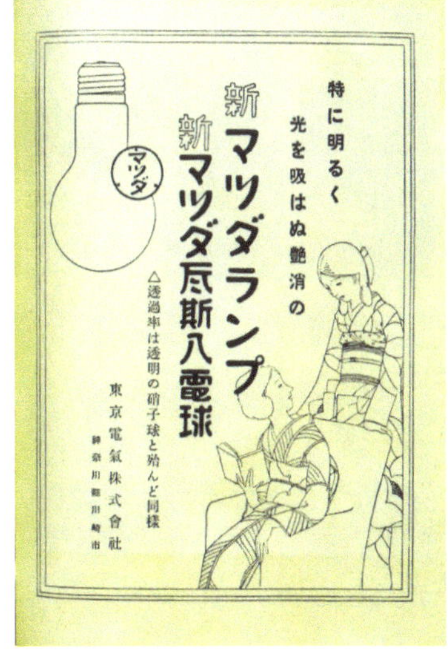

TOKYO ELECTRIC & MATSUDA LAMP ADVERTISEMENTS

Claude Neon began operations in Japan by 1929, after a costly franchise permit was obtained by Mr. Kouji Naito and associates. Claude Neon held a technical advantage as their products were already developed and patented. The business was set up swiftly as two American engineers came to Japan to setup and provide technical guidance. Claude Neon soon expanded into Osaka, and was eventually established in the major cities across the country.

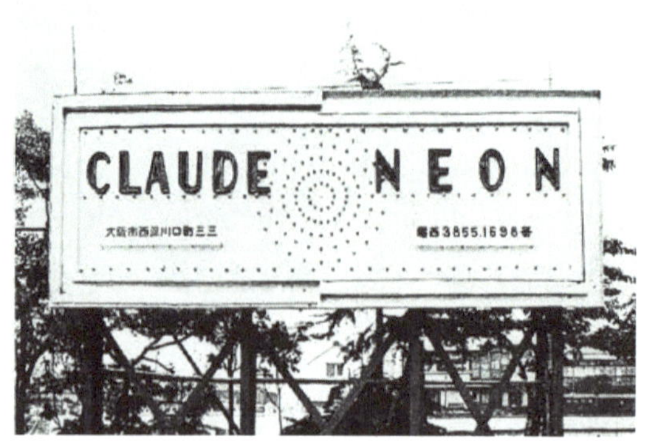

CLAUDE NEON ADVERTISEMENT, 1933

By the 1930s, numerous neon companies sprouted around Japan. Many existing companies considered transitioning to neon production. Even Toyota's predecessor, Toyoda Automatic Loom Works, had considered transitioning to the neon lighting business as it was one of the most advanced industrial fields at the time.

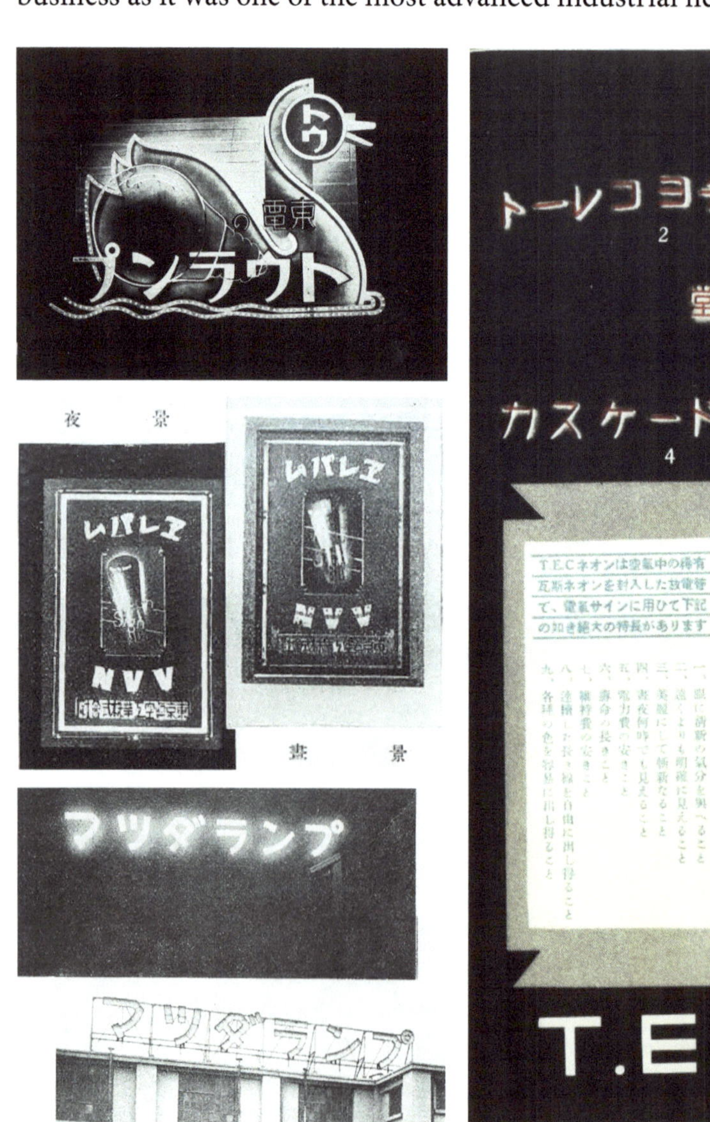

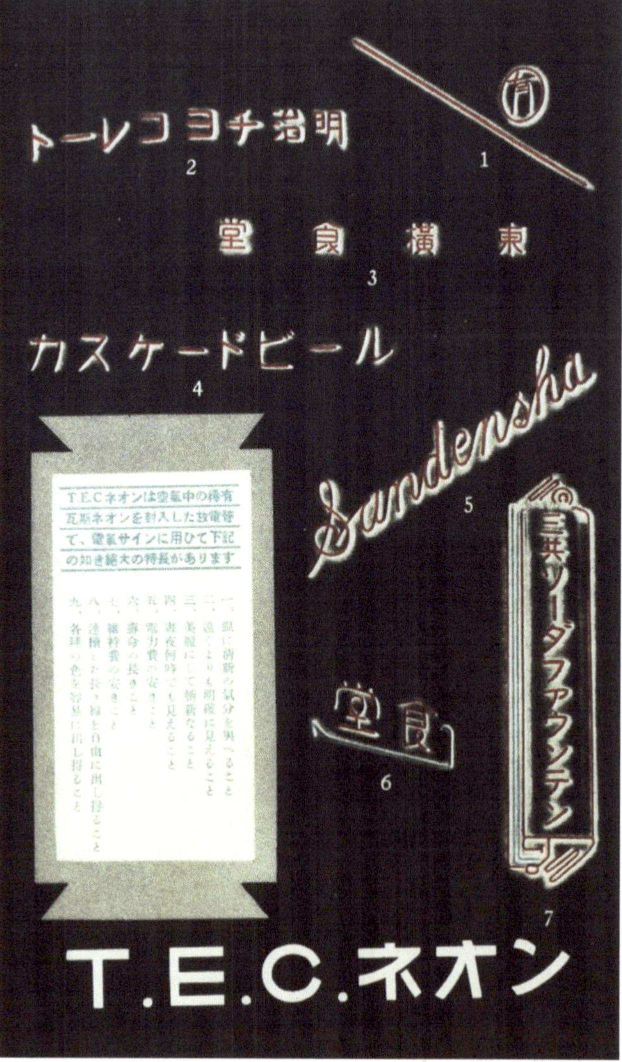

る圓消にマツダのマークに變り、最後に旗は消えてマツダのマークと、上部にはマツダランプ、下部にはマツダ眞空管とネオン管が點ずる設計で、新しい調光裝置を使用した點、觀衆の眼を奪ひ好評を博した。

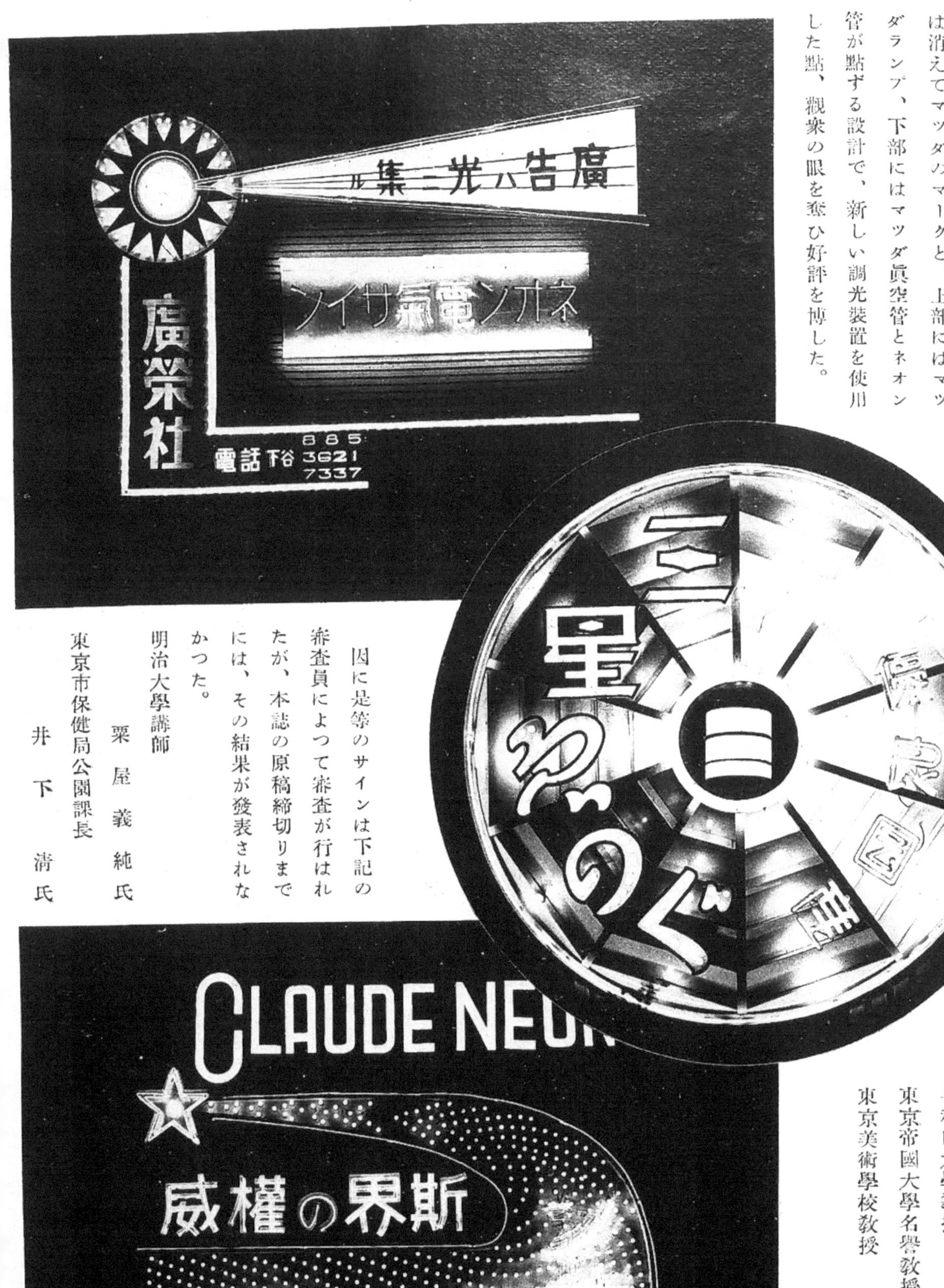

因に是等のサインは下記の審査員によつて審査が行はれたが、本誌の原稿締切りまでには、その結果が發表されなかつた。

早稻田大學教授　佐藤功一

東京帝國大學名譽教授　本田靜六

東京美術學校教授　和田三造

明治大學講師　栗屋義純氏

東京市保健局公園課長　井下清氏

In May 1927, the Electricity and Waves Exhibition was held at the Tokyo Metropolitan Electric Research Institute. A neon sign reading "Electricity and Waves" in Japanese was domestically produced by Tokyo Electric and installed on the building's rooftop. Until then, every neon sign in Japan glowed red with neon gas. The section "waves" glowed blue, as they used argon+mercury tubes for the first time in Japan. This sign was only lit temporarily for the exhibition, though it brought on many questions and issues for the use of neon signs:

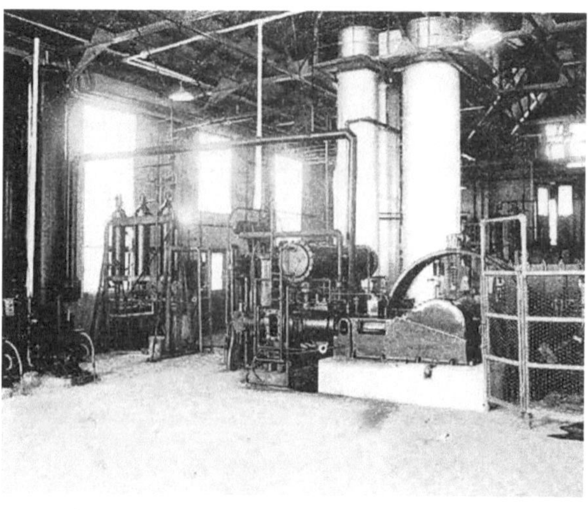

DOMESTIC ARGON PRODUCTION PLANT

Similar to the Shirokiya sign in Osaka, there was a lot of anxiety revolving around the unknown properties of neon signs due to the lack of testing. One of the main issues encountered was deciding upon a safe amount of voltage to use. The sign required 60,000 volts, and was originally denied by officials. It was agreed upon that they can use a maximum of 30,000 volts in a circuit. Tokyo Electric then split the sign into multiple circuits, allowing for the entire sign to be lit.

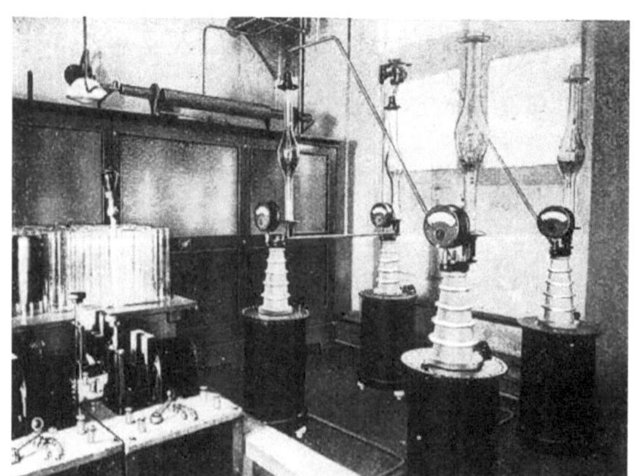

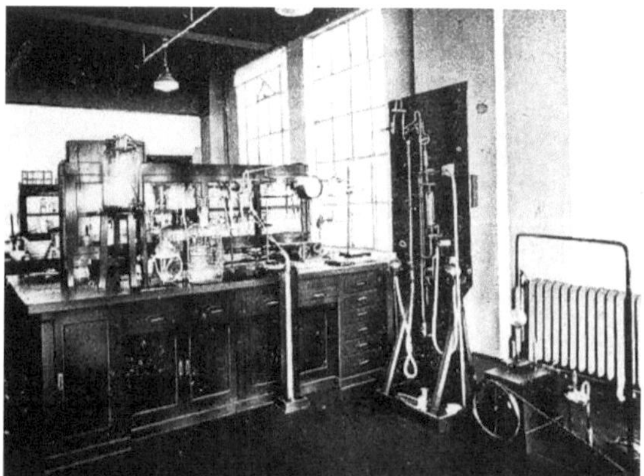

TOKYO ELECTRIC TESTING LABORATORY

There were also concerns about rainfall. They tested this by spraying the signs with a hose at the Tokyo Electric laboratory. They were instructed to cover the neon signs with plate glass, though it blurred the characters and hindered legibility. The sign was reluctantly installed without the plate glass.

Electrical problems continued for every neon company in Japan. With the help of government officials, Tokyo Electric ran experiments with high voltage transformers. 400 various animals were shocked by transformers to deem if they were lethal to humans. It was declared that 15,000 volts / 50 milliampere would be the maximum rating for a neon transformer. Much of the research done by Tokyo Electric contributes to the safety and allowances of Japan's current neon regulations.

The following year, in 1928, Tokyo Electric produced a neon sign for the Tokyo Asahi Newspaper in Sukiyabashi, Ginza. The sign used 1.2 square meter letters that were installed along the company's rooftop. In addition, a rotating, reflective sphere surrounded by spotlights accompanied the sign.

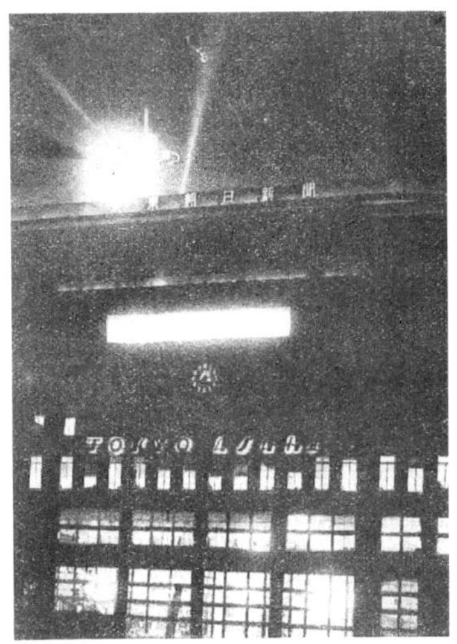

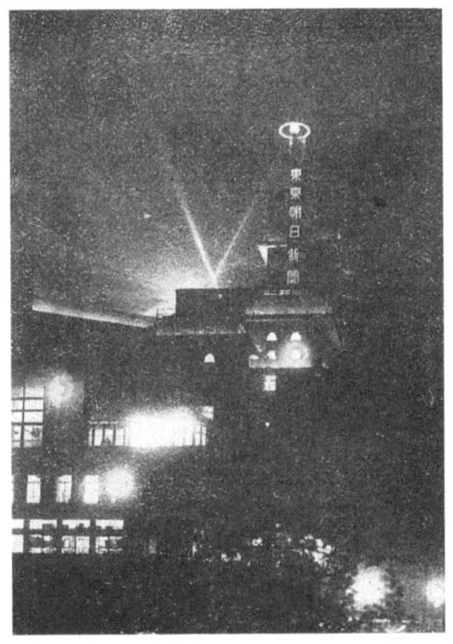

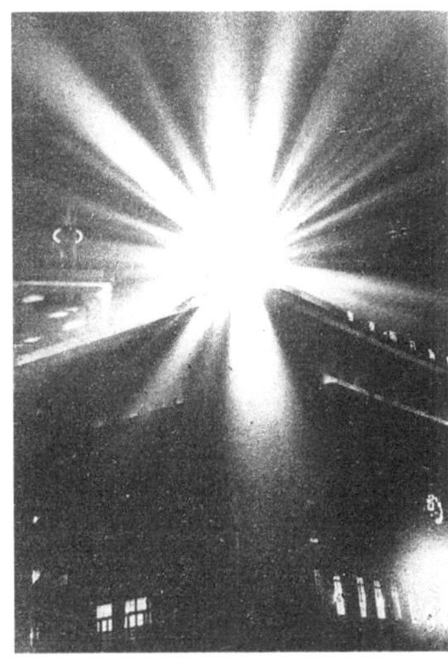

TOKYO ASAHI NEWSPAPER BUILDING,
EQUIPPED WITH A ROTATING REFLECTIVE SPHERE

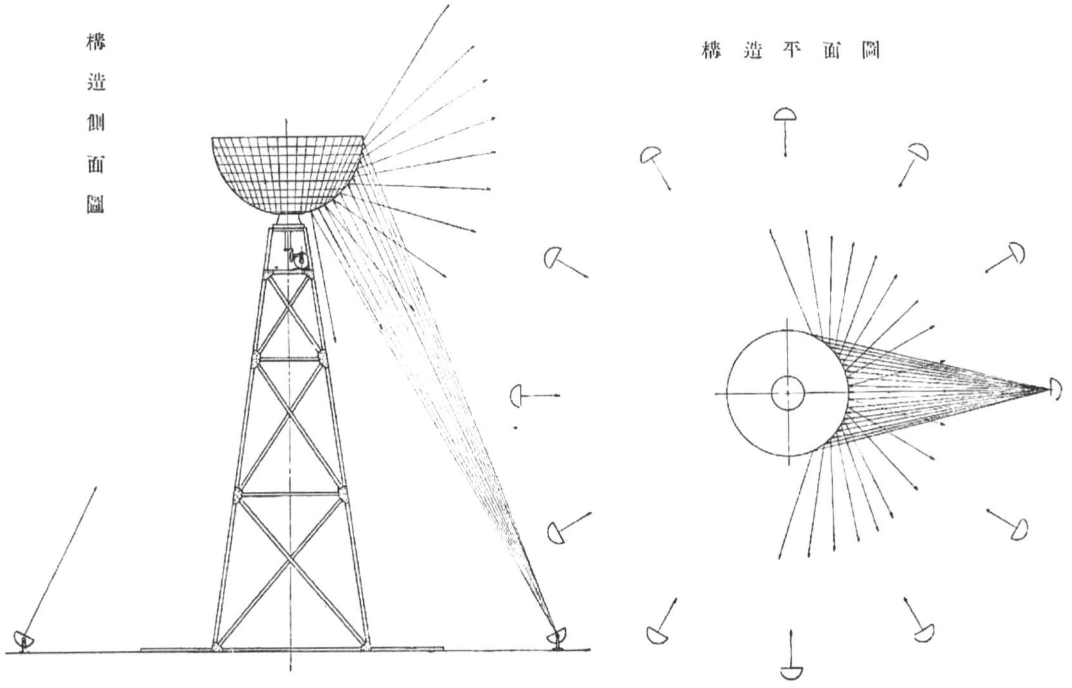

Domestic neon began to populate the streets around 1929. Within a couple of years, the spread of neon signs exploded. It was said that the amount of neon in Japan was comparable to the United States and parts of Europe. Some Japanese businessmen ventured to Korea, Manchuria and China to setup in the untapped markets.

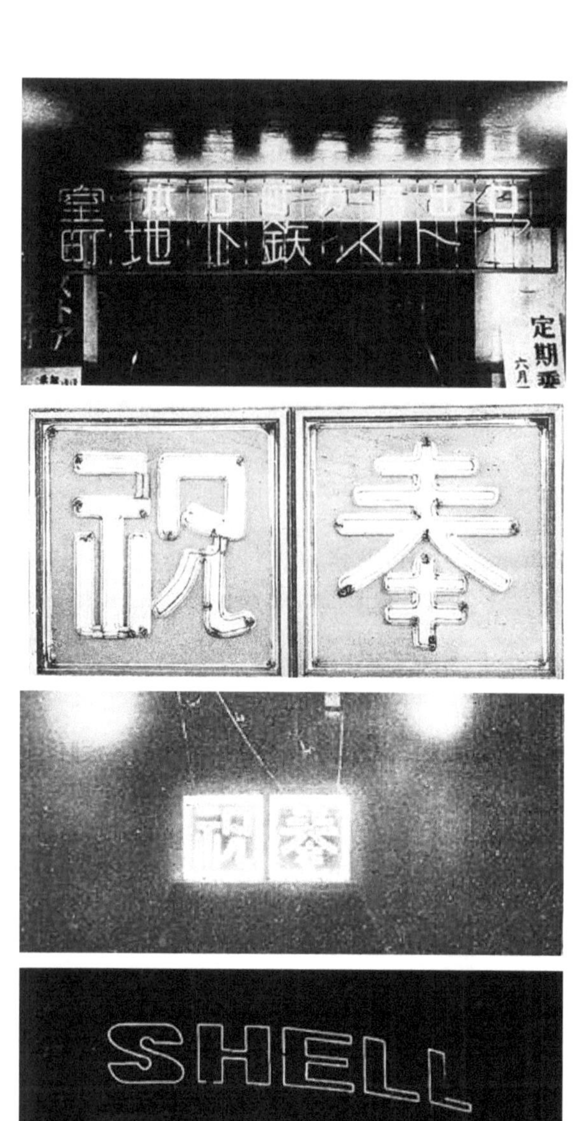
祝
奉
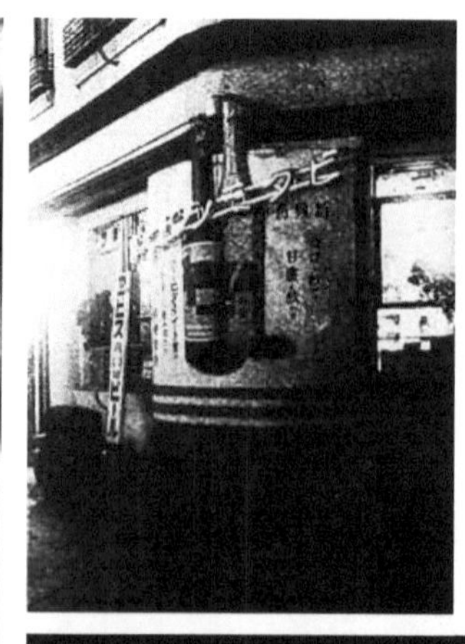
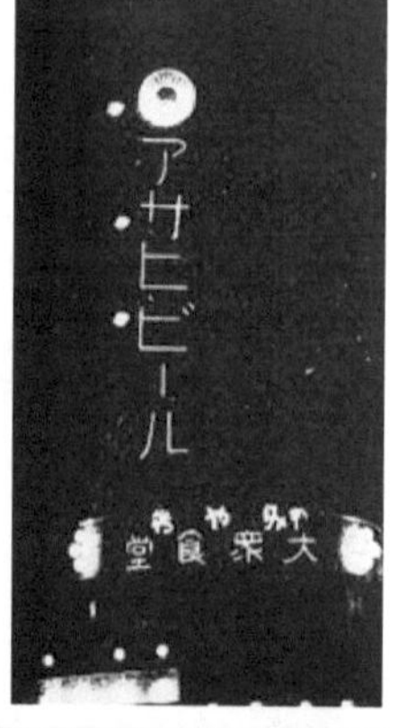
アサヒビール
大衆食堂
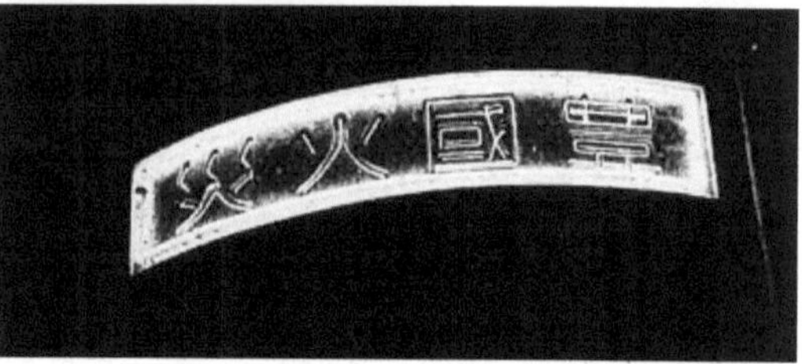
帝國火災
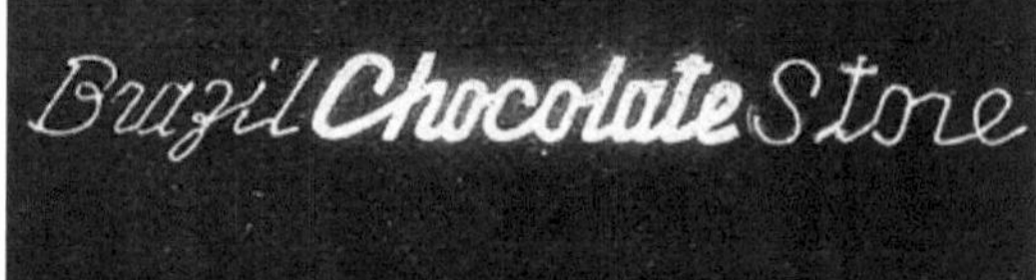
Brazil Chocolate Store
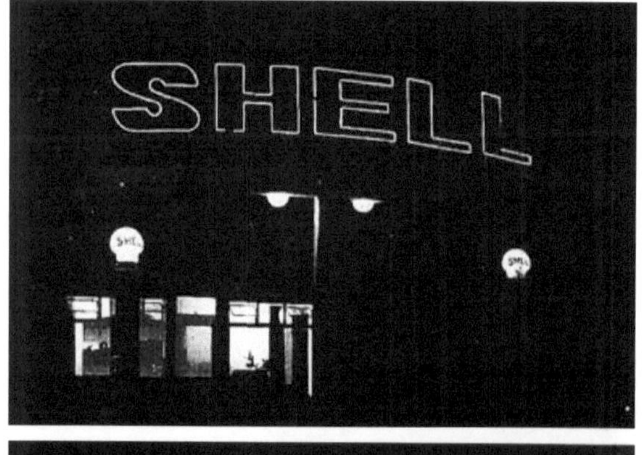
SHELL
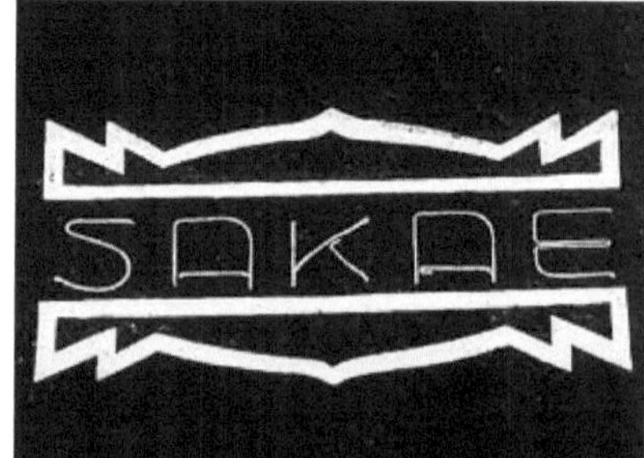
SAKAE
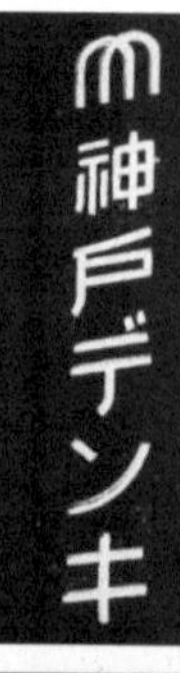
神戸デンキ
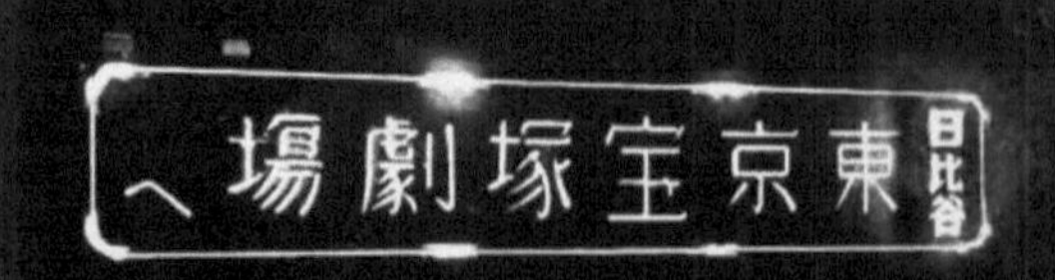
日比谷
東京宝塚劇場へ
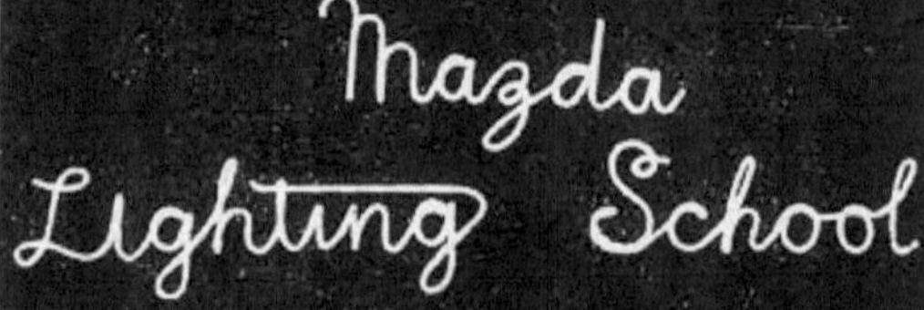
Mazda
Lighting School
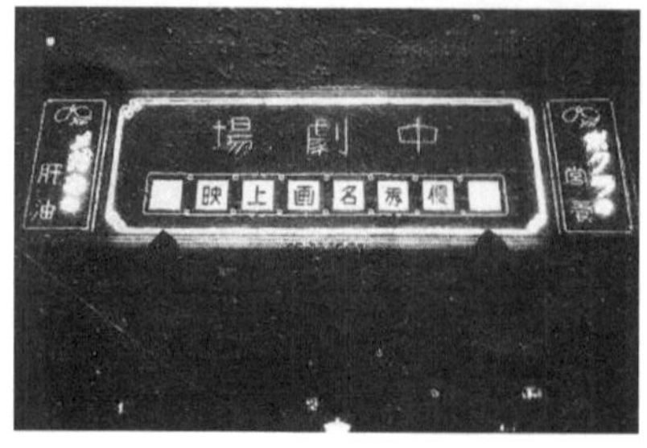
中劇場
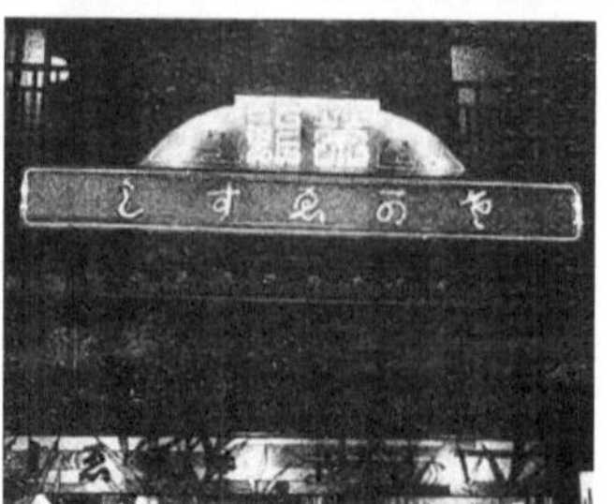
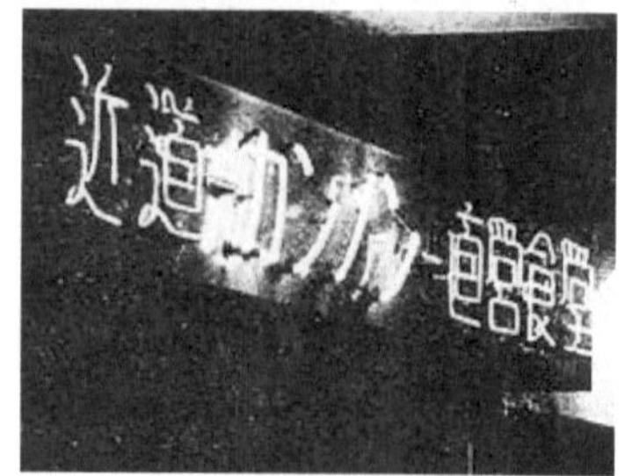

サイン用放電管

此の放電管は空氣中の稀有瓦斯ネオンを封入した放電管で、電氣サインに用ひて左記の如き絶大の特長があります

一、眼を奪ふ事
二、遠くよりも明確に見へる事
三、美麗にして總明なる事
四、晝夜何時でも見へる事
五、電力費の安き事
六、壽命の長い事
七、維持費の安い事
八、連續した長い線を自由に表はし得る事
九、各種の色を容易に出す事

東京朝日新聞社

（東京朝日新聞社の文字は一字三尺角）

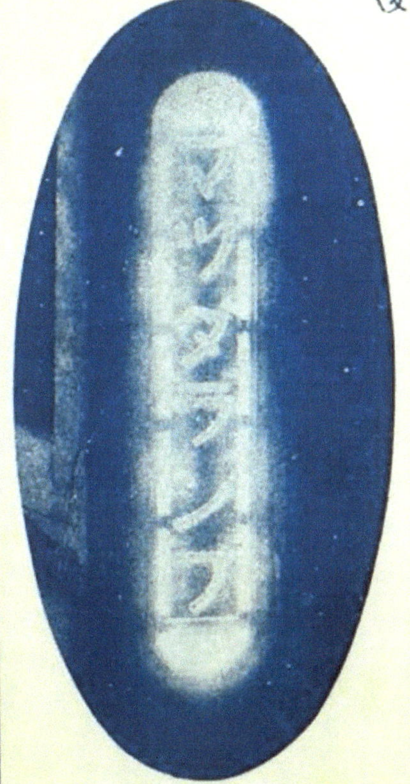

東京電氣株式會社
銀座販賣店

（マツダランプの文字は一字二尺角）

KIRIN-BEER

1

マーケット

2

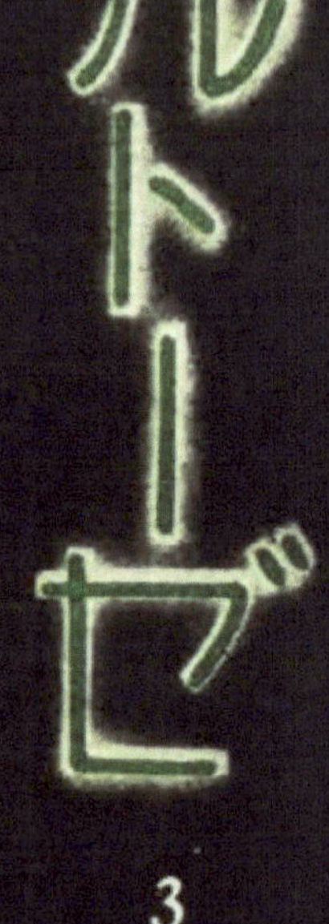

3

此の放電管は空氣中の稀有
瓦斯ネオンを封入した放電管
て、電氣サインに用ひて下記
の如き絶大の特長があります

一、眼に清新の氣分を與へること
二、遠くよりも明確に見えること
三、美麗にして斬新なること
四、晝夜何時でも見えること
五、電力費の安きこと
六、壽命の長きこと
七、維持費の安きこと
八、連續した長き線を自由に出し得ること
九、各種の色を容易に出し得ること

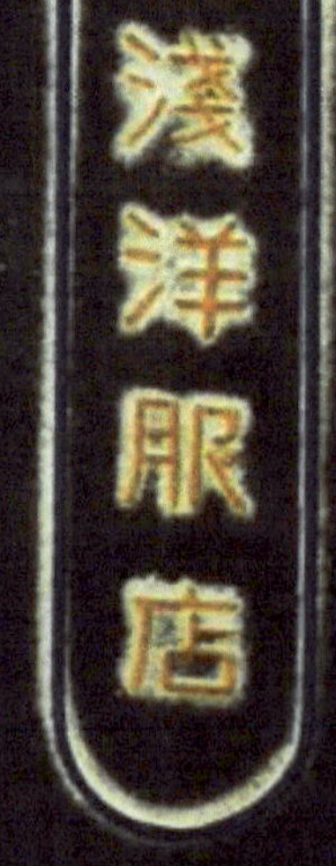

4

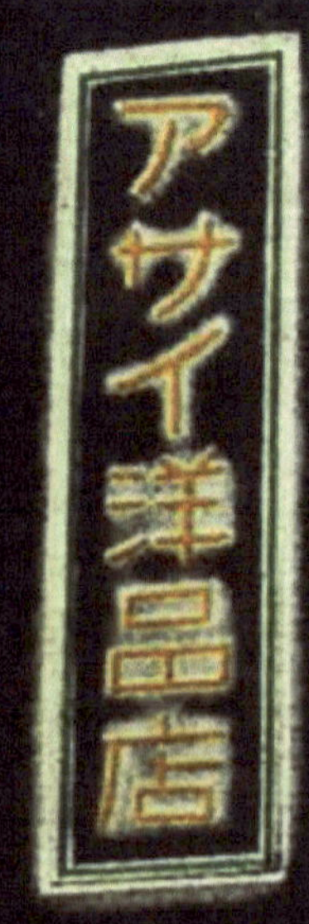

5

サイン用放電管

TECネオン

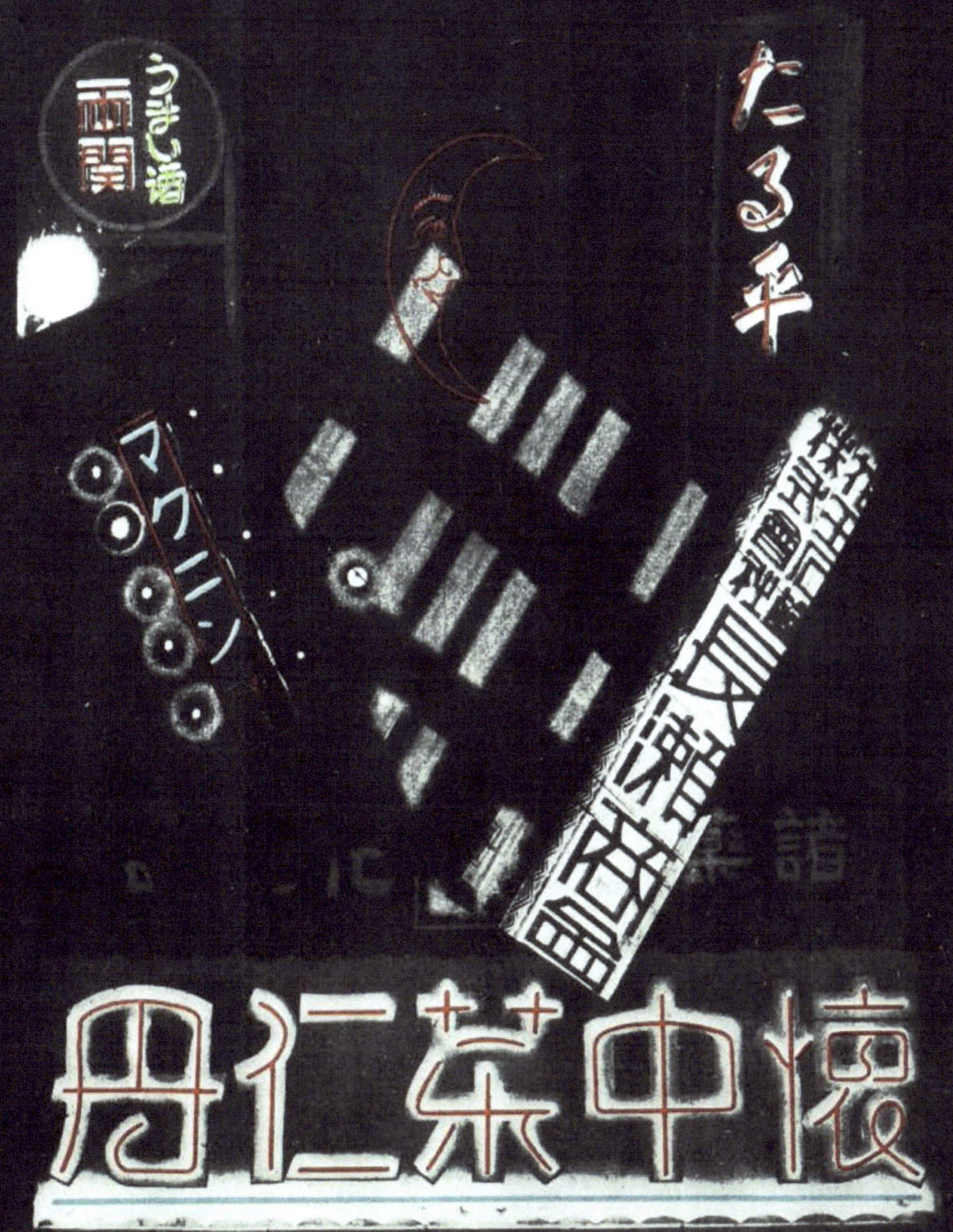

Early Materials

Japan initially relied exclusively on US imports for neon materials. Traders would import glass tubes, gas, transformers, insulators, and enameled wiring for neon signs. They were amazed to see green neon lights, as they hadn't thought about using colored glass for neon tubing. The industry was eager to start domestic production of neon materials as the imported glass tubing was routinely damaged due to rough freighting.

Neon gas was first imported from the United States and Germany. Initially, only neon gas was used for neon signs, soon followed by argon, helium, krypton and xenon. Around 1926, Tokyo Electric and Teikoku Oxygen produced the first domestic neon gas, but its purity was inferior to that of foreign products. Further development was put off until after World War II.

By 1928, neon tubes were being hand pulled from a glass furnace in Japan. Although the quality didn't match the imported product, it met the current quality demands of the industry. Tokyo Vacuum Glass Subsidiary was eventually established to mass produce neon tubes. In addition, Kimura Insulator Subsidiary created products from foreign samples. They supplied automatic flashers, insulators, and a number of other unique products to the industry.

Most of the neon transformers were imported from General Electric or Jefferson's company. The early transformers were large, heavy, and housed in a wooden box. Claude also supplied an adjustable transformer to its licensees. Transformers were studied by companies such as Osaka Transformer and Seidensha, and were soon imitated and produced. Osaka Transformer made one of the first outdoor type transformers that resembled an umbrella shape.

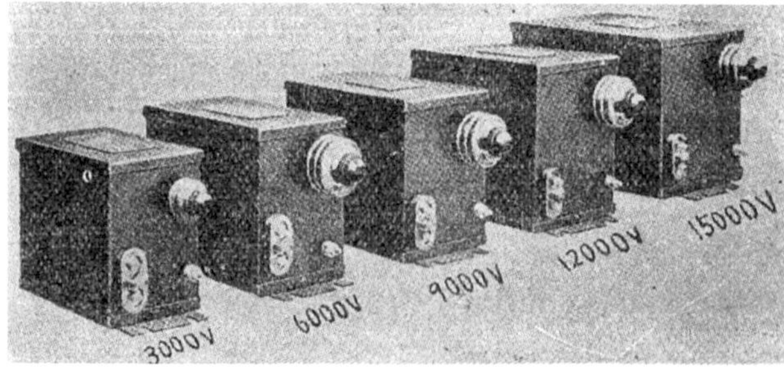

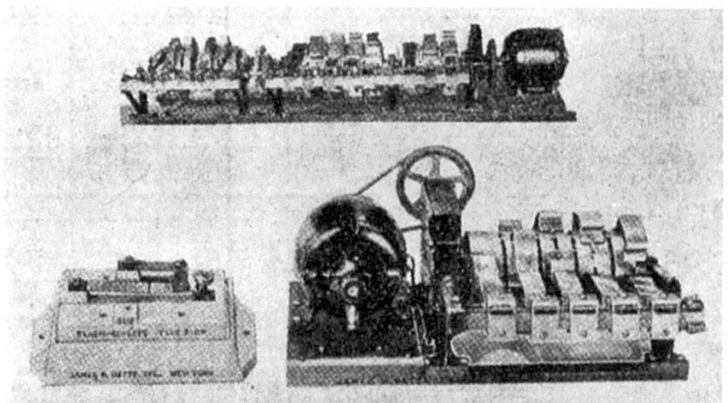

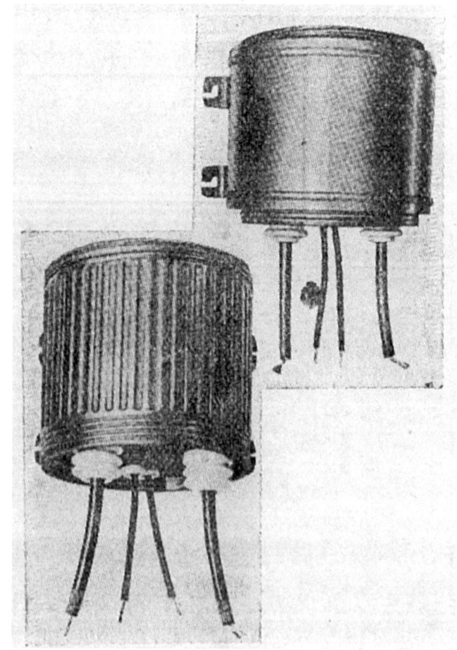

TOP: WESTERN STYLE TRANSFORMERS
BOTTOM: JAPANESE BULB FLASHERS

JAPANESE STYLE TRANSFORMERS

1930s

By 1930, neon lights were installed on the rooftops of Mitsukoshi and Matsuya department stores in Osaka. These lights were used as official beacon towers. The powerful glow of red neon would pass through strong fog for the benefit of aircraft visibility. About six of these beacon towers were installed in the vicinity. In addition, neon tubes were used along ports and coastal regions for marine navigation markers.

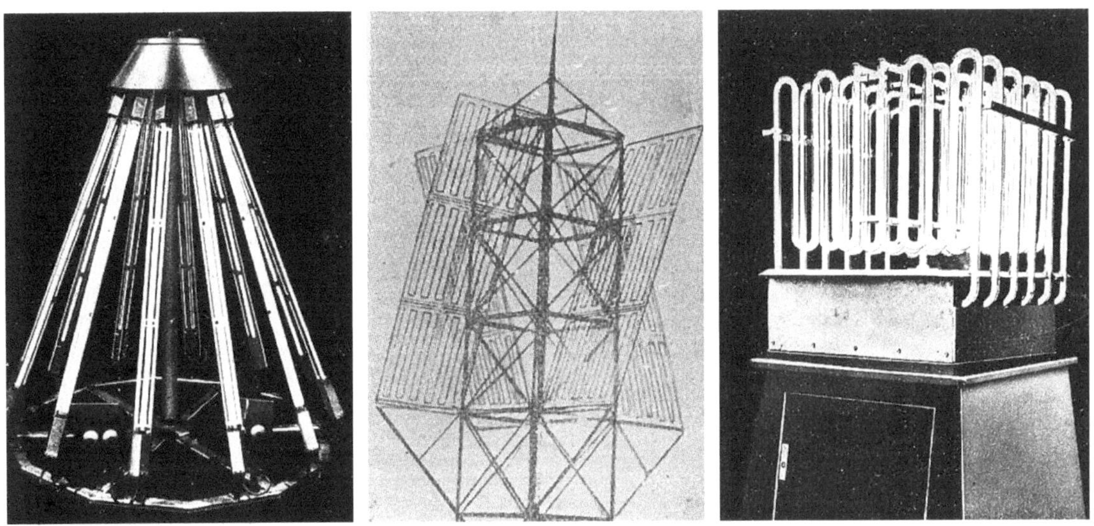

NEON BEACON TOWERS FOR AIRCRAFT

The neon signs that appeared on the streets were not much different from those of the United States. Arched signs and light post decorations lined shopping arcades throughout many neighborhoods across Japan. Universal symbols such as eyeglasses, shoes, tea kettles, kimonos, books, and medical crosses were made into neon signs to advertise a shops' products and services.

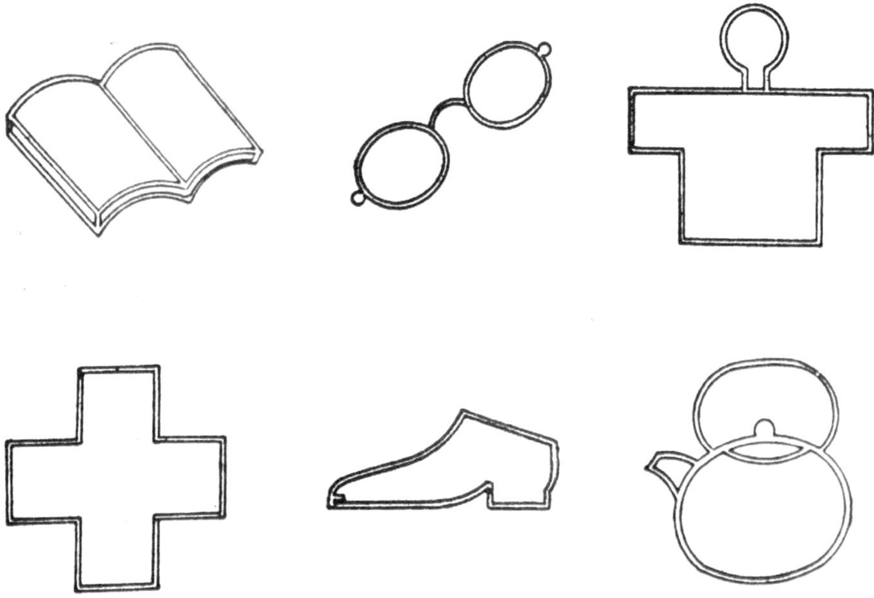

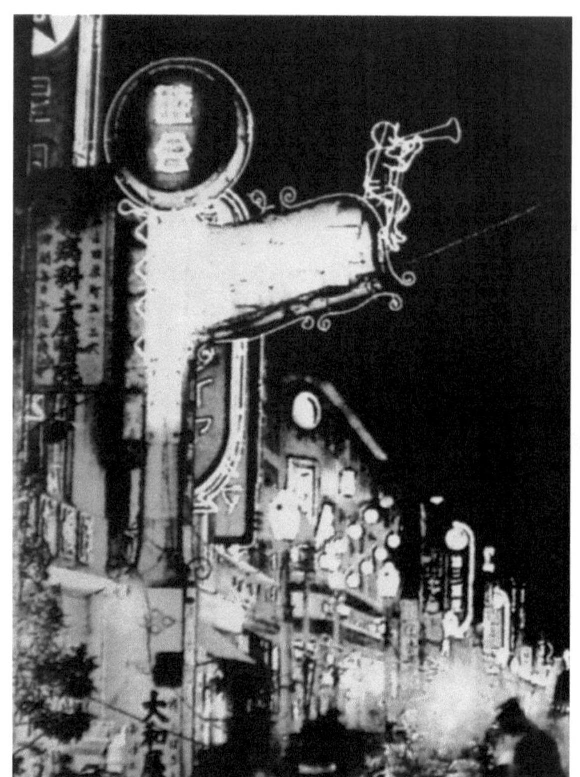

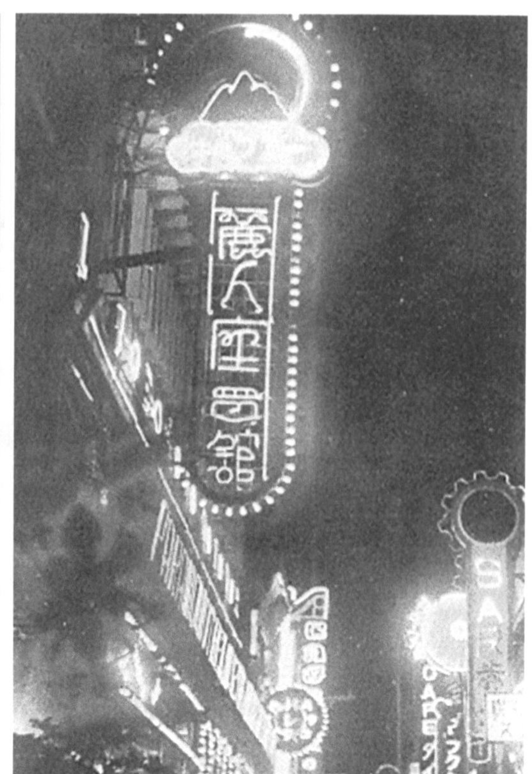

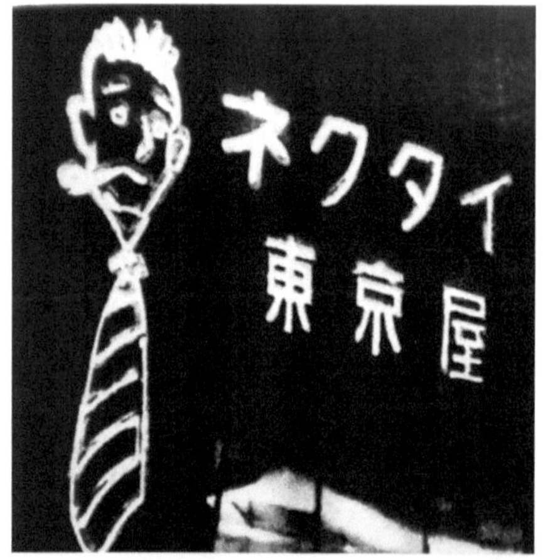
ネクタイ
東京屋

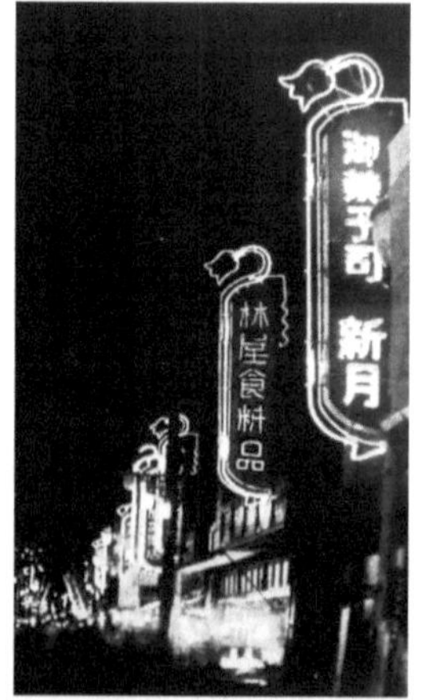
御菓子司 新月

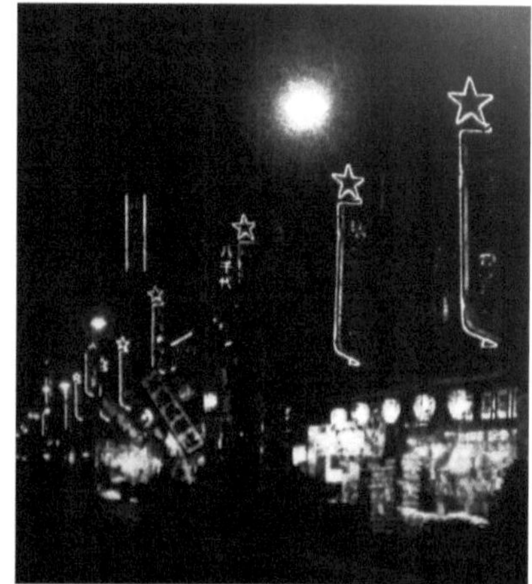

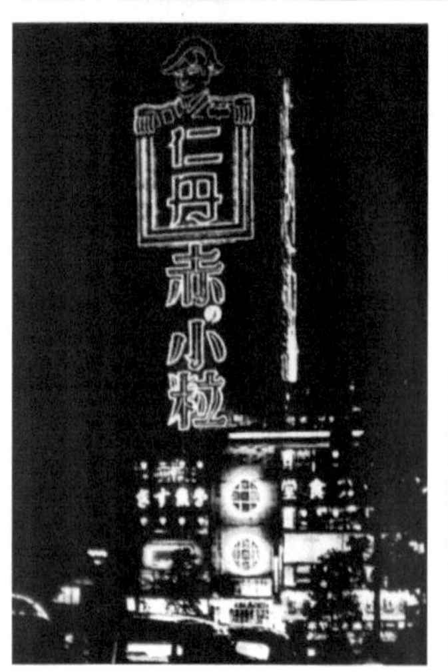
仁丹

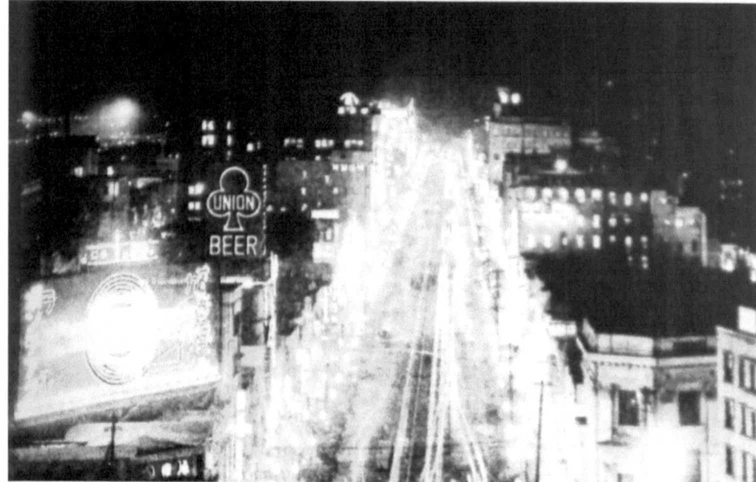
UNION
BEER

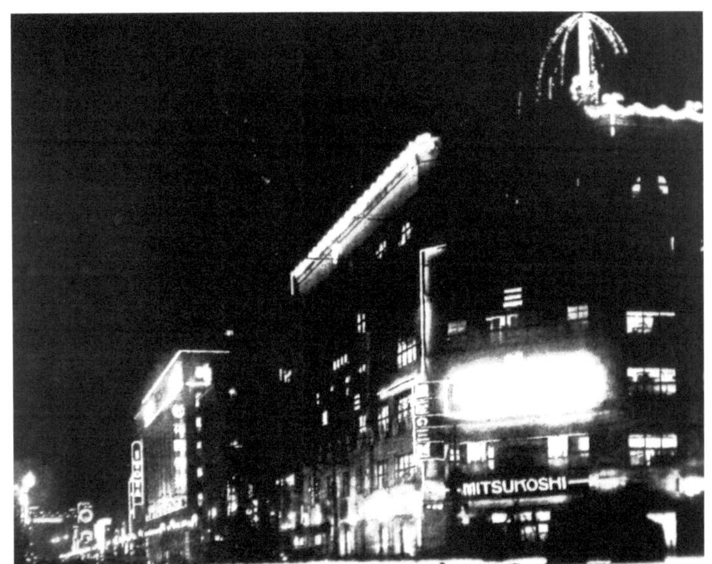

MITSUKOSHI

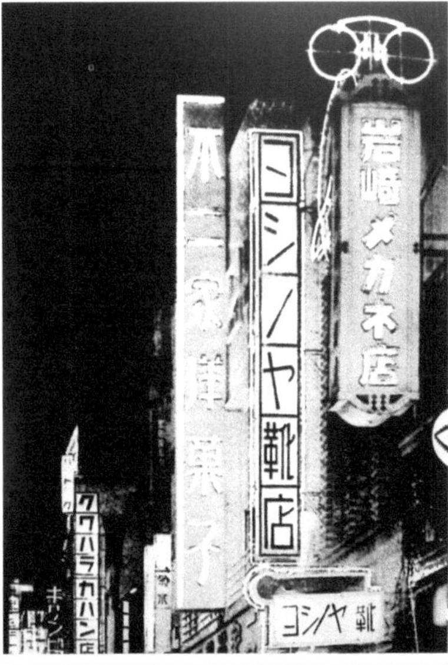

岩崎メカネ店
ヨシノヤ靴店
ヨシノヤ 靴

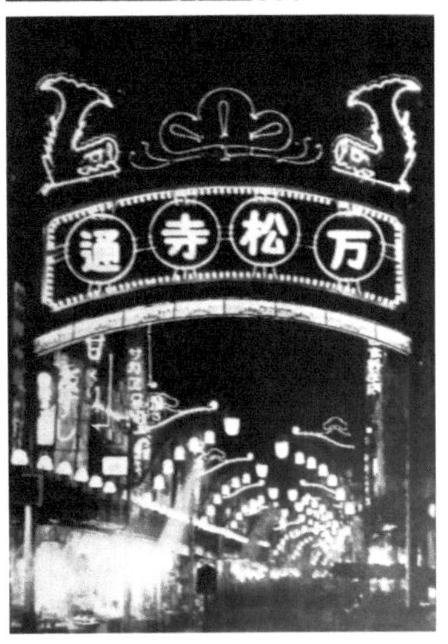

万松寺通

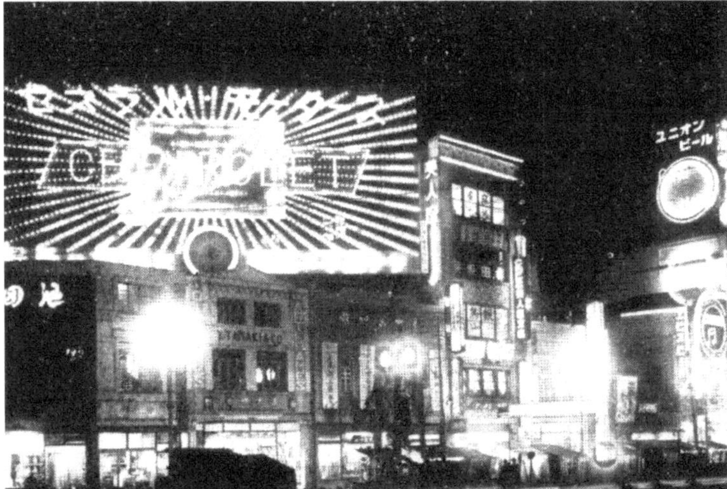

ユニオン
ビール

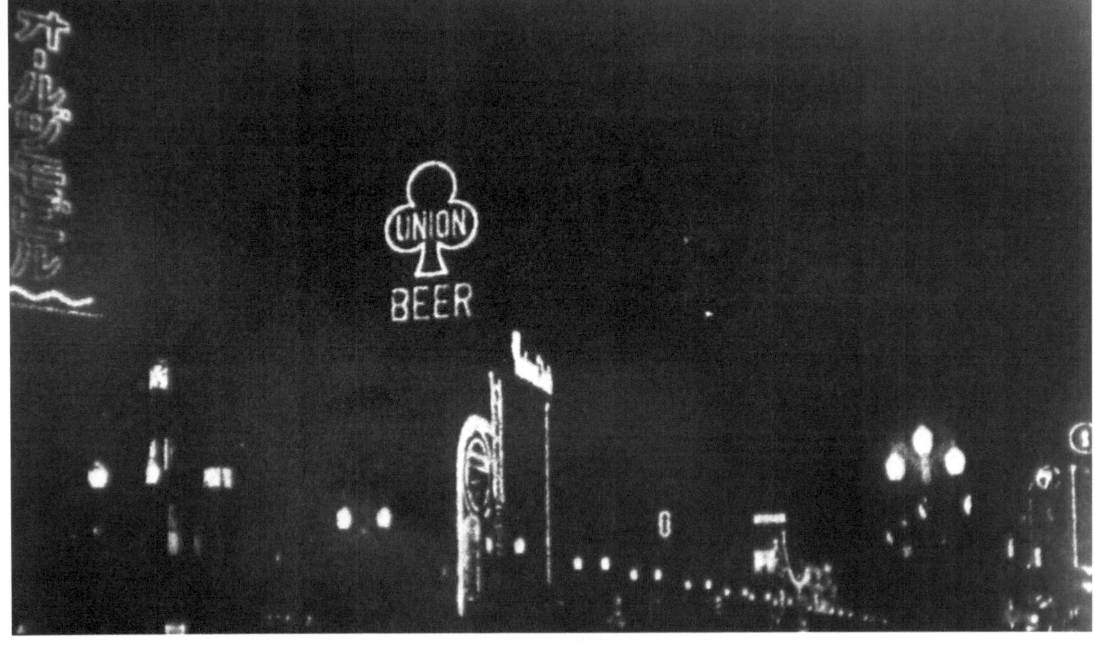

UNION
BEER

In February 1930, the GM spectacular made its debut in Ginza. The sign was made up of concentric circles, overlaid by the General Motors logo, Japanese characters and English characters. The sign reportedly cost 10,000 yen to build, and another 10,000 yen per year in media fees. The sign was updated three times, in 1931, 1933, and 1935. The glamor of the design increased as sign technology rapidly developed.

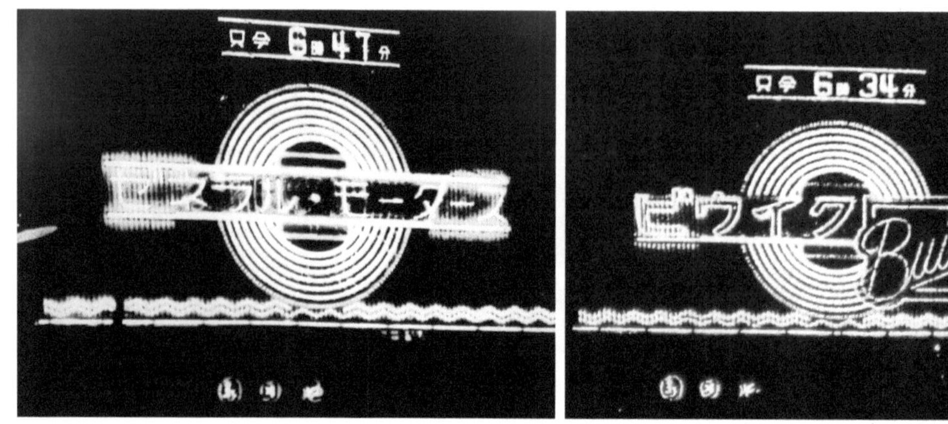

GM SPECTACULAR IN GINZA, TOKYO

In 1931, the Kao Soaps neon tower was constructed in Ueno, Tokyo. The Kao Soaps neon tower was bigger than the GM sign of Ginza, with a power rating of 32kW/hour. Nearby, the world's largest neon clock, at 18 meters in diameter, was constructed in front of the Ueno Subway Station.

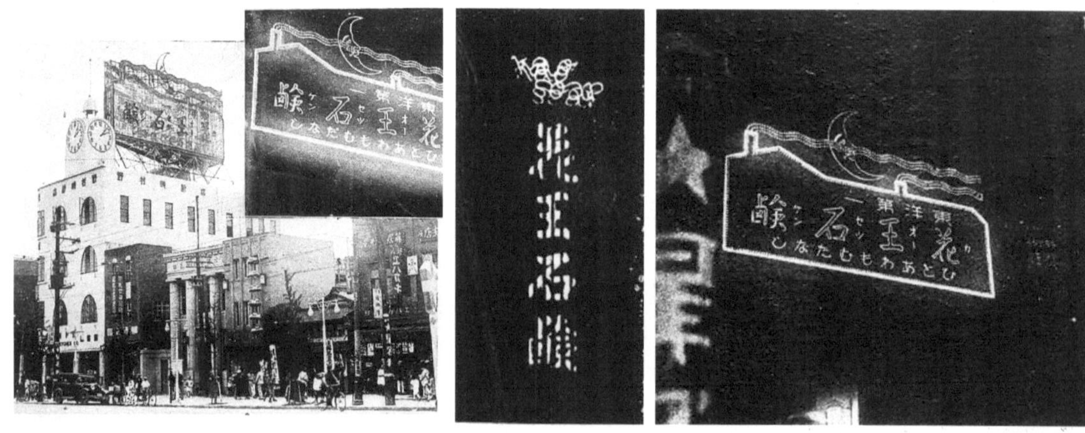

KAO SOAP SIGN IN UENO, TOKYO

A survey from 1931 that found that 55% of neon signs were used in cafes, cabarets, and restaurants. The use of electric signs held great significance for people, as it was a symbol of the new age. Illuminated sign competitions were held by the Tokyo Electrical Bureau, the Illuminating Engineering Society, and the Tokyo Electric Lighting Company. Neon manufacturers tested their abilities to make spectacular neon displays for the public. These neon signs were successful in attracting advertisers for alcohol, automobiles, medicines, and other consumer goods.

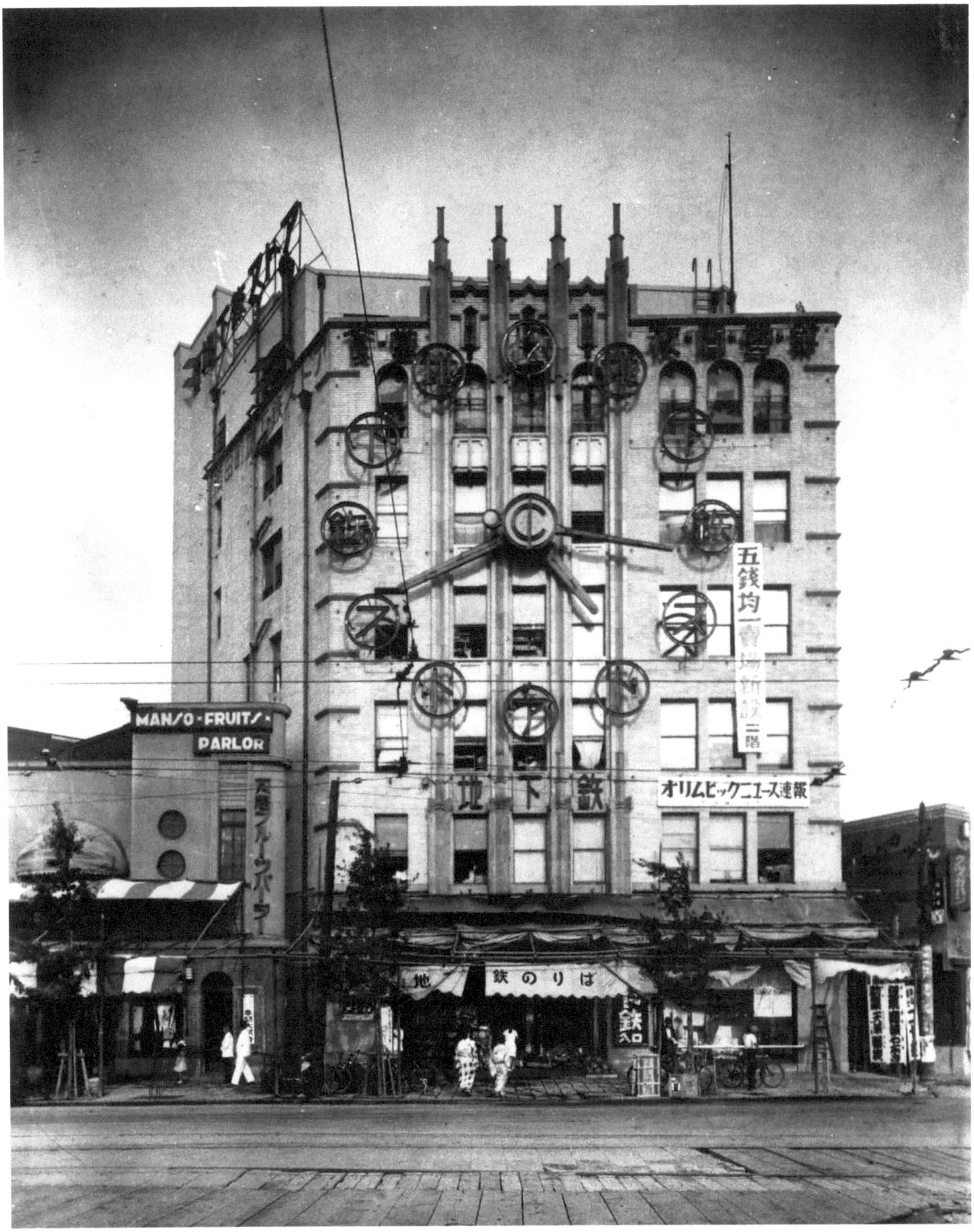

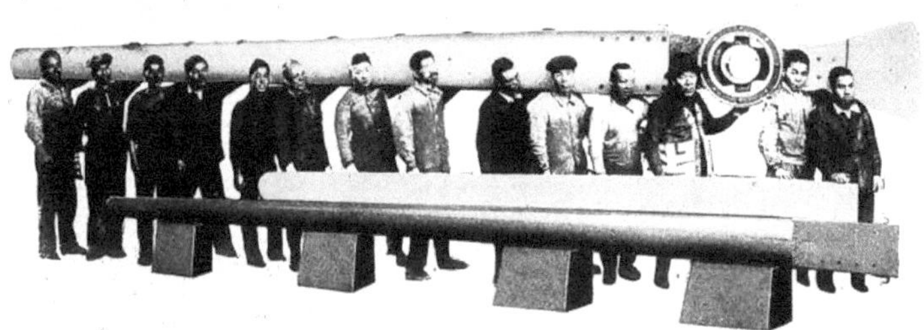

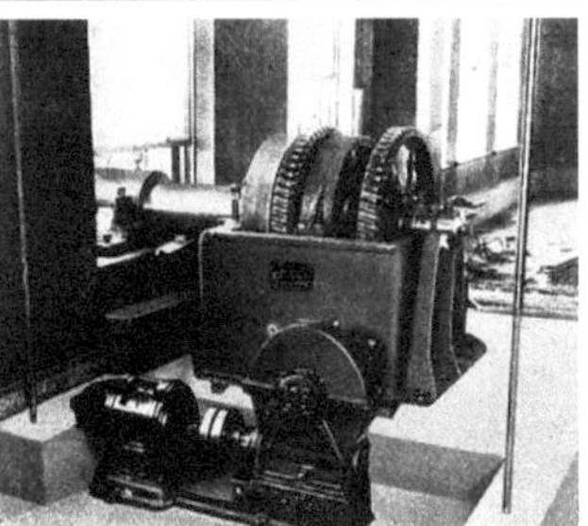

THE NEON CLOCK OF THE UENO SUBWAY BUILDING

Early Showa Era Neon Signs

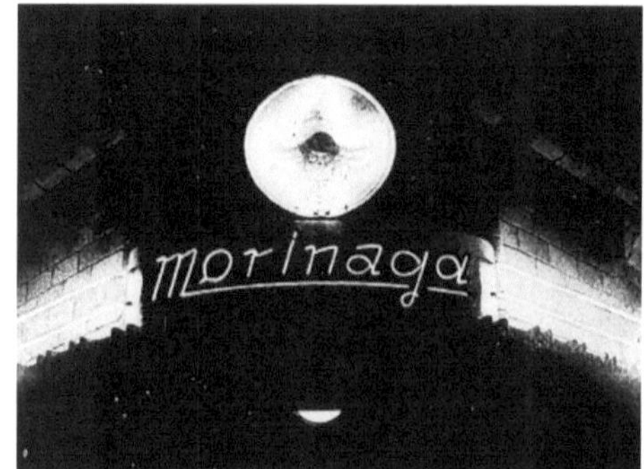

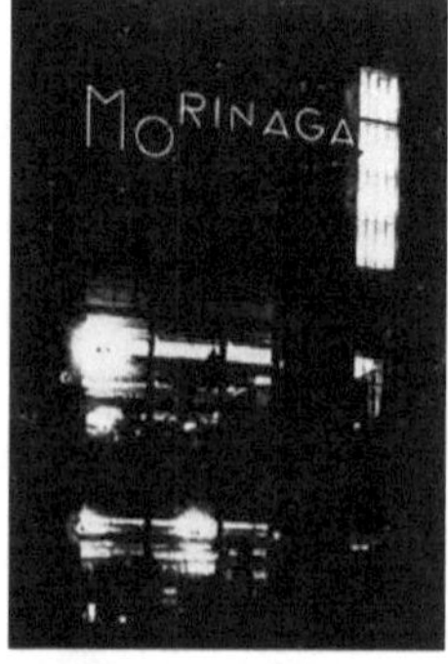

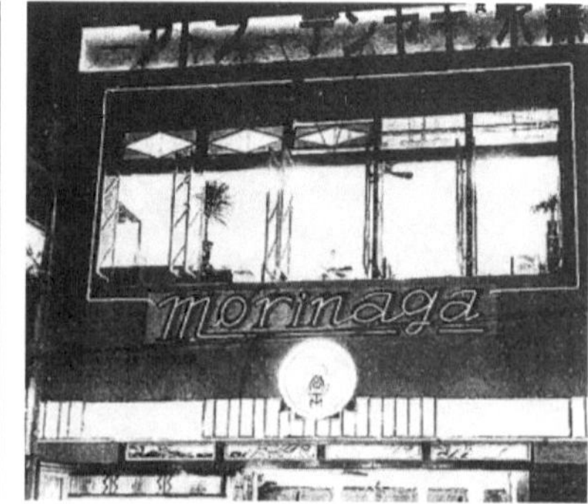

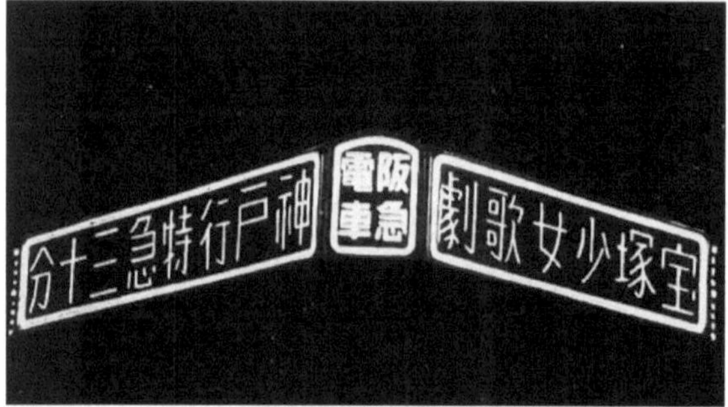

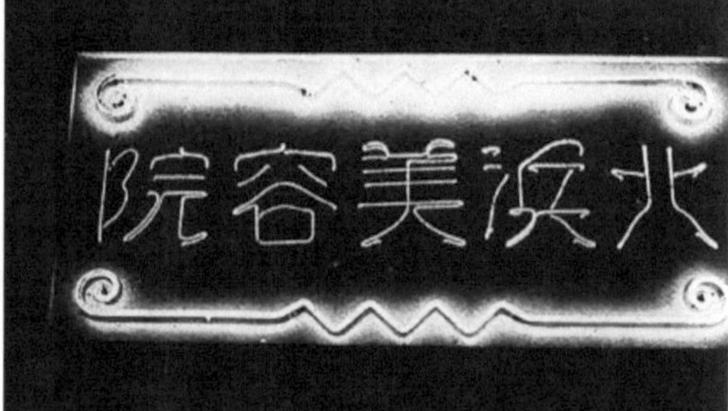

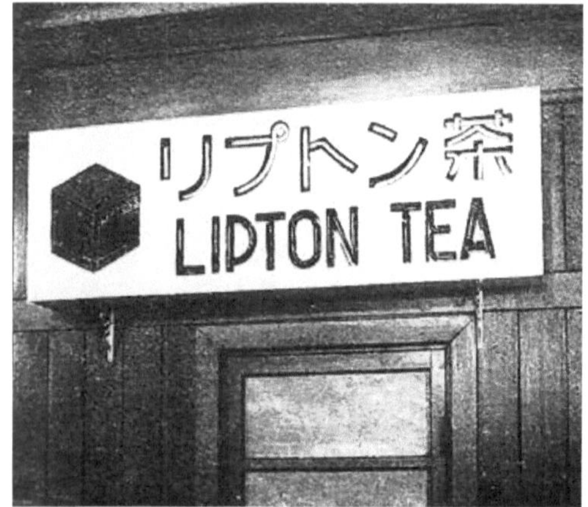

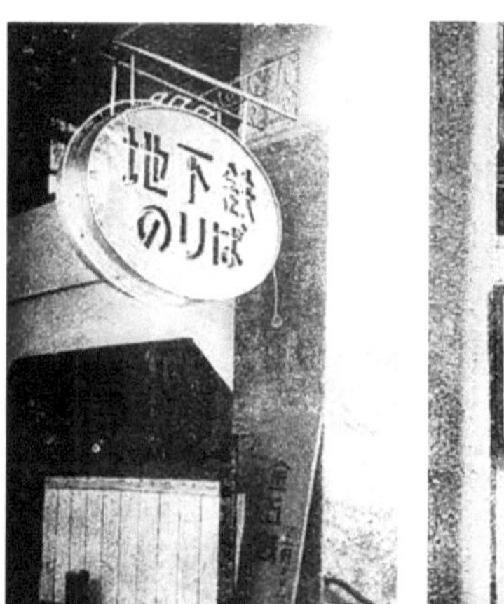

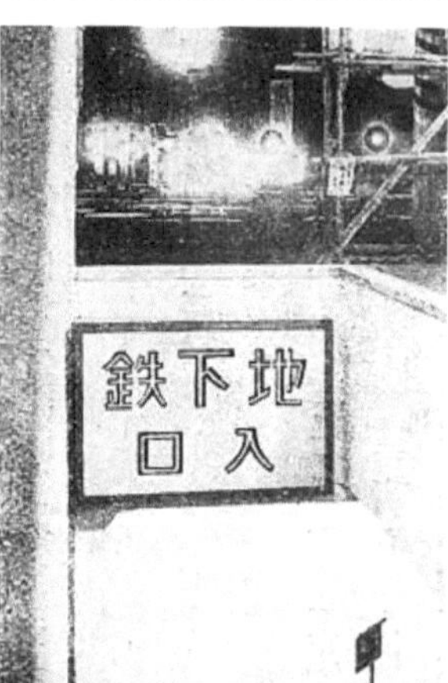

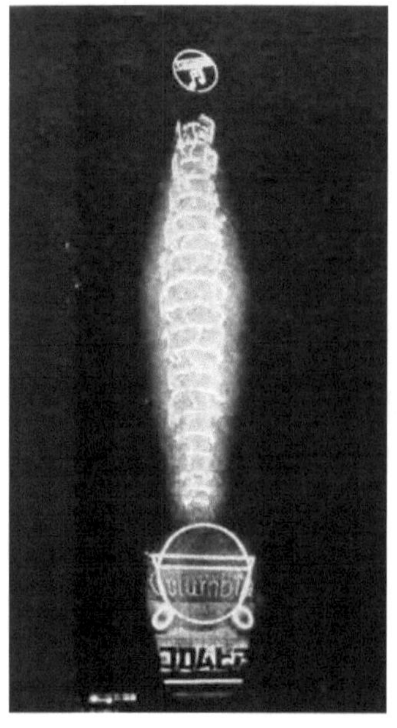

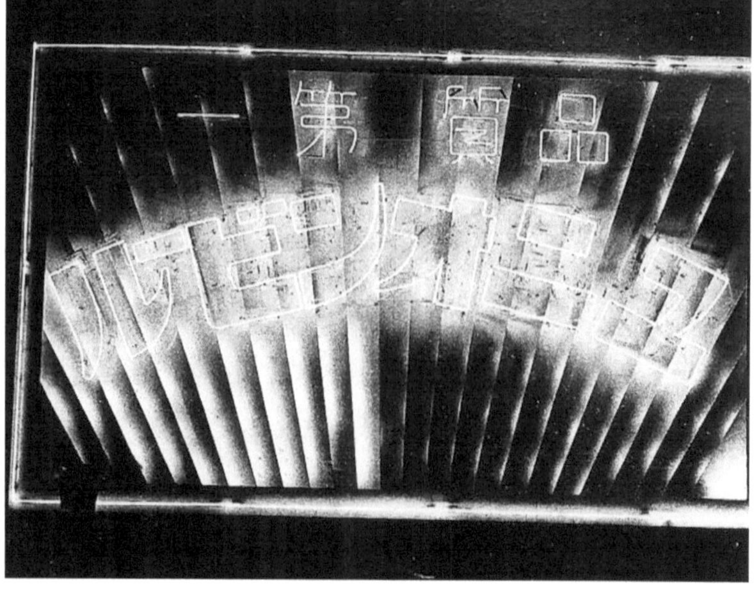

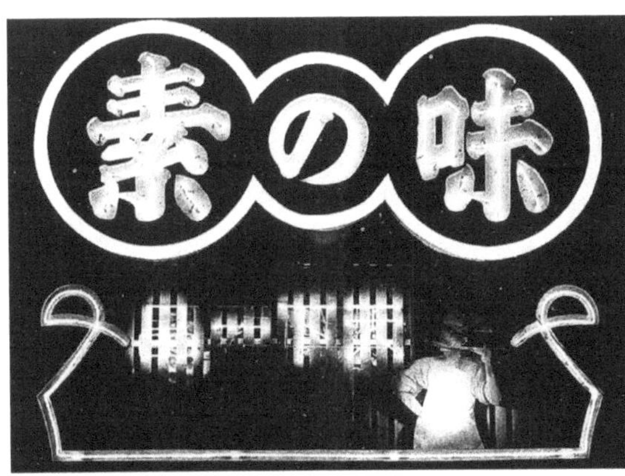
味の素

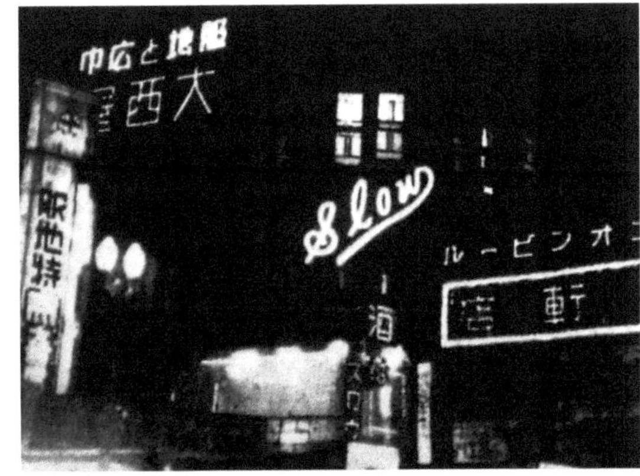
Slow
ユニオンビール

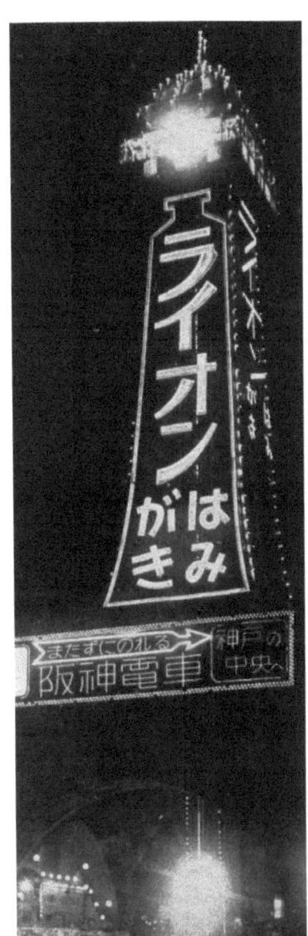
ライオンはみがき
またずにのれる
阪神電車
神戸の中央へ

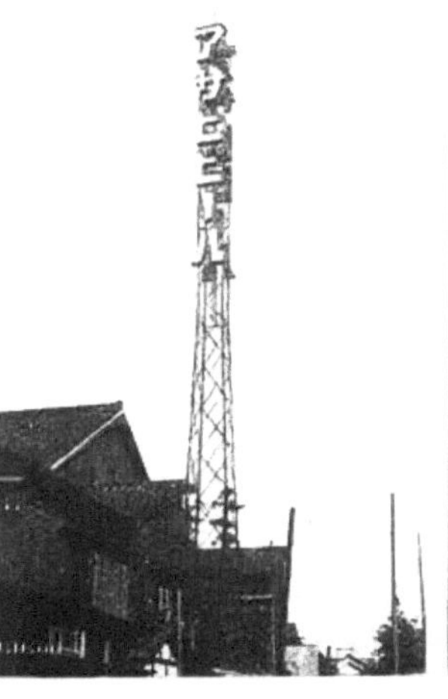

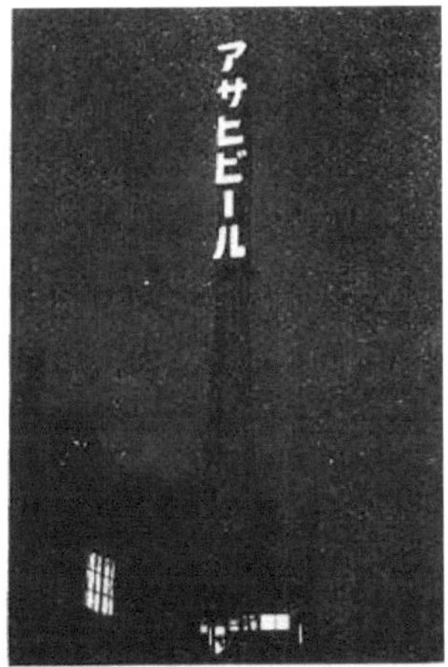
アサヒビール

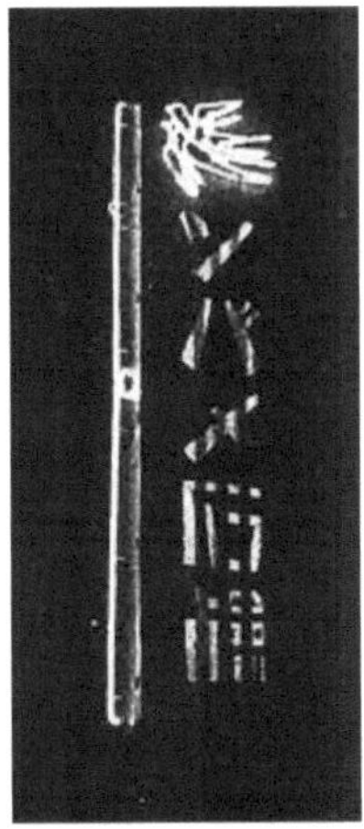

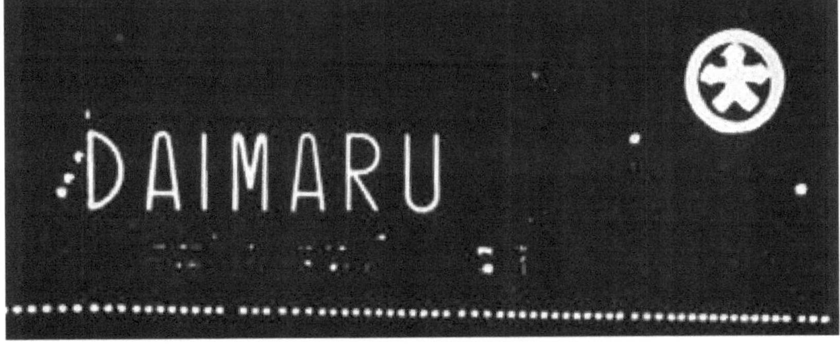
DAIMARU

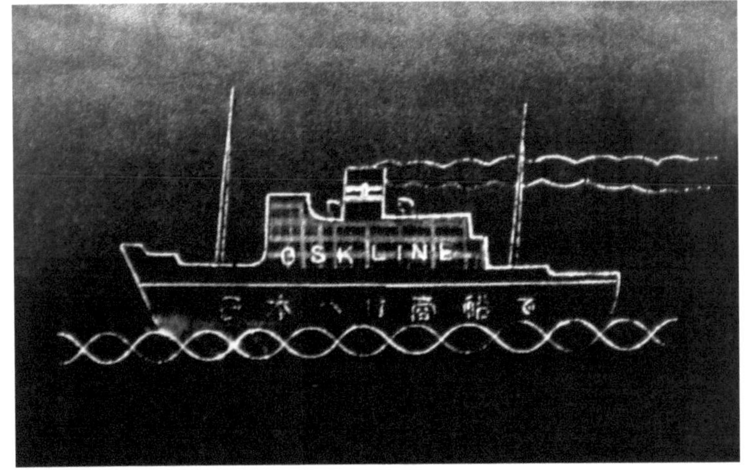
OSK LINE

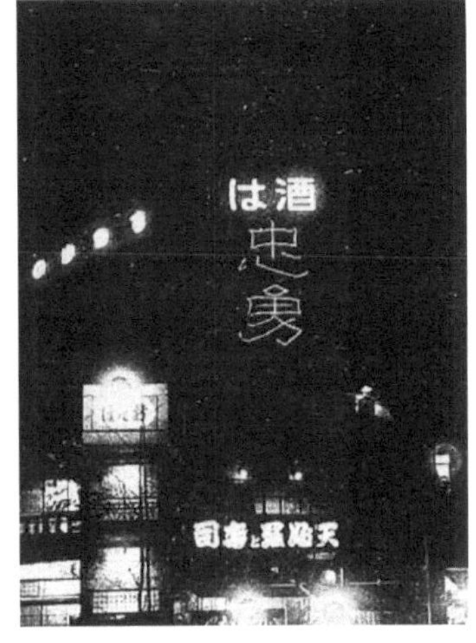
酒は
忠勇

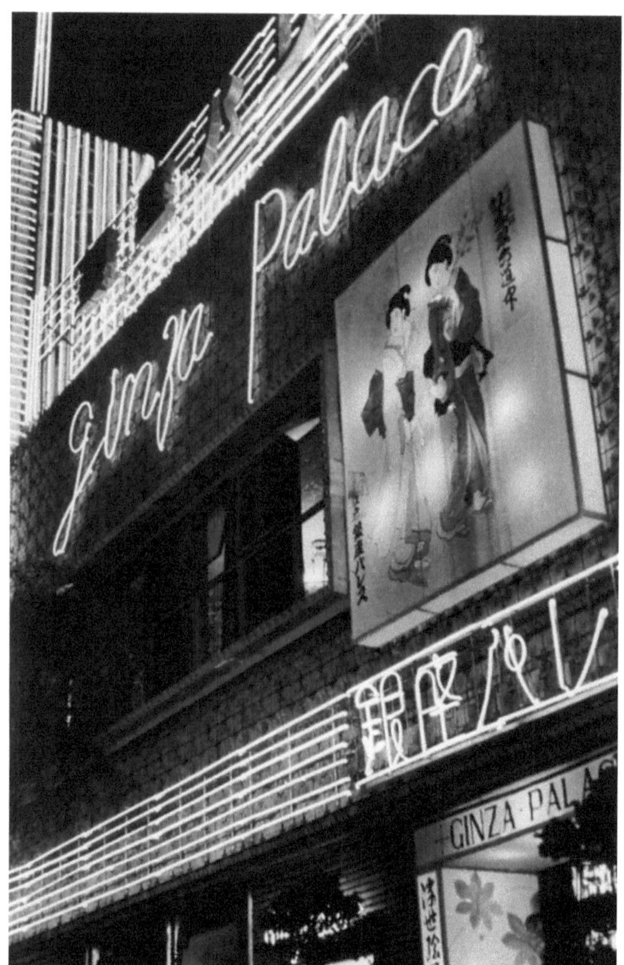

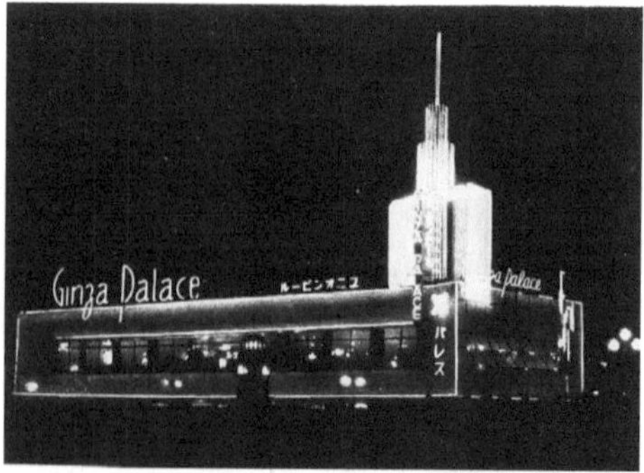

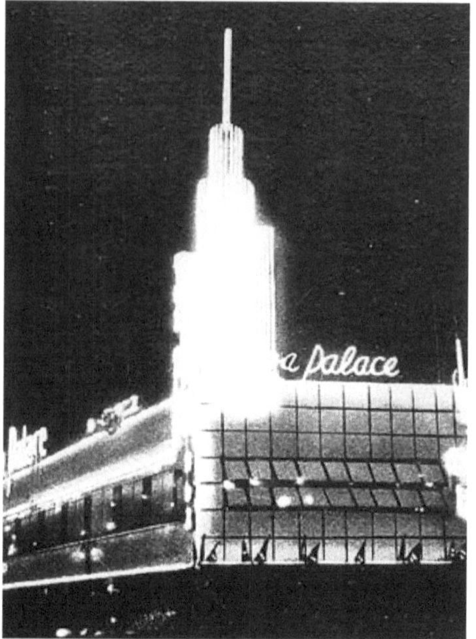

THE GINZA PALACE, TOKYO, 1936

Patent issues

Just as neon signs began to take off, a big patent dispute was filed by George Claude in 1933. He claimed that transformer that was produced by Tokyo Electric infringed upon his patent. A lawsuit was filed to invalidate the patent case at issue, though it wasn't upheld. George Claude disrupted the entire Japanese neon industry with this claim. The story gained a lot of attention from the press.

Nationwide suppliers and manufactures joined together to form the "Electric Club", the precursor to the national industry organization. Claude sent a notice to all companies involved and published articles in the newspapers requesting the cease of use. This lawsuit affected each company and the thousands of employees within Japan's neon industry.

The industry united to fight the claim. After years of disputing, a settlement was reached in 1938. This was a sensitive time as Japan was ramping up to engage in war with China. They felt that it was an inappropriate time to continue fighting, as world tensions were increasing.

By 1934, the Osaka Grand Palace set the world record for the largest amount of neon on a building. There was about 4000 meters of tubing along the club's facade. Tokyo Grand Ginza was just behind with about 3500 meters. In the same year, the electric railways started neon sign campaigns. A 8-meter tall sign by the Hanshin Railway appeared, advertising the quickest express train from Osaka to Kobe. After that, the Hanshin and Hankyu railways would engage in a neon battle. Every time one of the competitors would shorten the travel time of the express train, they would change their neon sign. This would happen multiple times per year.

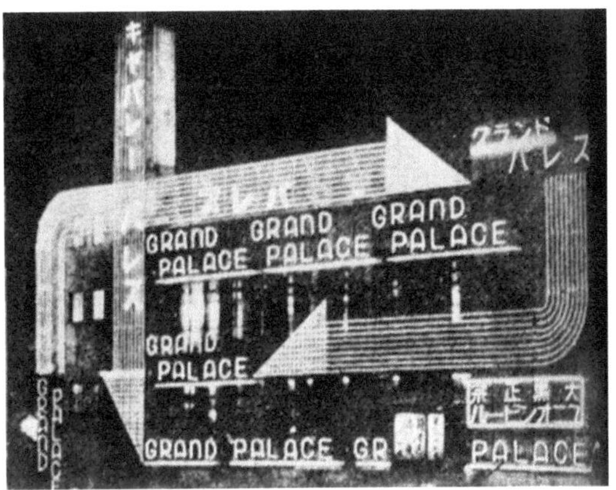

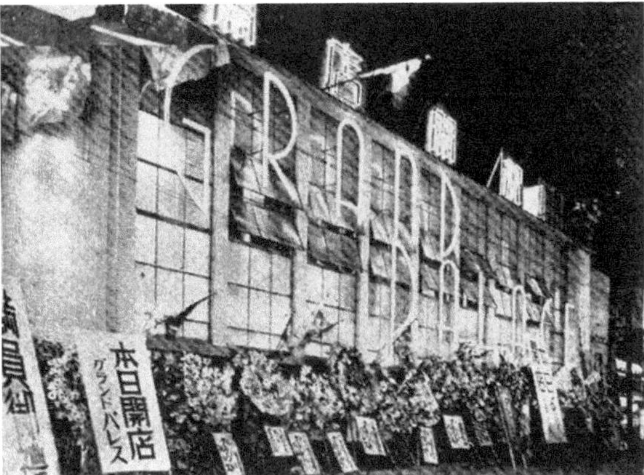

Companies that were traditionally active in newspaper advertising usually plunged into the "new medium". An even wider variety of companies such as manufacturers of chemicals, toothpaste, stationery, electrical products, and general stores were having neon spectaculars produced. This was before television made its way into households, so these emerging companies were desperate for ways to make a public appearance in a bright and colorful fashion.

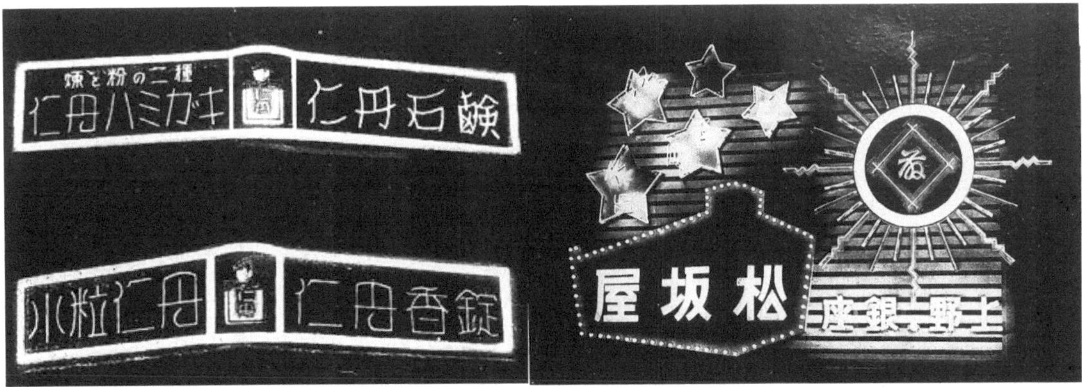

Due to the surge in signage, outdoor advertising ordinances were established in each prefecture, enacting standards for neon advertisements. This sparked the creation of local neon associations around the country that would combine forces to combat unreasonable regulations. From 1938, due to light control and construction regulations, only one large neon sign could be attached to a building's frontage. There were many critics that set out to preserve the cityscapes, especially in traditional areas.

Cafes, Clubs, and Cabarets

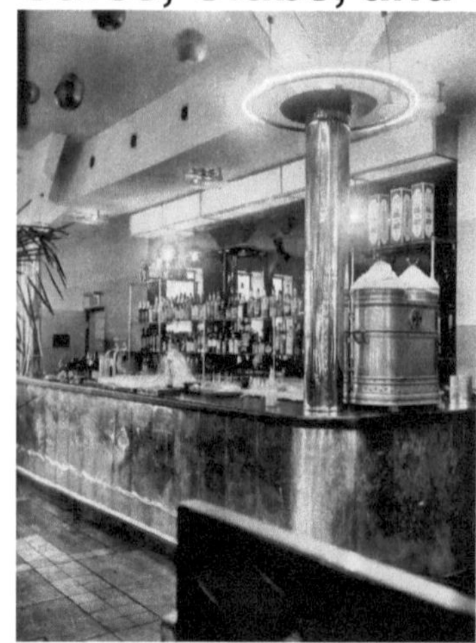

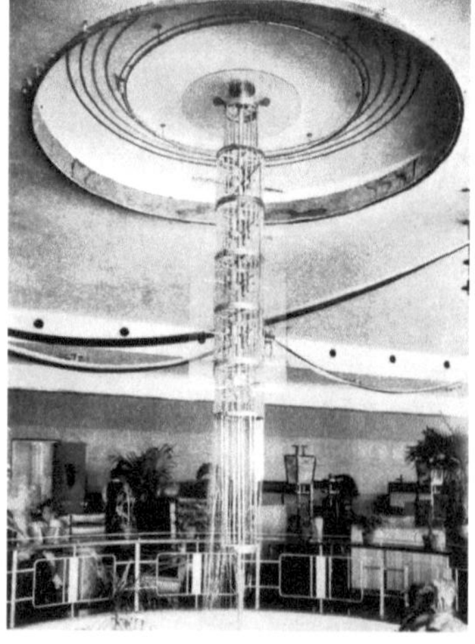

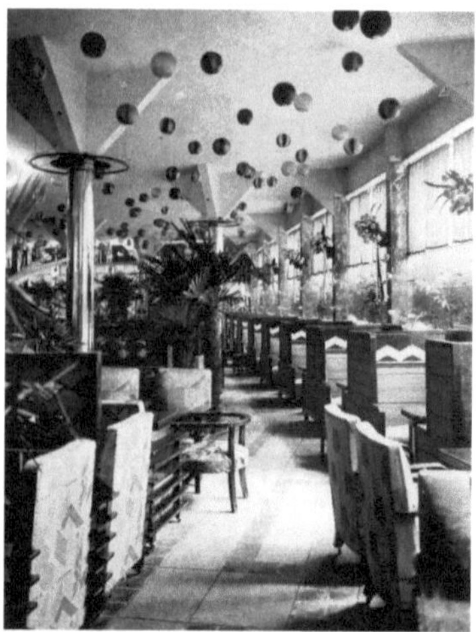

GINZA PALACE INTERIOR

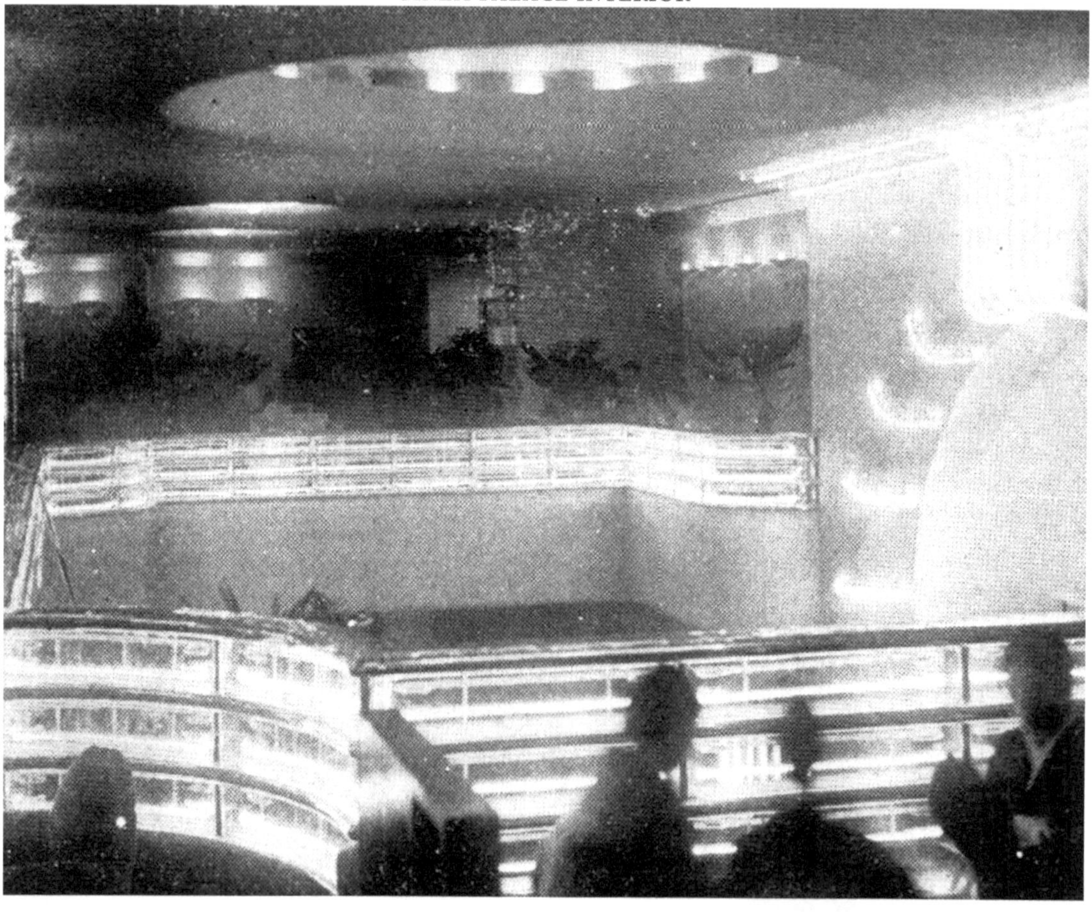

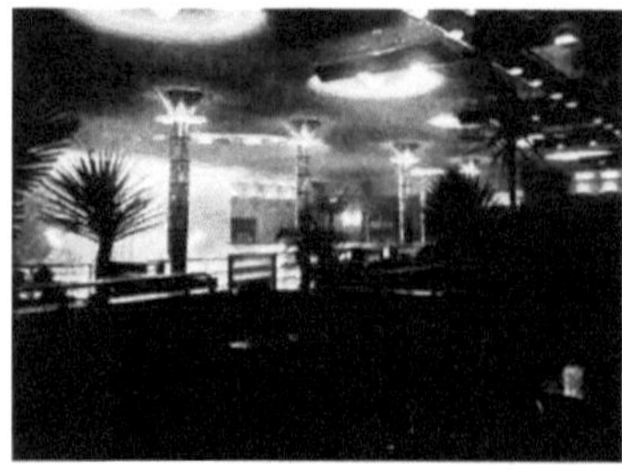

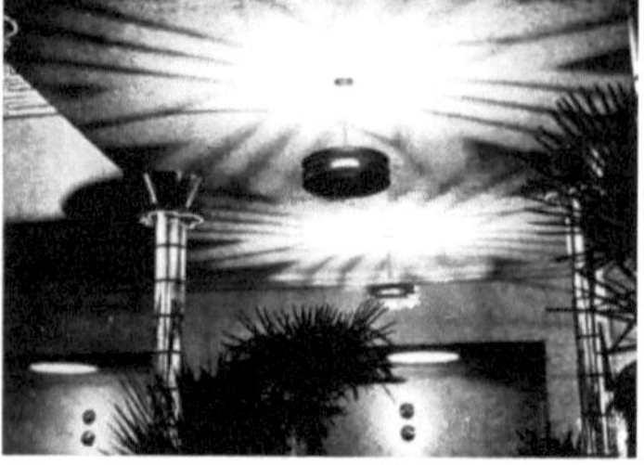

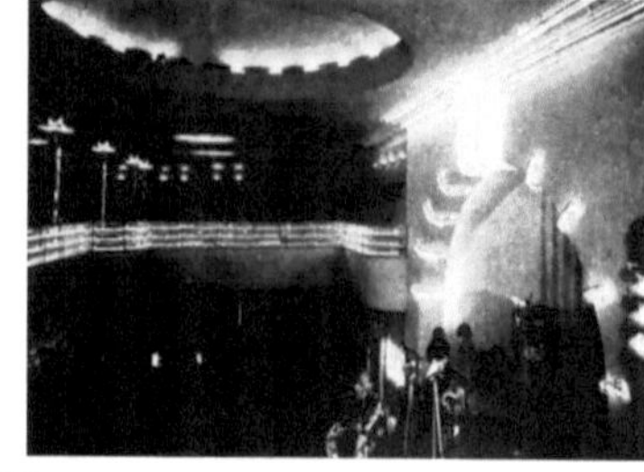

GRAND GINZA CLUB INTERIOR

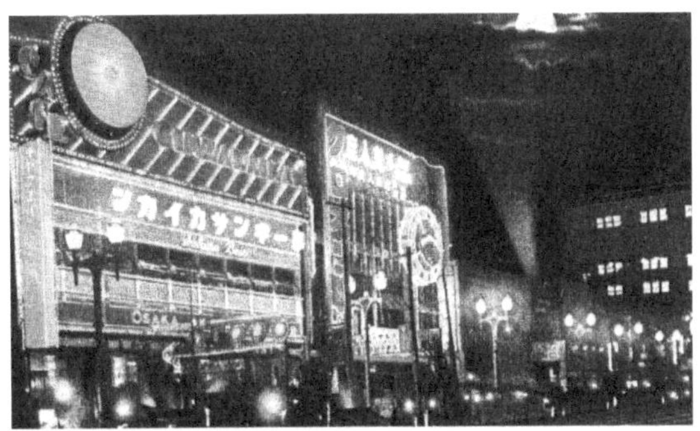

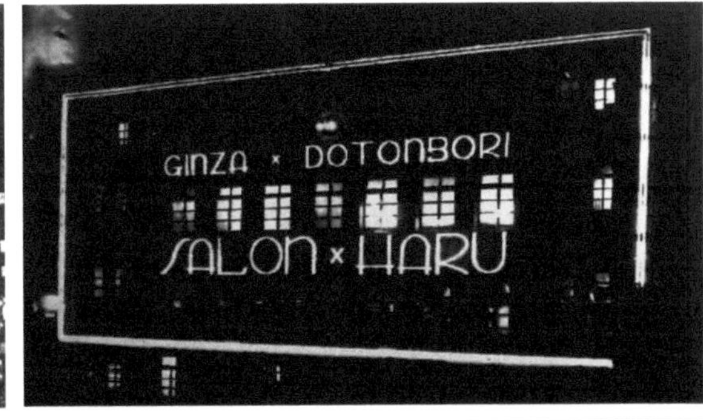
GINZA × DOTONBORI
SALON × HARU

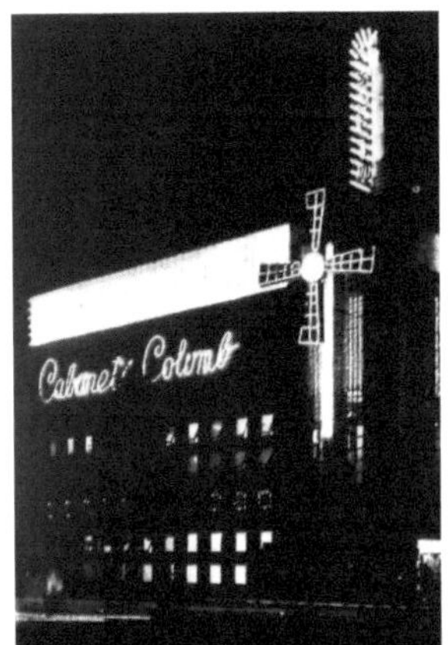
Cabaret Columb

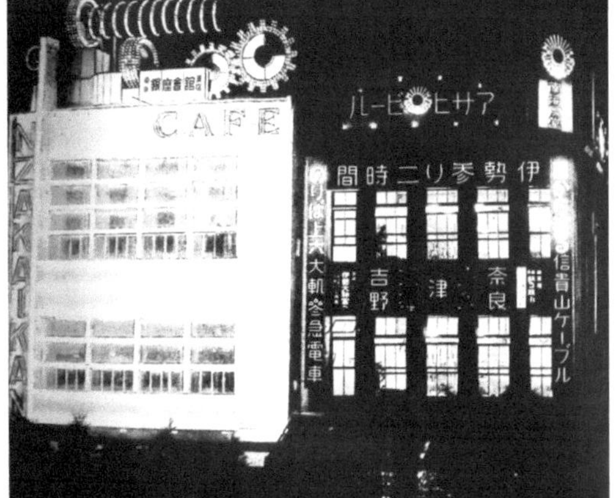
CAFE
アサヒビール
伊勢参り二時間
吉野
奈良
信貴山ケーブル
大軌参急電車

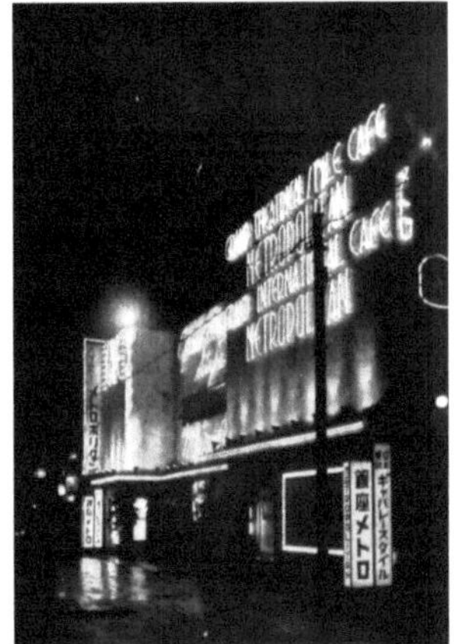

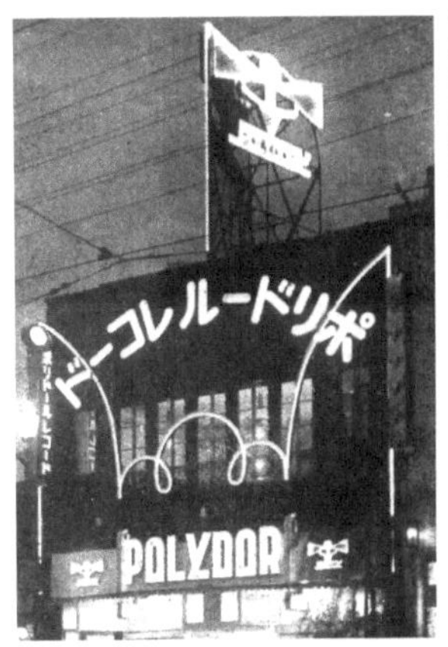
ポリドールレコード
POLYDOR

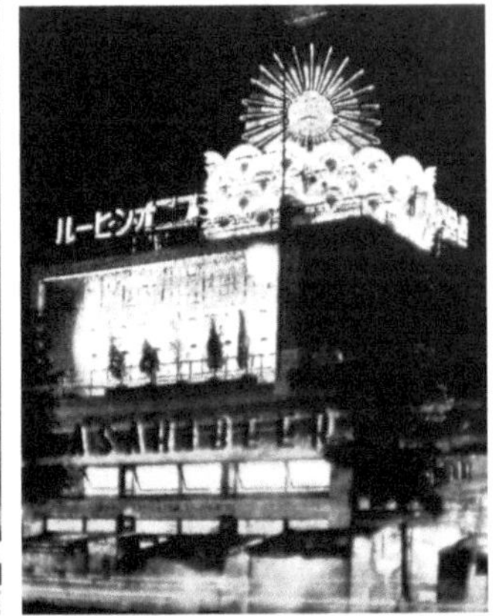

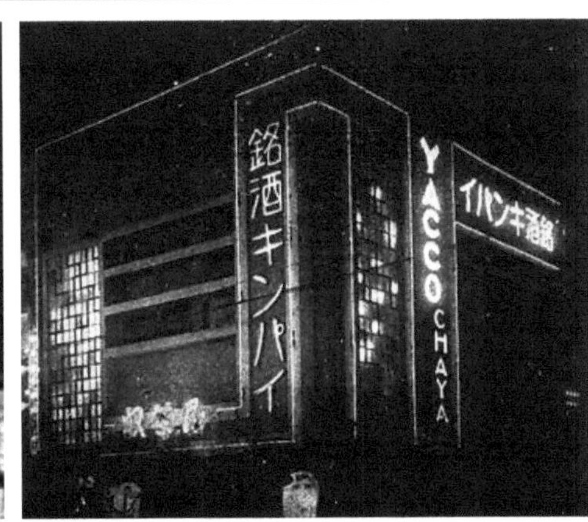
銘酒キンパイ
YACCO CHAYA
銘酒キンパイ

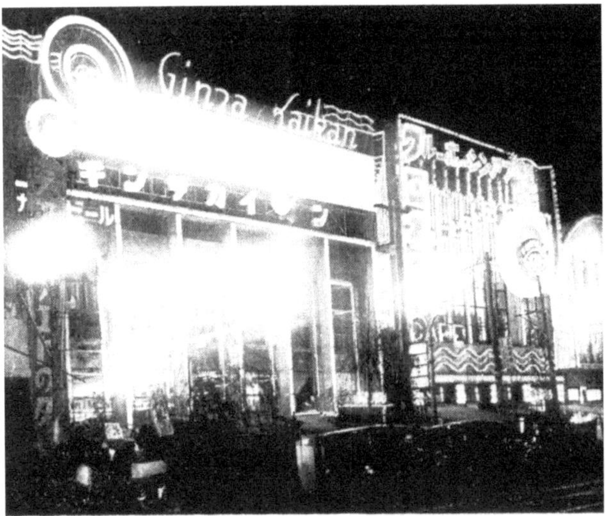
Ginza Kaikan

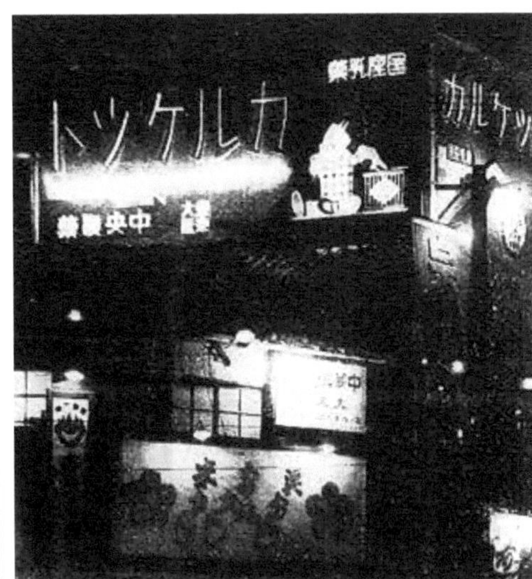
カルケット
カルケット

Illuminated Advertising Balloons

In addition to neon signs, many companies utilized advertising balloons during the early Showa Era. This method used a banner hung from a mooring balloon containing hydrogen or helium. The balloons were typically 3 meters in diameter, and flown at 20-50 meters high. Advertising balloons were also flown at night, with the banner and inside of the balloon illuminated with incandescent bulbs. The balloons were considered risky, and required monitoring at all times.

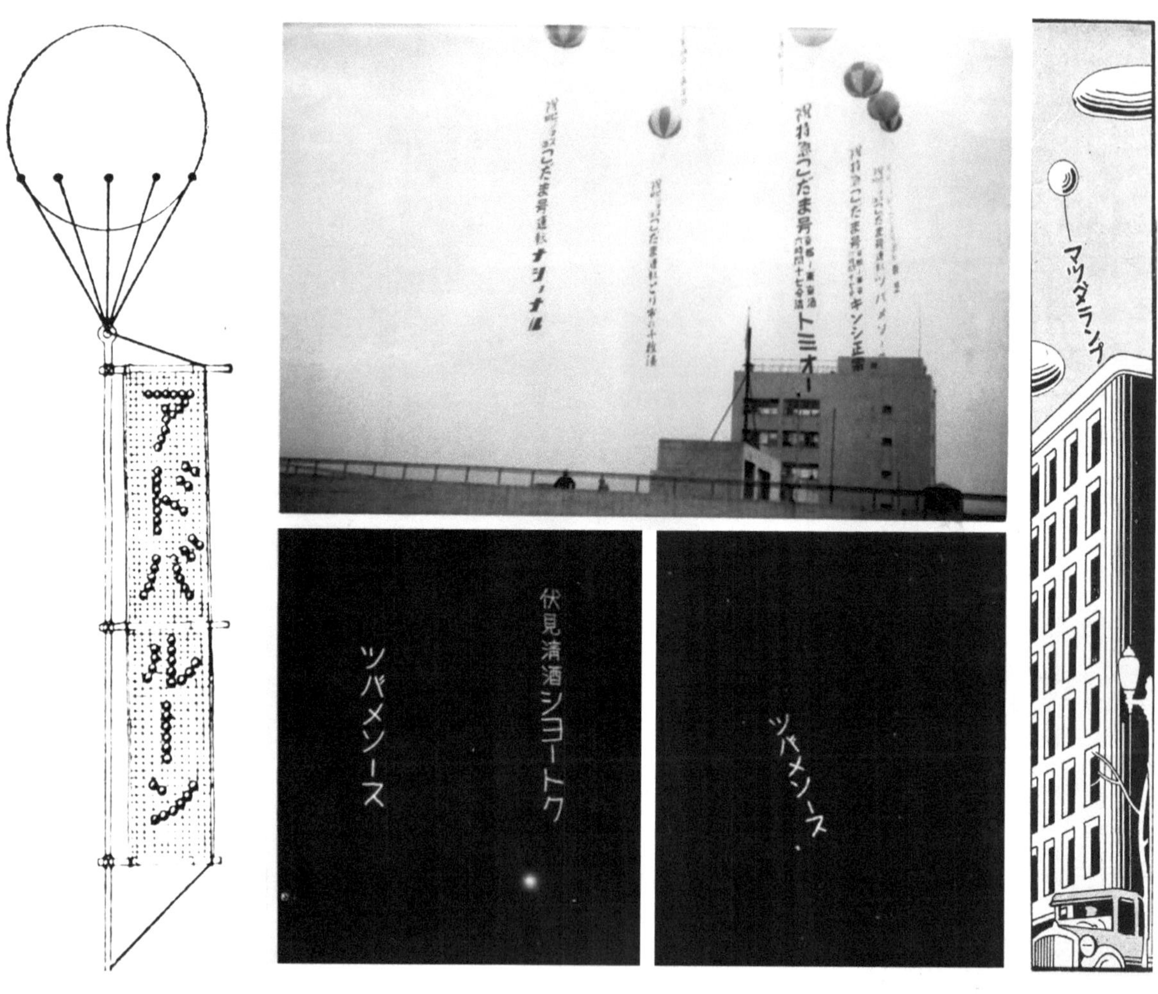

Advertising balloons used the same technology as moored balloons, often used for aerial photography, vertical surveying, environmental observation, and for inspection of overhead power lines. In the beginning, flammable hydrogen was used as the buoyant gas, but because of the risk of explosion, it was gradually changed to noncombustible helium.

Eventually regulations were enacted that prohibited the use of advertising balloons. As a result, many balloons were replaced by banners and other advertising mediums. Many companies shifted to using neon signs for their illuminated outdoor advertisements.

War Time

By the end of the decade, the heyday of neon lights reached its pre-war peak. A gradual decline set in as international tensions grew. Residual turbulence from the First Sino-Japanese War of the Meiji Era resurfaced in the 1930s following the Manchurian Incident. The Japanese expansion into China extended their control, allowing them to obtain additional materials for industry. In 1937, the Second Sino-Japanese War broke out following the Marco Polo Bridge Incident, where Japanese troops were fired upon while conducting military exercises.

The outbreak of war plunged Japan into an time of strong economic control. Electricity rations began as Japan heavily relied on foreign coal and oil. The National Mobilization Law came into effect during 1937, along with the National Service Draft Ordinance. The program had at its peak 1,600,000 men and women drafted, and about 4,500,000 workers reclassified as draftees.

At the beginning of the war, there were several places in the Manchurian mountains where neon air traffic beacons were installed. Electrical power was pulled up from the city to the mountains, allowing the beacons to flash in a Morse Code manner by remote control. The beacons were used to relay encrypted messages to other Japanese troops.

After the abolition of the Japan-US Trade Treaty in 1939, Neon signs other than public signs were banned in order to save electricity due to a shortage of coal. The law on stores was enacted, forcing closure by 10pm and limiting them to 10 kWh per month per light.

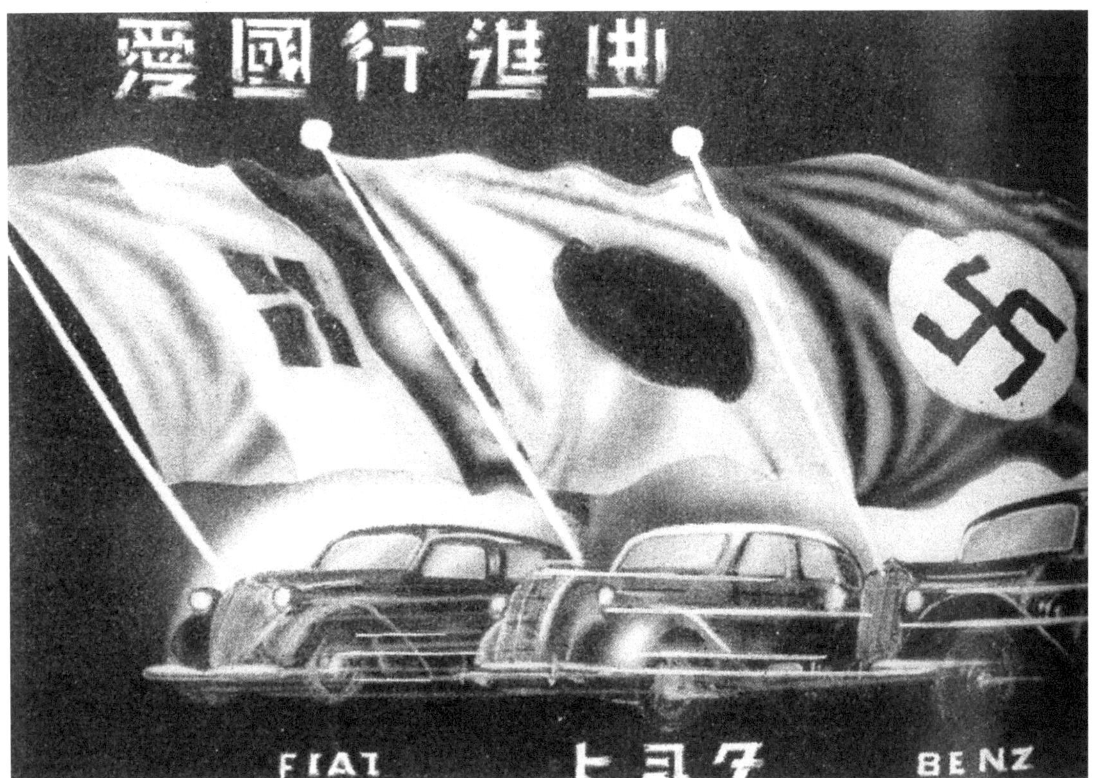

JAPAN BENEFITED FROM TECHNOLOGY SHARING FROM ALLIES IN WORLD WAR II

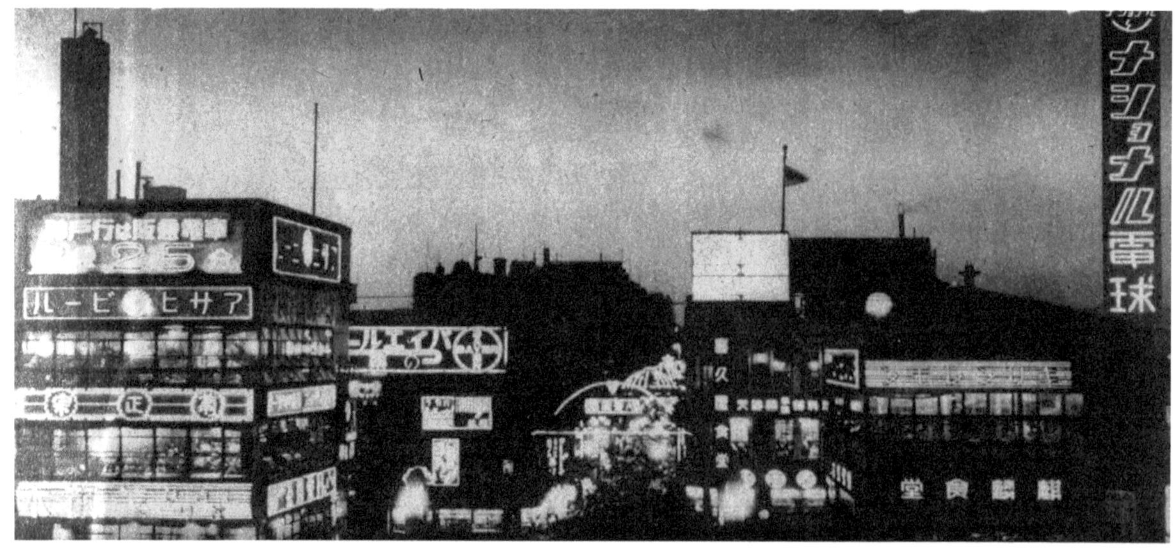

SHINSAIBASHI, OSAKA PRIOR TO LIGHTING RESTRICTIONS, 1939

The Lighting Adjustment Act

As a result of the incidents in China, the power supply for various industrial and export industries was closely observed. The decrease in hydroelectric power generation due to drought and the difficulty of obtaining coal for power generation created a power shortage. The situation soon became dire, and the government issued a power regulation order.

For Homes

1. Use a bowl shaped lamp shade to direct light to required areas
2. Reduce the amount of bulbs in each room
3. Turn off the lights when not in use.
4. Use good-quality light bulbs
5. Turn off garden lamps

For Shops

1. Avoid excessive brightness
2. Neon lights, sign illumination, and decoration lights are prohibited
3. Reduce corridor lighting
4. Turn off all lights after closing
5. Shops must close no later than 10pm

In the meantime, stores were to continue business at night with the minimum necessary practical lighting. In Tokyo, the Lighting Association in cooperation with the Tokyo Chamber of Commerce provided storefront guidance to reduce light use. Many store-owners lost enthusiasm as it grew harder to purchase merchandise. At the same time, the public grew concerned about the increasing price of light bulbs.

One day before neon was banned, the Victor RCA neon sign of a dog running debuted in Tokyo. It had to be shut off almost immediately, a tragic moment for the neon industry. This was one of the last commercial neon signs to be constructed in Japan until after the war.

In September 1939, Japan attacked the Chinese city of Changsha, but was pushed back for nearly a month. A stalemate was reached by 1940, and Japan was being drained of resources. Afterwards, the United States embargoed iron, steel and mechanical parts to Japan. Many neon signs and their steel structures were removed and salvaged for the war effort.

Neon companies were forced to shut their doors, as fabricating commercial neon signs was now against the law. Sign makers were forced to change their occupations, mainly to support the war effort. However, some neon contractors would receive orders for military lighting, such as air beacons, signs for infantry crossing operations, sea buoys, and lighting for the decks of aircraft carriers. The Excise Tax Law was subsequently put into effect to limit the amount of imported goods. The tax rate for neon tubes, neon transformers, and other related materials was at 60% of their value.

In the United States, neon signs were also turned off, gasoline was rationed, and numerous other regulations went into place. Tin cans and cigarettes wrapped in tin paper disappeared due to the sharp demand for tin.

Turbulence in Europe encouraged Imperial Japan to send troops to European controlled colonies in Southeast Asia. Japan quickly gained leverage, and was able to negotiate oil supplies from the East Indies. This threatened the United States and Britain, uniting them for the defense of their territories in Asia. They reacted by placing a complete oil embargo on Japan.

In 1940, Tokyo Electric completed their first hot-cathode discharge tube. The 20-watt fluorescent lamp was used for interior lighting of naval submarines. Fluorescent tubes were favored over incandescent bulbs as they did not create as much heat inside of the vessel.

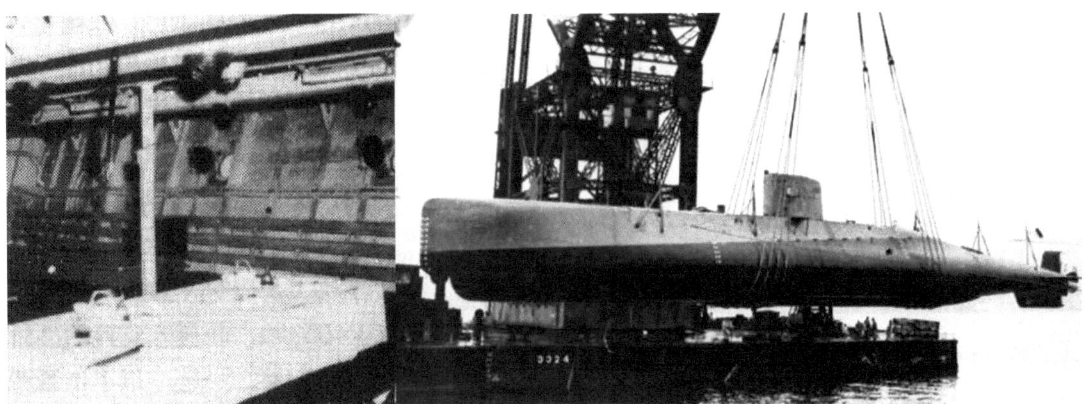

EARLY FLUORESCENT LAMPS WERE FIRST USED INSIDE OF JAPANESE SHIPS

A resolution was proposed to solve the conflict. Japan demanded the end of American aid to China, and for the embargo to be lifted. The counter offers demanded Japan to sign a non-aggression pact requiring abandonment of their ambitions in China and throughout the Pacific. The offer was ignored, and Japan continued to overtake the European and American colonies.

In 1941, Japan attacked US and British holdings around Southeast and Central Pacific Asia. The attack of Pearl Harbor on December 7th led the United States, Britain, and the other allies to formally declare war on Japan. Both sides engaged in brutal combat that resulted in mass casualties. By 1945, American forces moved towards Japan, taking Iwo Jima by March, and Okinawa by the end of June. American submarines cut off Japanese imports, reducing Japan's ability to supply its overseas forces.

On August 6th, 1945, the United States dropped an atomic bomb on the city of Hiroshima, followed by another in Nagasaki on August 9th. In addition, the Soviets invaded Japanese-held Manchuria and defeated the largest Japanese fighting force. The Japanese surrendered on August 15th, with the official documents signed in Tokyo Bay on the deck of the American battleship USS Missouri on September 2, 1945.

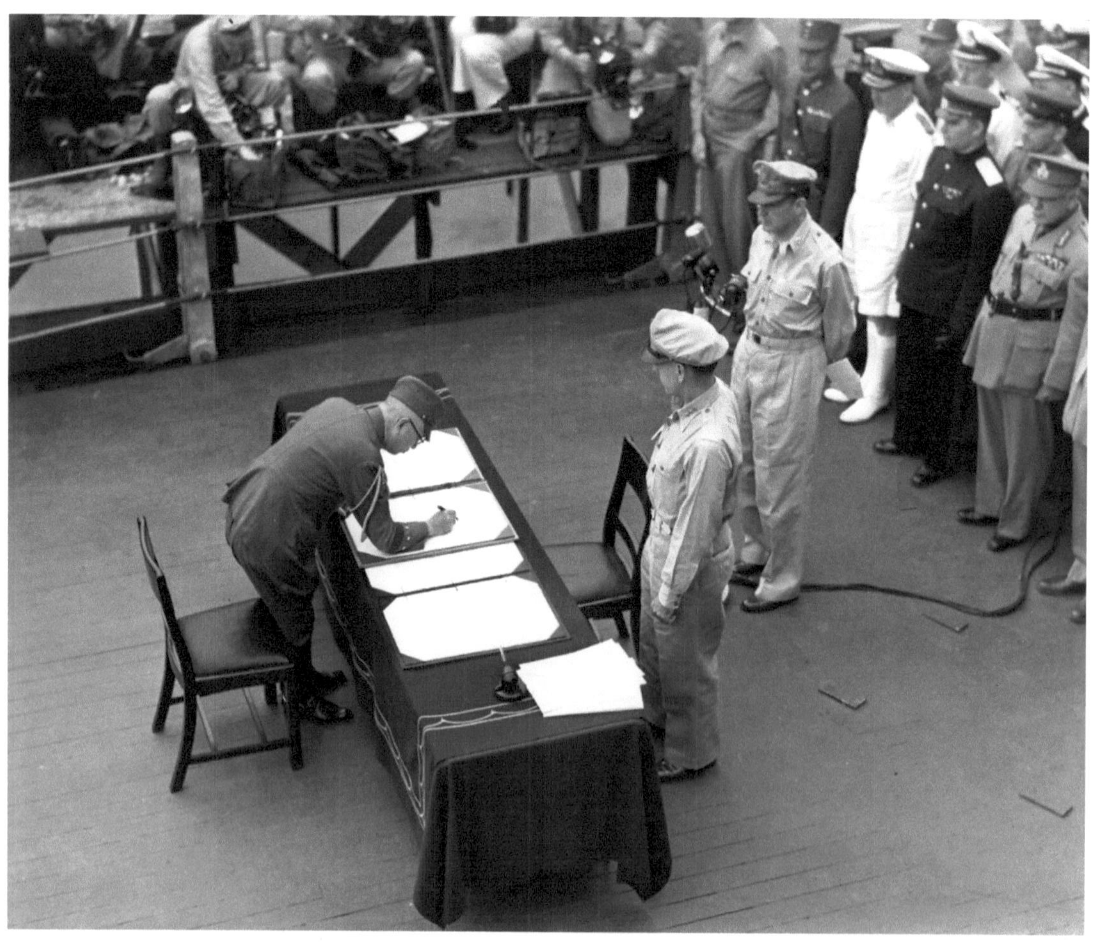

SIGNING OF THE JAPANESE INSTRUMENT OF SURRENDER

Post War

Japan suffered heavy damages from bombings throughout the war. Industry was devastated, many people lost their homes, and food shortages occurred. The once advanced Japanese economy would have to be rebuilt from the ground up. The political and social systems underwent drastic changes, as Japan was occupied by a foreign government for the first time in history. American Forces occupied Japan until 1952, and provided monetary aid and advisory services for reconstruction, similar to the Marshall Plan in Europe.

As soon as the war ended, orders for neon lights slowly picked up for military and government uses. Signs were constructed along the Kanmon Straits, the waterway between the two islands of Honshu and Kyushu. The signboards used flashing neon tubes bent into triangular spiral shapes to visibly define to coast for passing ships.

During the first year of occupation, US troops ordered neon signs for postal exchange stations, also known as "P.X.". By 1947, big orders were placed for three letter signs, reading "R.T.O.", for the Railway Transportation Offices nationwide. Several neon companies negotiated with each other and decided to manufacture them separately. The organization of neon companies is what became the parent of the soon-to-be All Japan Neon Sign Association.

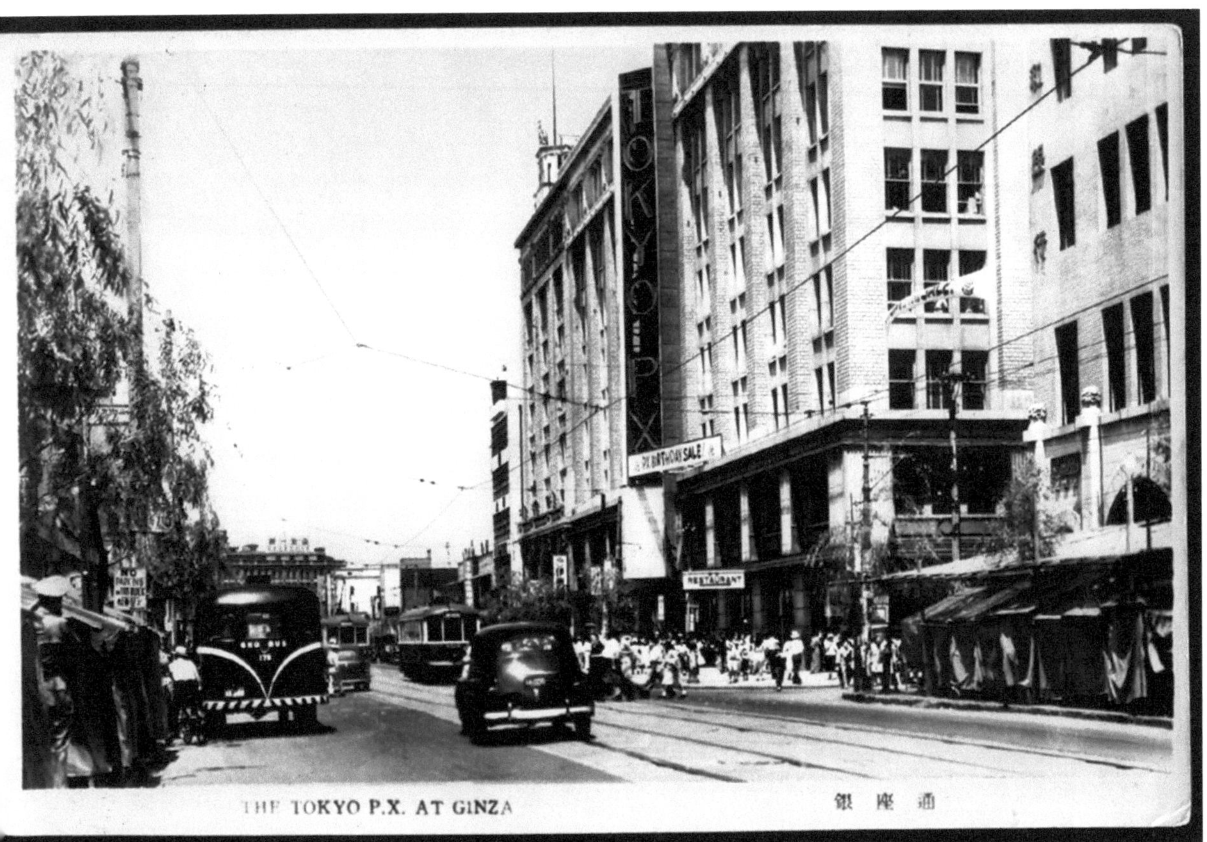

1946 - NEON SIGN FOR A POSTAL EXCHANGE OFFICE IN GINZA, TOKYO

These companies had to be resourceful as supplies for manufacturing were scarce. Burned-out transformers were taken out of old signs and rebuilt for use. Mr. Hirobe of Tokyo Neon secretly buried a reserve of gas inside of a bomb shelter during the war, preserving 90 liters of neon and argon together. Nippon Light Bulb supposedly had only 30 liters of neon gas saved. Shortly afterwards, production of glass tubes and insulators expanded, and more neon gas was imported. Although the initial production was painstaking, it was a great pleasure to revive neon lights. Stimulated by the resurgence, other companies across the country rushed to restart operations. The material suppliers once again became busy.

By 1947, domestic production of fluorescent tubes began to meet the needs of neon makers. The colored phosphors used in fluorescent tubes were adopted, making colors for neon more diverse than from before the war, as Japan was mostly limited to the red of neon and blue of argon+mercury. Tokyo Neon was one of the pioneers in Japan to begin the fluorescent coating of neon tubes. These new colors painted the night sky, a sight that gave hope to people. This contributed greatly to the rise of neon lights after the war.

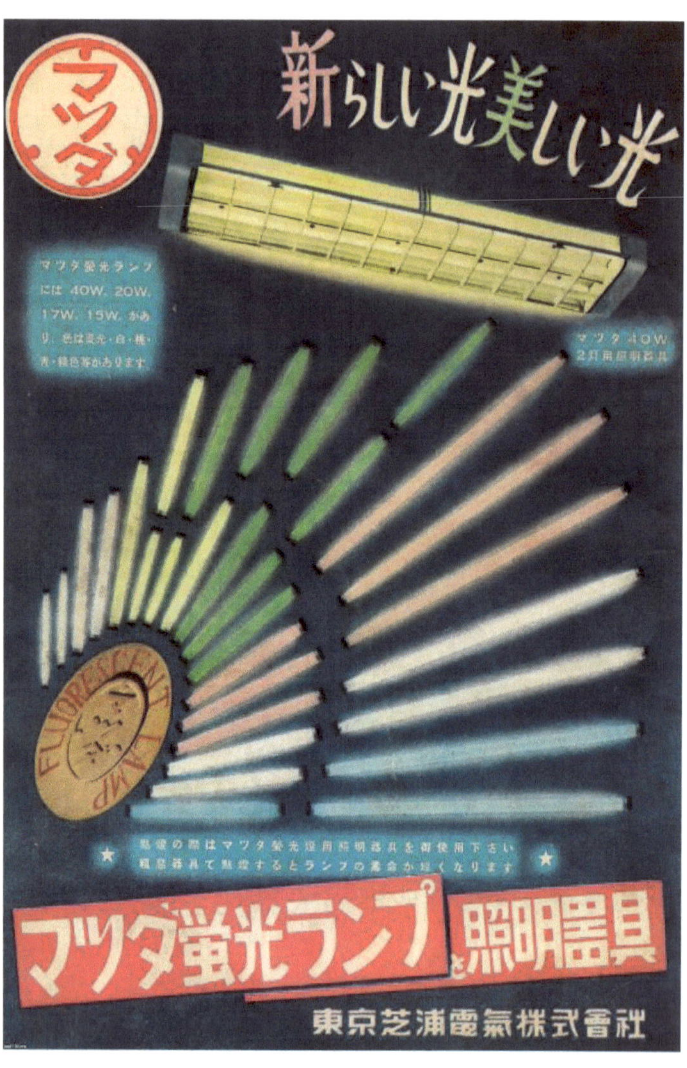

1950 - Matsuda Lamp, a division of Tokyo Electric, advertising their new product, colored fluorescent lamps

Unfortunately, the power shortage that plagued Japan during the war persisted, and ordinary neon signs were not yet officially approved, though smaller neon signs were being produced. The ban was due to the continual lack of power from the drought, as Japan relied heavily on hydroelectric power generation. The situation finally improved in 1949, and the ban was lifted for most of Japan.

With the release of the prohibition, the construction of large neon towers resumed. Two monumental signs were built on the corner of Ginza 4-chome, Tokyo. The advertisement of Kona Milk, where a bottle comforts a crying baby, is an example of the emergence of story-like animations. The idea attracted attention because of the narrative, compared to conventional signs that simply flickered on and off. In addition to Kona Milk, Nippon Beer's bubbling glass was a spectacular display of unprecedented color and animation.

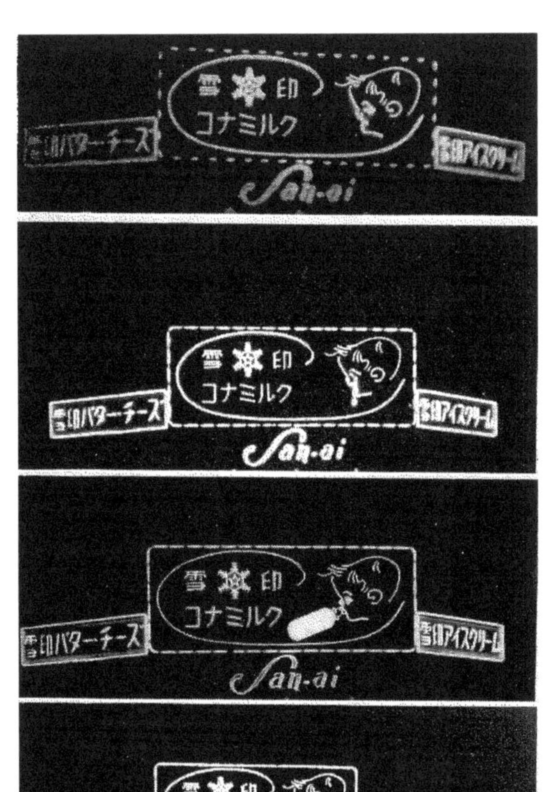

THE KONA MILK SPECTACULAR

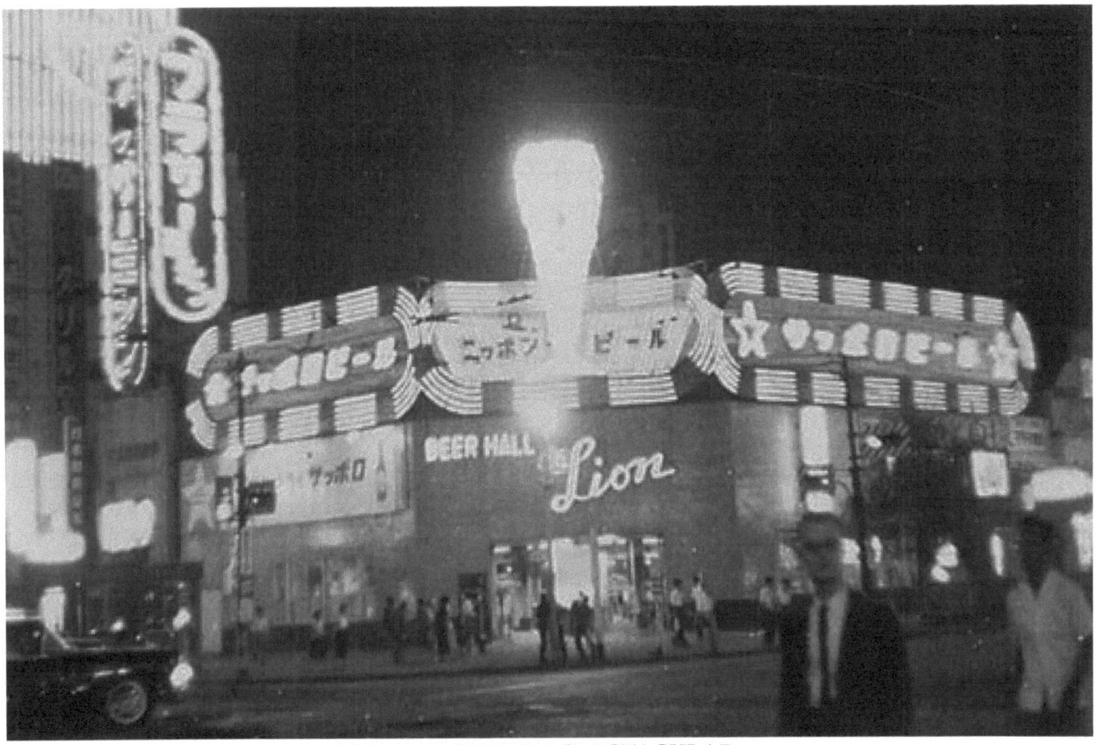

Following Kona Milk, storytelling neon animations became a trend of the time. After World War II, the United States brought new advertising ideas to Japan, including the concept of public relations. Instead of simple company and product name advertisements of the past, it was understood that making a connection between the product and the public would promote sales and business prosperity.

THE NIPPON BEER SPECTACULAR

The All Japan Neon Sign Association

The formation of the All Japan Neon Sign Association germinated before the Pacific War, when the industry was threatened by the patent litigation cases of George Claude. That was the first time the industry united, with smaller unions and federations beginning to organize. The All Japan Neon Sign Association was officially formed in 1951 as a central union, made up of regional associations. The national association provides a lobby to combat industry limiting laws and regulations, standardize materials and installation methods, and research neon products and advertising.

The All Japan Neon Sign Association in conjunction with the Association of Urban Artists also participated in setting up neon sign competitions. These events allowed sign companies to exhibit their work in an effort to advertise their abilities and bring public support to neon signs.

Taxes

The movement to eliminate import taxes after the Pacific War was the main cause of the association's formation. Sign companies and material traders felt strongly about fighting the tax as it dampened the industry. The tax was initially enacted to curb material usage while ramping up for wartime in 1938. It applied to goods that were deemed to be unnecessary or luxury. Even though the production of neon was banned, neon tubes and transformers were taxed at 60% of their value. The tax survived the war and continued to plague the industry for years. The association was successful in reducing the tax, and ultimately eliminating it by 1966.

Standardization

Following the war, there were a handful of inconsistencies that made it difficult to do business. Material prices greatly varied among traders, which caused pricing issues for sign companies. The All Japan Neon Sign Association succeeded in standardizing materials such as neon tube colors and transformers, making it easier to decipher colors between projects. It was requested that the Association manage the production of fluorescent phosphors for glass tubes, although it never came to be.

A big topic for the Association was pricing. At the time of the formation, the price of neon tubing was based on orders from the military facilities. The calculations were inconsistent as costs fluctuated, therefor it was difficult to settle a unit price per neon tube. One unit (one tube) ranged from 300 yen to 1500 yen (about \$3-\$15). The price differences caused excessive competition among sign companies, which disturbed the harmony of the association. A standard price was set to seek the cooperation of union members, although it was not favored by material traders.

Safety in neon products and installations had become a primary focus for governmental authorities. The association set up a subcommittee for technological improvement research. This included trial production of special fuses and conducting various experiments on electric wires and ferrules, contracted through electric testing laboratories, electric wire associations, and insulator manufacturers.

From March 1950 to June 1952, there were 14 fires caused by neon transformers in Tokyo alone. These fires gradually increased with the spread of neon signs. They were usually the result of high-voltage wire passing through material, energizing the metal through current leakage, and generating heat. Any combustible material such as paper or wood nearby has the ability to catch on fire. These fires were reason that safer technologies were developed, which in turn have eliminated many of the dangers.

In 1957, the neon association revised the testing system for manufacturing licensees, and set up a recommendation system for products of qualified manufacturers. The All Japan Neon Sign Association set out to design and defend the rights of material traders, sign makers, and riggers while communicating with relevant government agencies for firefighting, traffic, and radio interference prevention, all while cooperating with the outdoor advertising industry.

Sign Regulations

A major revision of the planning system took place around 1948. The main authority for outdoor advertising was transferred to the Ministry of Construction. New laws and regulations were established in each prefecture. The ordinances were designed to maintain the aesthetics of cities and to ensure safety against typhoons and earthquakes. For example, the size of neon advertising towers became limited to a percentage of the building height.

During this time, the Association of Urban Beauty Engineers was founded in Tokyo to conduct technical research and guidance proposals on urban aesthetics. In addition, the Tokyo Metropolitan Government launched the Tokyo Metropolitan Outdoor Advertising Market, with the aim of improving the aesthetics of outdoor advertisements.

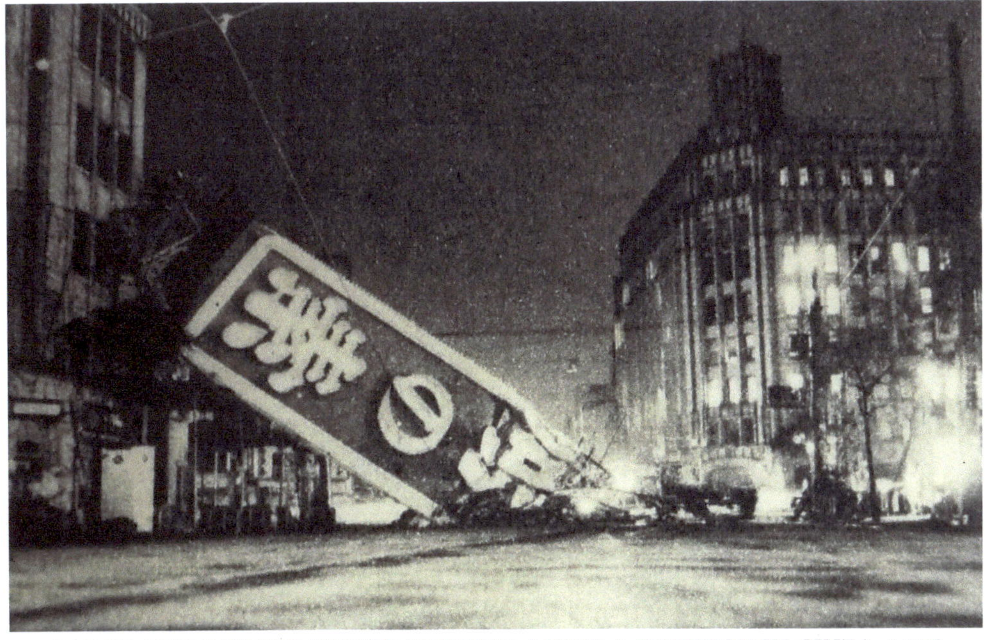

LARGE ADVERTISING TOWER TOPPLED AFTER A TYPHOON IN GINZA, 1953

As infrastructure further developed, tighter regulations on outdoor advertising were enacted by the Ministry of Construction's Deputy Secretary. Like anything in excess, neon signs have the ability throw off the balance of a cityscape. Laws and regulations were put in place to manage the aesthetics of the city, as well as the general safety of pedestrians. The outdoor advertising law and advertising ordinances stipulated by local municipalities varied by city. For example, Tokyo and Osaka were more lenient as large cities, and Kyoto was quite strict as traditional city.

Above all, the government needed to ensure compliance with the regulations. The amount of advertising was enormous, so routine sweeps were carried out to remove reported violations. It was important for municipalities to stay vigilant as some signs created a public safety hazard if not maintained well.

In addition to safety, neon signs created a significant amount of light pollution. It was unavoidable that light leakage would occur, therefor zoning for bright signs was necessary to prevent disturbances in residential areas. In addition, signs were mandated to be turned off during the late hours of the night in certain areas.

The subjective issue of sign design came into question as authorities preferred advertisements that were harmonious with the environment. This was more strict in traditional areas, as certain colors and designs became prohibited. It was believed that neon signs should be designed to be inconspicuous and not too noisy, adding to the environment in a positive manner.

In attempt to influence design to fit local aesthetic, several local governments, including the Tokyo Metropolitan Government, held outdoor advertising contests to recognize outstanding signs that improved cityscapes. In each region, the neon association worked with the government to raise awareness and provide guidance on the observance of ordinances meant to maintain urban aesthetics. However, there were many so-called outsider sign companies that did not belong to an organization, and did not abide by the recommendations.

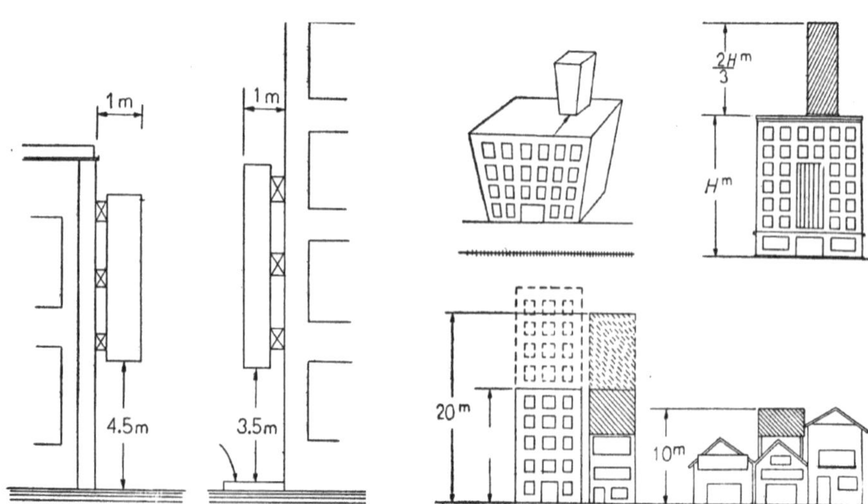

Tokyo Outdoor Advertising Ordinance

ROOFTOP ADVERTISING TOWERS

1. Advertising article height shall not be more than 2/3 of the building height
2. The height from the ground surface to the upper end of the advertising tower must be 52 meters or less (33 meters or less in Class 1 and Type 2 semi-residential areas)

WALL SURFACES

1. The distance to the upper end of the advertisement must be 52 meters or less (33 meters or less in Class 1 and Type 2 semi-residential areas, etc.)
2. The area of the advertisement surface must be 100 square meters or less
3. When there are multiple advertisements on one wall of a building, the total area of those advertisements must be 30% or less of the wall of the building

ADVERTISING MATERIALS PROTRUDING FROM THE BUILDING

1. The distance to the top of the advertisement must be 52 meters or less (33 meters or less in Class 1 and Class 2 semi-residential areas, etc.)
2. The width from the road boundary is 1 meter or less
3. The lower end of the advertising material must be at least 3.5 meters above the ground if there is a sidewalk, and at least 4.5 meters if there is no sidewalk
4. The total display area of the advertising material displayed on the object is the total wall of the building It must be within 60% of the total area (total amount regulation)

DIRECTLY INSTALLED ON LAND

1. Up to the upper end of advertising material must be 10 meters or less (13 meters or less for private advertising material in commercial area)
2. The lower end of the advertising material is 3.5 meters or more above the ground if there is a sidewalk, and 4.5 meters or more if there is no sidewalk
3. Type 1 and 2 residential exclusive beauty and scenic areas are prohibited areas. Only very small items are allowed as exemptions, where the use of neon tubes is completely prohibited and the use of exposed neon tubes, the use of red light and the flashing of light sources is prohibited

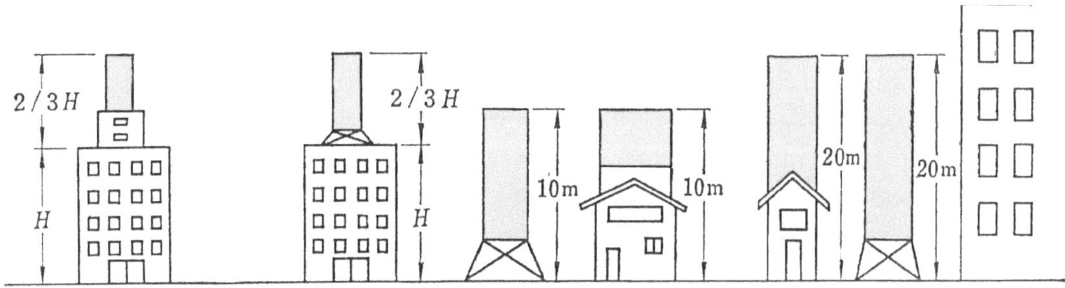

Keiretsu

Keiretsu, a network of companies with joint business relationships and shareholdings, were formed following the war due to the collapse of family-controlled monopolies known as "zaibatsu". Before the war, Japan's industrialized economy was controlled by four families: Mitsubishi, Sumitomo, Yasuda and Mitsui. They focused on steel, banking, international trading and other key sectors. They worked closely with banks that provided funding for their ventures.

After World War II, under the American occupation, sixteen zaibatsu were targeted for dissolution, and handfuls more for reorganization. The controlling families' assets were seized, holding companies were eliminated, company names were changed, and anti-monopoly laws were enacted. Complete dissolution of the zaibatsu was never achieved as the United States realized that they were essential for re-industrializing Japan. It was believed that communism would spread to Japan if the economy didn't recover. Many of these companies were renamed during reorganization, further increasing the demand for neon signs.

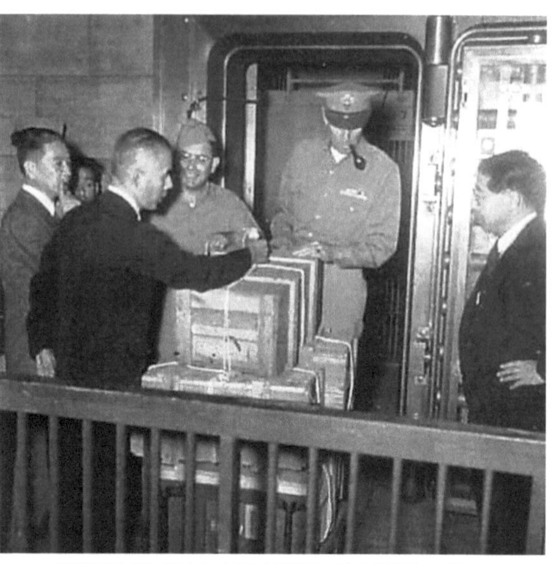

SEIZURE OF ZAIBATSU FAMILY ASSETS

In 1947, the Ministry of International Trade and Industry permitted the use of the former names of the zaibatsu. Many companies reverted back to their old names in order to secure former credit lines. As a result, companies split into those who did and those who did not keep their new names after the war. Mitsui, Mitsubishi, and Sumitomo restored their old zaibatsu names, thus resulting in more demand for updated neon signs.

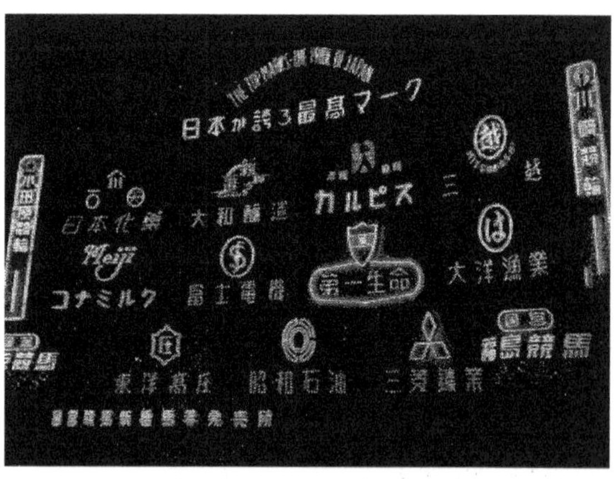

POST WAR NEON SIGNS

Today, banks and trading companies remain in control of many corporations, although shareholders now replace family control of the cartels. For example, the Mitsubishi Group consists of car manufacturing, insurance, banking, plastics, metals, and handfuls of other companies across a range of industries. Mitsubishi is the parent organization of well-known companies such as Kirin and Nikon.

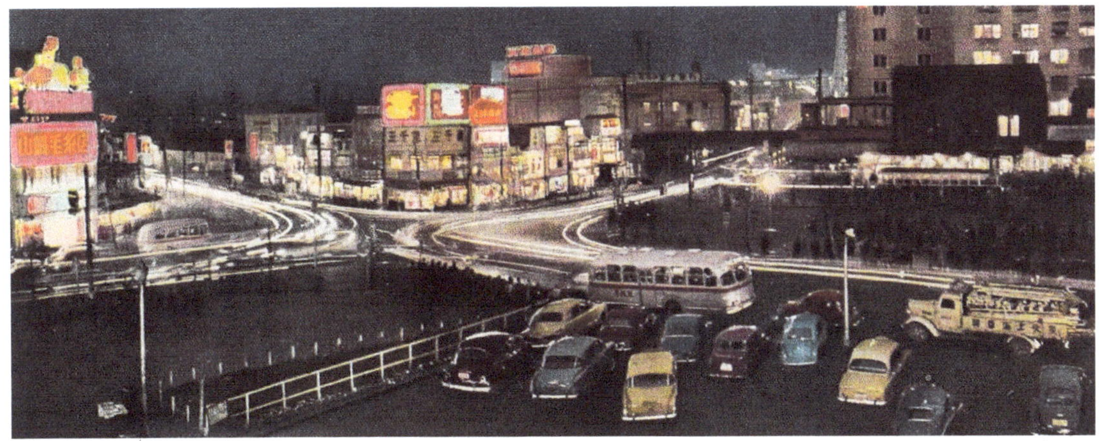

SHIBUYA STATION SQUARE, 1955

The Booms of the 1950s

In June 1950, North Korean troops crossed the dividing line of the Korean Peninsula, sparking the Korean War. The focus in Asia shifted towards fighting communism. The United States placed major orders for supplies from Japan, which caused their first economic boom of 1950s.

The benefits Japan received were in the form of large orders of food, textiles, construction materials, and other products and services. The value of the exports totaled around three billion dollars over a three-year period, doubling Japan's production capabilities. Japan's most popular exports at the time, known as the "three treasures" of the 1950s were radios, motorcycles, and sewing machines. Large-scale neon advertisements began to revamp as many companies were created by dismantling the conglomerates.

It was expected that when Korean War ended, Japan would head into a recession, though the economy continued to perform well. The "Jinmu" boom lasted for 31 months from December 1954. This boom is believed to have been driven by private investment in companies. Japan set its sights on modernization and technological innovation with a similar die-hard passion exhibited during the Pacific War. Neon was supported by this economy and experienced rapid development, thus sparking the post-war golden age of neon.

1955 was a significant year for the Japanese economy. Per capital GDP surpassed the pre-war levels as exports of textiles, chemical fertilizers, ships, and radios increased. Japan then developed their first national economic plan, in which they declared its goal to attain economic independence without having to depend on U.S. aid and war-related activities.

Japan experienced the "Iwato" boom which started in 1959 and lasted 42 months. Japan's industrial developments were the main contributor to their successes. Steel plants were constructed, lower-cost energy generation was adopted, and industrial zones were developed. This had a great impact on the automobile and machinery industries, which Japan became widely known for.

The Second Heyday

By 1952, there were about 200 companies specializing in electric signs, approximately 12,000 union employees, and 70 companies specializing in neon tube manufacturing. The top five companies had monthly outputs of over 12,000 feet of tubing. Design, structure, and materials were rapidly developed as the demand for large neon signs increased. Unique sign forms of all shapes and sizes were constructed to compete for the attention of the city's inhabitants.

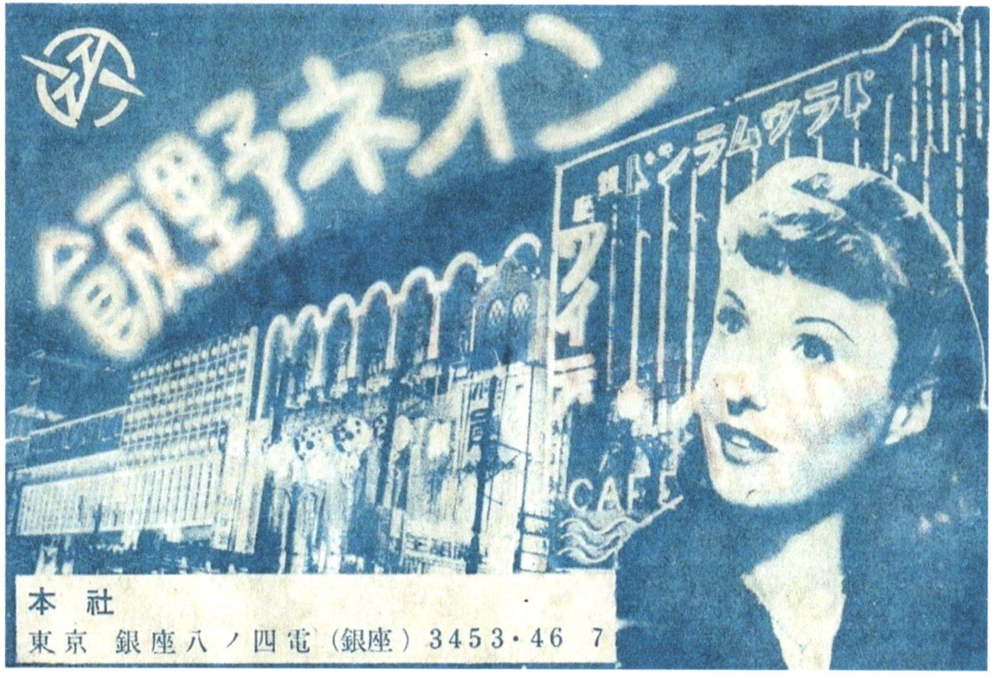

IINO NEON COMPANY ADVERTISEMENT

Neon signs became the most effective means for commercial advertising following newsprint. By the 1950s, a plethora of industries such as confectioneries, breweries, cosmetics, electronics, automobiles, bicycles, and appliances utilized outdoor advertising. Neon was also widely used in schools, cinemas, public spaces, restaurants, aquariums, and theaters.

The export industry was the driving force for many of the rooftop towers across Japan. Specifically, radio and television manufacturers were among the most common to employ extravagant towers. These companies positioned their advertisements along railways and airports in effort to establish their brand image. The development of highways created valuable real estate for advertisers, as towers were commonly erected on rooftops beside roads.

A single neon tower could have thousands of neon tubes and hundreds of transformers. At one point, the towers were densely erected in large and small cities around the country. The upbeat economy encouraged retailers to utilize electric signage. Although neon was mainly used for advertising and publicity purposes, cold cathode tubes were also used for general lighting and electrical embellishment for offices, factories, and store interiors.

Large sign companies would design, construct, and erect their own signs, with the exception of the steel structures. Channel letters, three dimensional letters and shapes made of steel, were commonly found on outdoor signs. Plastic was introduced in the early 1950s, but there was uncertainty as to how it would hold up to the outdoor elements. Mid-century designs paired with advancing technology made for some vivacious signs with effects such as color cross fading and complex animations.

Most signs primarily used neon tubing for illumination, though some were covered with a number of floodlighted square or triangular reflectors. Many signs made use of indirect or cove-lighting styles, utilizing the effect of light on three-dimensional shapes. Sometimes signs would use fluorescent lamps and incandescent bulbs depending on the application. Advertisers were interested in unconventional lighting techniques as they wanted to set their brand apart from the others, which helped to justify the big costs associated with outdoor signage.

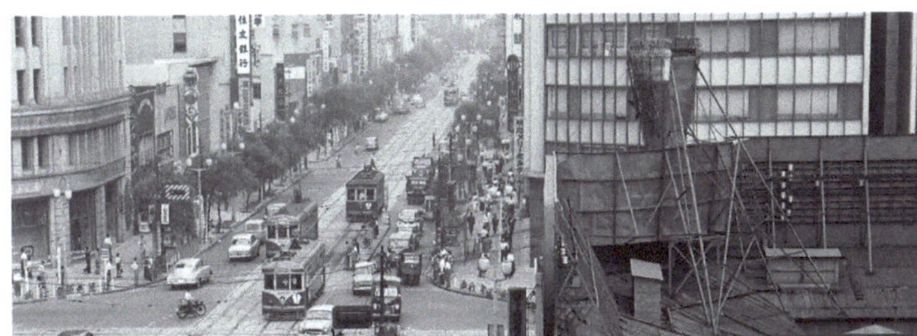

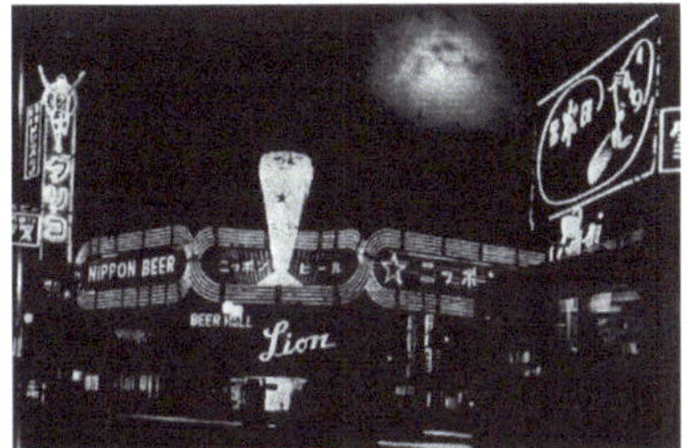

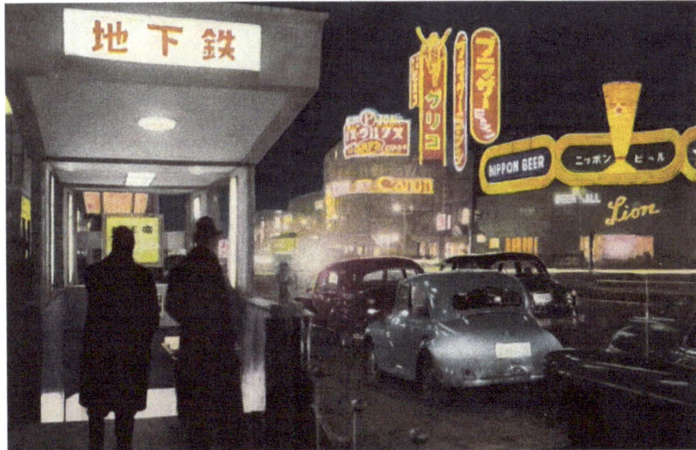

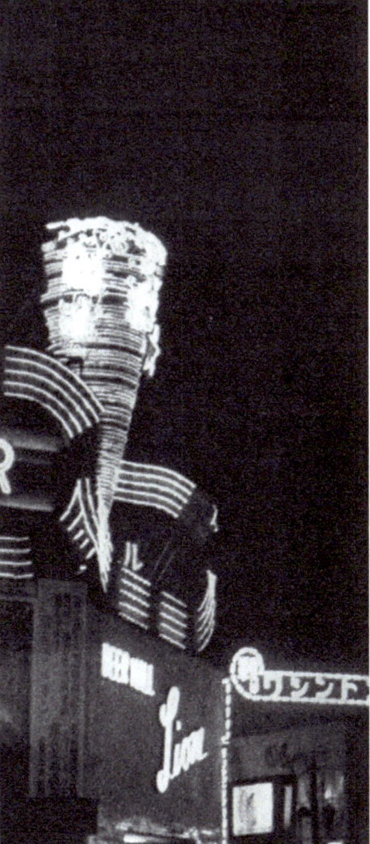

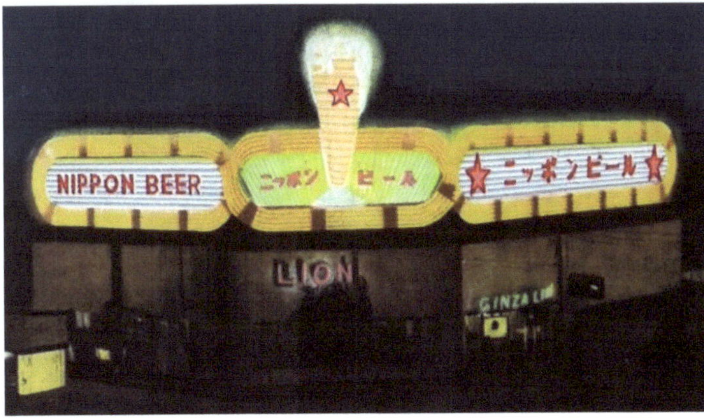

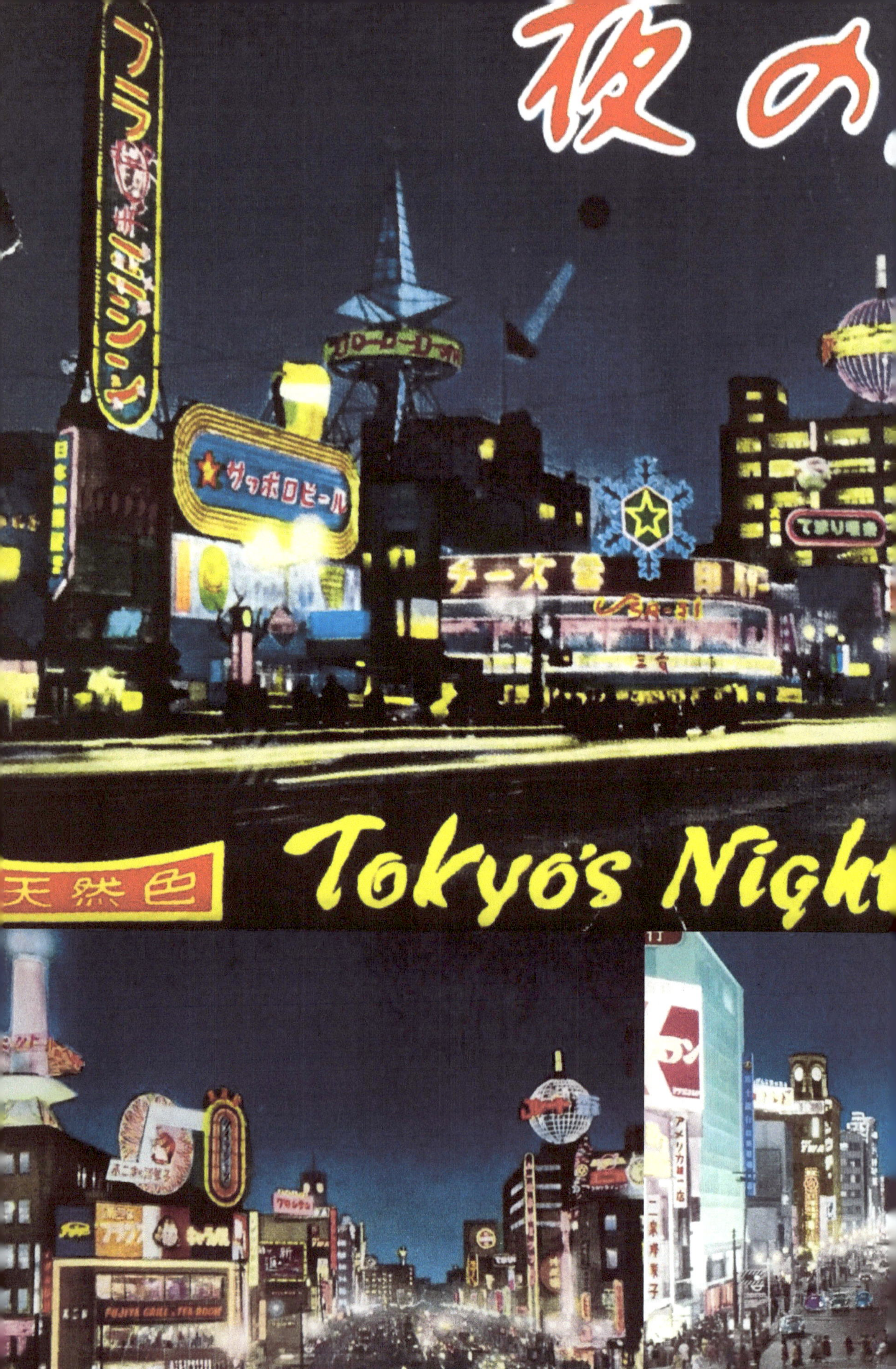
夜の
サッポロビール
Tokyo's Night
天然色

京

in Colour

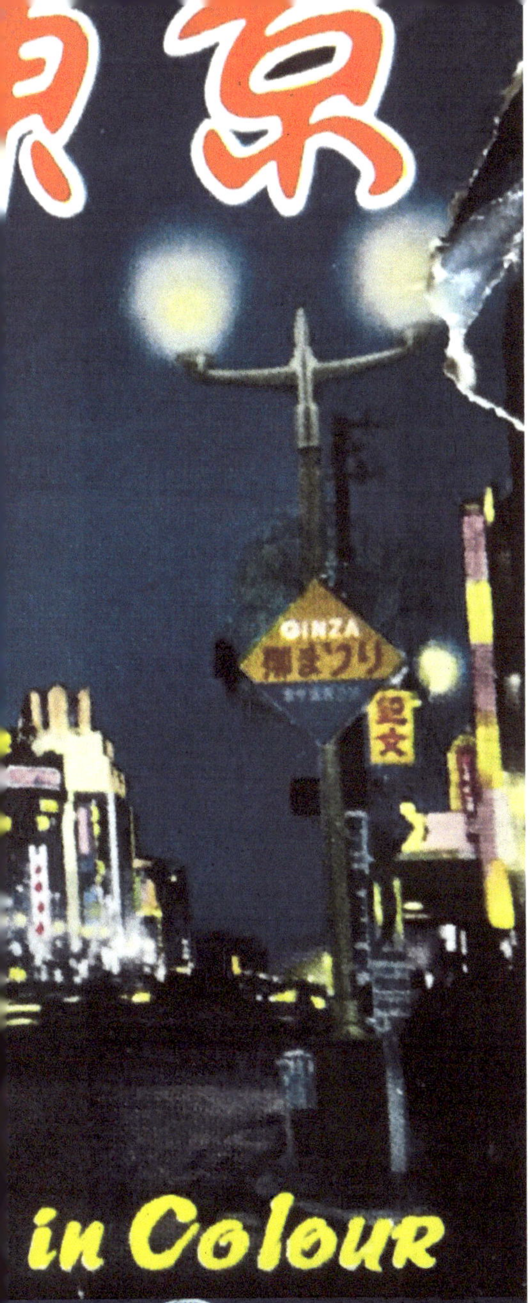

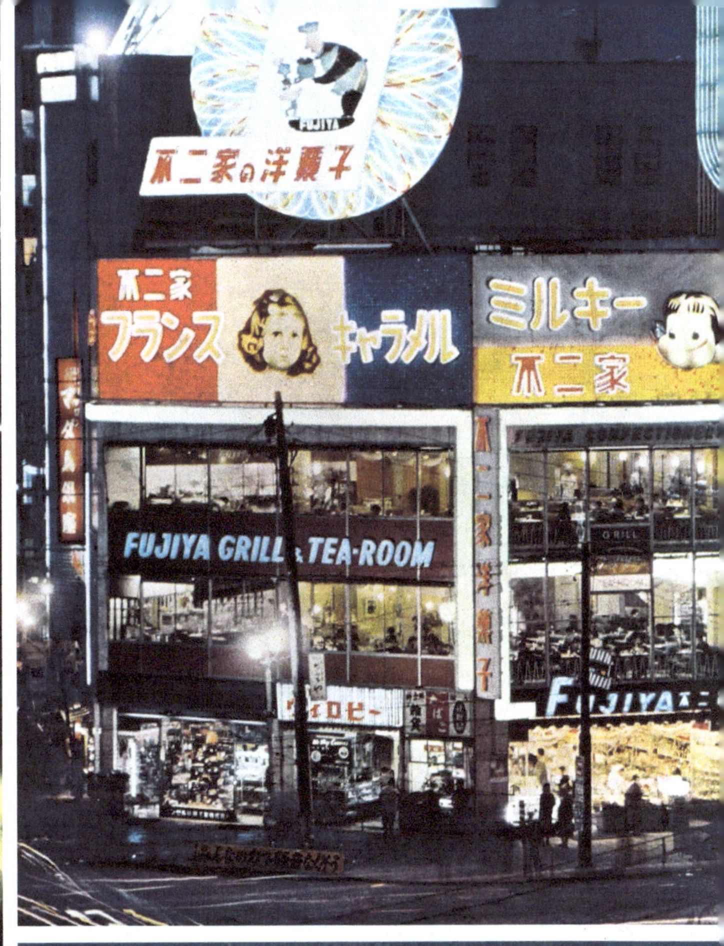

FUJIYA
不二家の洋菓子
不二家
フランス
キャラメル
ミルキー
不二家
FUJIYA GRILL & TEA-ROOM
不二家洋菓子
FUJIYA

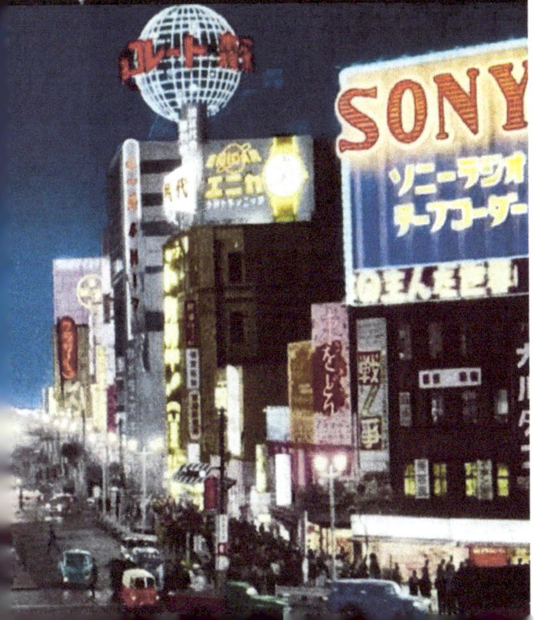

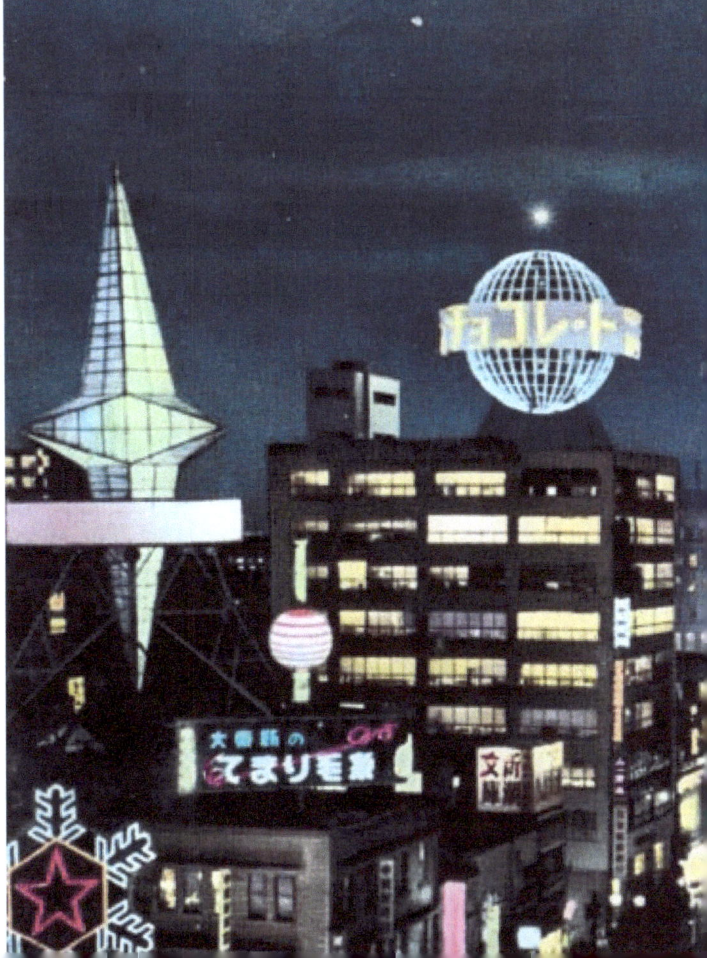

チョコレート

Structures

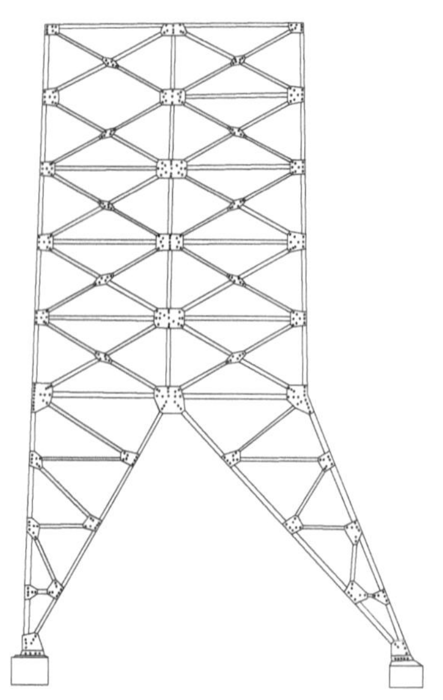

Intricacy of sign structures depended on the project, some were made using the minimum necessary steel members, and others would use large steel members, overbuilt to a sufficient margin. It would usually reflect the economic situation. In the times of high steel prices, structures would be built lightly with thinner members. In addition, it would depend on whether the sign was a special order or part of a bidding war. People in the industry would feel that the sign's structure reflected the creator's heart, revealing the personality of the designer and manufacturer. The morphology of the structure adds to the overall design, as it's the foundation of the project.

As orders increased, sign structures became more intricate and robust. Unconventional signs were difficult to design structures for, as they were not evenly loaded. The first large-scale rotating band was built for the National star tower in Ginza. The structure was designed by Yujiro Hasuoka, who worked on a large number of sign structures nationwide, including the globe of Morinaga. A common issue with the signs that used moving parts was the loud noise they produced.

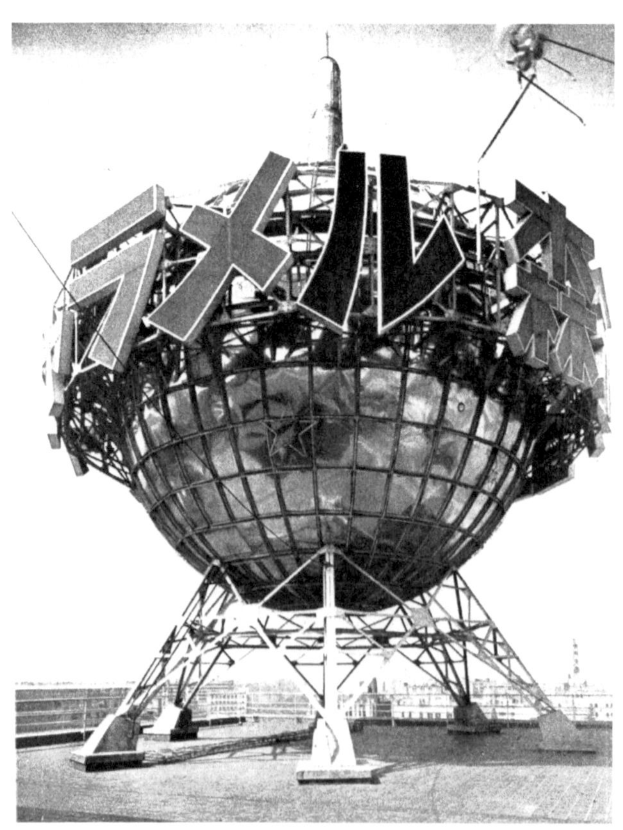

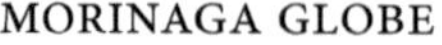

MORINAGA GLOBE

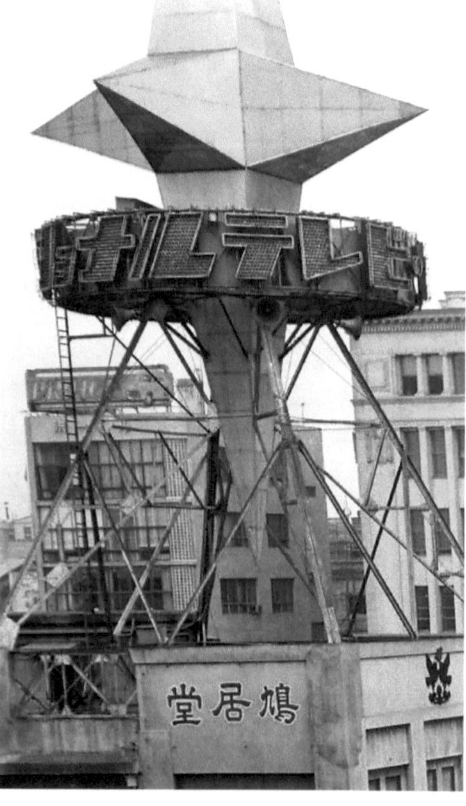

NATIONAL STAR

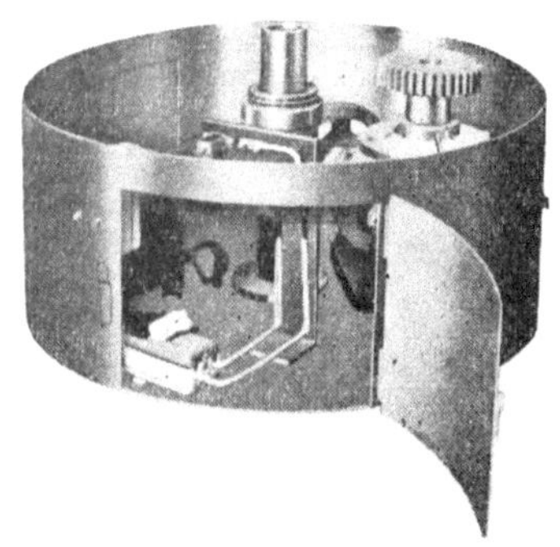

MOTOR BOX FOR THE ROTATING BAND OF THE NATIONAL STAR

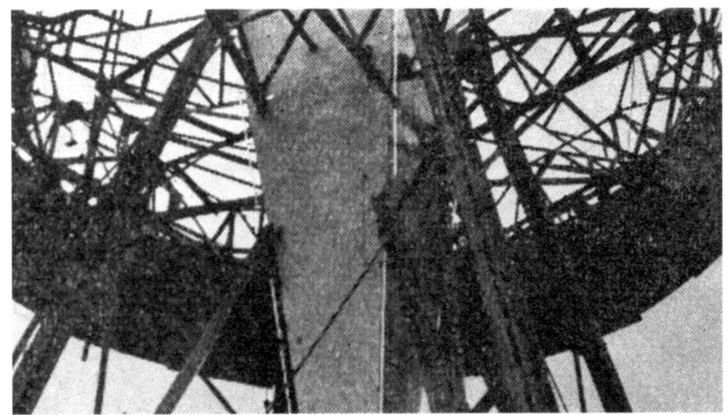

STEEL MEMBERS CONNECTED TO THE BODY OF THE NATIONAL STAR SIGN

Rebuilding of Tsutenkaku

The Tsutenkaku of Osaka was rebuilt after local citizens rallied for its return. It officially reopened in 1956. The new tower measured 338 feet tall, about a third taller than the original structure. The new Tsutenkaku was designed by architect Tachu Naito, the same architect of the Tokyo Tower. The original sponsor of the building was the Lion Toothpaste Company, though Hitachi Corporation took over the sponsorship of the new tower.

The updated tower was covered in neon lights, which underwent renovation every few years. The lights on top of the tower show the weather forecast, and the east side of the tower was the home of Kansai's largest clock, measuring nearly 20 feet in diameter. The tower still stands today, though it has been mostly taken over by LED lights.

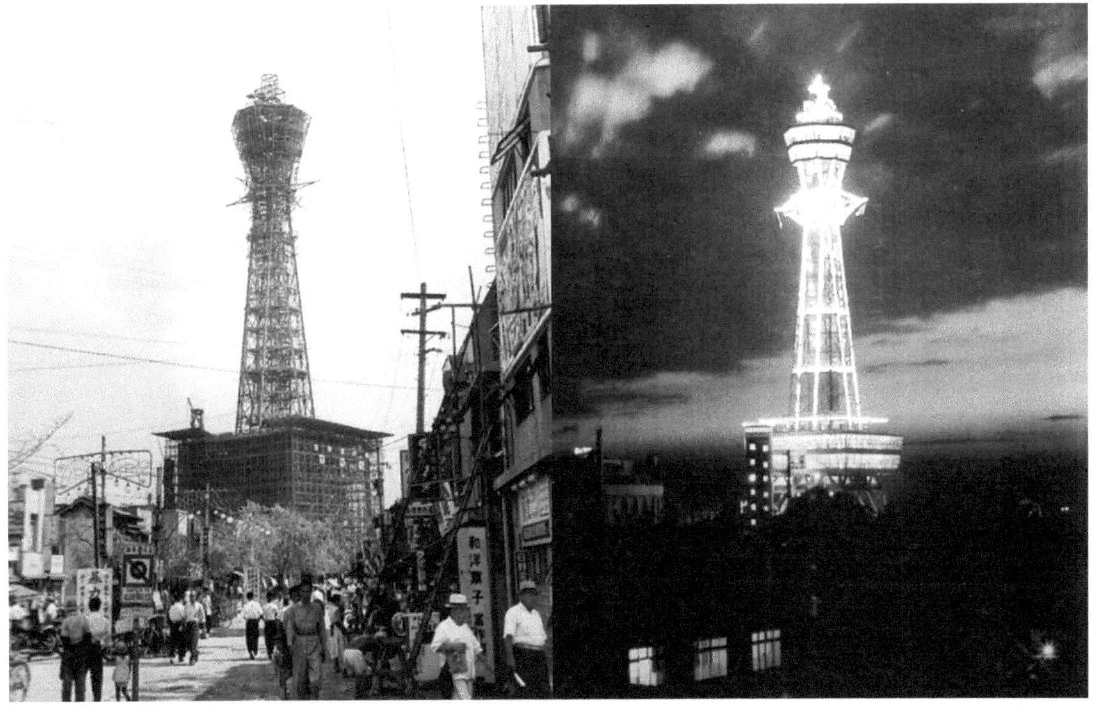

TSUTENKAKU BEING CONSTRUCTED IN 1955

OPENING ILLUMINATION IN 1956

Designers Participation

As the industry matured, leading designers and artists became involved in sign design. The decision to outsource design led to many radical concepts, creating a challenge for fabricators and engineers. "The key to the neon resurrection is in art" are the words of Japanese painter, Misao Yokoyama. He believed neon would become more accepted into the cityscape if it were aesthetically pleasing and captivating.

In 1953, Morinaga, a confectionery company, erected a globe-shaped neon tower in Ginza, Tokyo. The globe was installed on the roof of the Fujikoshi Building. It measured 36 feet in diameter, 48 feet in height, 148 feet from the ground, and originally had 10,000 feet of neon tubing. The sign reportedly cost about 30 million yen in 1953, a significant investment at the time. The globe became the landmark of Ginza, and gave Japan a feeling of postwar recovery. The sign was designed by a Japanese painter, Misao Yokoyama, before he was widely recognized for his artwork.

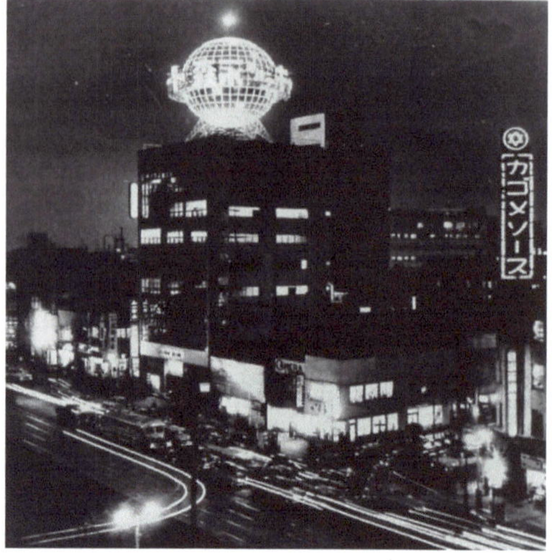

The sign was constructed of sheet metal stretched over steel arches running up, down, and across the sphere, simulating longitudinal and latitudinal lines. Steel channel letters spelled out "Morinaga Milk Caramel" and "Morinaga Chocolate" across the equator, and rotated around the sphere. Special decorations were applied during Christmastime, the wedding of the Crown Prince (1959), and the Tokyo Olympics in 1964. The Morinaga Globe Neon Tower could be called the symbol of Japan at the time.

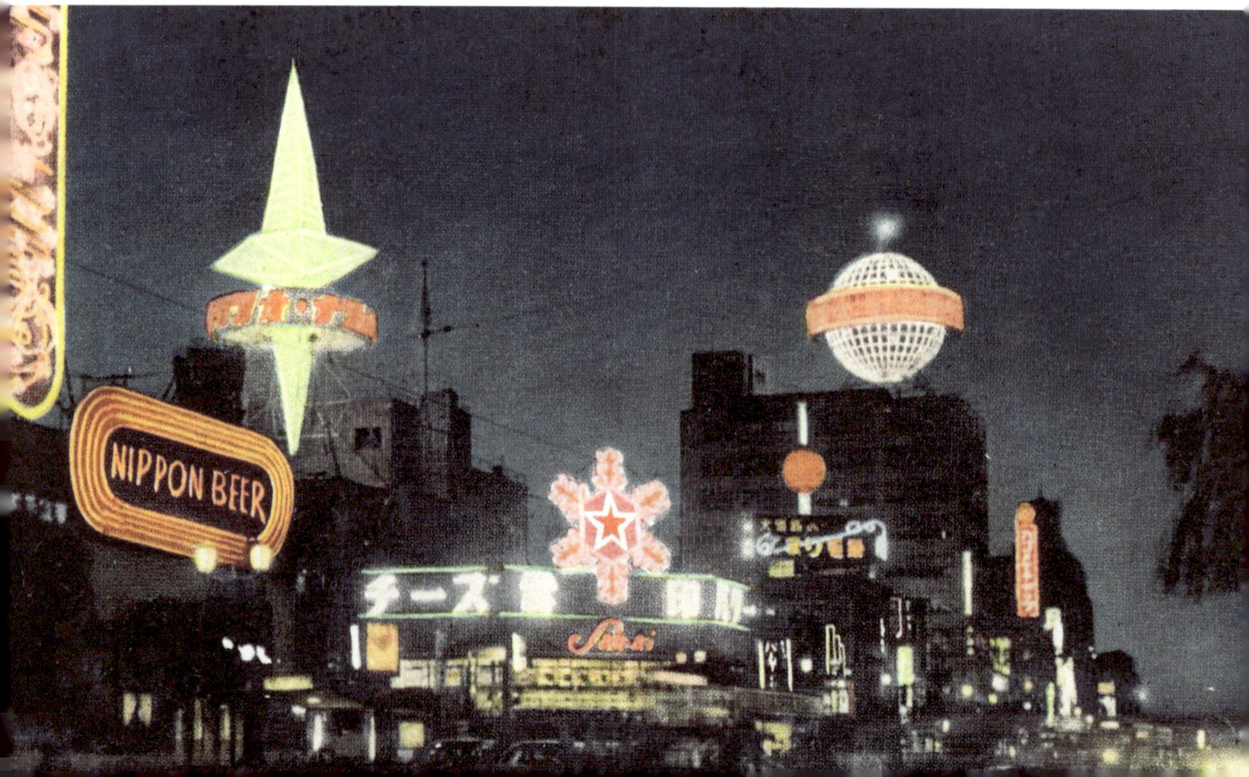

The makers of the Globe, Fuji Neon, played an active part in the neon industry before the Pacific War. It was said that the president, Iyoji Kawase, was a strong man who had a horse racing horse named Neon. The designer, Misao Yokoyama, lived in detention in Siberia after the war. He claimed that he was creating concepts for the Morinaga Globe before the opportunity came about. It wasn't until 1950 that he became a member of the Fuji Neon team. The neon tower was finally erected in 1953, and won the Advertising Dentsu Award for that year. Yokoyama was given a studio space at Fuji Neon for his achievements.

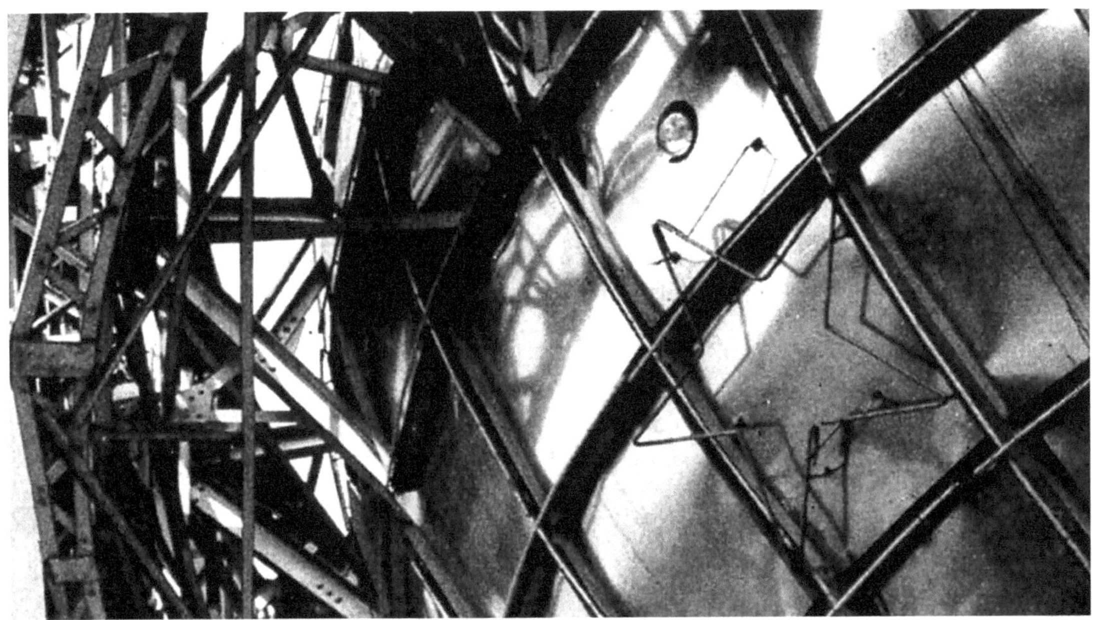

The Morinaga globe became a frequently renovated sign in order to keep a modern sense of color and style. New techniques such as indirect lighting and plastic facing were applied one after another. In addition to Ginza, Morinaga also erected signs in Osaka, Nagoya, Takamatsu, Shimonoseki, and other cities around the country. The original Morinaga Globe Neon Tower was active for about 30 years (1953-1983). It is said that a building collector kept the remains of the globe after it was removed from the building.

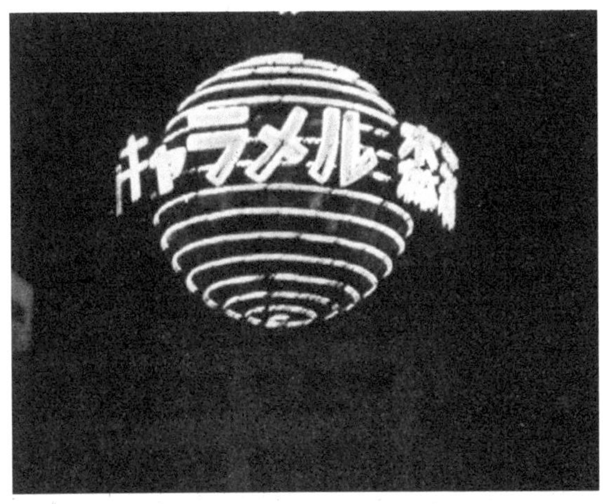

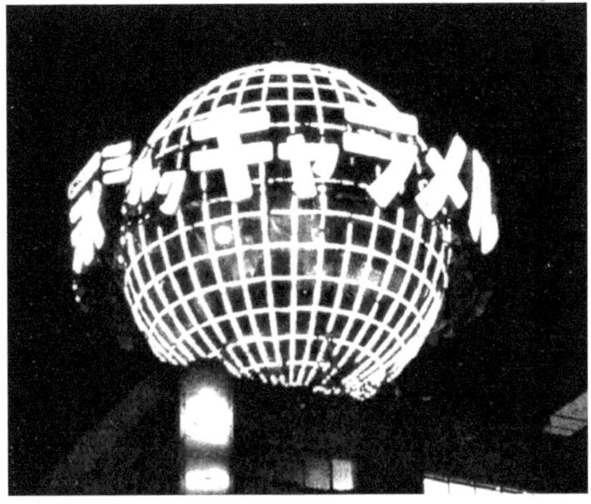

The neon star of National was erected in Ginza, Tokyo in 1954. This neon tower is an example of the eye-catching, spaceship-like signs that appeared around Japan during this era. Unconventionally, the design was commissioned to an independent designer outside the company for the first time. Ryoichi Takeoka, director of the advertising department of Matsushita Electric (National), was asked to pick from the top graphic designers, and Kenji Itoh's design was chosen. This neon tower was a star-shaped structure unlike the any other tower ever built. A banner revolved around the star, advertising National brand television sets. The star was well recognized for improving the cityscape's aesthetic .

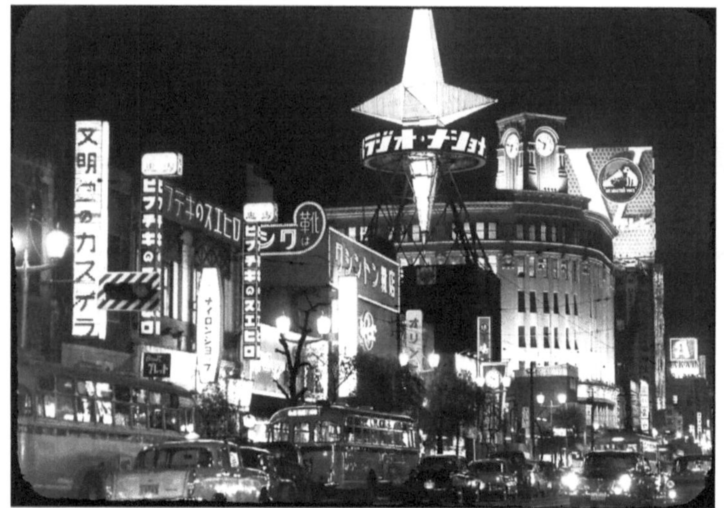
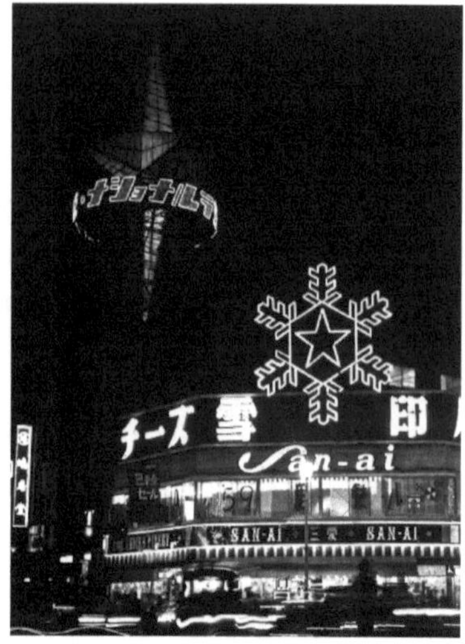

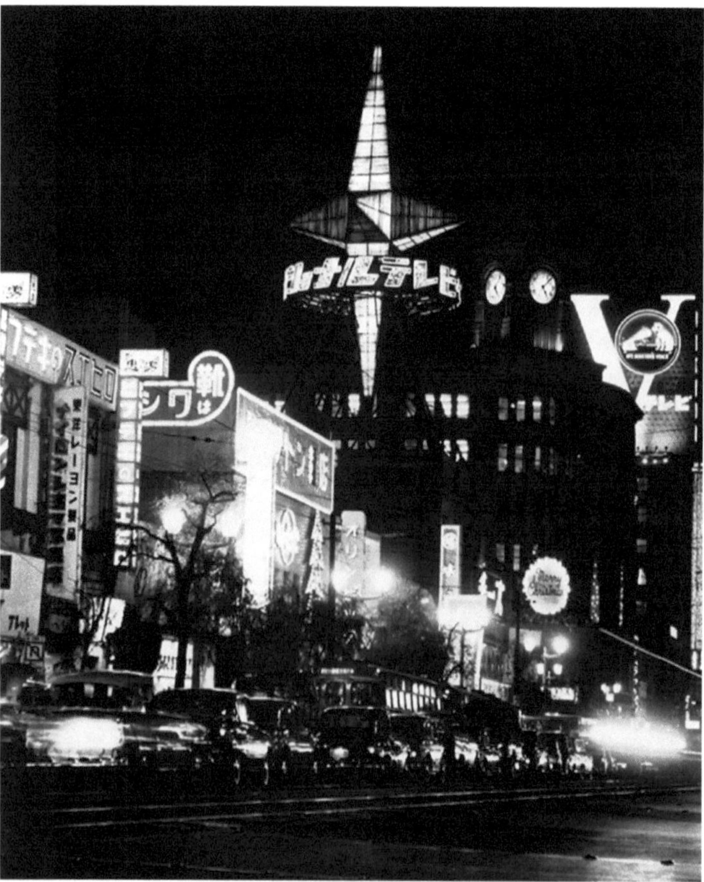
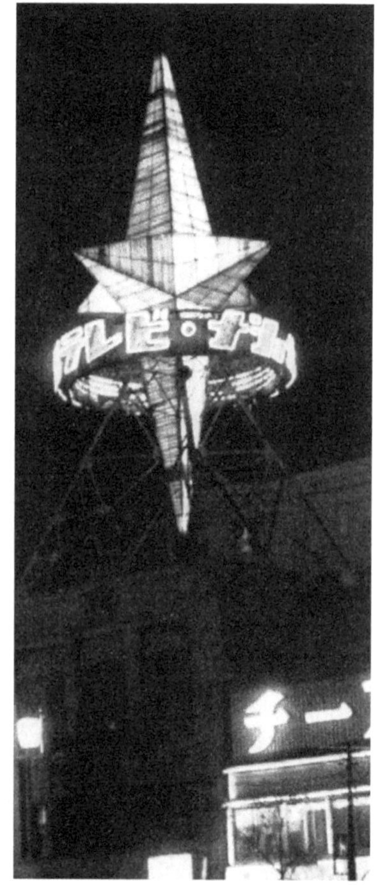

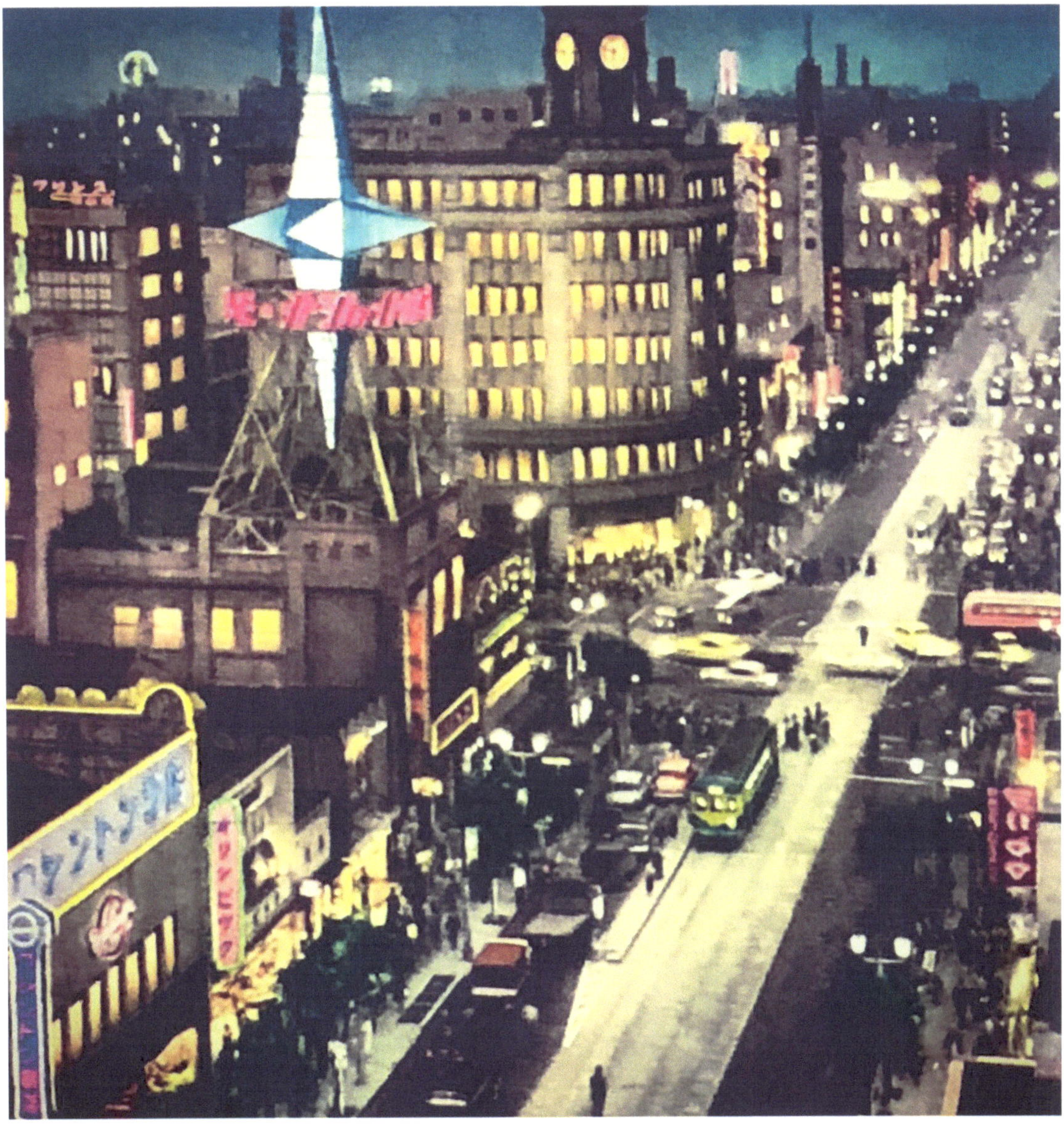

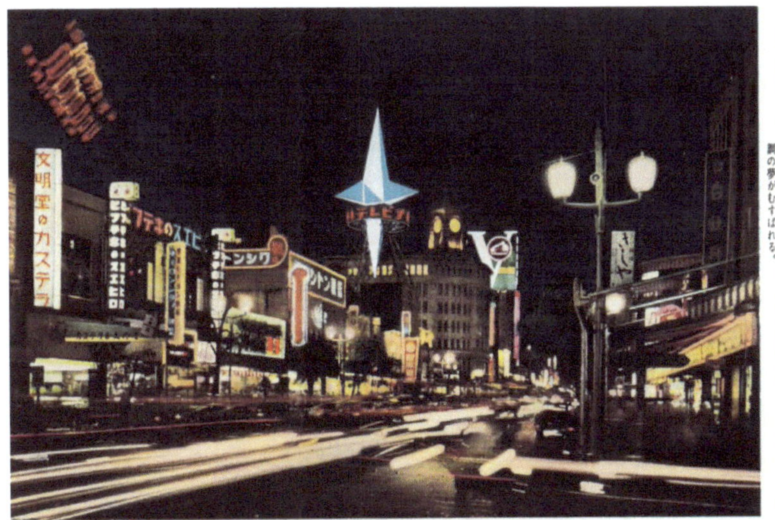

GINZA STREET (SHOPPING CENTER OF TOKYO)

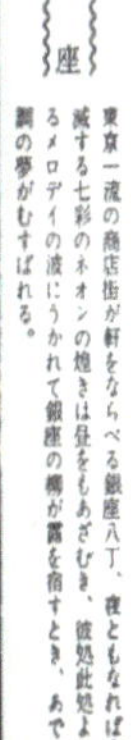

銀座

東京一流の商店街が軒をならべる銀座八丁、夜ともなれば夜空に明滅する七彩のネオンの煌きは昼をもあざむき、彼処此処より流れでるメロデイの波にうかれて銀座の柳が露を宿すとき、あでやかな情調の夢がむすばれる。

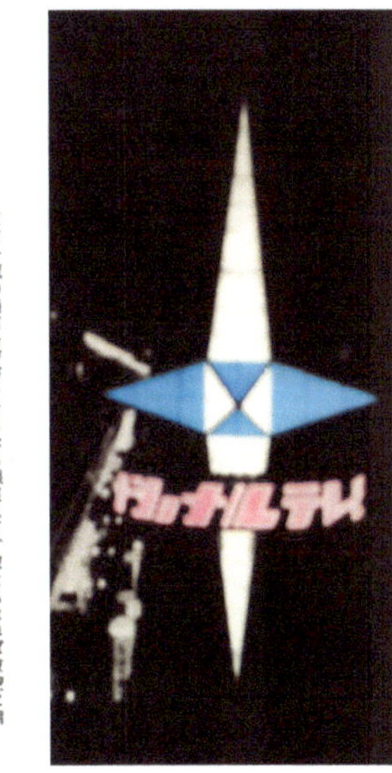

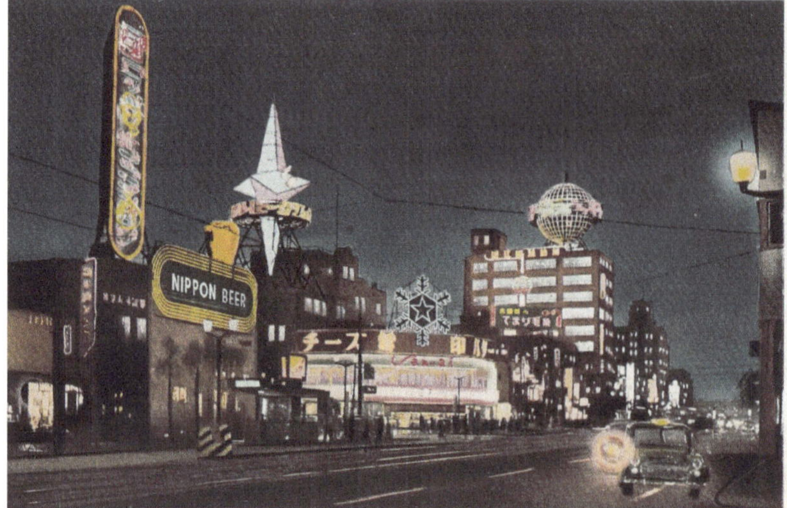

View in Night Ginza

銀座夜景

銀座の美しさは夜にある。ネオンの光芒に不夜城の盛観は、歓楽の果てるをしらない

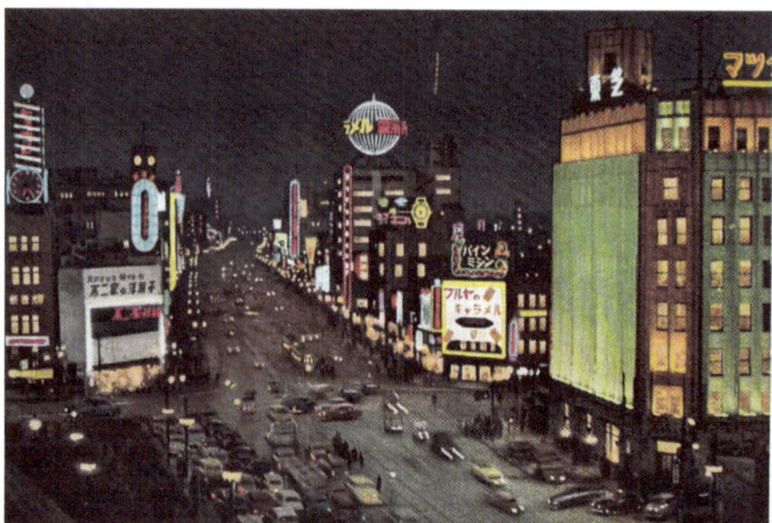

Ginza Street (Shopping Center of TOKYO).

銀座

東京一流の商店街が軒をならべる銀座八丁。夜ともなれば夜空に明滅する七彩のネオンの煌きは昼をもあざむき、彼処此処より流れでるノロデイの波にうかれて銀座の柳が露を宿すとき、あでやかな情調の夢がむすばれる。

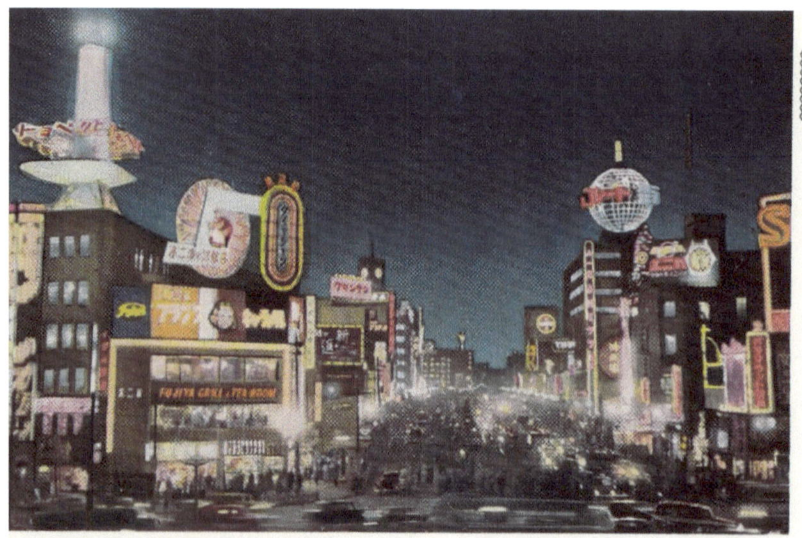

View in Night Tokyo at Ginza

夜の東京

ネオンの光芒に昼をあざむく夜の銀座

たくましい体力を

そのまゝ表現した、新しいデザインのネオン塔を、有樂町日劇前につくりました。高さは四十五尺、この結び目をとけば百尺に達します。使用した高輝度ネオン管は、従來のネオンに比べて四倍の明るさをもち、世界で始めて使つたものです。お出かけの節には、ぜひご高覧下さい。

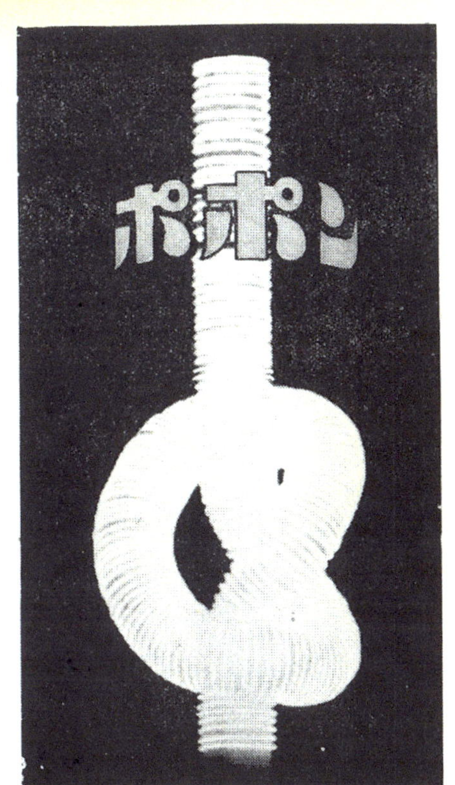

高単位綜合ビタミン・ミネラル剤

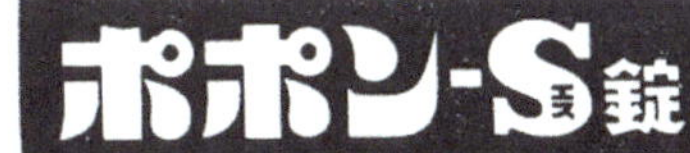

他に錠・末・液　15錠 350円 50錠 950円

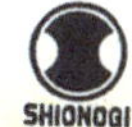

東京都日本橋本町　塩野義製薬株式会社

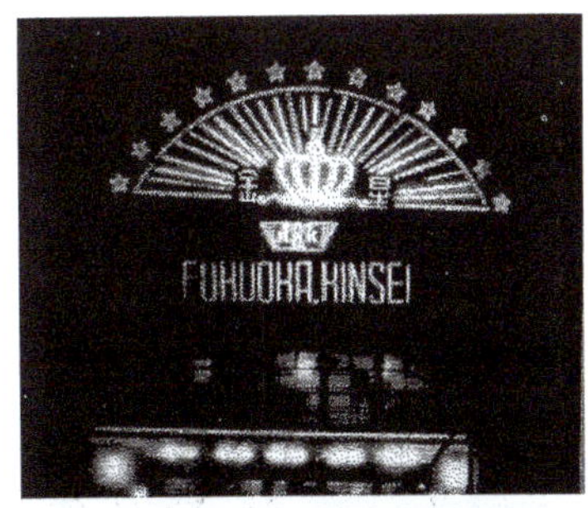

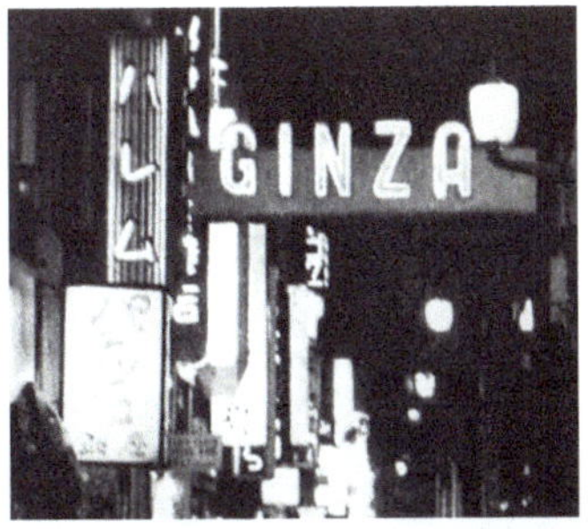

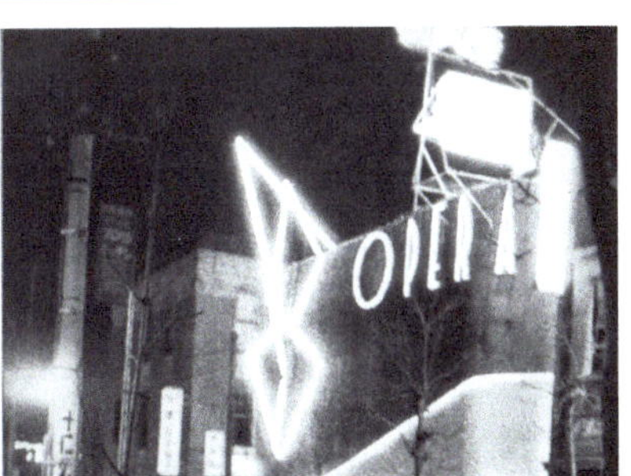

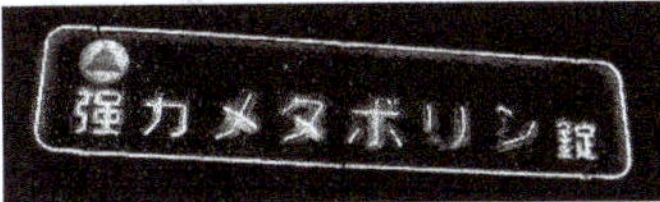

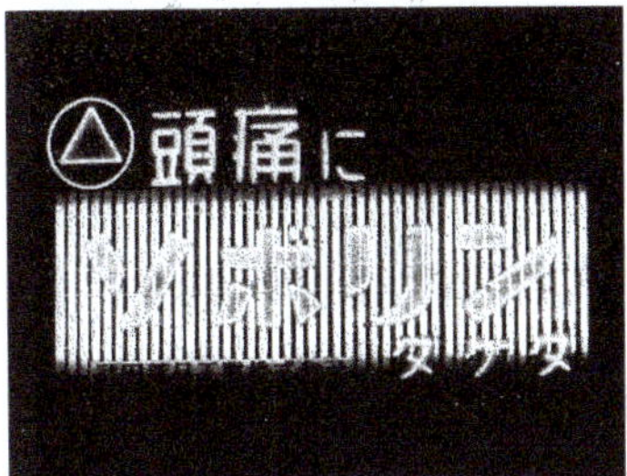

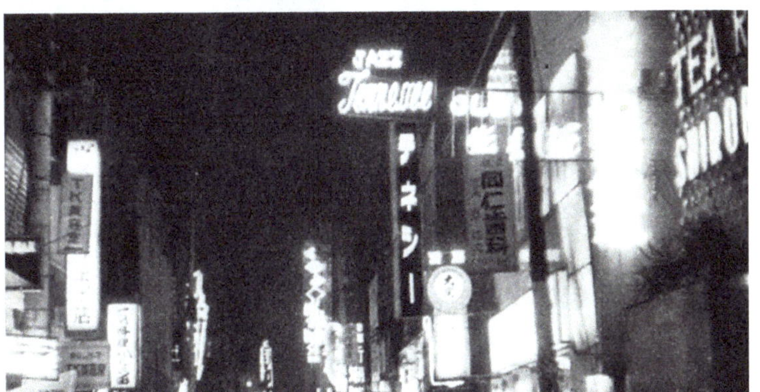

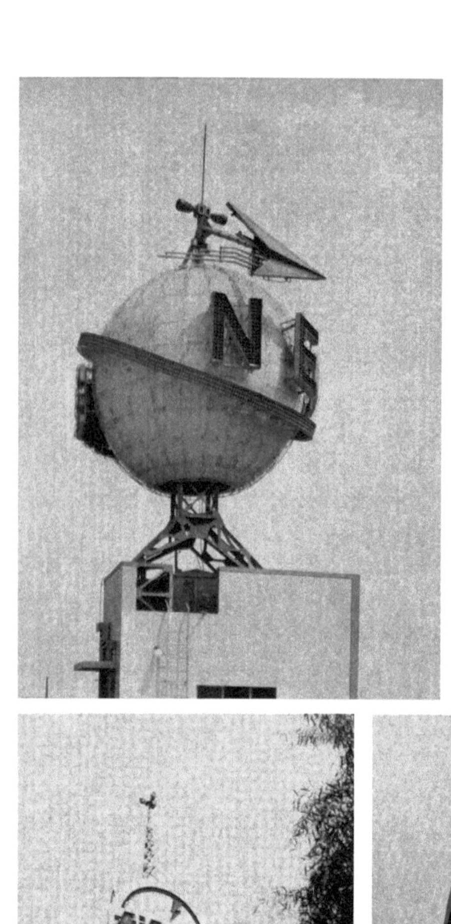
NE
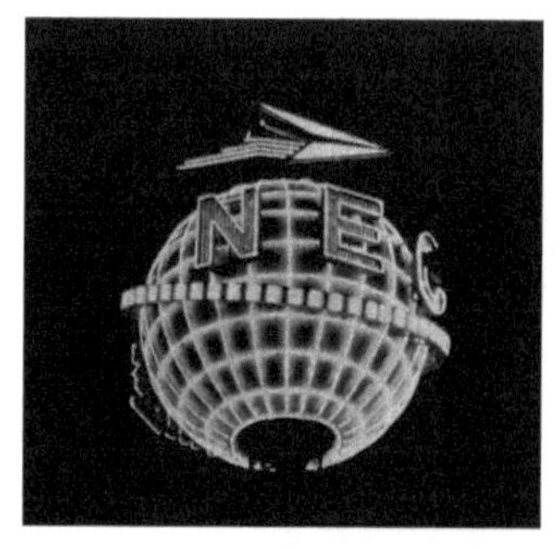
NE
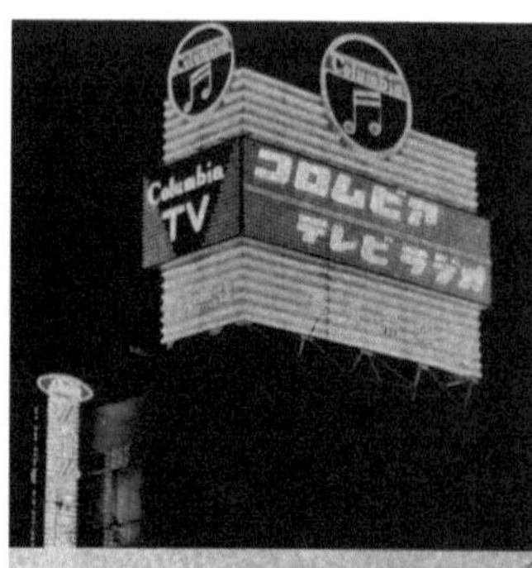
Columbia
Columbia TV
コロムビア
テレビ ラジオ
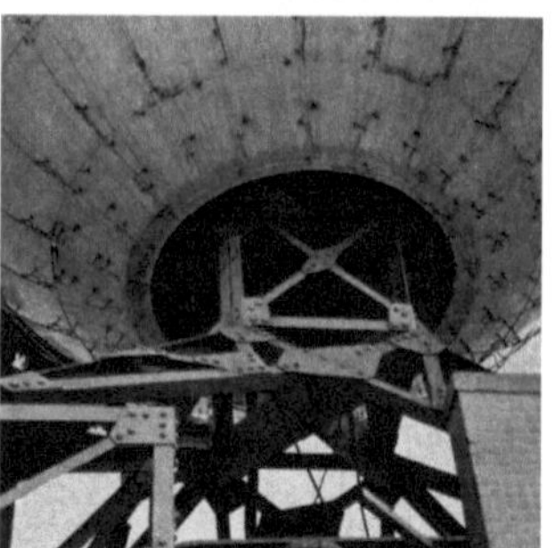
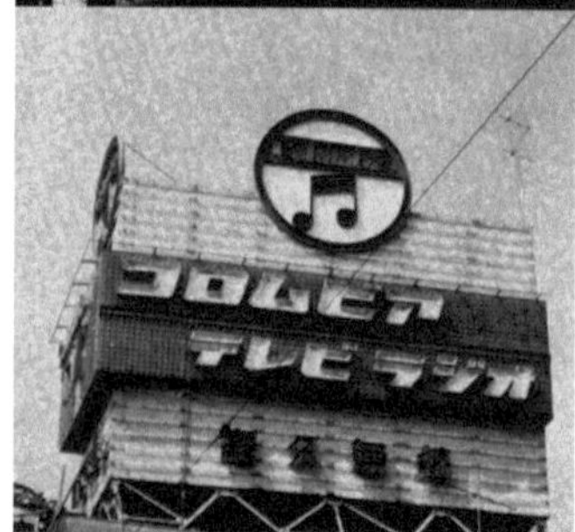
コロムビア
テレビ ラジオ
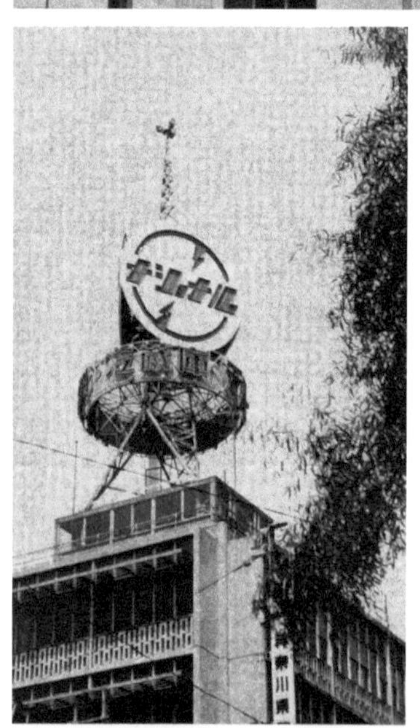
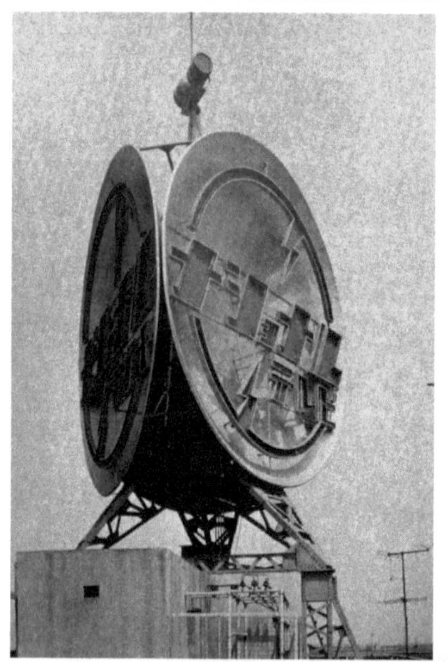
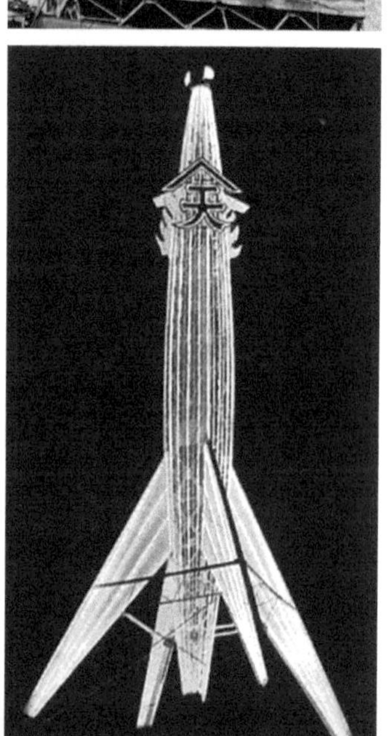
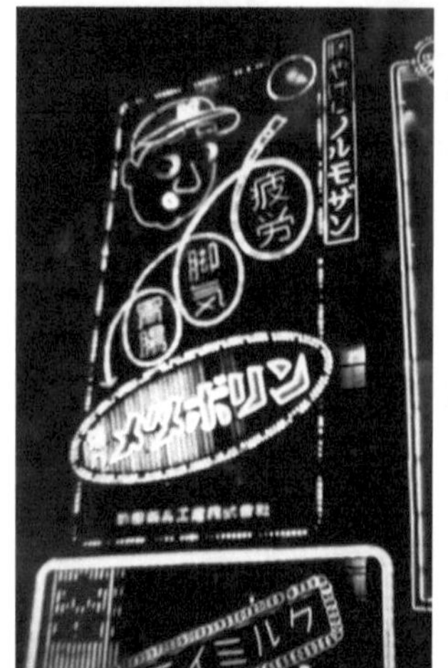
ノルモザン
疲労
脚気
ポリン
ミルク
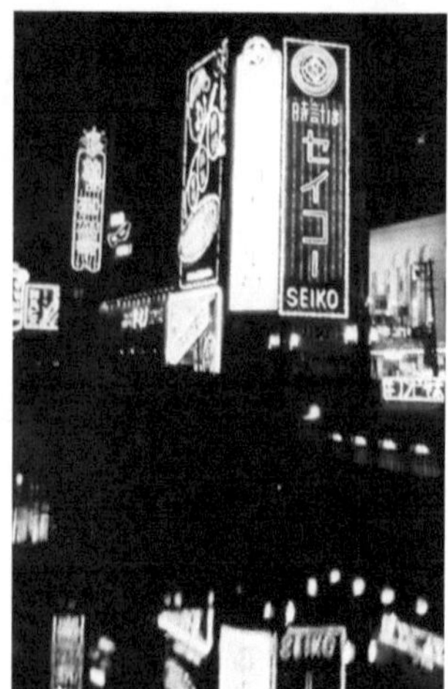
セイコー
SEIKO
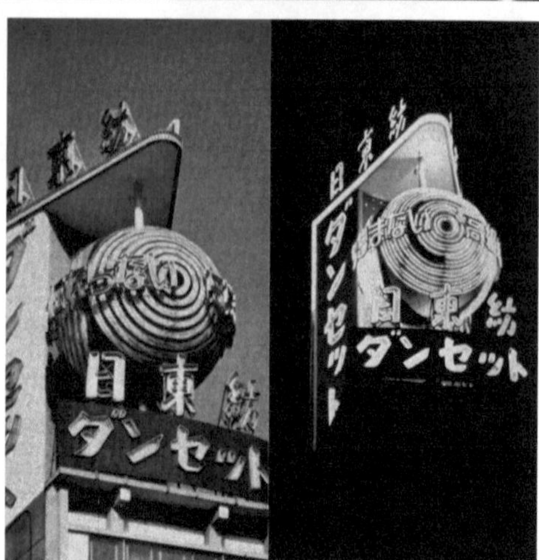
日東紡
ダンセット
日東紡
ダンセット
ダンセット

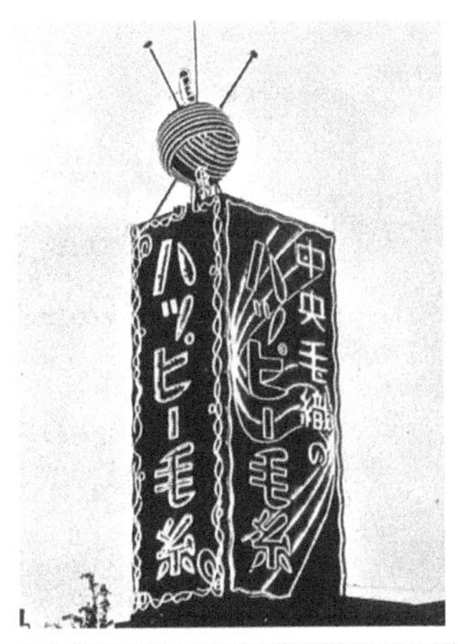
ハッピー毛糸
中央毛織の
ハッピー毛糸

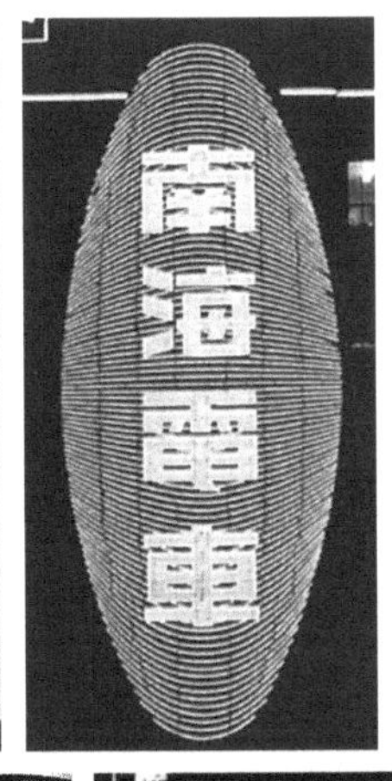
南海電車

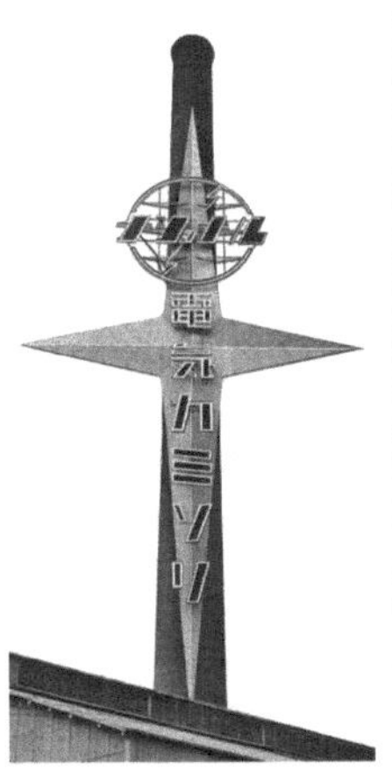
電気カミソリ

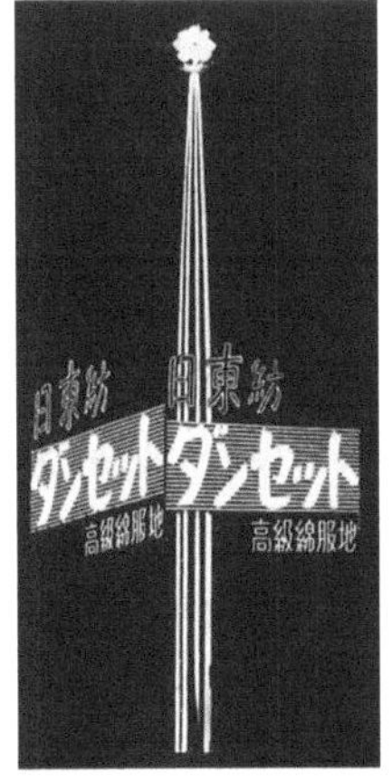
日東紡
ダンセット
高級綿服地
日東紡
ダンセット
高級綿服地

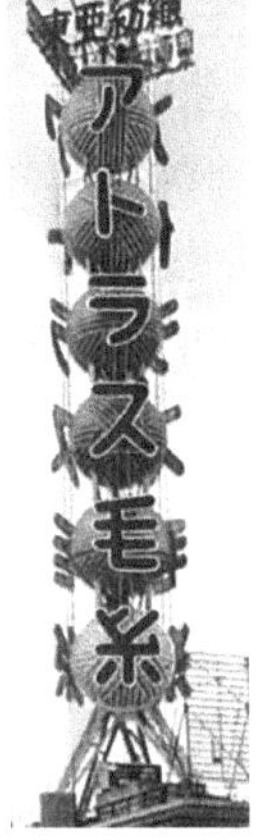
東亜紡織
アトラス毛糸

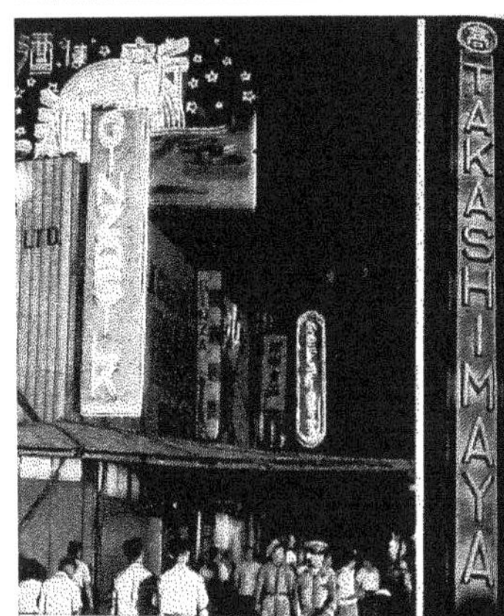
TAKASHIMAYA

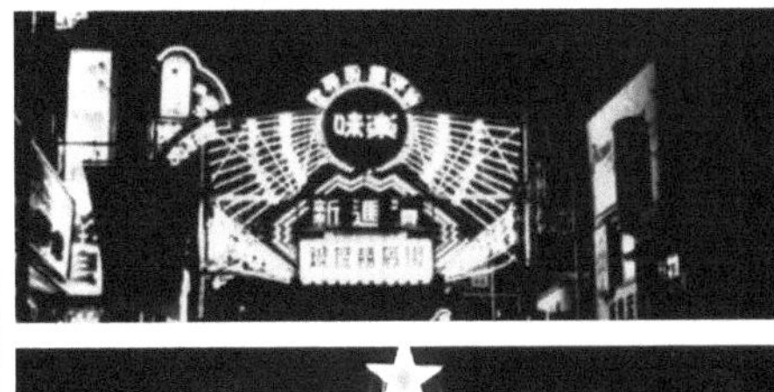

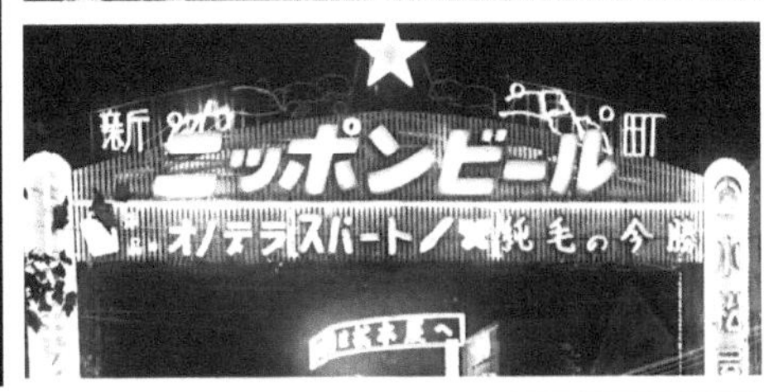
ニッポンビール

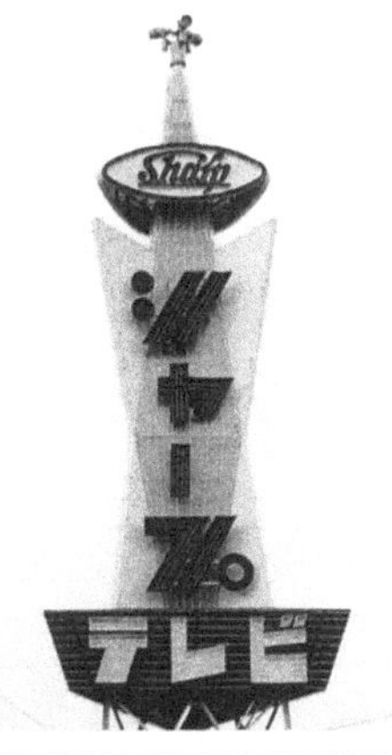
Sharp
シャープ
テレビ

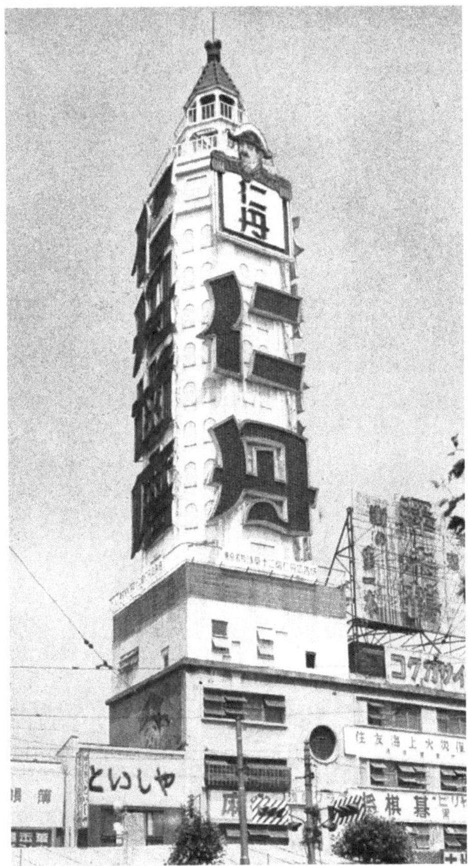
仁丹
仁丹
といしや

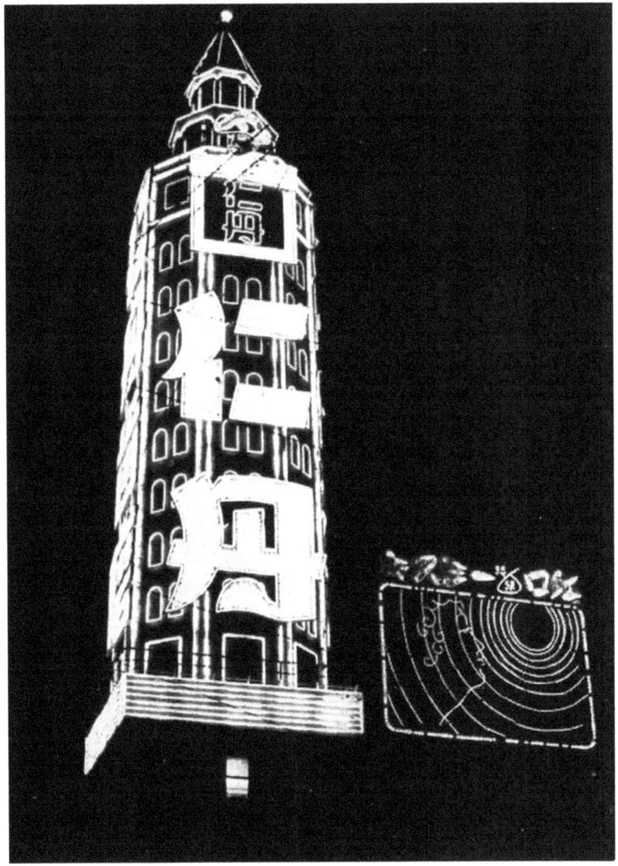
仁丹
仁丹

Toshio Kobayashi

Toshio Kobayashi (1921-2007) was an eccentric entrepreneur that helped sell the idea of a brighter Japan in the form of neon lights. Kobayashi worked as an advertising producer and TV filmmaker. He was the representative director, president and former chairman of the advertising firm Nobuhirosha.

Kobayashi started his career working for his father's advertising company. He was drafted to serve in World War II and was sent to mainland China as a heavy machine gunner. He would eventually take over his father's company, growing it into an advertising agency focused on outdoor advertising.

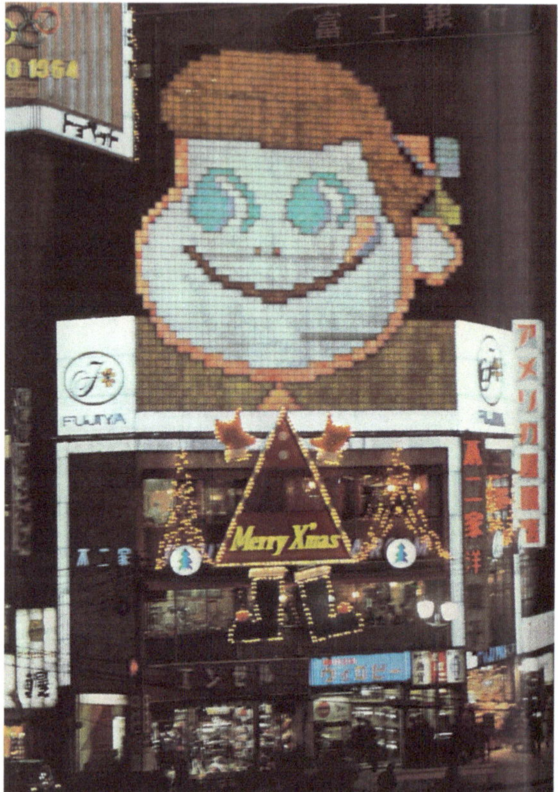

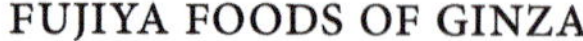
FUJIYA FOODS OF GINZA

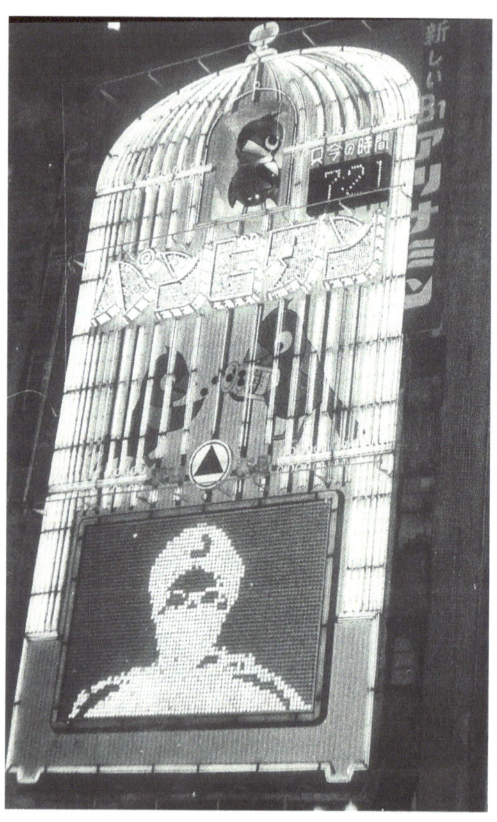

PANBITAN MEDICINE, OSAKA

When he returned from the war, he was stunned to see Tokyo in burnt ruins. Inspired by the neon lights of Times Square published in an American magazine, he wished to "give a bright light" to his war-torn country, and ventured into the neon business. After a series of high-profile projects, Kobayashi became known as the "man who brightened Ginza". He worked on signs for Toshiba, Takeda Pharmaceuticals, Sony, Fujiya, and other notable companies. His projects went as far as Hong Kong, New York, Singapore, and Bangkok. In addition, he founded a successful television production company, which filmed in many overseas locations.

Sony

Totsuko, short for Tokyo Telecommunications Engineering Corporation, wished to appeal to the global marketplace as a quality brand. Japan carried a reputation for poor manufacturing at the time, so they sold their exported products under an American brand. Executives at Totsuko decided to create their own brand name in effort to become renowned, re-branding as Sony.

The name Sony was adopted in 1955. The brand slowly gained recognition, and as such management felt the need to advertise. They decided that a neon sign would be the best way to portray their brand, and they would need a prominent place to display it. Sony eventually secured an advertising spot at the entrance to Ginza, the Sukiyabashi Bridge.

Morita, one of the co-founders of the company, filmed neon signs during his visit to New York City. Management studied the neon lights of Broadway, taking inspiration from the famous smoke ring puffing Camel sign, and other spectaculars alike. Aspiring to match the signs of New York, Sony commissioned designers from leading sign makers in Japan. They reviewed 19 designs, and reached a decision within four days.

Within two months, including considerable delays from preparing the building, the sign was installed on December 19th, 1957. The lighting ceremony that took place on that cold winter evening was a turning point for one of the world's top electronic manufacturing brands. The neon sign helped them achieve their goal of becoming world renowned.

The neon sign was about 32'x32', and weighed roughly 5,000lbs, with each letter of the name weighing 600lbs. The sign cost about 20 million yen to produce, though it proved its worth in the years to come. The giant advertisement was relayed by NHK Television on New Year's Eve throughout Japan.

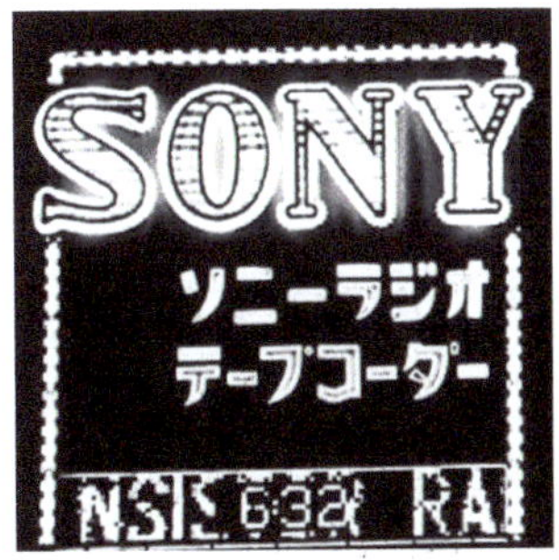

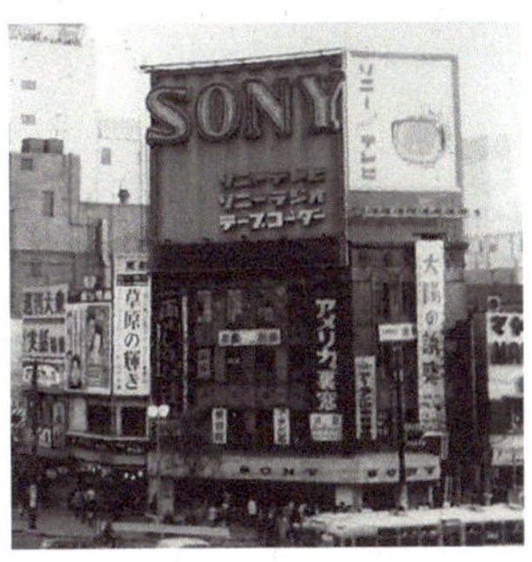

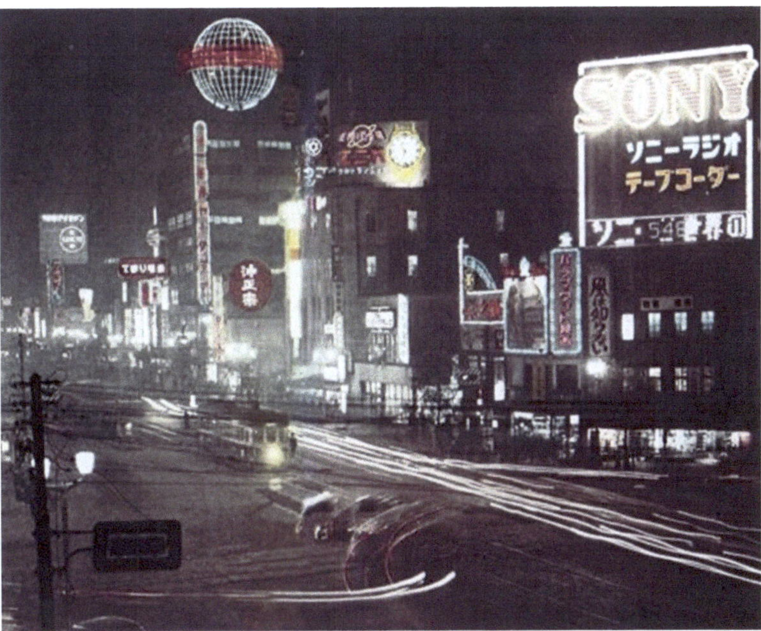

Innovations

Numerous neon engineers invented unique concepts to garner visual attention. Innovations such as the ripple tube, the glittering tube, and the scripting tube are examples ingenious concepts that gave companies a competitive advantage in the market place. Advertisers and retail shops were eager to employ the most captivating products to attract customers.

Inventors Rinji Tate, Keiichi Kubo, and Masao Nishiyama came up with the idea to bend two or more tubes into wavy lines, with each tube of the same or different color. The tubes would be connected to an automatic switching blinker, causing the neon to appear as fluctuating in a waveform when the tubes are turned on and off alternately. The inventors speculated that this would increase the value of an advertising display significantly.

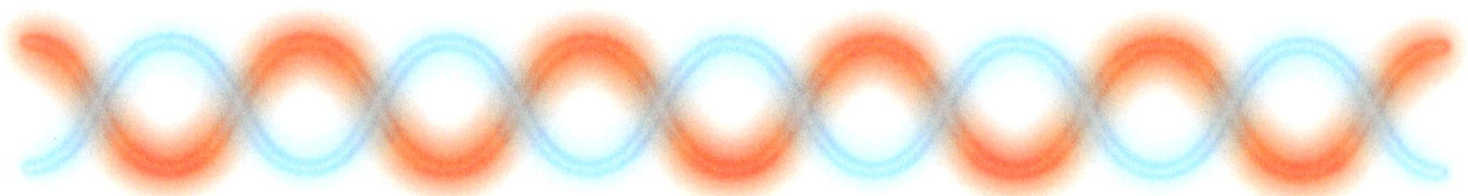

Toho Photo Studios invented "flowing neon", an effect that flowed the electrical discharge of the neon light in a fluid motion across the tube as if someone were writing. This effect was expensive to produce, and it couldn't be made at a large scale as the frequency violated radio laws. Nonetheless, the invention was used on smaller signs, and still had a captivating effect.

In attempt to save energy on neon signs along railway lines, a prototype of an automatic device that turns on the advertisement when a train was passing was developed. The device was activated by the loud noise generated by the train to switch on the neon advertisement for a 20 second time period. It consisted of a dynamic microphone, a sound level meter, and a main unit that completed the electrical circuit when a sound level of 60 decimals was sensed. The device was mounted on the Hitachi neon sign along the Tokaido line in Totsuka. The sign operated successfully, and received much interest from various fields.

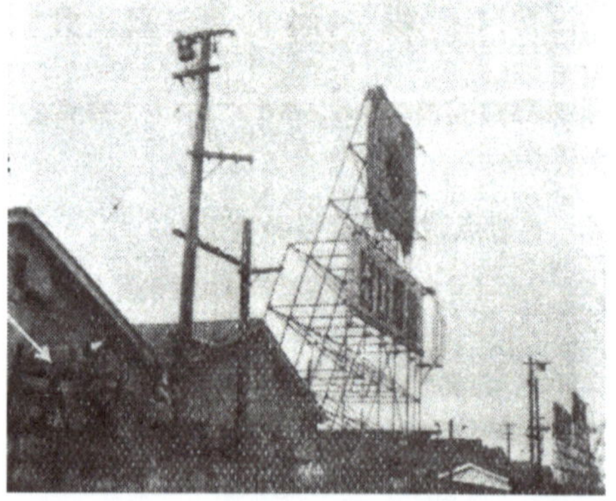

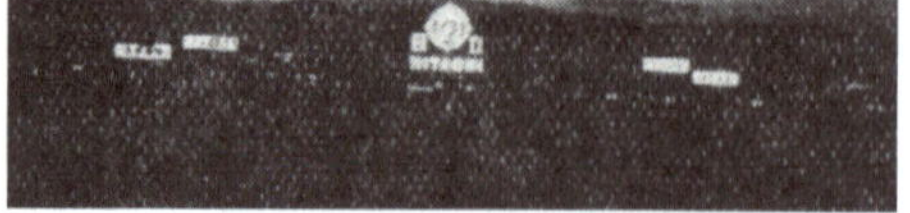

Another innovative concept used in neon advertising was surface design. Some signs used mirrors and reflective surfaces on the faces and backsides to shape light into interesting patterns. Other signs would utilize spotlights to shine from under to define geometrical shapes. This style was used for decades after becoming popular in the 1960s.

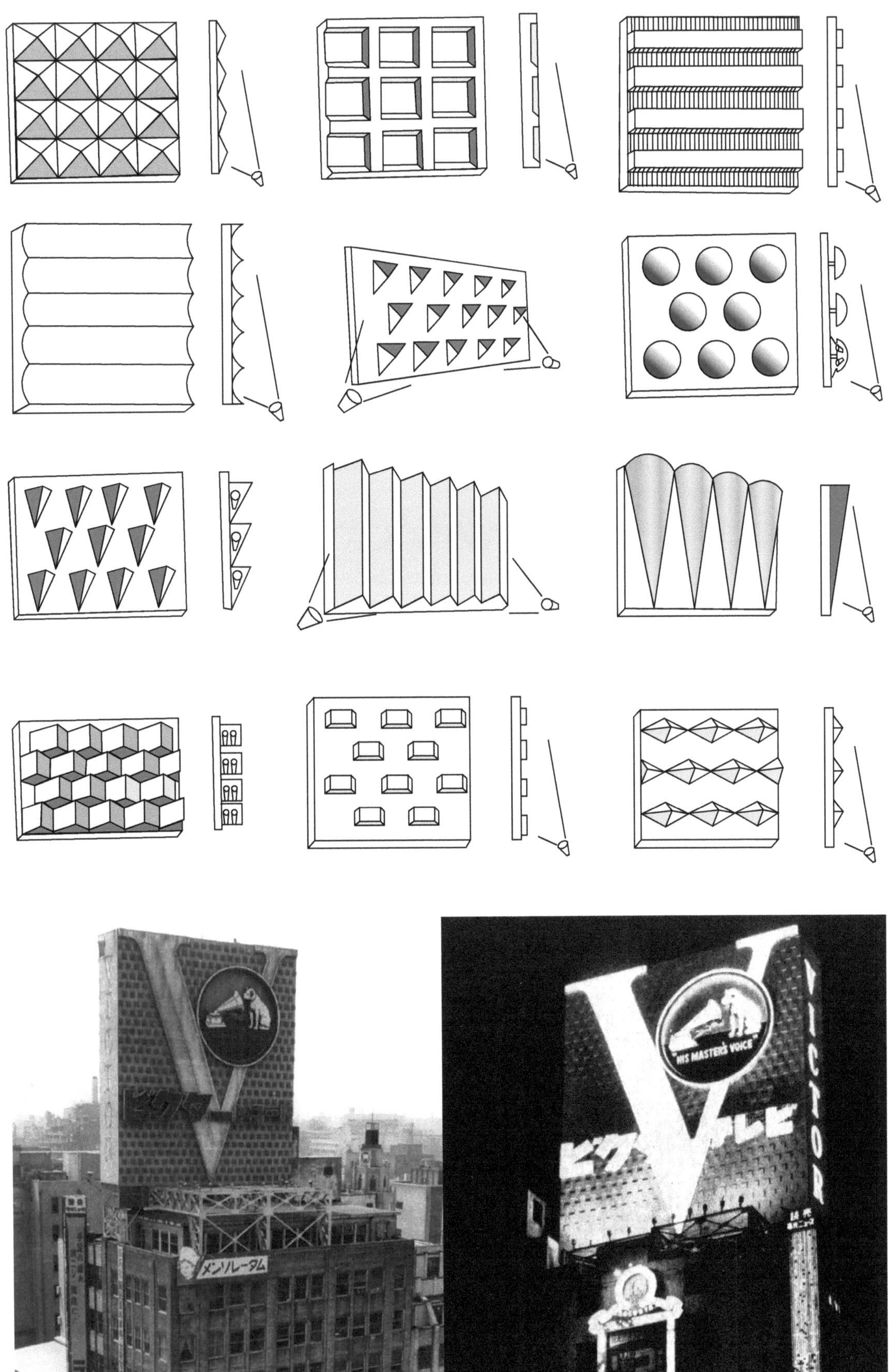

メンソレータム
"HIS MASTER'S VOICE"
VICTOR

The Golden Years

Japan's economy was taking off with annual growth rates over 10%, setting Japan on its path to become a leading world power. Japan's economic prosperity continued into the 1960s, though it came in waves similar to the past decade. Nuclear power had recently been adopted, which helped to relieve fears of future energy shortages. The most popular export products during the beginning of the decade were the refrigerator, washing machine, and television.

Infrastructure developed greatly in anticipation of the 1964 Tokyo Olympics. The development of roads and urban planning became widespread, leading to an increase of signs along the highways instead of along railway lines. The construction of the Metropolitan Expressway began in Tokyo during 1962, causing a great competition for advertising space along this route. In addition to the new highway, the Shinkansen, Japan's high-speed train was opened in 1964. The changes in infrastructure made neon companies nervous as the government took control of advertising spaces, increasing the fees and regulations.

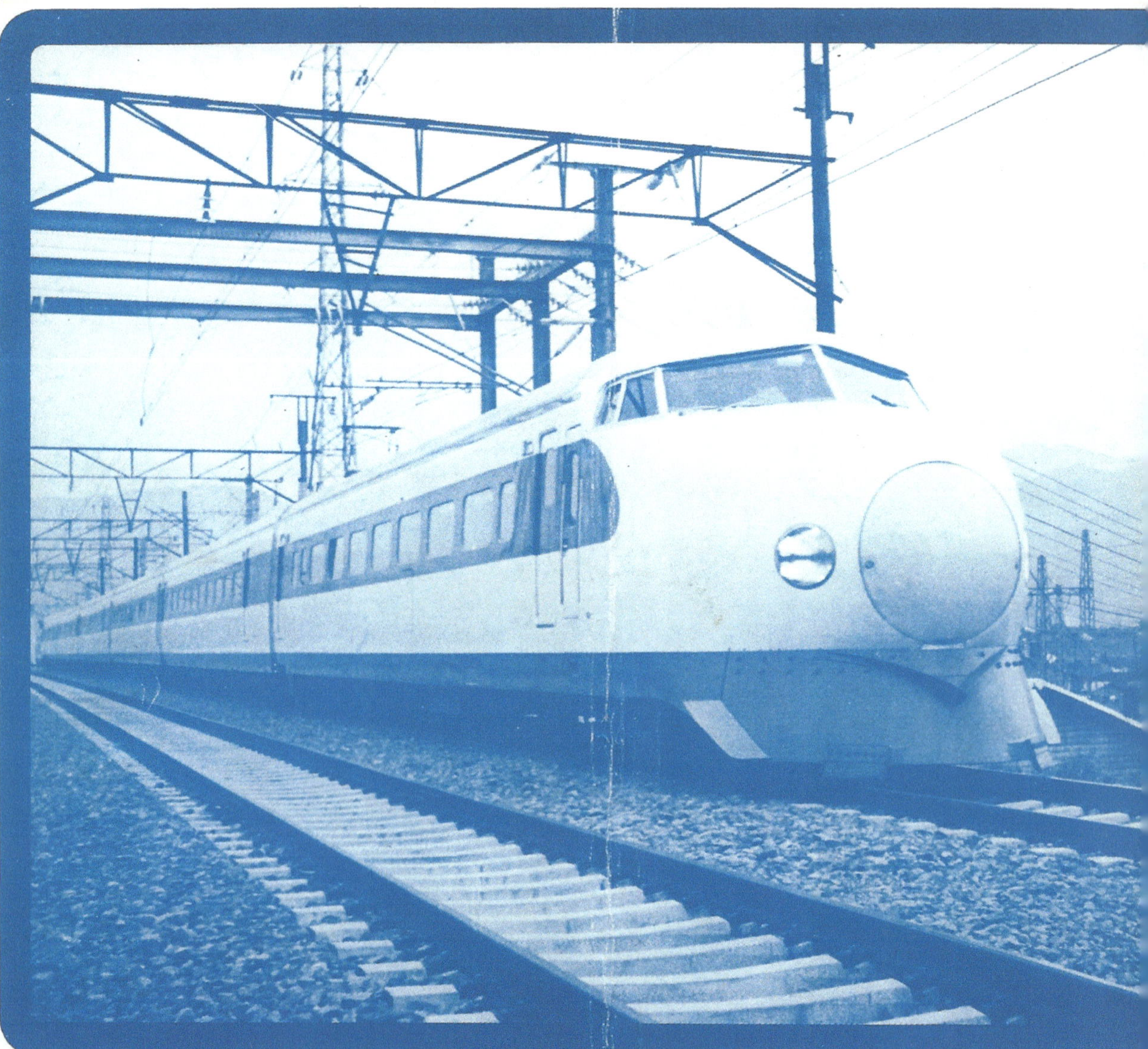

Super-speed services on the New Tokaido Line are commenced on October 1st.

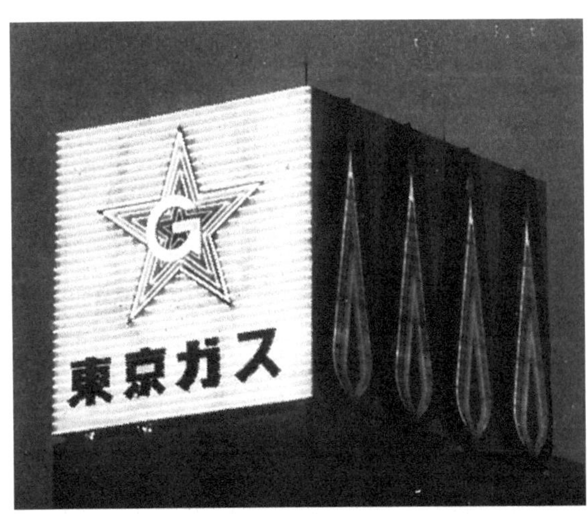
G
東京ガス

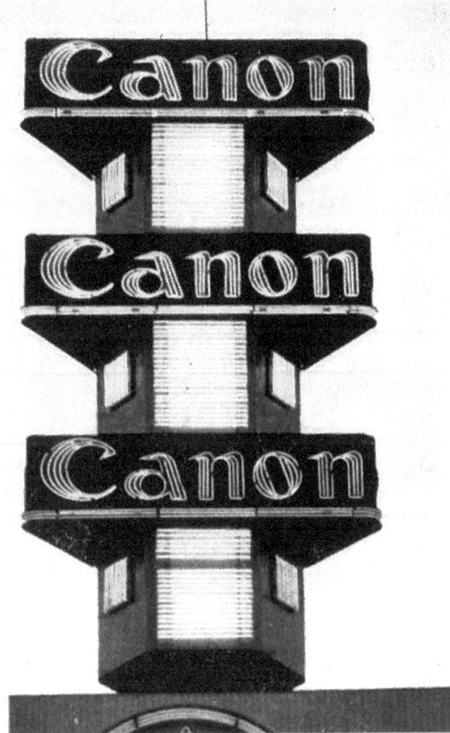
Canon
Canon
Canon

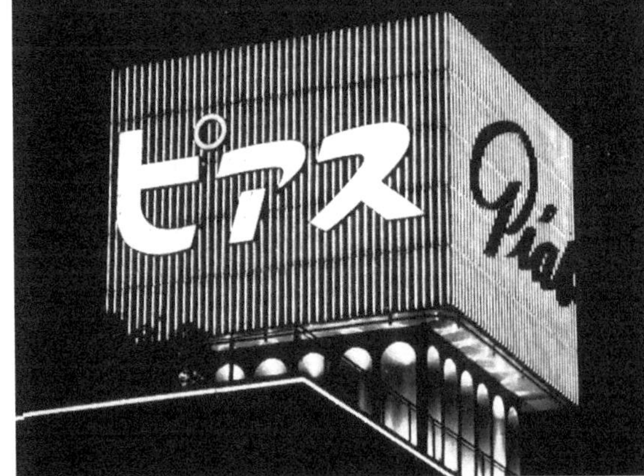
ピアス

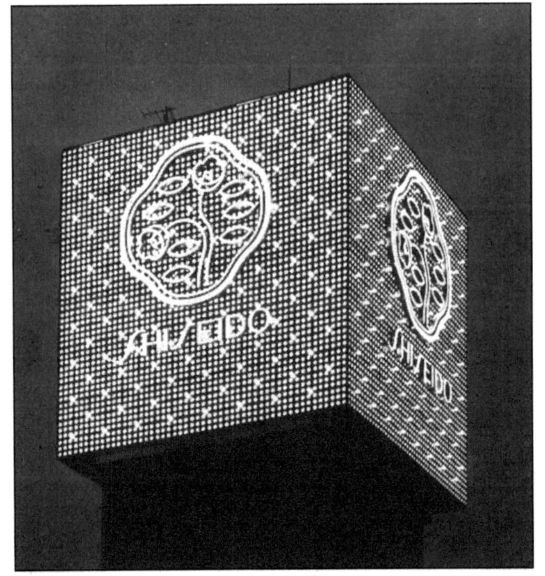
SHISEIDO
SHISEIDO

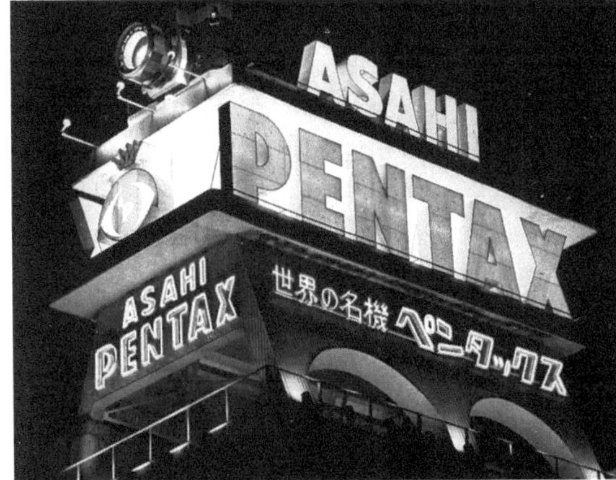
ASAHI
PENTAX
ASAHI
PENTAX
世界の名機 ペンタックス

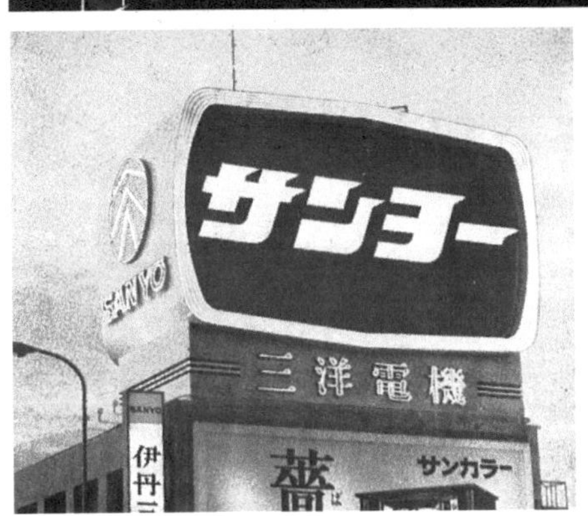
SANYO
サンヨー
三洋電機
サンカラー

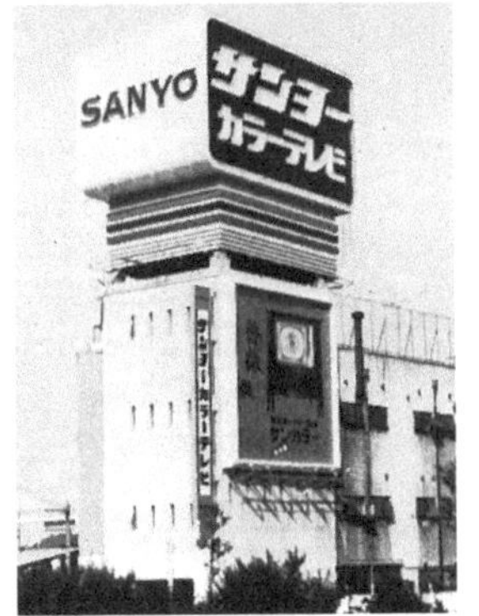
SANYO
サンヨー
カラーテレビ

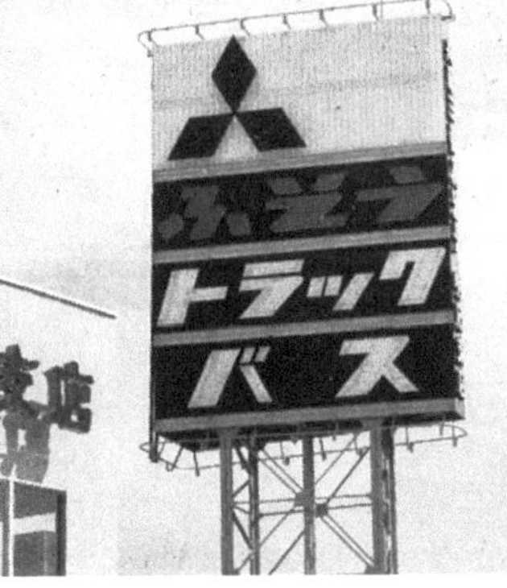
トラック
バス

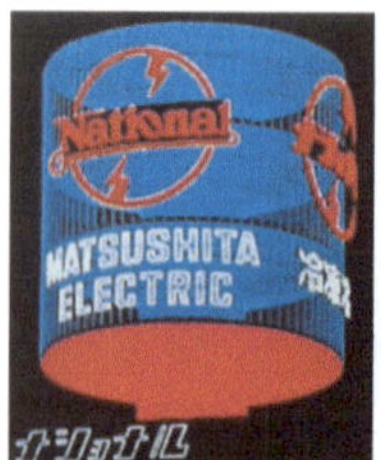
National
MATSUSHITA
ELECTRIC
ナショナル

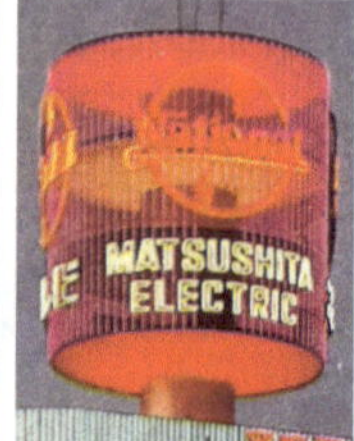
National
MATSUSHITA
ELECTRIC

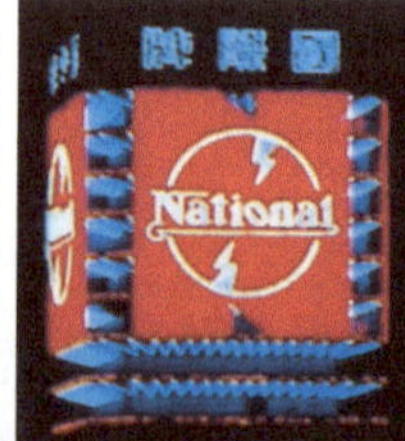
National

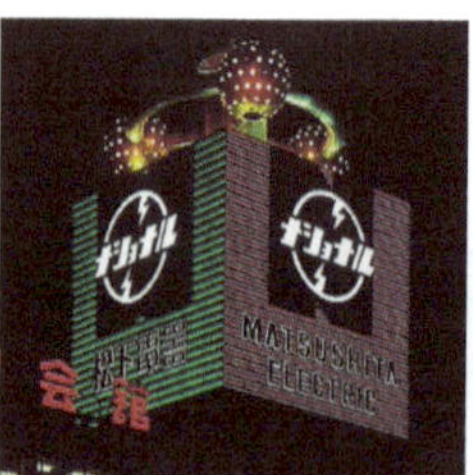
ナショナル
ナショナル
MATSUSHITA
ELECTRIC

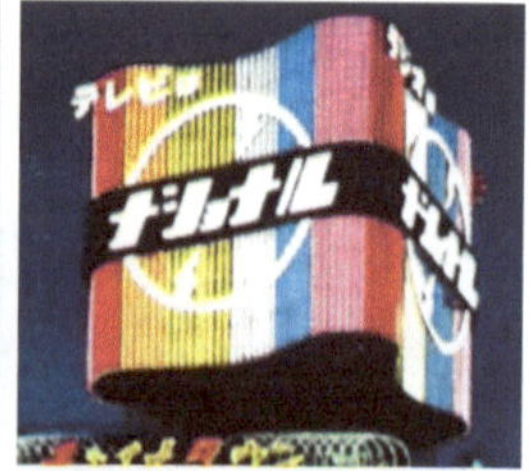
ナショナル

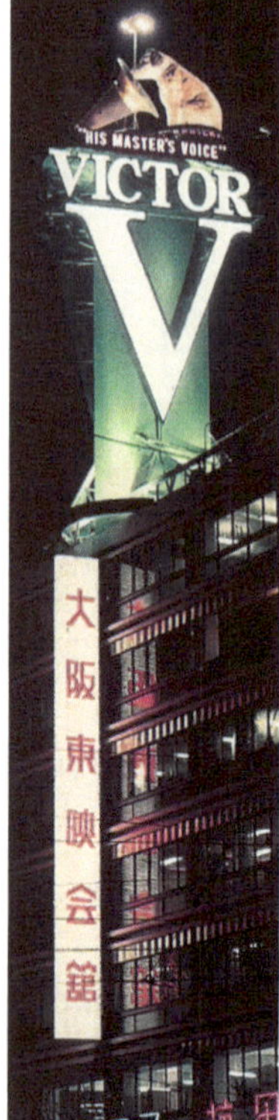
"HIS MASTER'S VOICE"
VICTOR
V
大阪東映会館

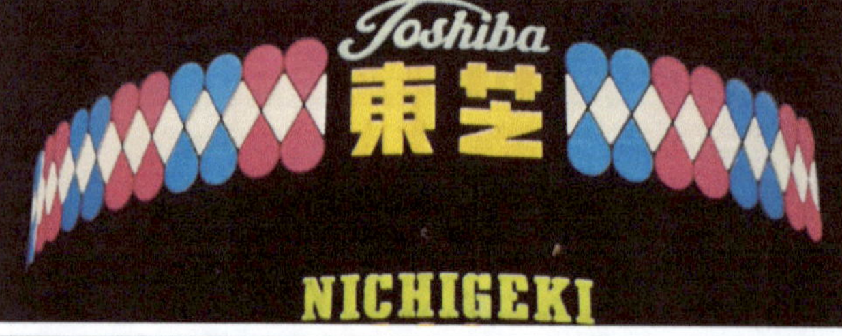
Toshiba
東芝
NICHIGEKI

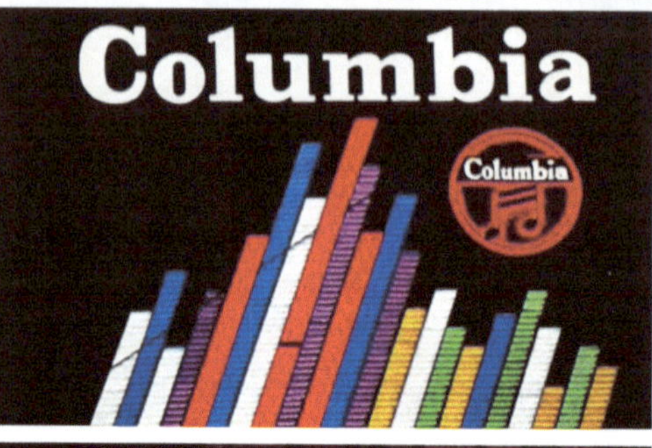
Columbia
Columbia

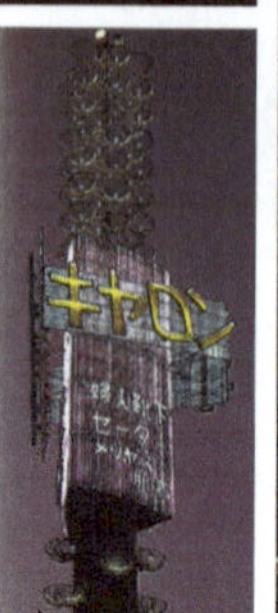
キヤノン

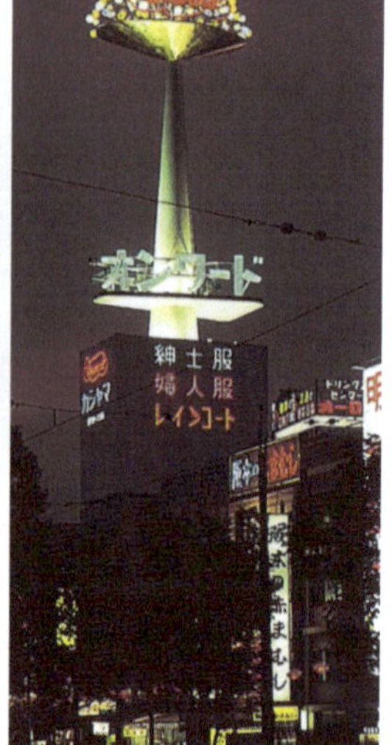
紳士服
婦人服
レインコート

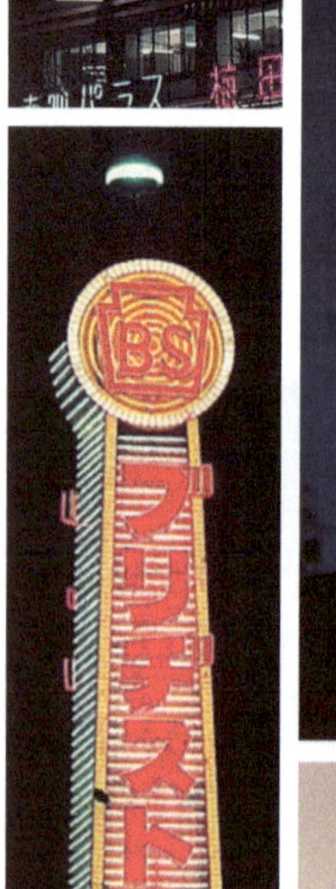
BS
ブリヂストンタイヤ

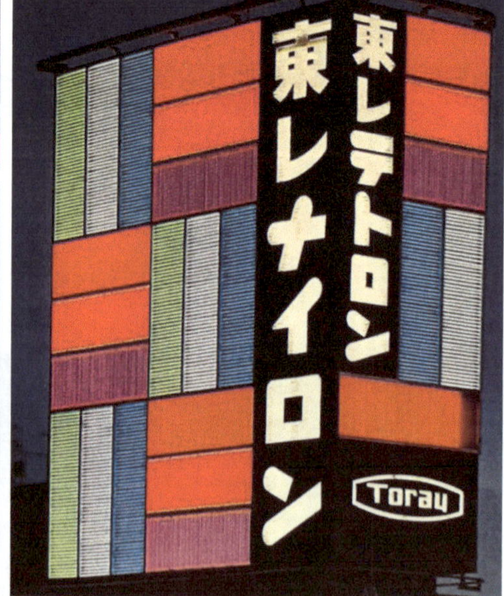
東レテトロン
東レナイロン
Toray

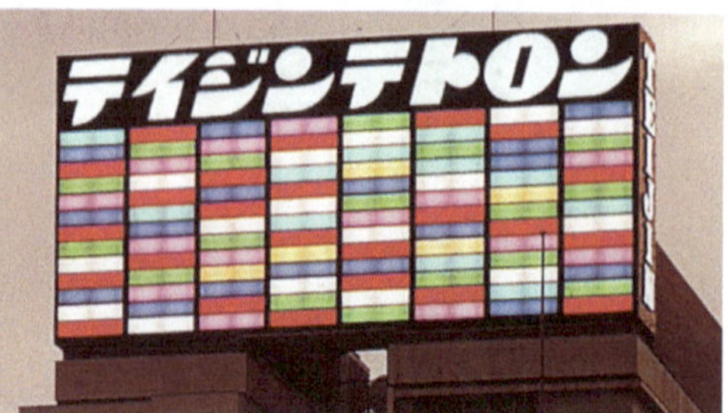
テイジンテトロン

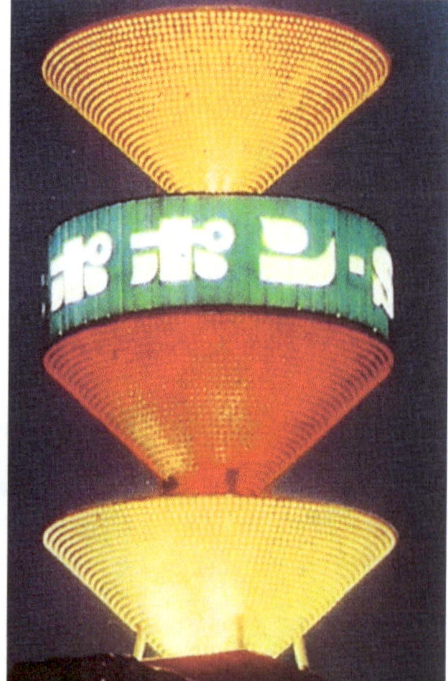
ポポン-S

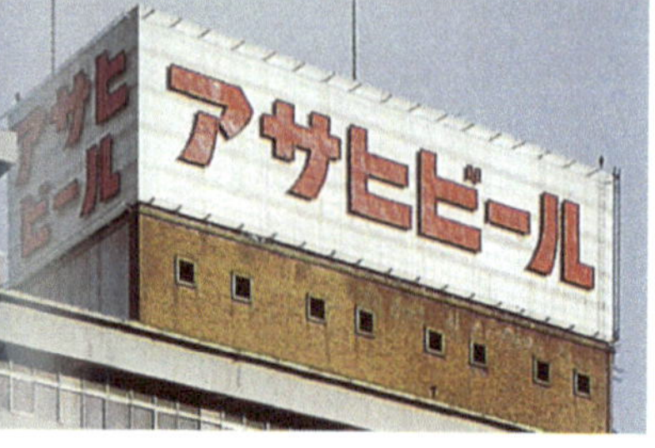
アサヒビール
アサヒビール

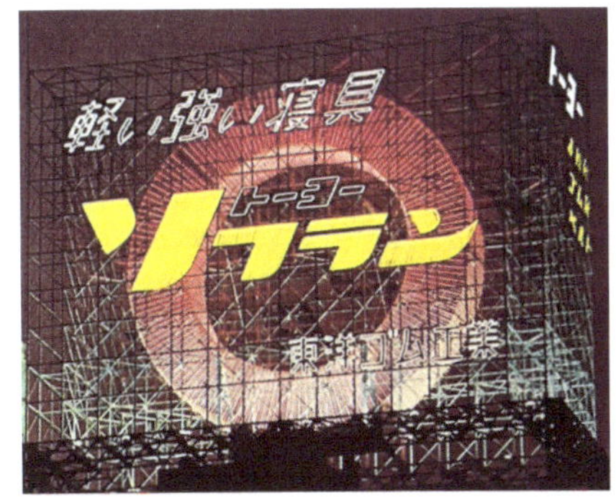
軽い強い寝具
トーヨー
ソフラン
東洋ゴム工業

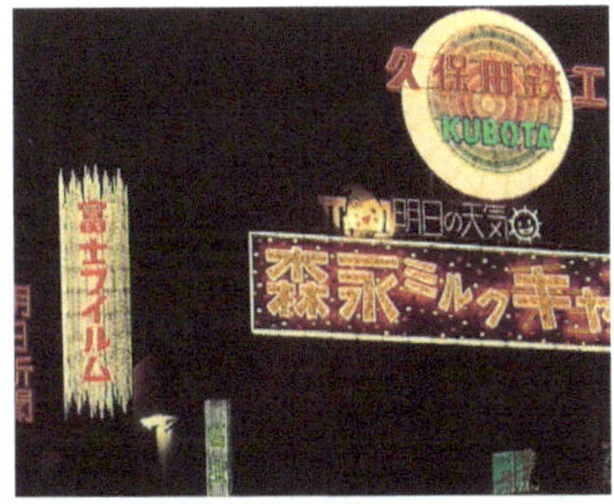
久保田鉄工
KUBOTA
明日の天気
富士フイルム

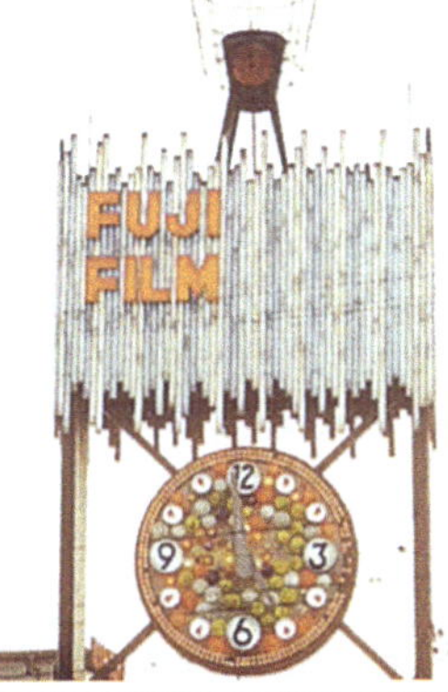
FUJI
FILM

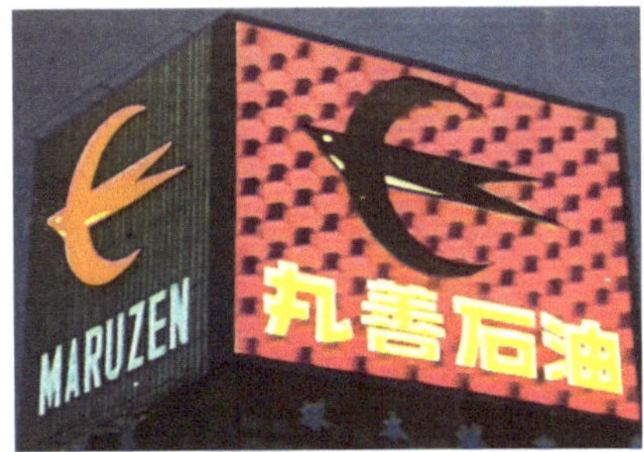
MARUZEN
丸善石油

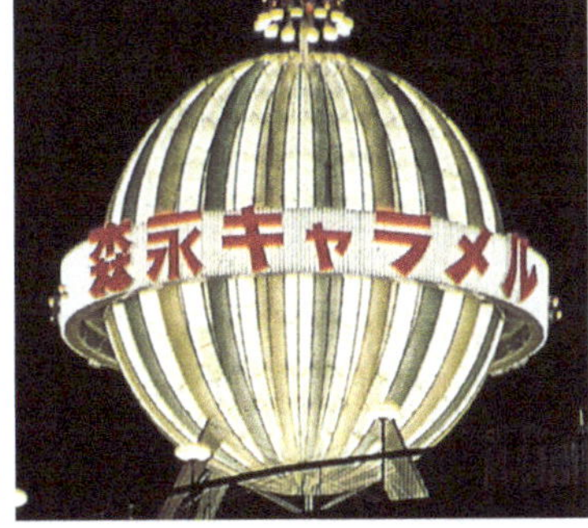
森永キャラメル

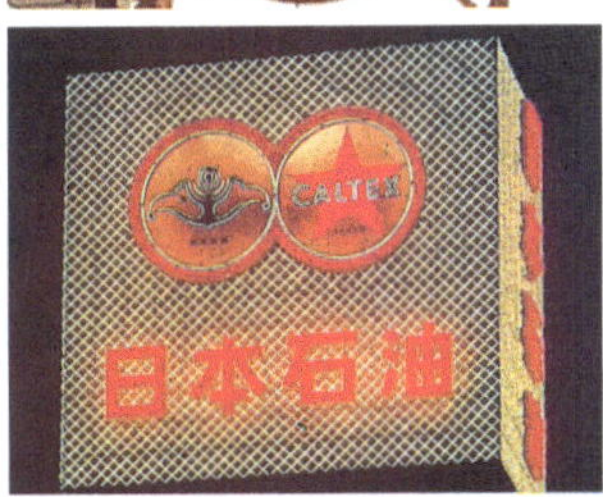
CALTEX
日本石油

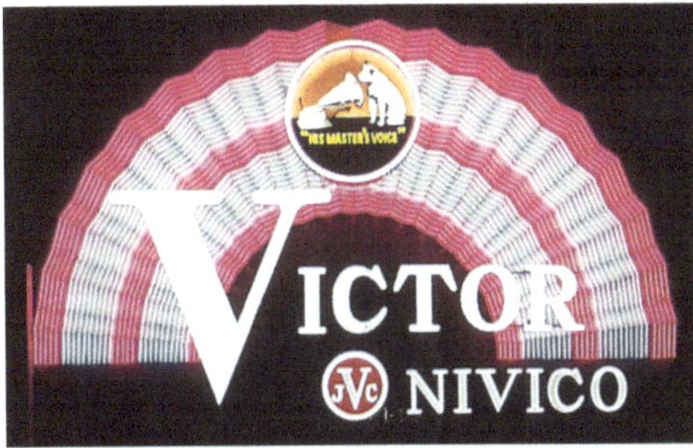
VICTOR
JVC NIVICO

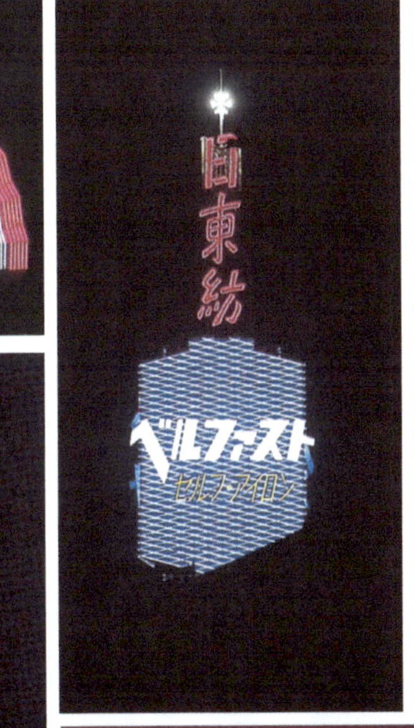
日東紡
ベルファスト
セルフアイロン

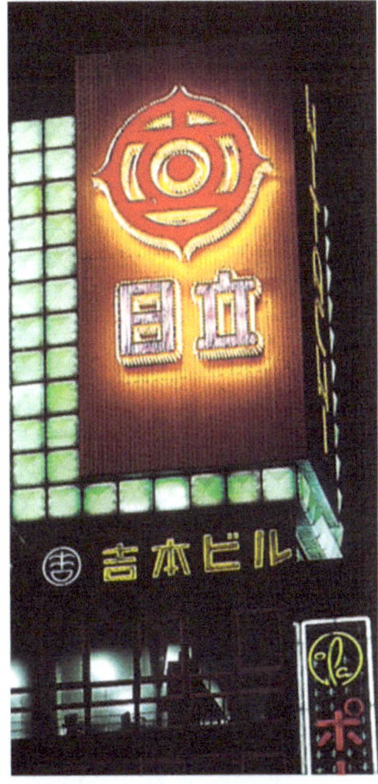
日立
吉本ビル

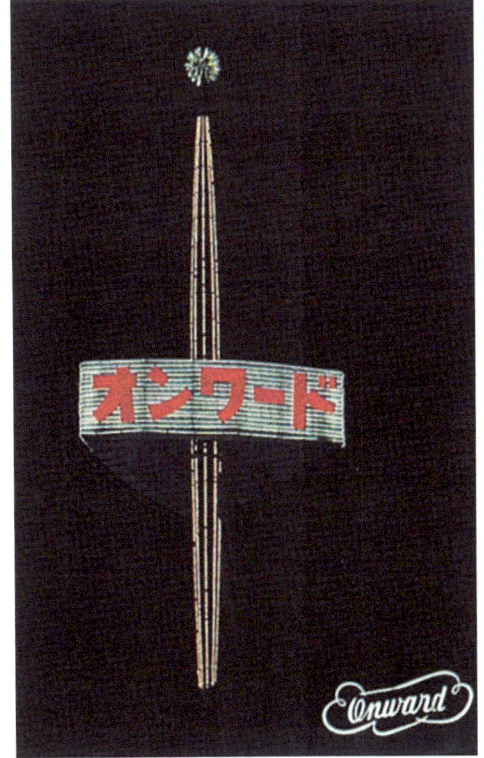
オンワード
Onward

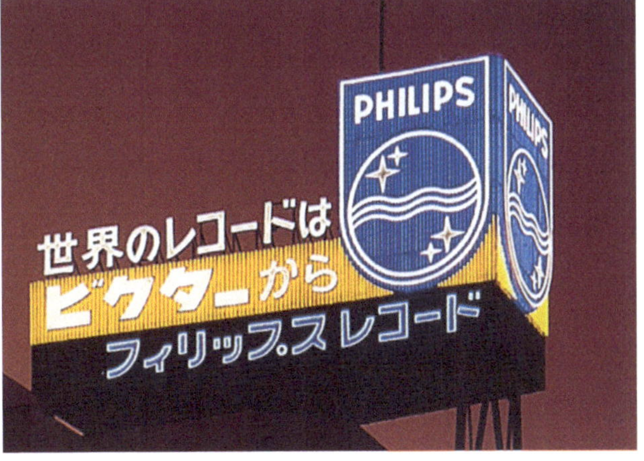
PHILIPS
世界のレコードは
ビクターから
フィリップスレコード

Many new signs were erected along the highway leading to Haneda Airport and the Olympic venue. In addition, many neon signs along Ginza were renovated. Signs made to appeal to tourists were built around the country. This was the "Olympic Boom" for sign companies. Some companies employed over 50 craftsmen and still couldn't keep up with the demand.

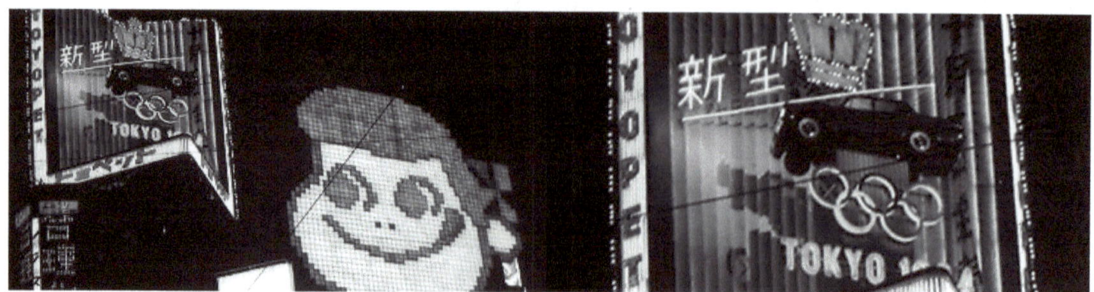

TOYOTA'S 1964 OLYMPIC ADVERTISEMENT IN GINZA

After the Olympics, Japan experienced another boom known as the long "Izanagi Economy", which lasted from 1965-1970. Investments made by companies led to new factories and sales offices, resulting in nationwide mass production of goods. The demand for neon advertisements expanded in parallel. Advertisers began to utilize psychological research for advertising to create the most effective neon signs for their clients. The progression of neon technology advanced with the development of new product materials, especially plastics and aluminum. Japan's treasured products for the latter half of the decade were the automobile, color television, and air conditioners.

The World Exposition held in Osaka created another great boom for sign companies. The economy was still doing great at this point. As many companies merged, there were many orders for new signs. Many existing signs were modified to show the countdown until the opening day, and neon towers were produced by sponsors for the exposition in major cities. Similar to the highway connection between Haneda Airport to the Olympics venue, signs were placed along the highway connecting the Osaka airport and the World Expo venue.

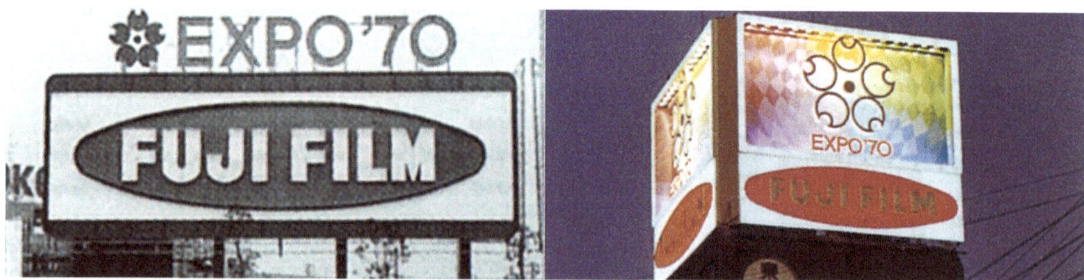

The industry started to hit some bumps early into the 1970s. Although production costs soared, the industry recorded the highest sales ever. However, troubles began to appear, as a sudden rise in costs of various materials began. Due to an explosion of a petrochemical factory, a shortage of plastics occurred and affected the industry tremendously. Vinyl wires, transformers, PVC boards, and paint become more expensive, followed by steel frames, rising 20% to 30% from the previous year's price.

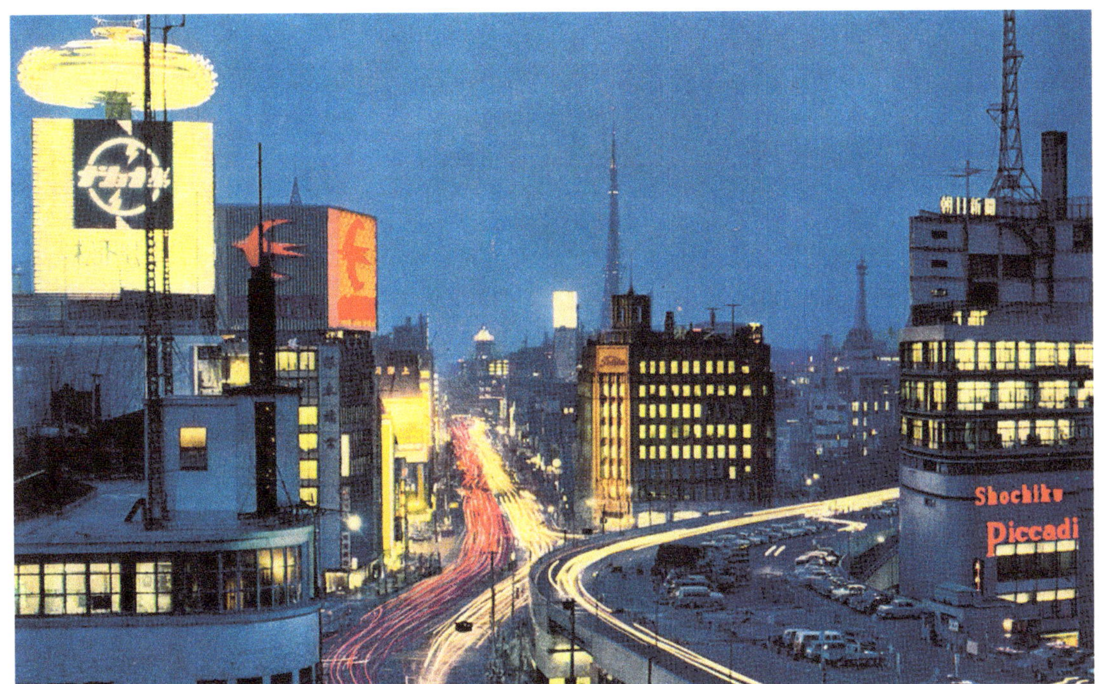
Shochiku
Piccadi

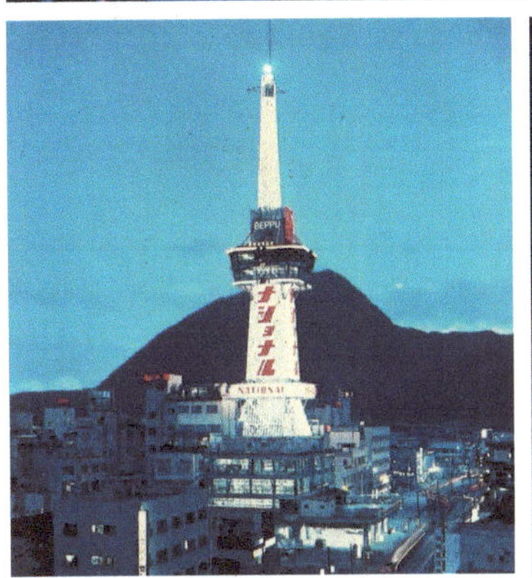
ナショナル

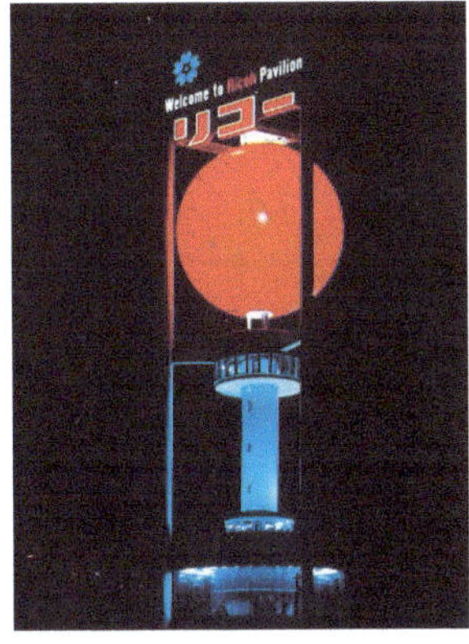
リコー

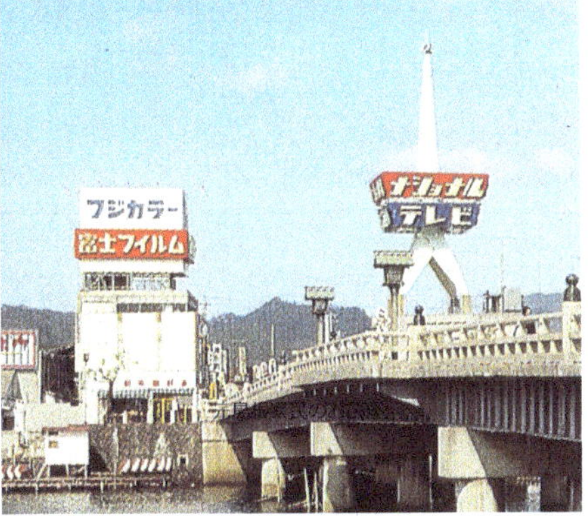
フジカラー
富士フイルム
ナショナル
テレビ

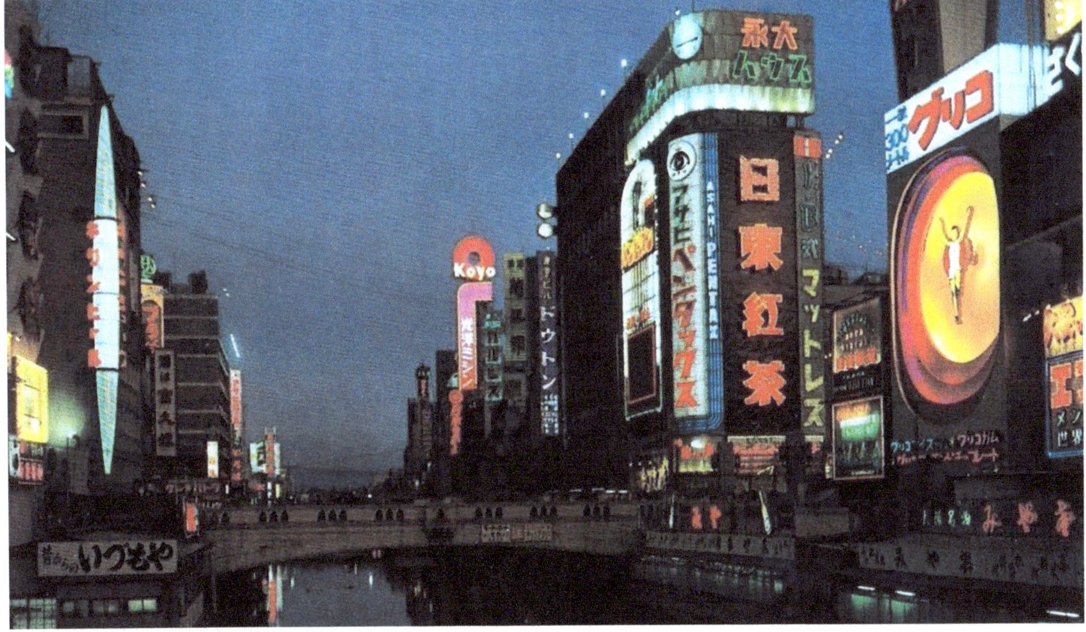
グリコ
日東紅茶
アサヒペンタックス
Koyo
ドウトン
マットレス
いづもや

The Glico Running Man
Dotonbori, Osaka

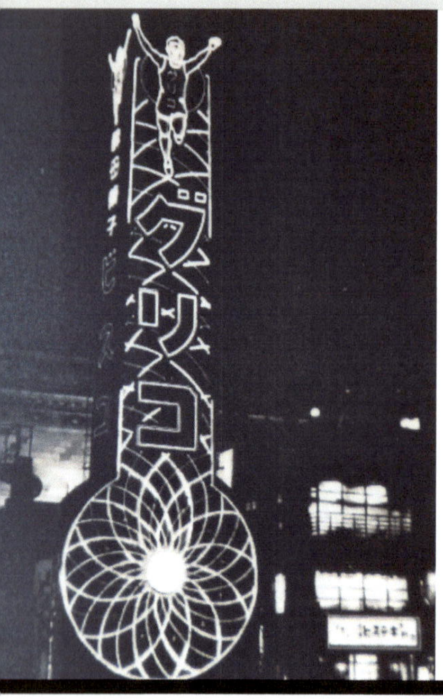

▼ Second Generation, 1955-1963

The 2nd generation sign was constructed 10 years after the war. It had a height of 21.75 meters, and was partially built using the base of the original sign that was dismantled for the war. The neon tower was unique because of its stage at the base of the arch, where a big doll crocodile played a piano, preformed a puppet show, and held a rockabilly competition.

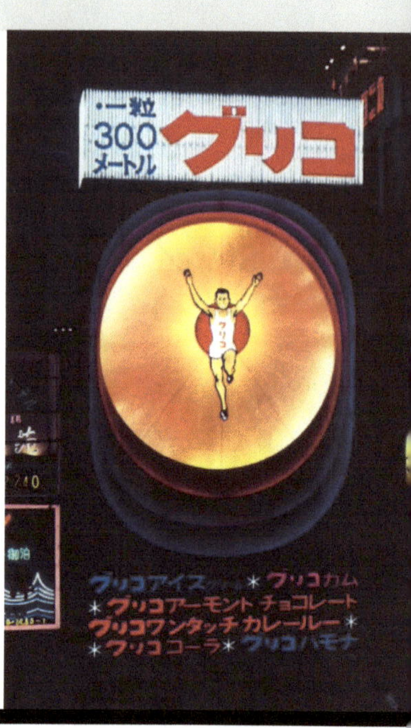

▲ First Generation, 1935-1943

In 1935, Glico founder Riichi Ezaki discovered this location in Dotonbori, Osaka, where over 200,000 people pass by each day. The first neon tower measured 33 meters high, which was unconventional for the time. It was one of the most unusual neon signs around. The tower was dismantled in 1943 to supply iron for the war effort.

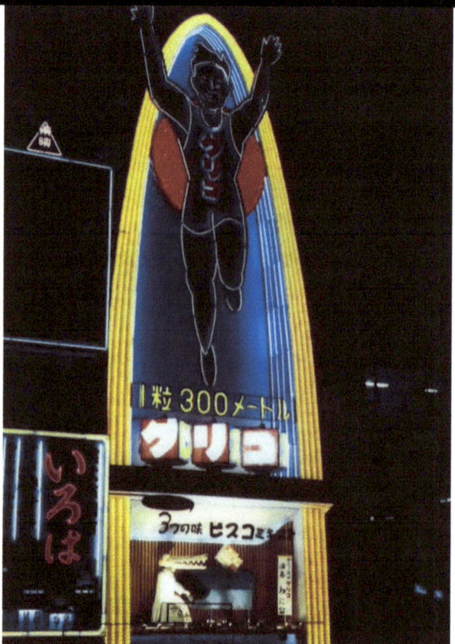

▲ Third Generation, 1963-1972

The 3rd generation sign had a height of 18 meters. It was designed as a fountain neon tower. It employed a cove lighting style, with 400 lamps of 12 colors that created a beautiful rainbow pattern. The sign squirted tons of water out of the waterwheel nozzle behind the running man.

Glico was founded in 1921 with the creation of the Glico-Caramel. The caramels were named after glycogen, a type of energy stored in humans. The candy used glycogen extracted from shellfish, and was marketed as a great source of energy. Each candy contained enough calories to run 300 meters, a catchphrase that was advertised on many Glico advertisements. On the box was the original Glico running man crossing the finish line and winning the race.

Glico has become a major food company, with a wide range of products from ice cream, candy, supplements, and soft drinks. The Glico sign of Dotonbori has stood for decades as one of the main symbols of Osaka. Scores of tourists take photographs at the popular destination emulating the running man on a daily basis.

▼ Fourth Generation, 1972-1996

The 4th generation sign was 17 meters tall, and was animated to appear as though the athlete was moving along the track. The trademark running man became alive, as the sign became famous. It appeared in movies and television until 1996, when it was removed for the purpose of renovating the supporting building.

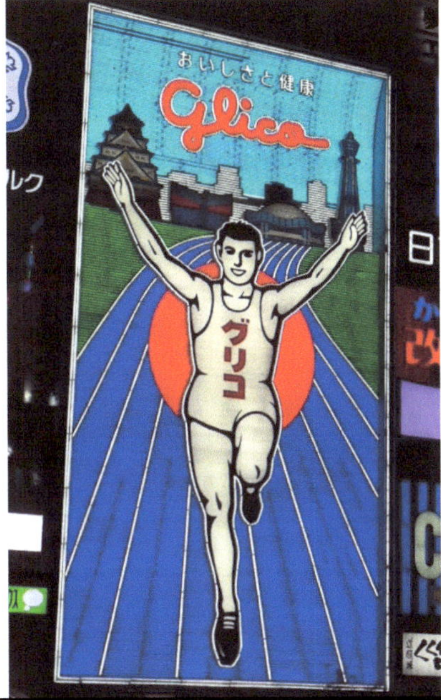

▼ Sixth Generation, 2014-Present (as of 2020)

The 6th generation sign measures 20 meters tall by 10 meters wide. The newest sign uses 140,000 LEDs in lieu of neon tubes. The sign now displays the running man making a journey around the world, and a variety of other scenes that are programmed for special occasions.

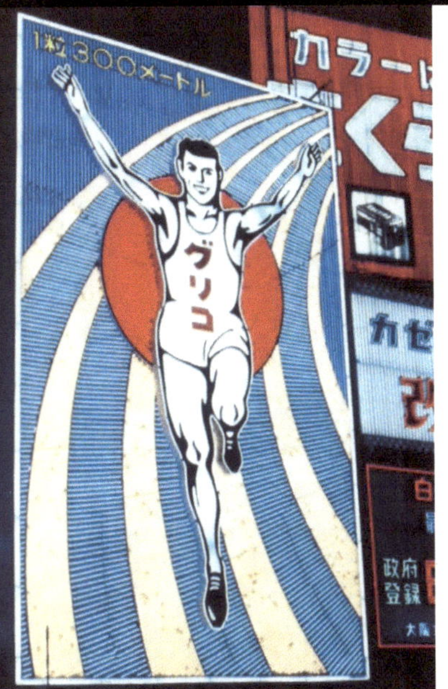

▲ Fifth Generation, 1998-2014

The 5th generation sign was 20 meters tall. It was turned on for the first time in two and a half years after the building's renovation. In the background of the runner are some of Osaka's famous landmarks. In 2003, the sign itself was designated as an official landmark of Osaka City.

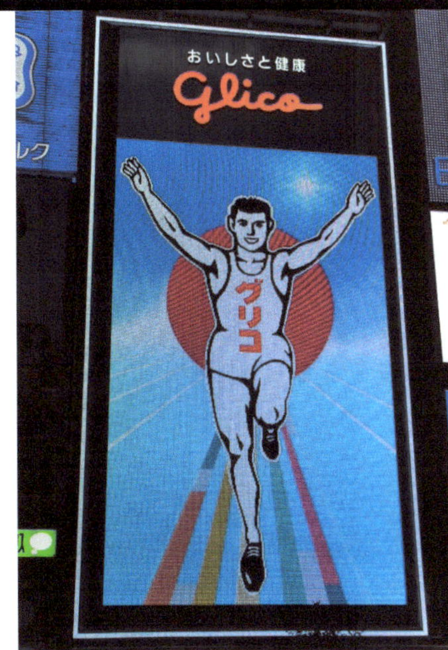

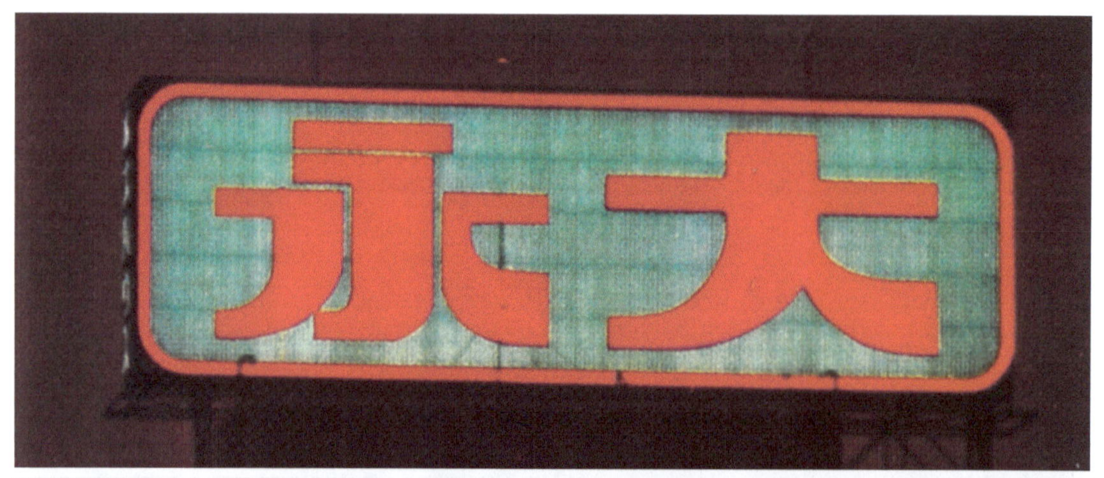
永大

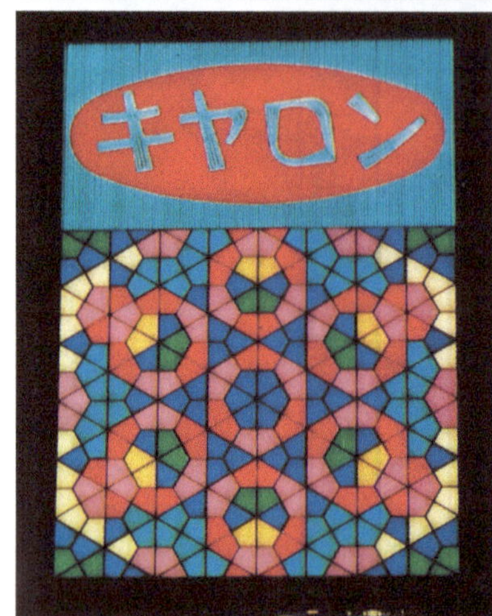
キヤロン

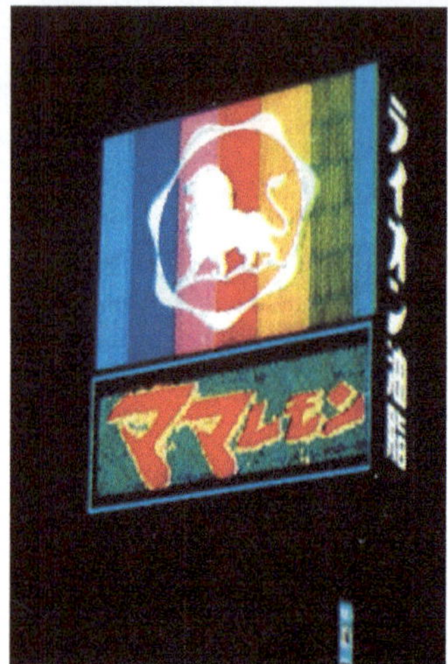
ライオン油脂
ママレモン

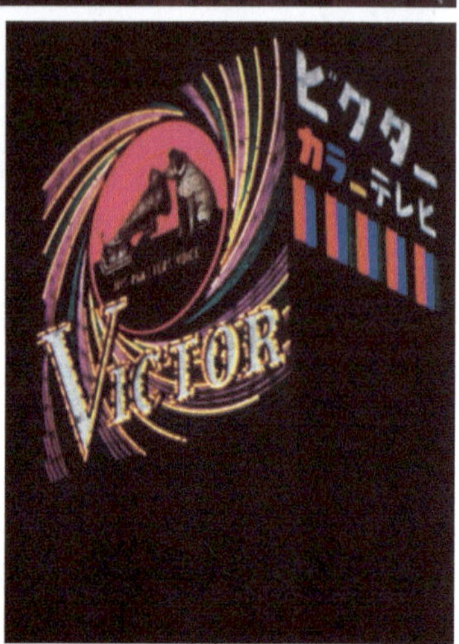
ビクター
カラーテレビ
VICTOR

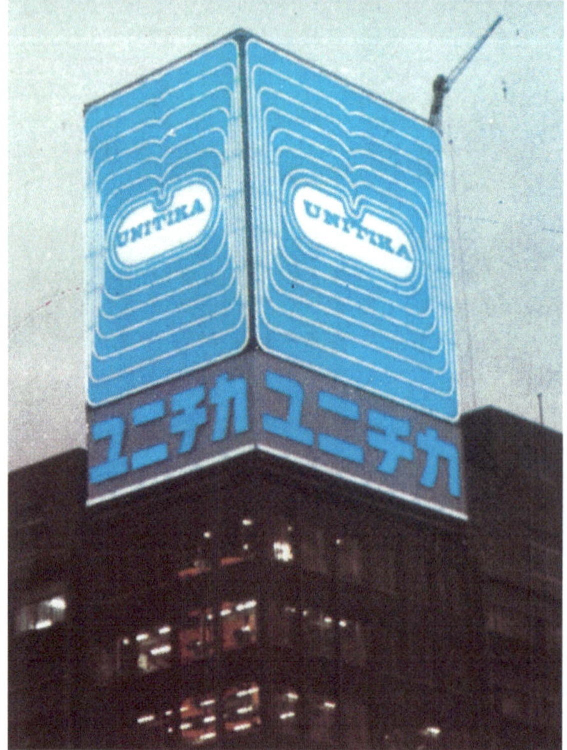
UNITIKA
UNITIKA
ユニチカ
ユニチカ

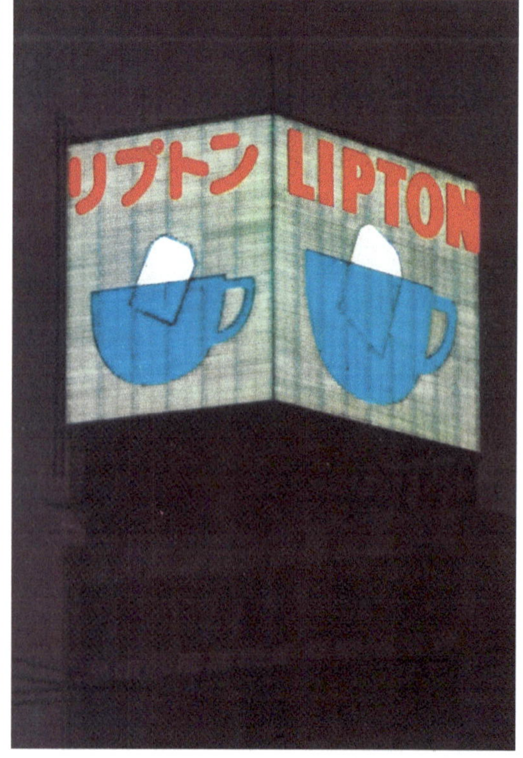
リプトン
LIPTON

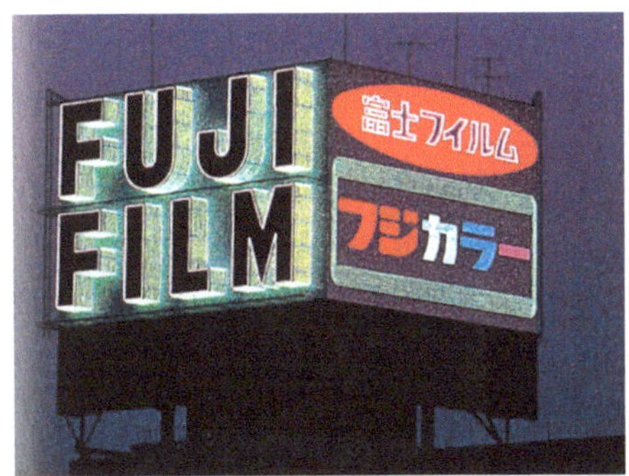
FUJI
FILM
富士フイルム
フジカラー

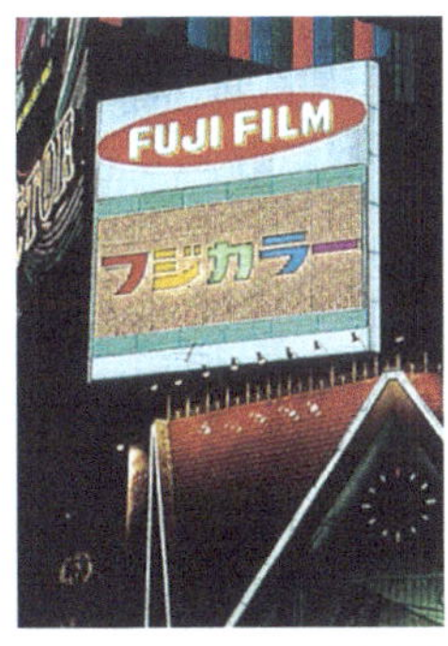
FUJI FILM
フジカラー

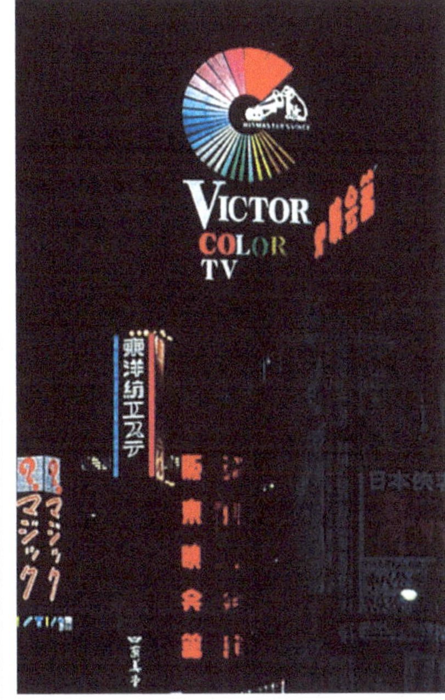
VICTOR
COLOR
TV

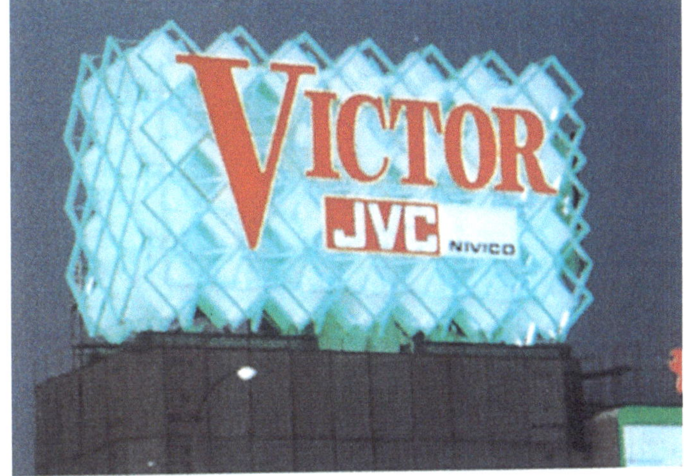
VICTOR
JVC
NIVICO

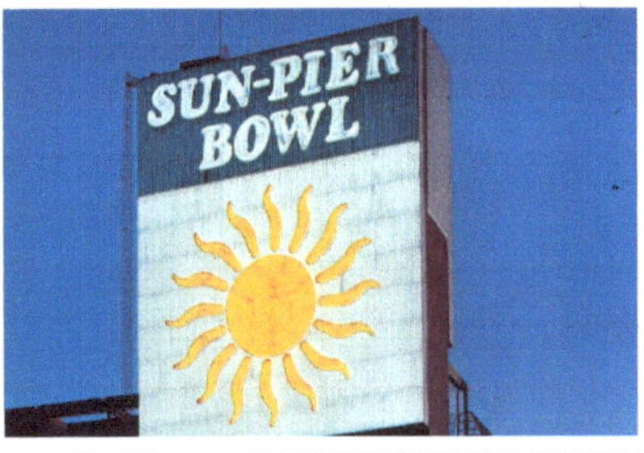
SUN-PIER
BOWL

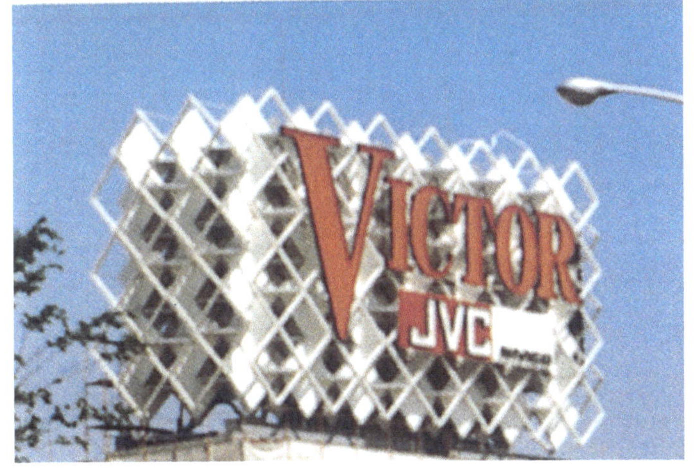
VICTOR
JVC

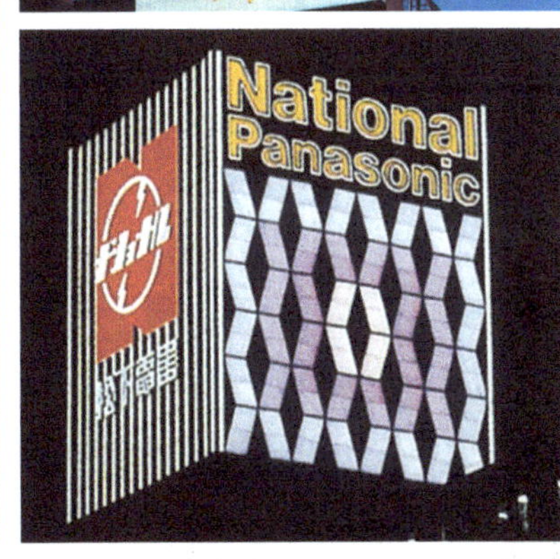
National
Panasonic
ナショナル
松下電器

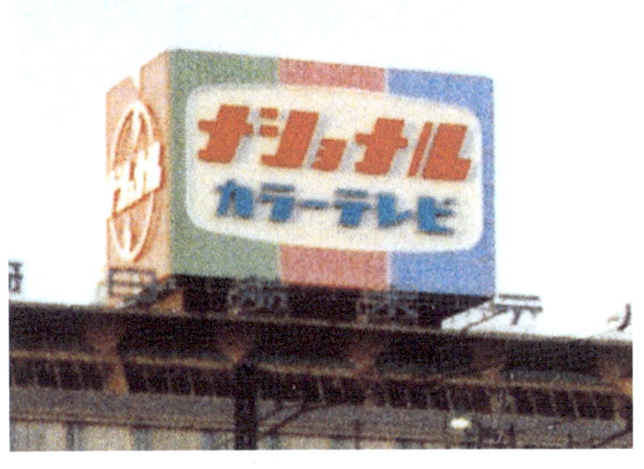
ナショナル
カラーテレビ

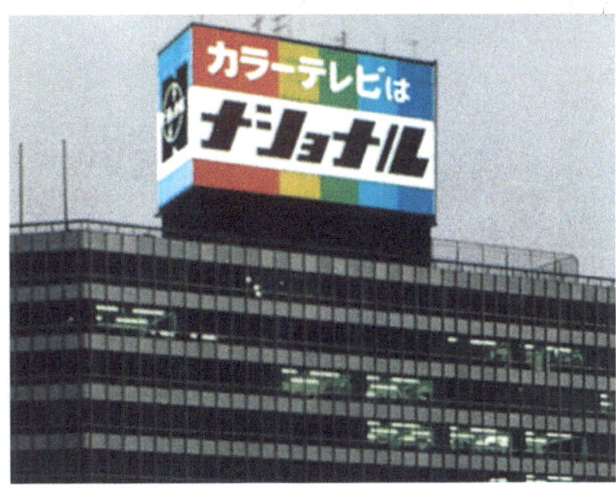
カラーテレビは
ナショナル

Troublesome Years

The "Oil Shock" began in October 1973 when exporters of oil in Arabia proclaimed an oil embargo on countries that were perceived as supporting Israel. The embargo caused a 70% rise in oil prices, resulting in a huge ripple on the world's economy. Japan was very dependent on Arab oil, and was heavily affected by the situation. Prices of commodities continued to rise, affecting production output thus hurting the national economy.

The neon industry had worries of neon lighting bans due to the power limitations. The Association responded by insisting that the power consumed by neon signs was comparatively small and that there was no point to turn off the signs. It was eventually decided to prohibit the use of neon lights, floodlights and other illuminated advertising except for the display of store names. Lighting restrictions were once again in place for the first time in decades. The entire industry suffered a heavy blow that took several years to recover from.

Companies began layoffs and wages cuts as the economic crisis escalated. Cancellations of neon media contracts followed the lighting restrictions. It became a depressing scene as the removal of outdoor advertising exposed the bare steel frames of advertising towers.

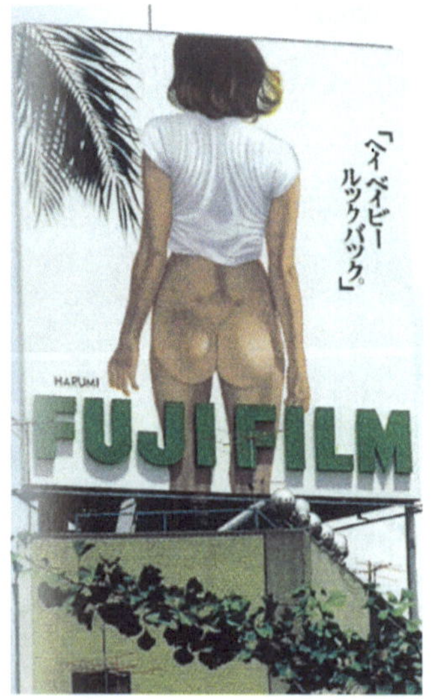

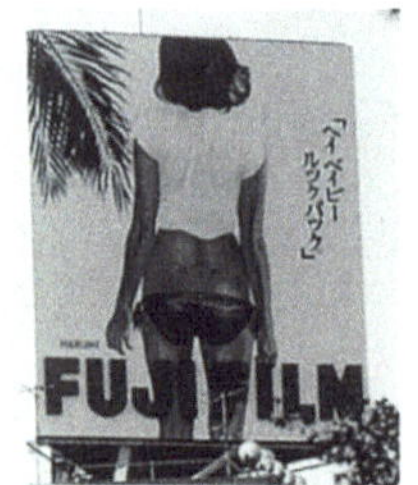

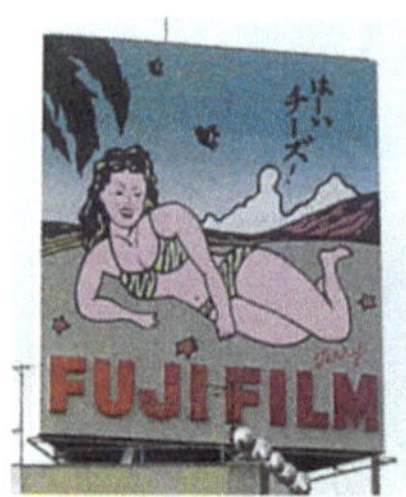

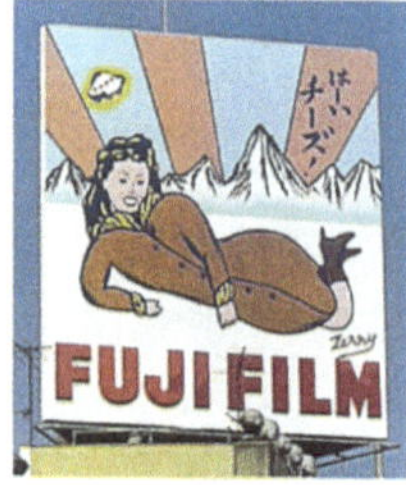

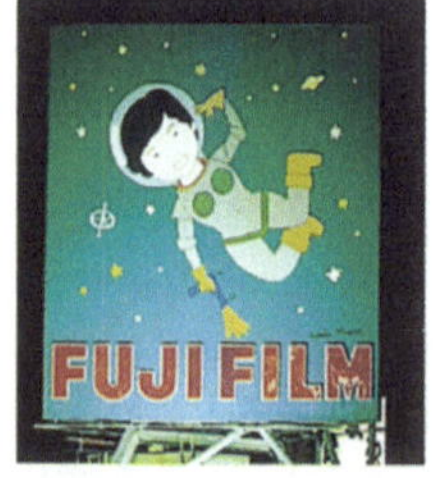

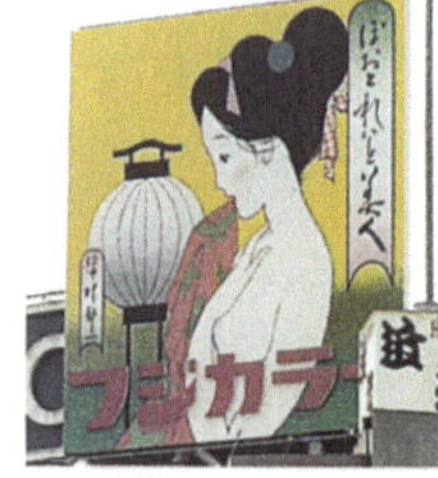

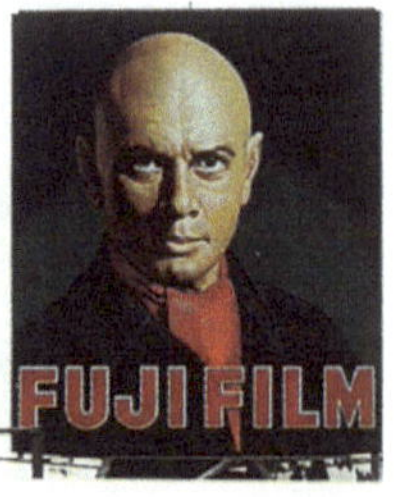

MANY COMPANIES SWITCHED TO SPOT LIT ADVERTISEMENTS AROUND THE OIL SHOCK

Companies were reluctant to deal with neon signs because of the economic downturn. Subsequently, new production and refurbishment work was postponed. Usual advertisers with a history of utilizing neon signs became shy to continue using them. Such neon towers stayed unlit for up to six months after the lighting restrictions loosened in September 1974. Many neon signs in downtown areas of large cities, such as Ginza, were not turned on until the end of the year. Even if a large sign was produced, they used minimal amount of neon, and the colors were reduced, which simplified the designs.

The economy could not recover until the end of 1974. In Japan, the opening of the Sanyo Shinkansen between Okayama and Hakata, the end of the Vietnam War, and the Okinawa International Ocean Expo provided some optimism that the situation was improving. Neon was considered to be a barometer of the shape of the economy. It made a gradual comeback as businesses recovered.

The Bubble Economy

The economy recovered from the Oil Shock, though the price hikes on commodities stayed. 1975 was marked by an unusually strong outflow of trade, which injected some life back into the neon industry. Inquiries steadily rose as restrictions were nullified. The industry quickly returned to the state it had been before the oil crisis. Neon advertisements were replaced more frequently than in the past decade, with bigger and more intricate signs. Neon signs spread from city centers to the suburbs and rural areas.

Advertising sponsors that were reluctant to deal with neon during the crisis were once again turning on their signs. Most were in need of maintenance due to neglect over the past couple of years. Those who had forfeited their advertising space made room for new companies to advertise. Sign structures could be reused to an extent, making it much less expensive than to have started from scratch.

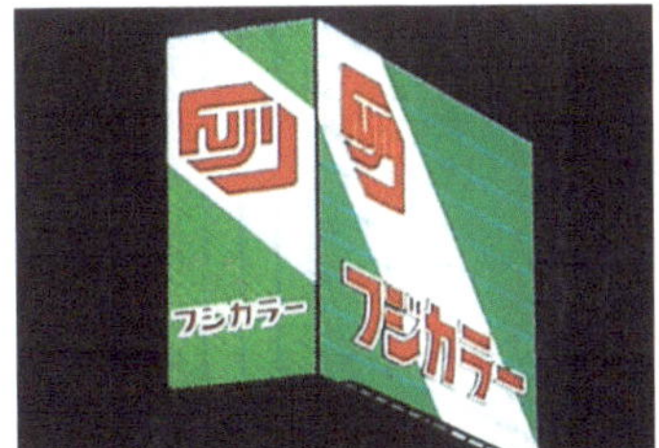

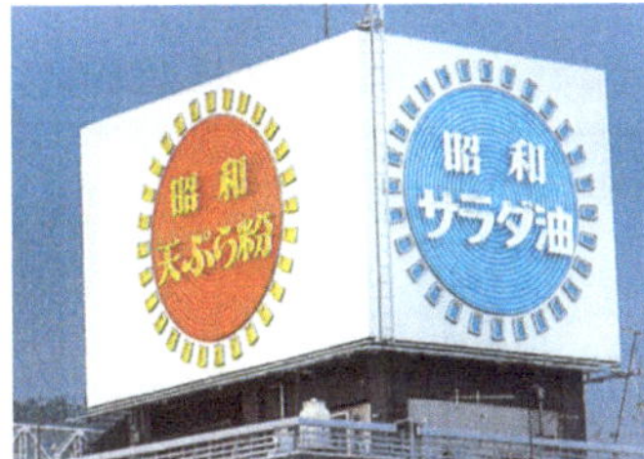

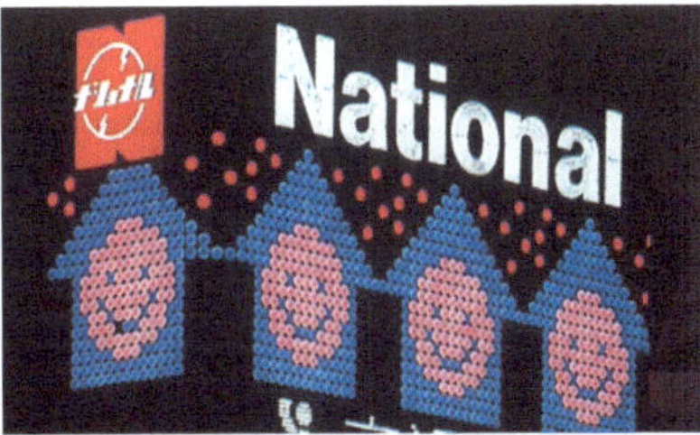

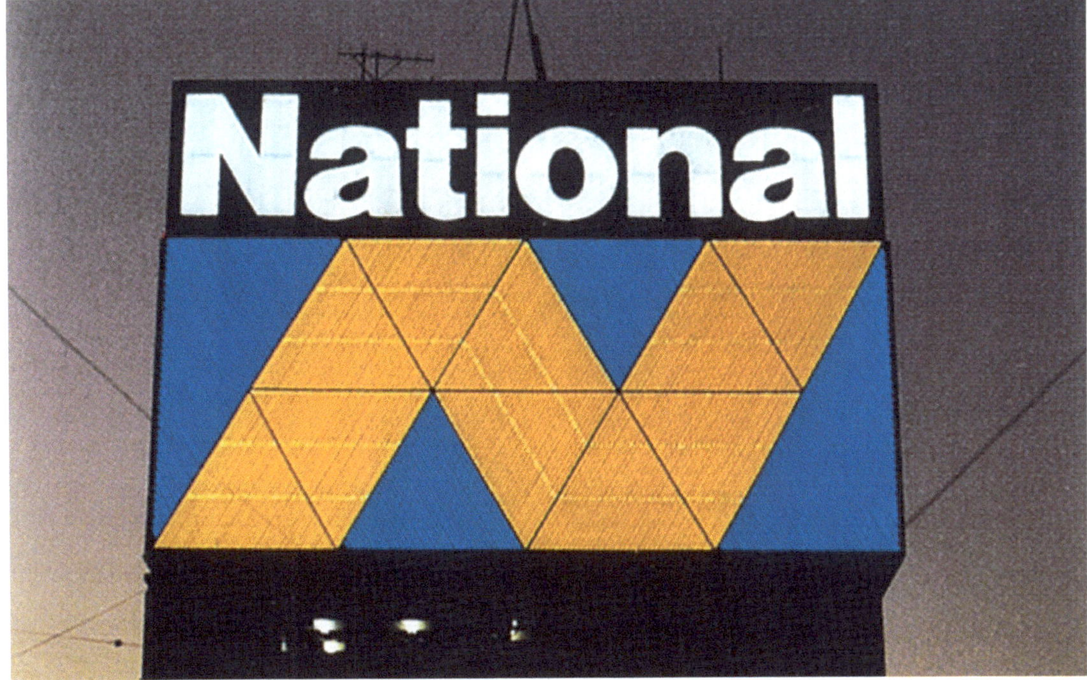

Many of the neon signs that were constructed during the 1964 Tokyo Olympics were also renovated. Construction was carried out on a nationwide scale in order to update brand appearances. It was rare that so many signs undergo renovation at the same time. In addition, many companies began to use their updated neon signs for television commercials.

Japan's economy continued to grow into the 1980s, and developed into what is known as the "Bubble Economy". This was caused in part by the Japanese government attempting to stimulate domestic demand by providing inexpensive loans. The price on land, which was used as collateral for the loans, escalated to exorbitant levels. For example, the Imperial Palace's plot of land in Tokyo was worth more than the state of California in 1988. Japan achieved fame for being one of the wealthiest countries at the time.

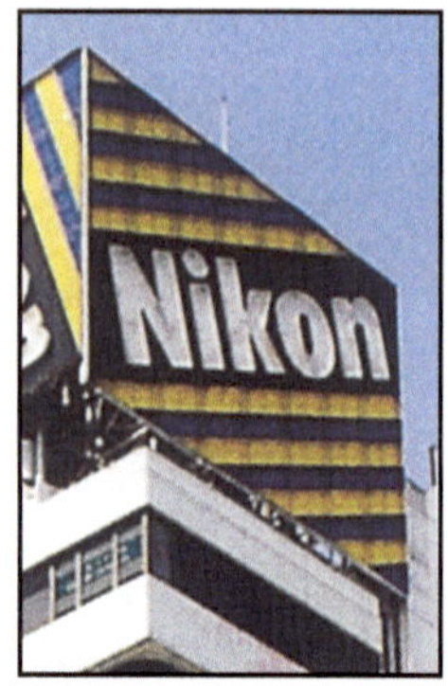

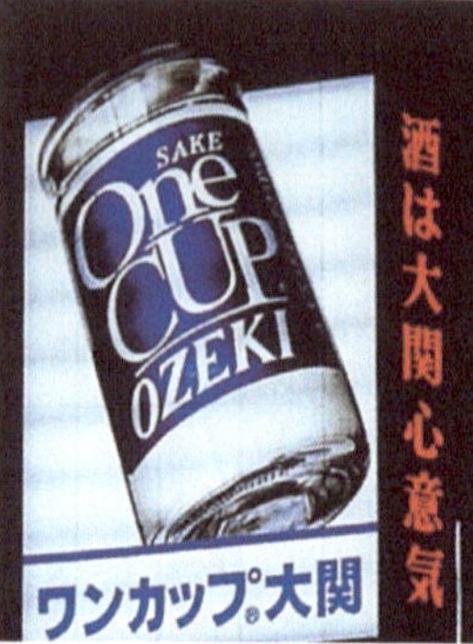

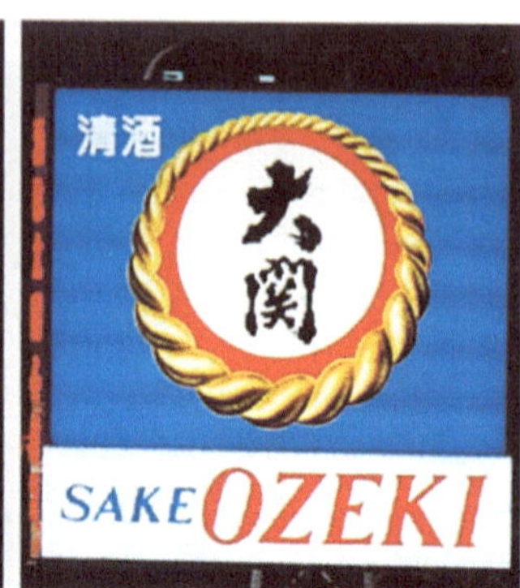

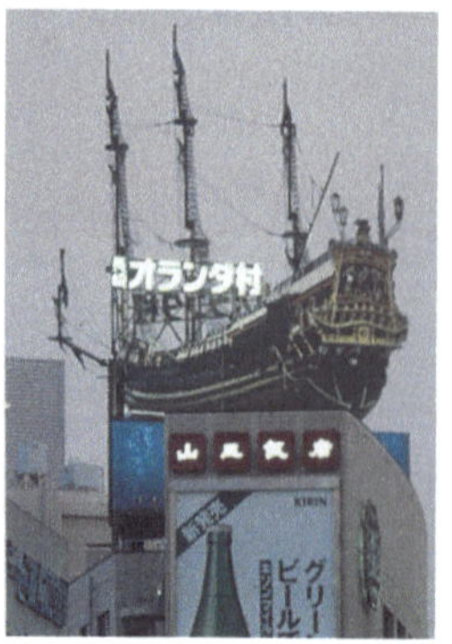

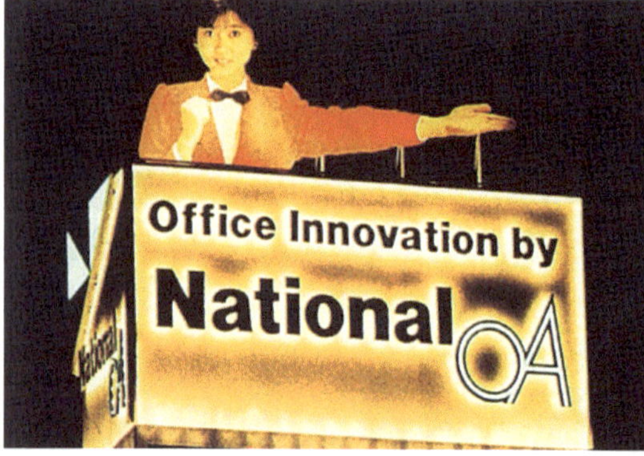

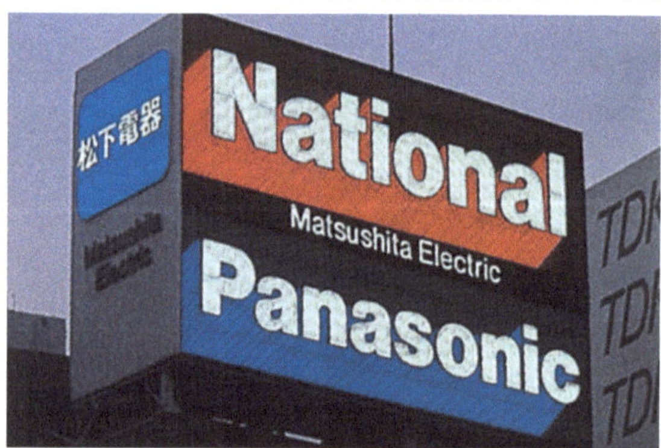

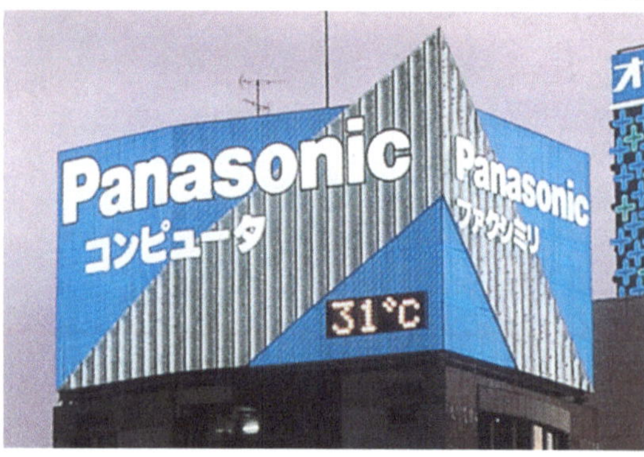

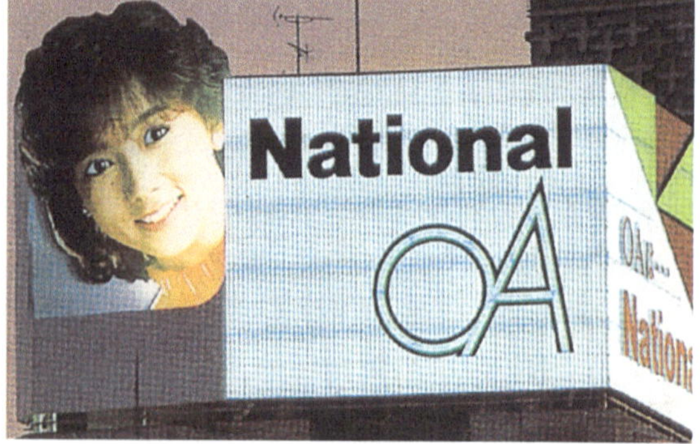

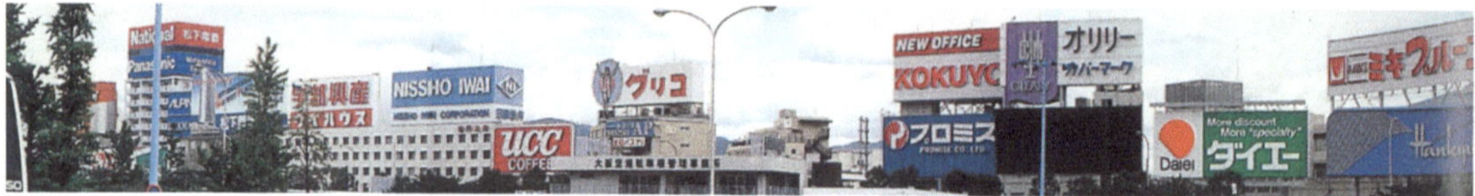

The neon industry followed the boom. The most popular signs were for pachinko parlors (slot casinos), "love hotels", CD rental shops, and bank loan services. Smaller companies might have a production output of 5,000 neon tubes per month, while larger companies could produce over 30,000 tubes per month. Some neon companies ran 24 hours per day, with employees working in shifts to meet the production demands. Glass benders, electrode splicers, and tube processors would work in an assembly line fashion.

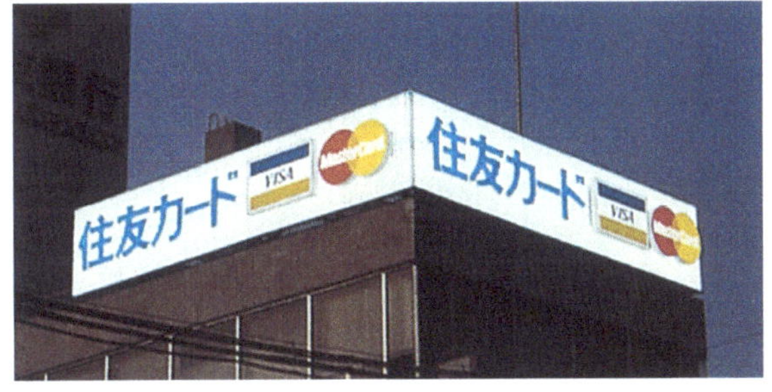

Pachinko, a game similar to slot machine gambling, was one of the fastest growing mass entertainment industries after the war. Large pachinko parlors sprung up all around the country. Their signs represented 60% of the demand during the peak, and often emulated the large and gaudy style signs of Las Vegas.

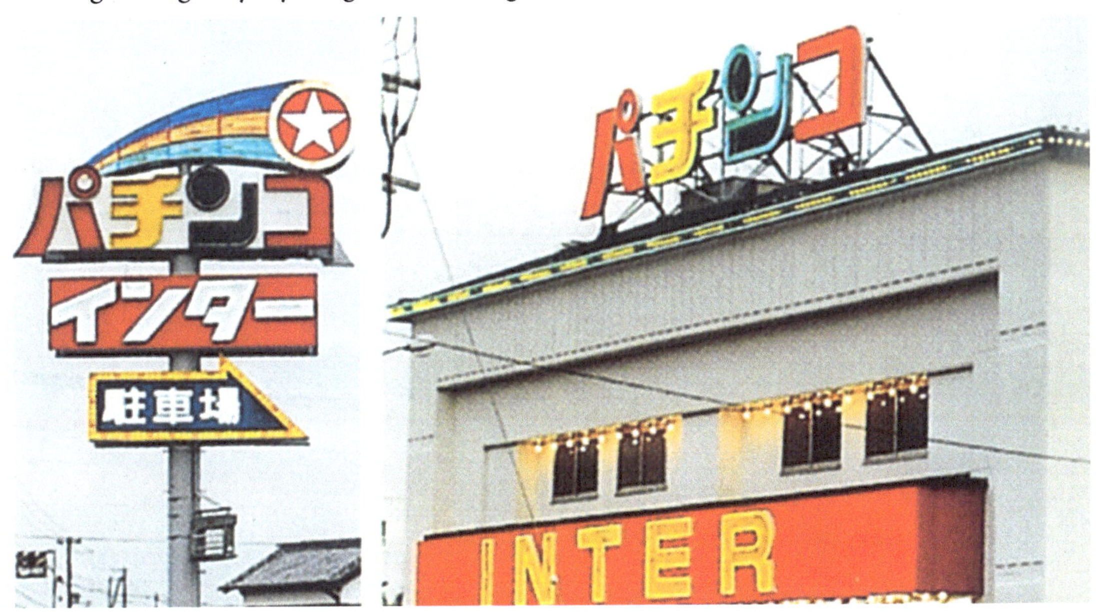

TYPICAL SIGNAGE OF A PACHINKO PARLOR

There was a large demand for labor at this time. Neon making requires trained motor skills, which take years to develop. A small number of neon schools were set up by neon equipment manufactures as a promotion to sell their production equipment. Classes would run from 1-2 months teaching basic bending techniques and processing abilities.

The Showa Era came to an end in 1989 following the death of Emperor Hirohito. Advertisers were instructed to turn off the neon lights nationwide during the time of mourning. In December, the Japanese bubble economy began to burst, plunging the country into a recession. This marked the end of Japan's post war economic growth. The neon industry was severely affected, causing many neon companies to close.

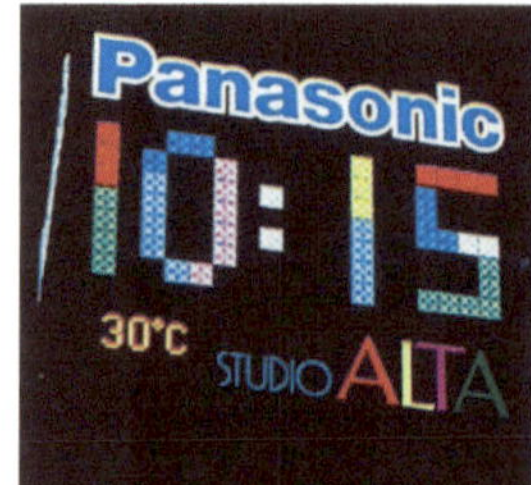
Panasonic
10:15
30°C
STUDIO ALTA

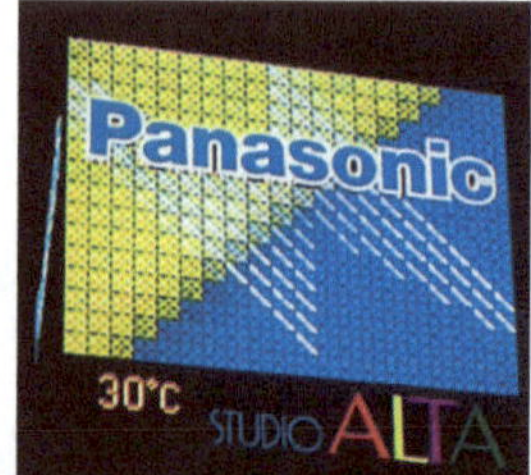
Panasonic
30°C
STUDIO ALTA

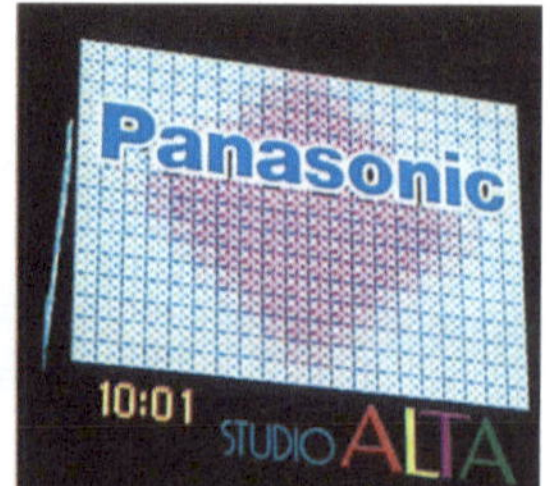
Panasonic
10:01
STUDIO ALTA

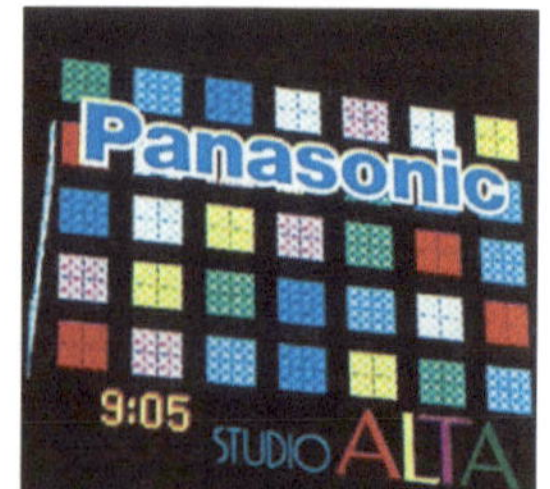
Panasonic
9:05
STUDIO ALTA

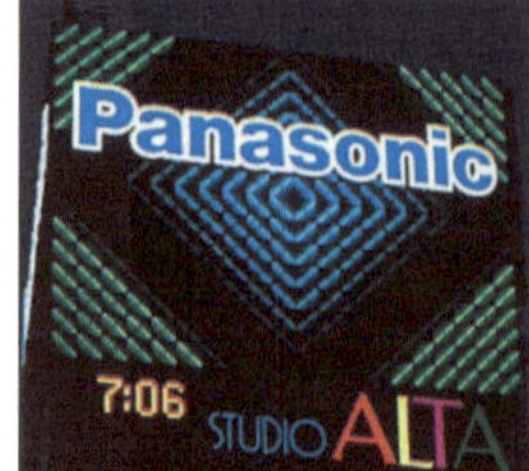
Panasonic
7:06
STUDIO ALTA

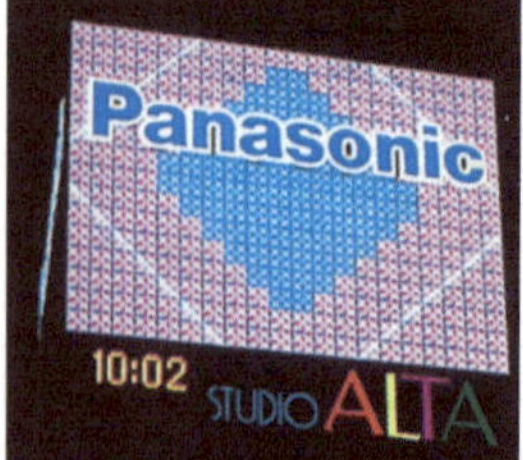
Panasonic
10:02
STUDIO ALTA

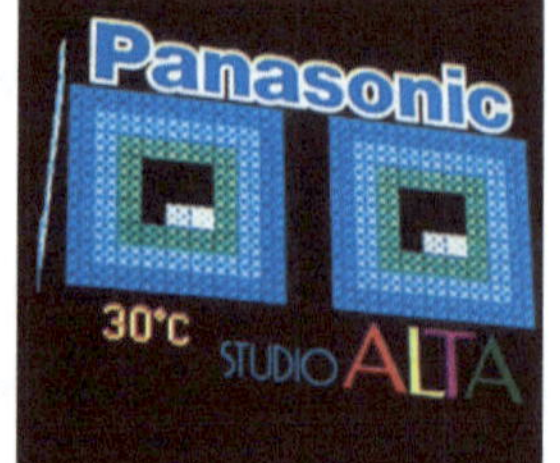
Panasonic
30°C
STUDIO ALTA

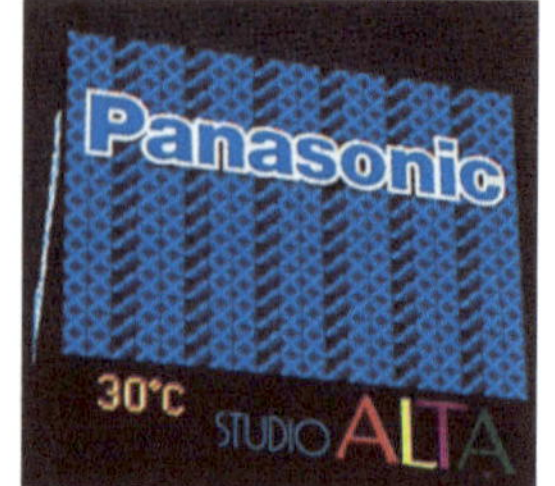
Panasonic
30°C
STUDIO ALTA

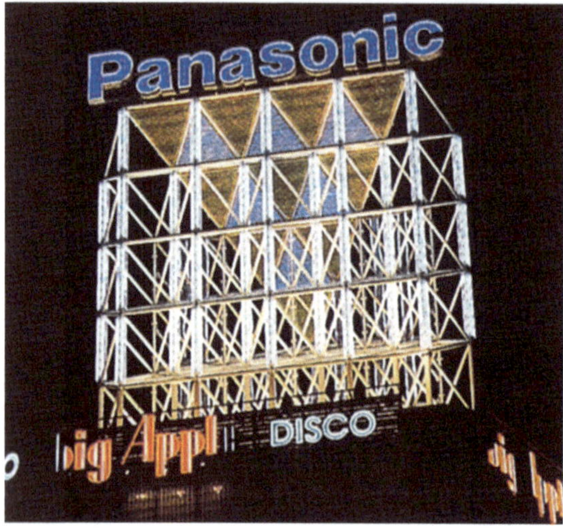
Panasonic
DISCO

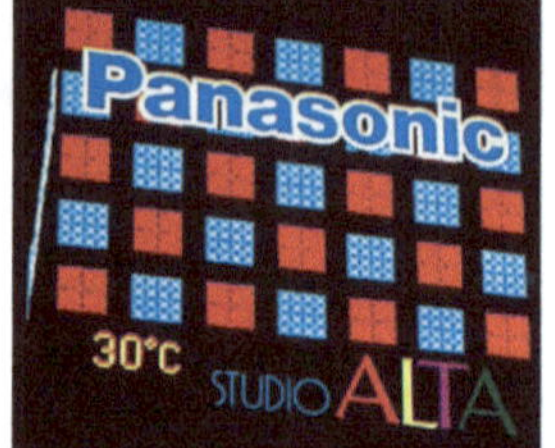
Panasonic
30°C
STUDIO ALTA

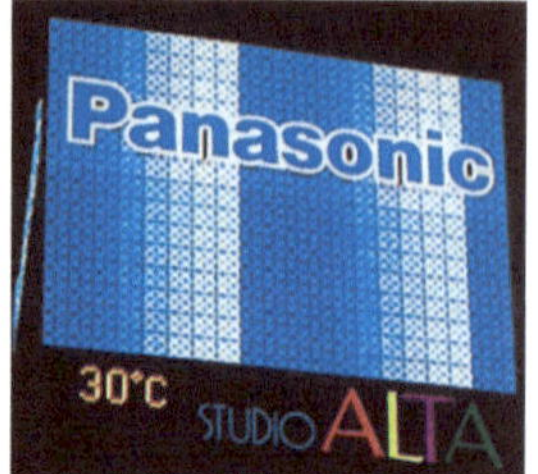
Panasonic
30°C
STUDIO ALTA

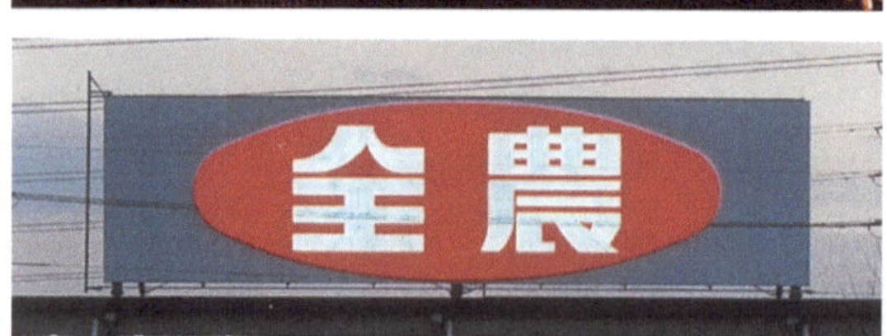
全農

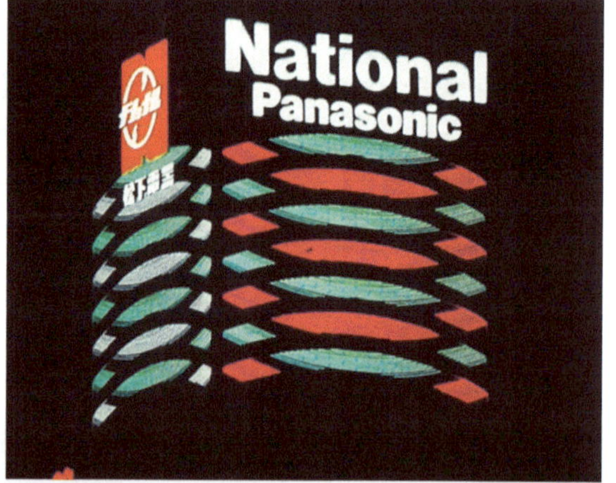
National
Panasonic

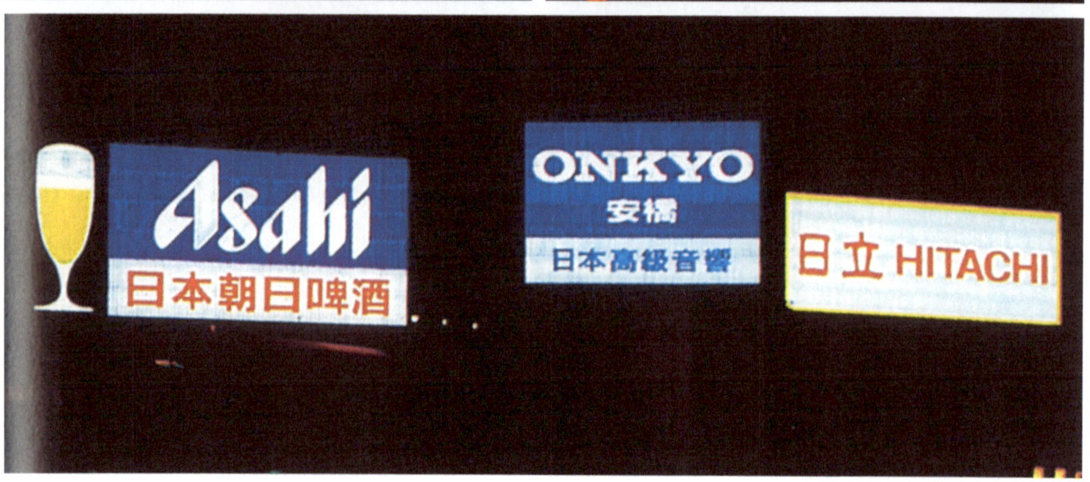
Asahi
日本朝日啤酒
ONKYO
安橋
日本高級音響
日立 HITACHI

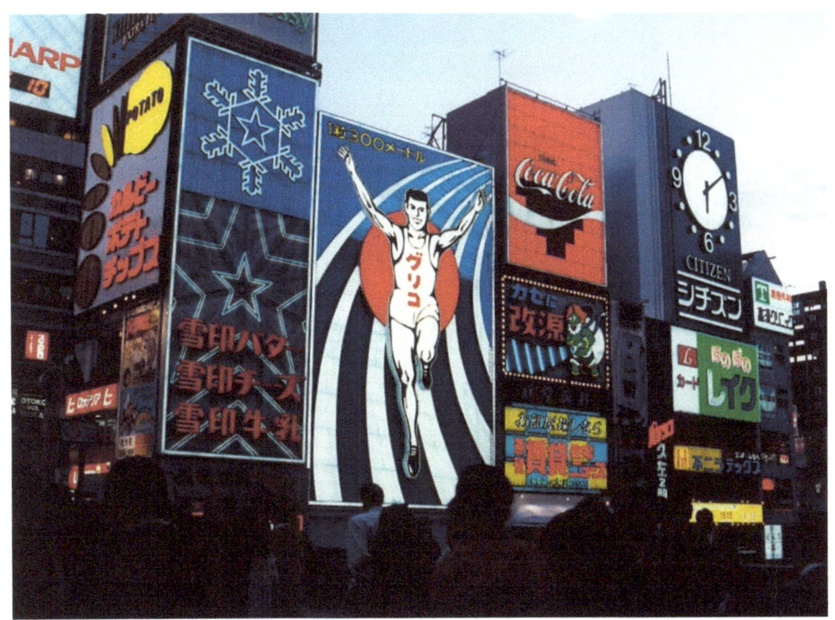
POTATO
カルビー
ポテト
チップス
雪印バター
雪印チーズ
雪印牛乳
1粒300メートル
グリコ
Coca-Cola
CITIZEN
シチズン
レイク

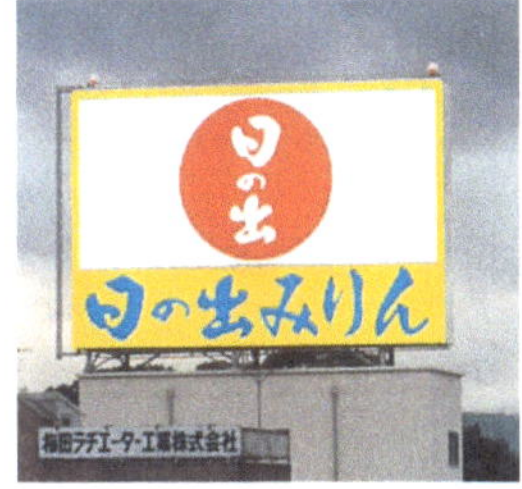
日の出
日の出みりん

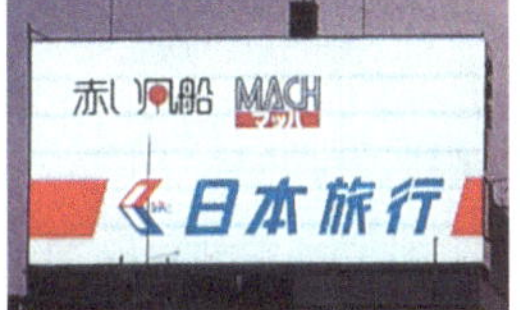
赤い風船
MACH
日本旅行

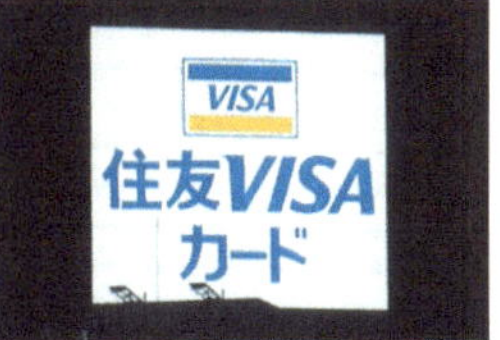
VISA
住友VISA
カード

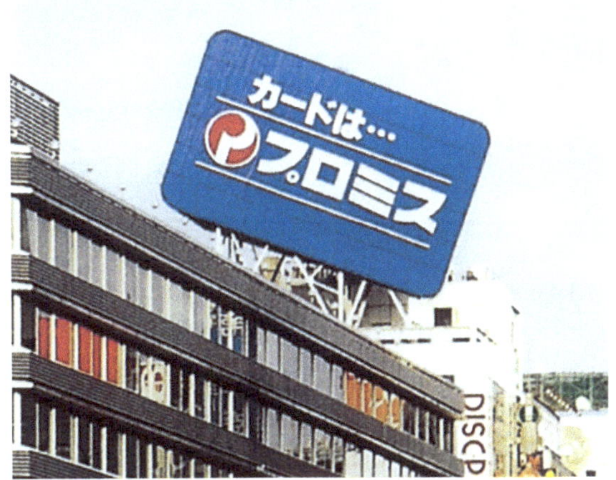
カードは…
プロミス

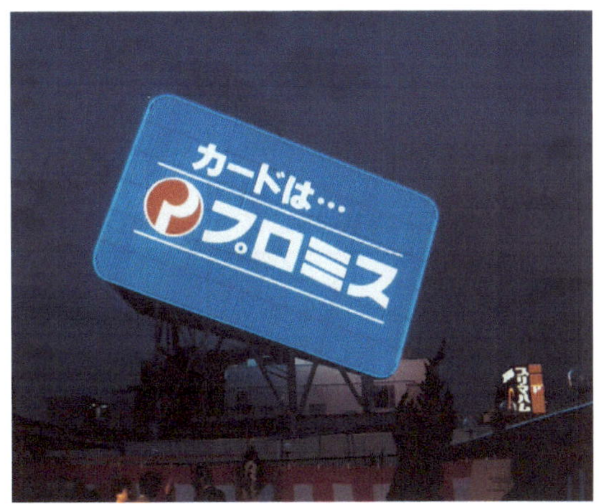
カードは…
プロミス

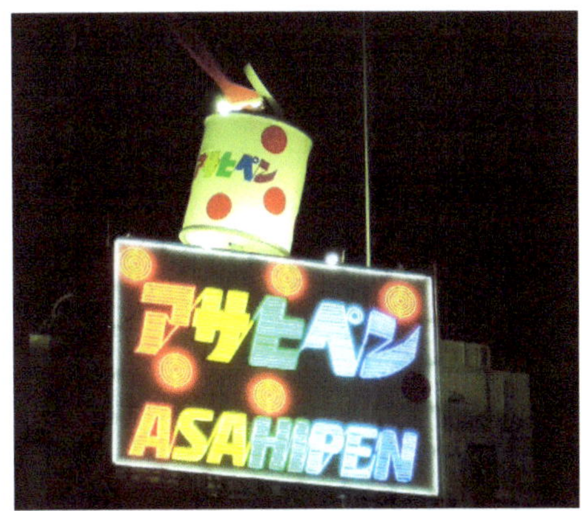
アサヒペン
ASAHIPEN

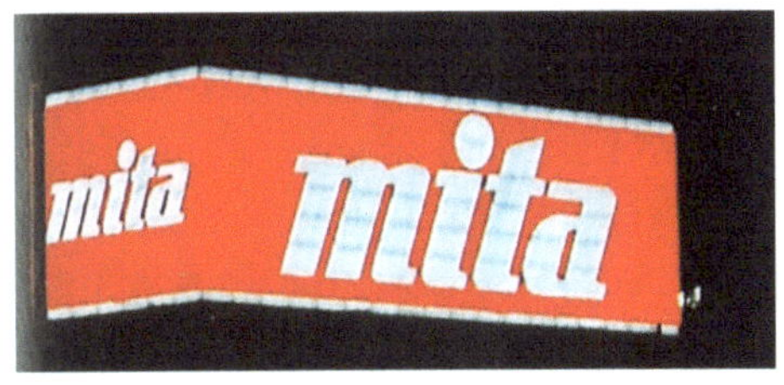
mita
mita

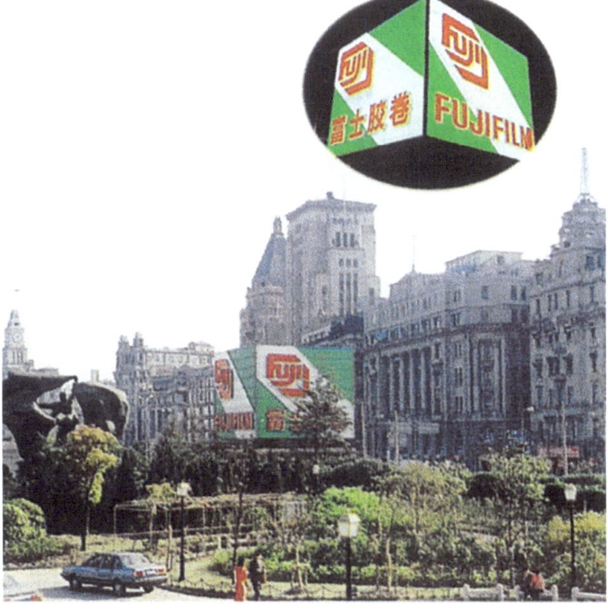
富士胶卷
FUJIFILM

The New Era

Threats to the Industry

The economic bust could have been the final blow to neon spectaculars across Japan. It's unlikely that the massive sphere and star shaped signs wrapped in neon will be constructed again. New technologies allow for more versatile and efficient forms of outdoor advertising. The reduction of energy use, the increasing strength of typhoons, and the aging workforce among neon workers make options such as LED screens, spot lit billboards, and back lit panels favored among outdoor advertisers.

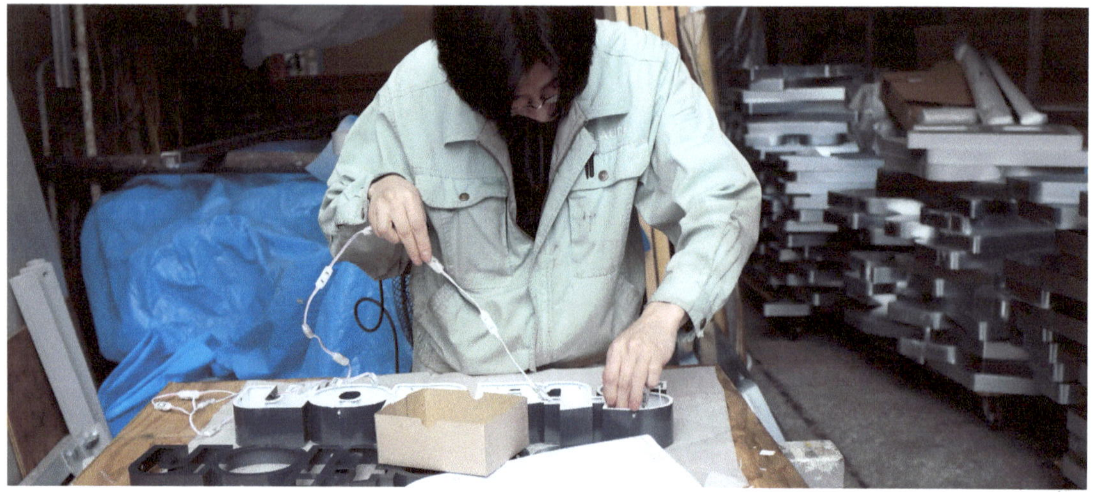

INSTALLATION OF LED MODULES INTO A SIGN

The demand for large neon signs dropped significantly, causing many companies to close or adapt their production. Pachinko parlors reduced the use of neon from 60% down to 10% for exterior signage. Similar to the effect of the oil crisis, many neon tradespeople have been forced to change their occupation, many becoming general sign builders. General sign companies were more likely to survive as they could adapt to the current trends of the market, unlike companies that specialized in neon tubing.

At the turn of the millennium, LED screens and back-lit panels took precedent in the outdoor advertising industry. It is cheaper and easier for advertisers to rent a 30 second time slot on an LED screen, than a 10-year commitment that requires an extensive maintenance. When sign companies consider which medium to use, neon may seem inconvenient. In addition, most LED signs conserve more energy than their neon counterparts, reducing the monthly energy bill for the advertiser. Considering the amount of outdoor advertising in Japan, the combined reduction in energy usage becomes significant.

Autumn is typhoon season in Japan, and the storms seem to get stronger every year. Sign companies often experience a "typhoon bubble" of repairs and renovations after the season. The storms often put signs into states of disrepair, and when the customer is faced with purchasing a new sign, they usually opt to replace with LED, as most sign companies do not offer neon services anymore. In some cases, customers have a nostalgic feeling about neon and continue to use the trusted medium.

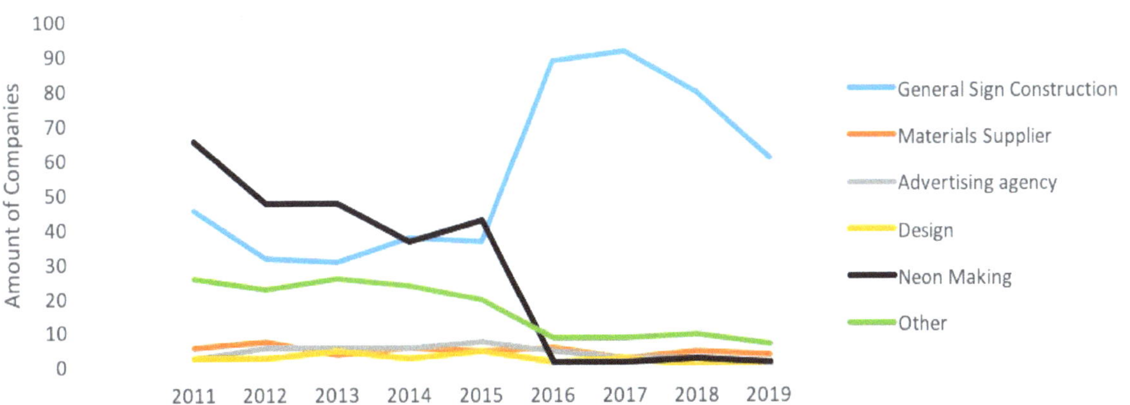

Another threat to the industry are the looming restrictions on the use of mercury. The Minamata Convention is an act that is lobbying against the use mercury, calling for the ban of on non-essential products worldwide. The convention is named after Minamata City in Kumamoto Prefecture, Japan. It was there that industrial wastewater containing methyl-mercury was released into the Minamata Bay, contaminating the water. Methyl-mercury accumulated in the fish of the bay, which was consumed by the local population. The tragedy resulted in generational mercury poisoning among the citizens of the city, severely disabled many people. Although the use of mercury in neon signs is small, and the elemental state that is used is far less dangerous than methyl-mercury, it does still present an occupational and environmental hazard. Restrictions on the use of mercury is a realistic threat to the industry.

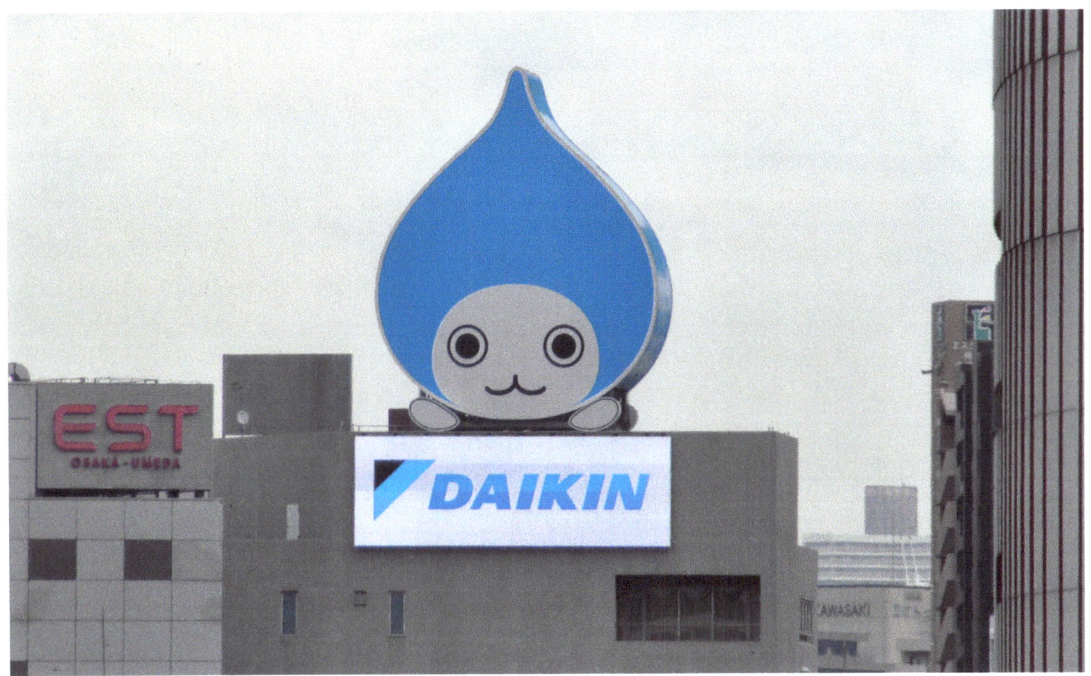

LED SIGN NORTH OF OSAKA STATION

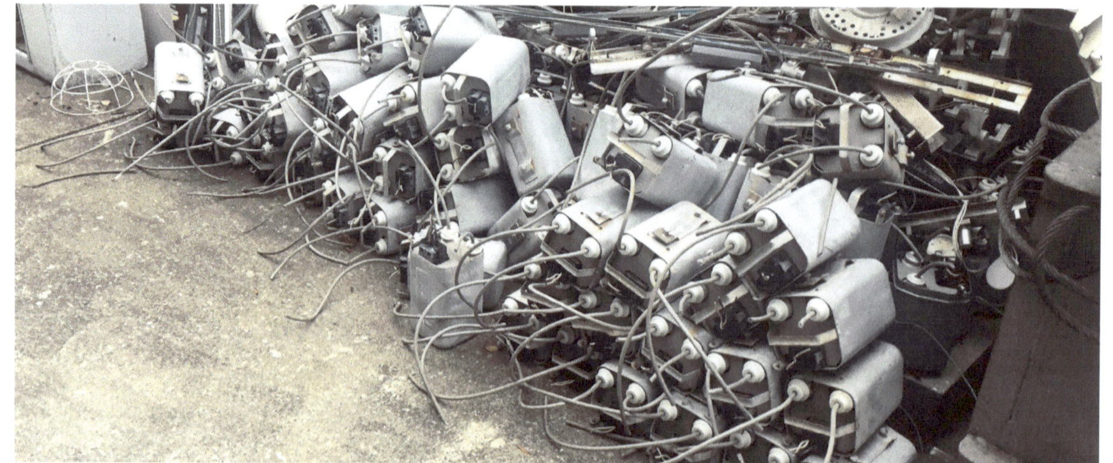

TRANSFORMERS FROM A SCRAPPED NEON SIGN

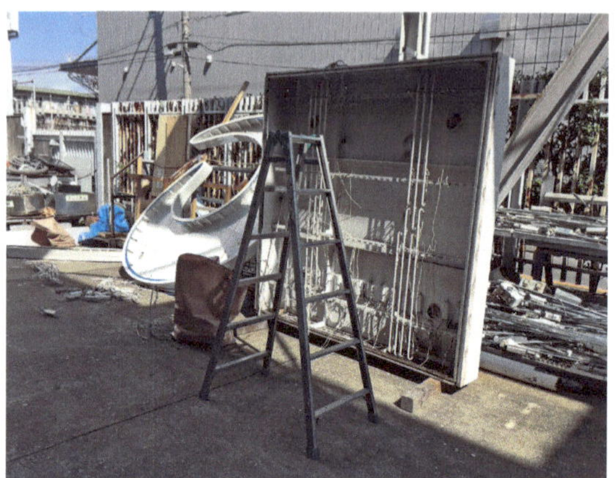

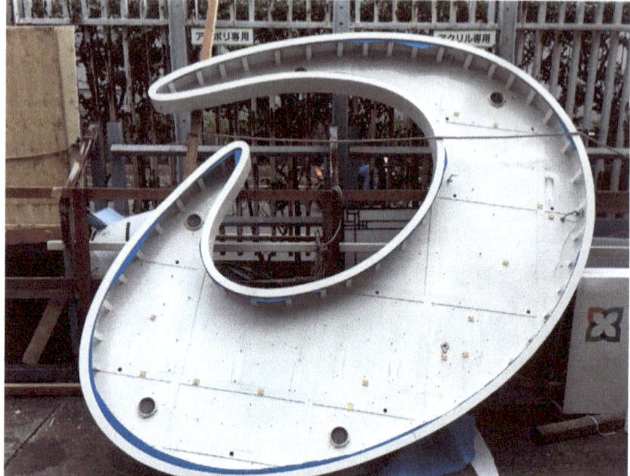

RETROFITTING NEON SIGNS WITH LED MODULES

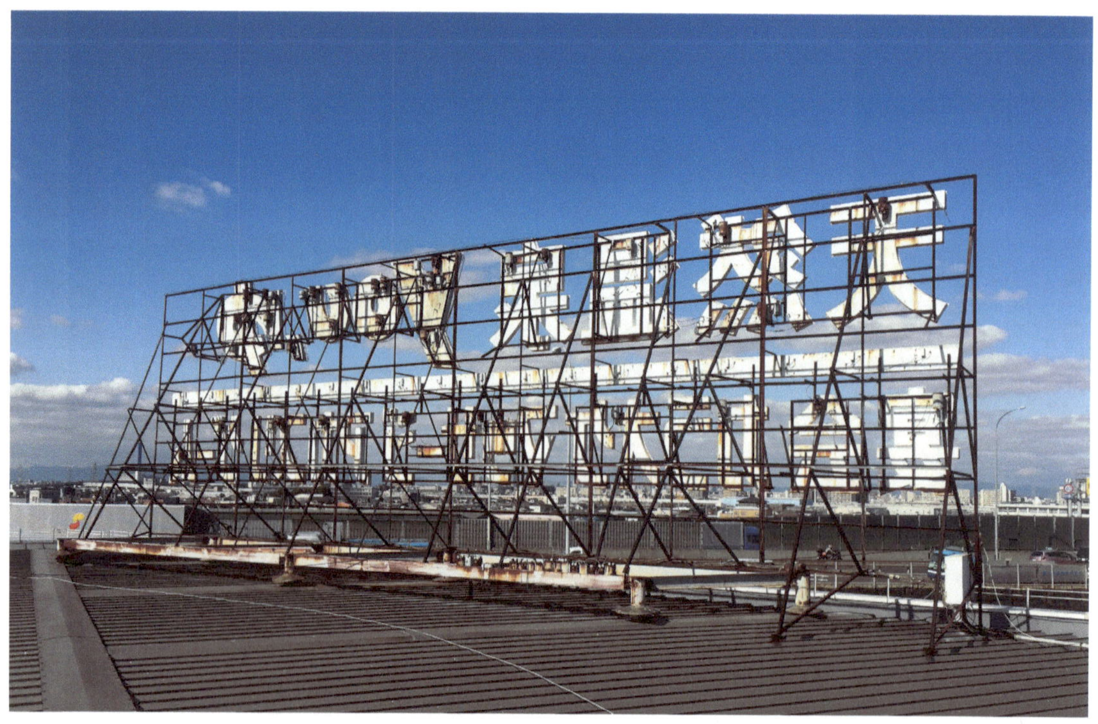

ROOFTOP NEON SIGN ENTERING A STATE OF DISREPAIR DUE TO CORROSION

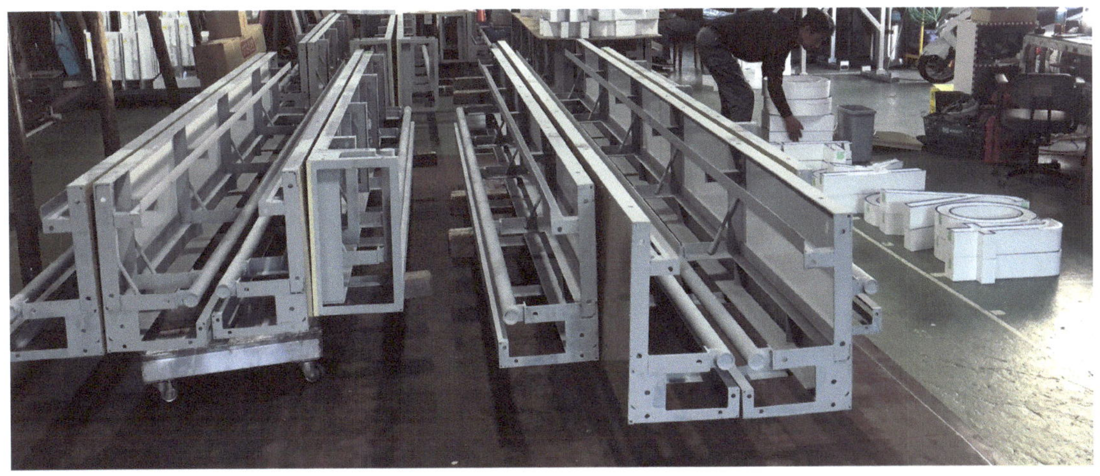

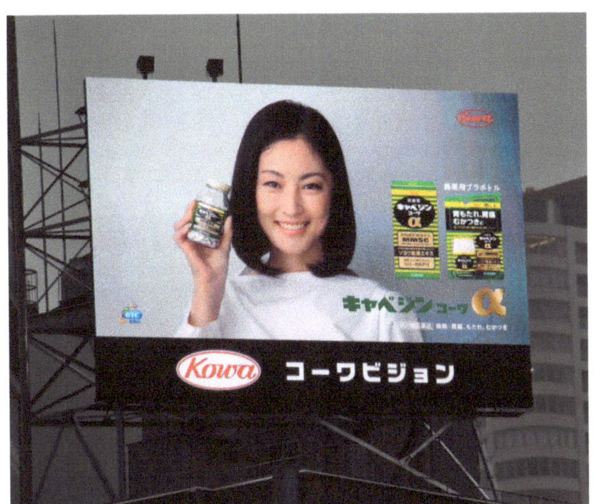

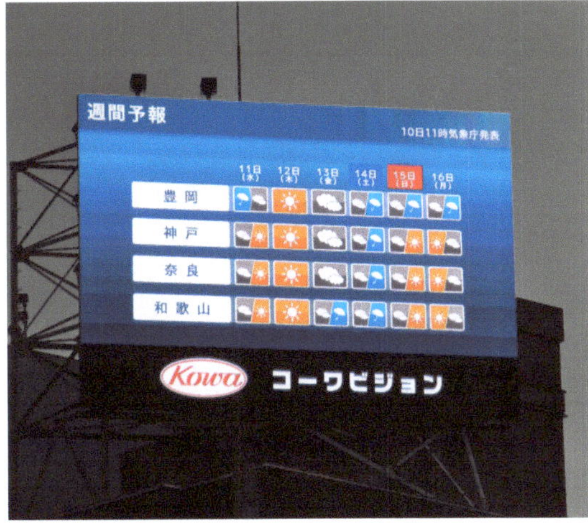

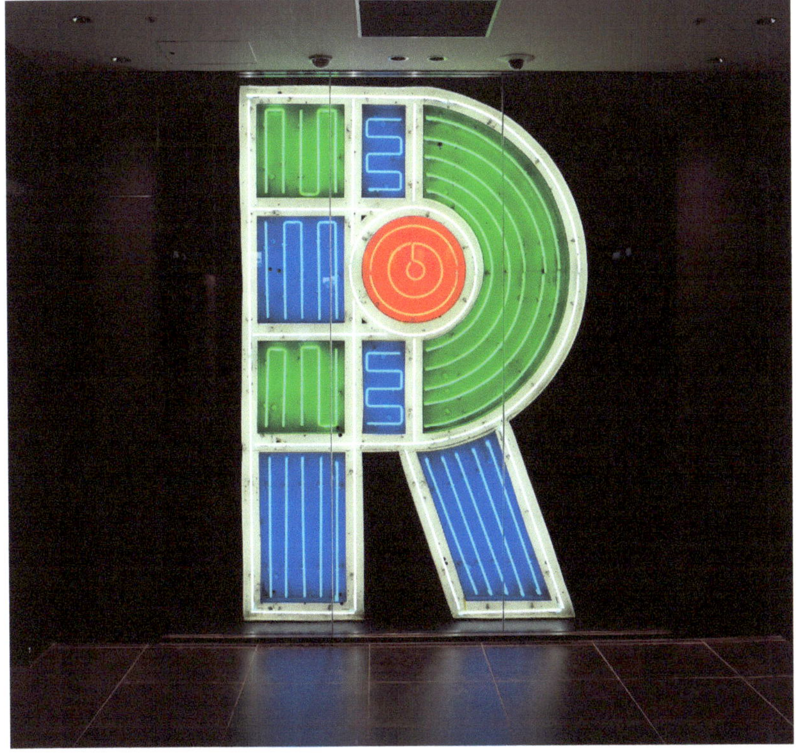

TOP: FRAMES FOR LED CHANNEL LETTER SIGNS

MIDDLE: LED VISION BOARD DISPLAYING TELEVISION ADS

LEFT: THE TOKYO DEPARTMENT STORE, PARCO, RENOVATED THEIR OLD NEON SIGN FOR USE AS A DISPLAY INSIDE OF THE STORE.

The Bright Side

Many large sign companies have decided to leave neon manufacturing to the specialists. Neon companies of the past were made up of many types of craftsmen, designers, salesmen, engineers, etc. Today, for the most part, this has all boiled down to a couple of people. Quite frequently, neon shops are one-person operations.

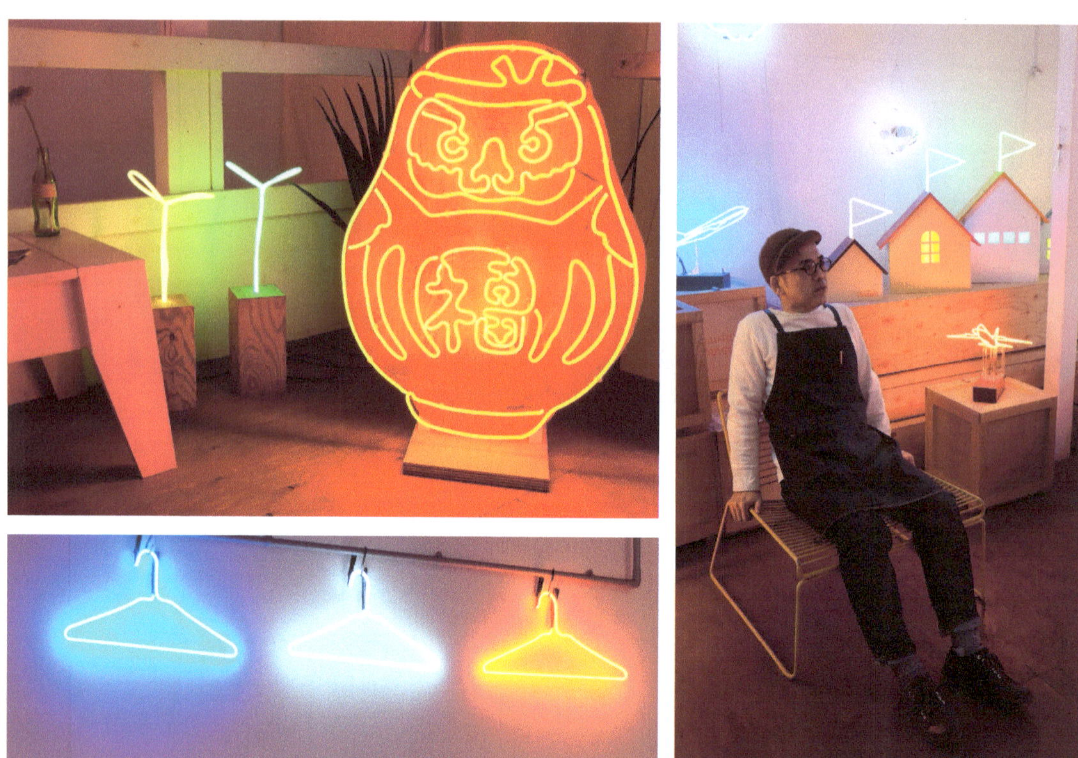

YUICHI YAMAMOTO OF MAVERICK, NEON ART STUDIO IN OSAKA

The typical clientele for neon signs today are retail shops, modern cafes, hair salons, art galleries, bars and clubs. Neon is still recognized for its original purpose, to attract people and to enhance an environment. Many people love to share their shopping experiences over social media, and frequently take pictures of a store's neon sign.

Neon has been used as a medium in contemporary art for years, and has continued to grow in popularity. Many people take interest in neon with respect to the craftsmanship that goes into its creation. Artists such as Waku Fukui, of Tokyo, uses neon as the primary element for his artwork. Mr. Fukui has used the principles originally practiced by advertisers in conveying concepts through his work.

One of the positive outcomes is that neon benders can focus on projects that offer a better return on investment for their time. A single neon tube in a large neon advertisement may cost less than $20 per tube, whereas one tube in a custom logo for a retail store could cost hundreds of dollars. It's also much less tedious, as neon benders aren't stuck making thousands of straight tubes every month. Making custom signs for shops is often more mentally rewarding than producing a wholesale batch of tubes.

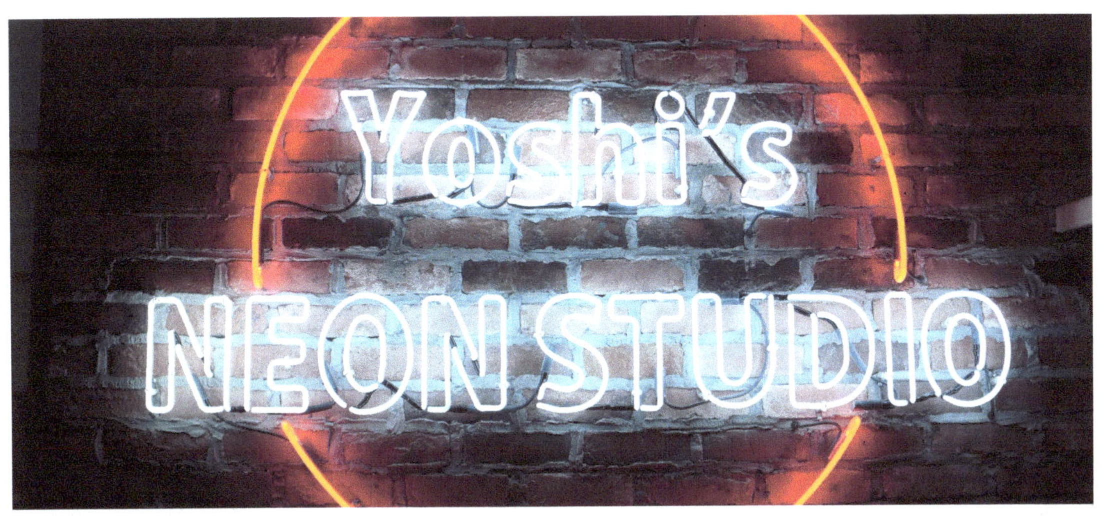

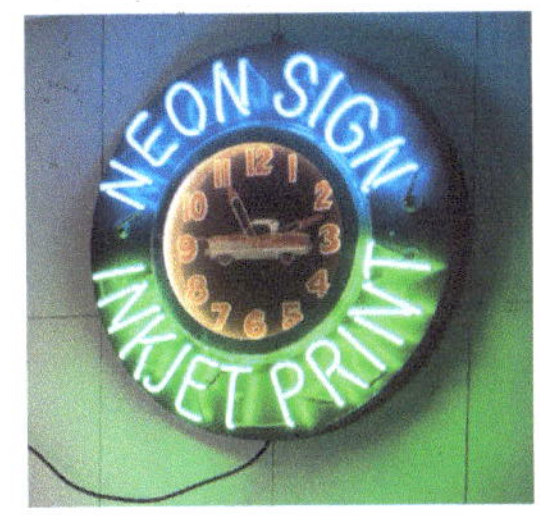

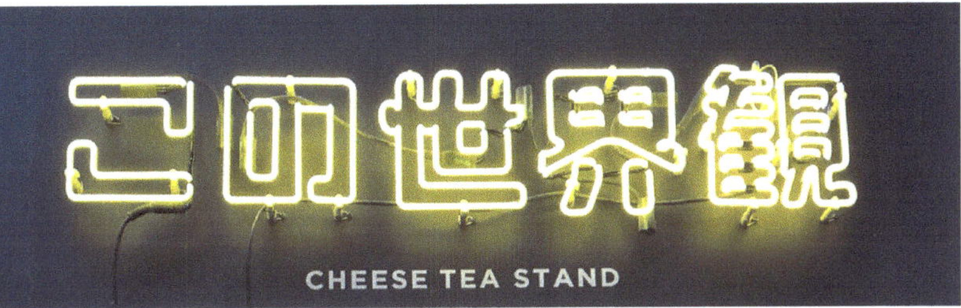

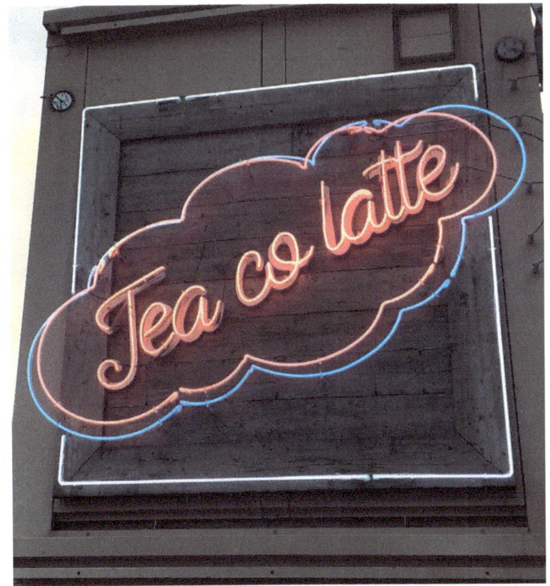

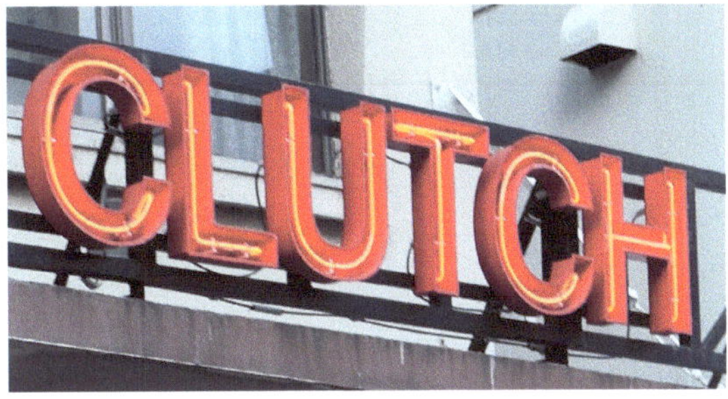

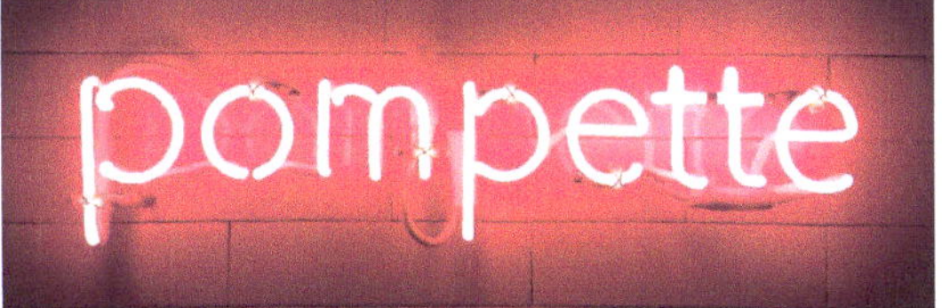

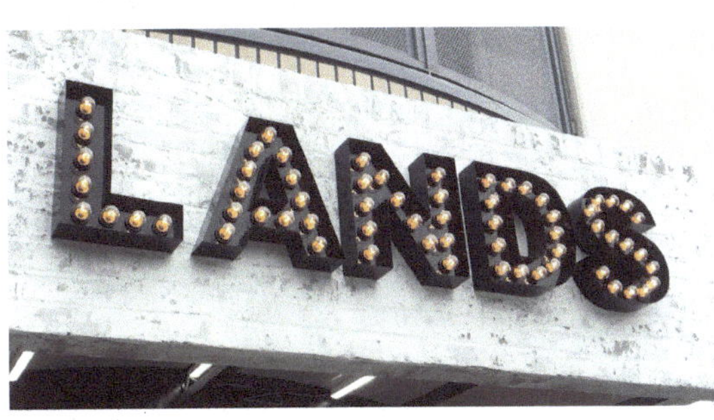

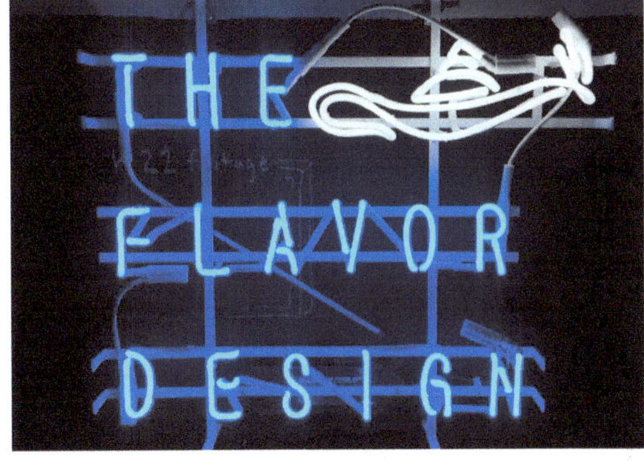

WORK OF YOSHIHITO YASUTOMI OF YOSHI'S NEON STUDIO, OSAKA

Artwork of Waku Fukui

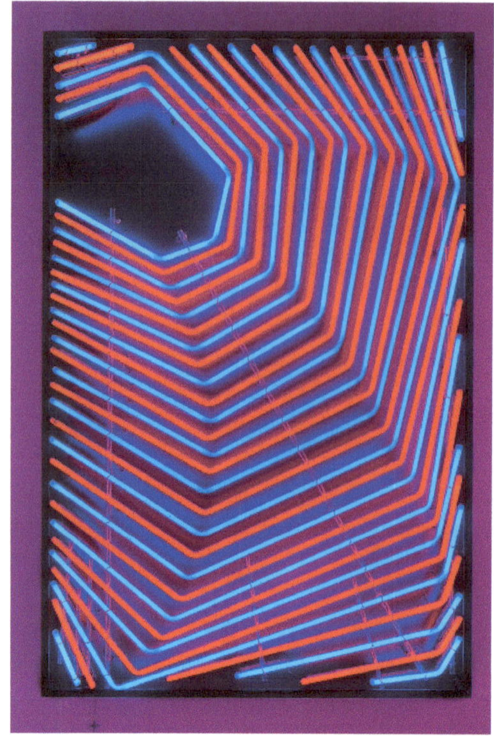

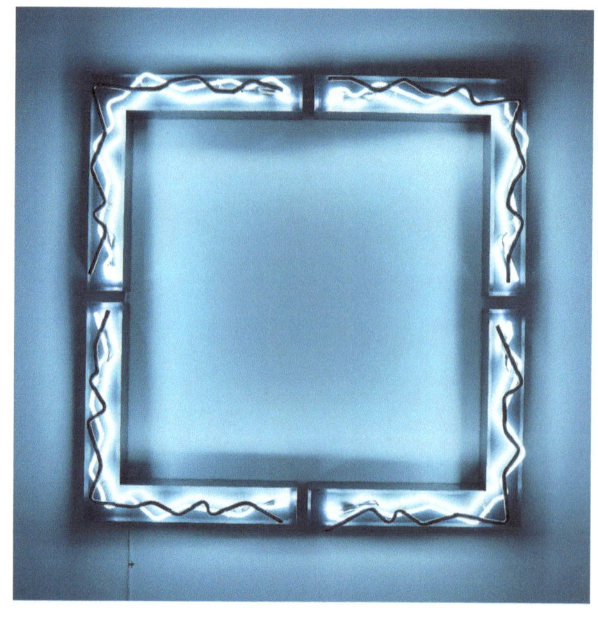

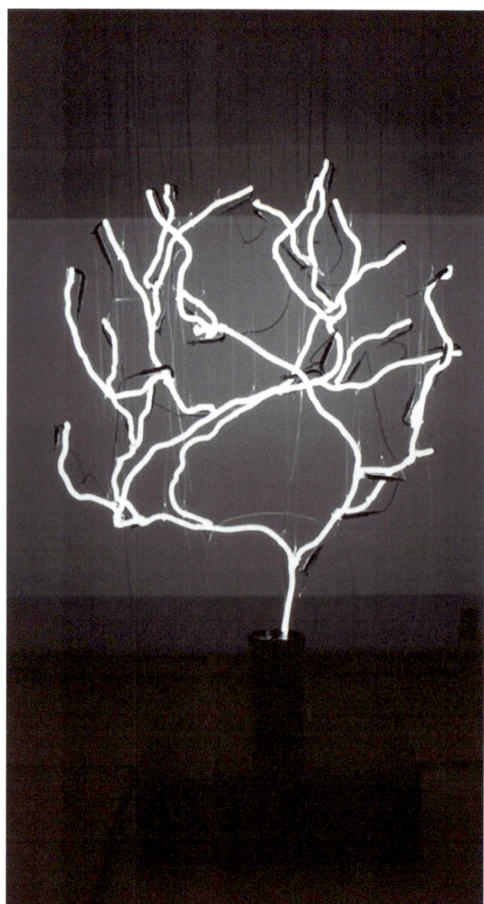

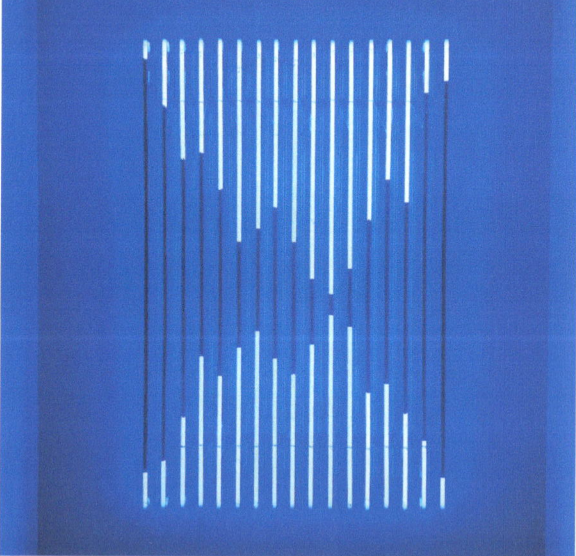

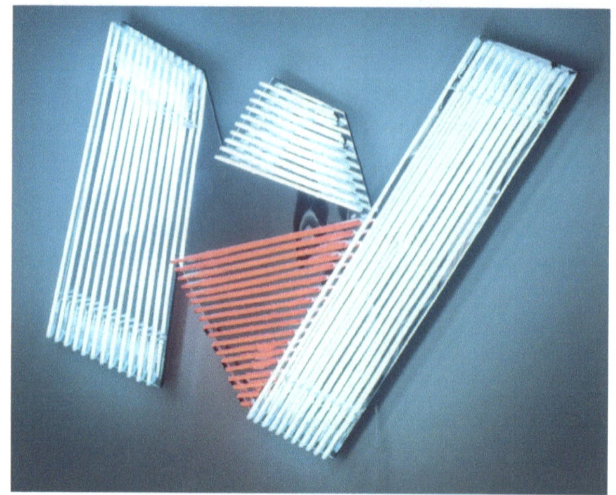

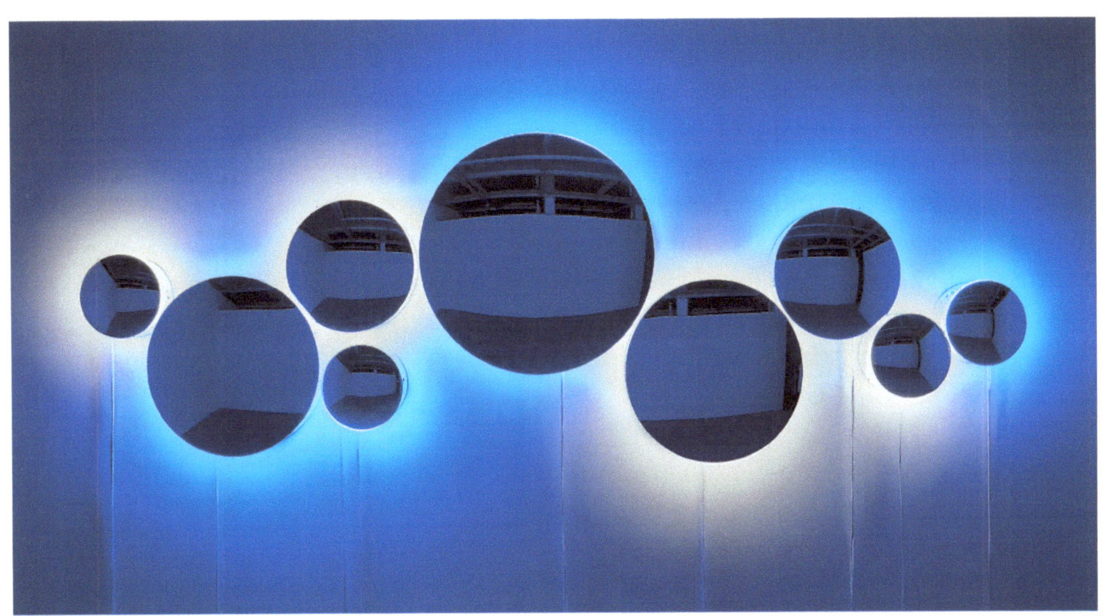

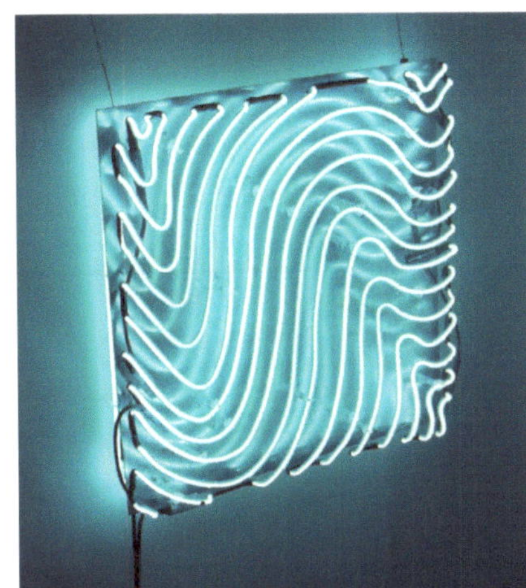

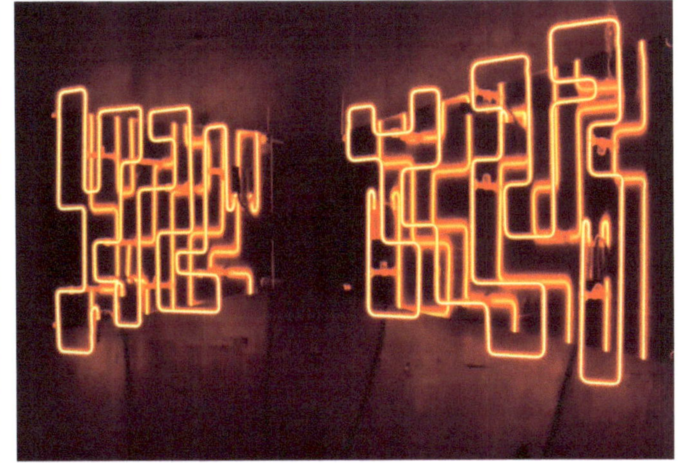

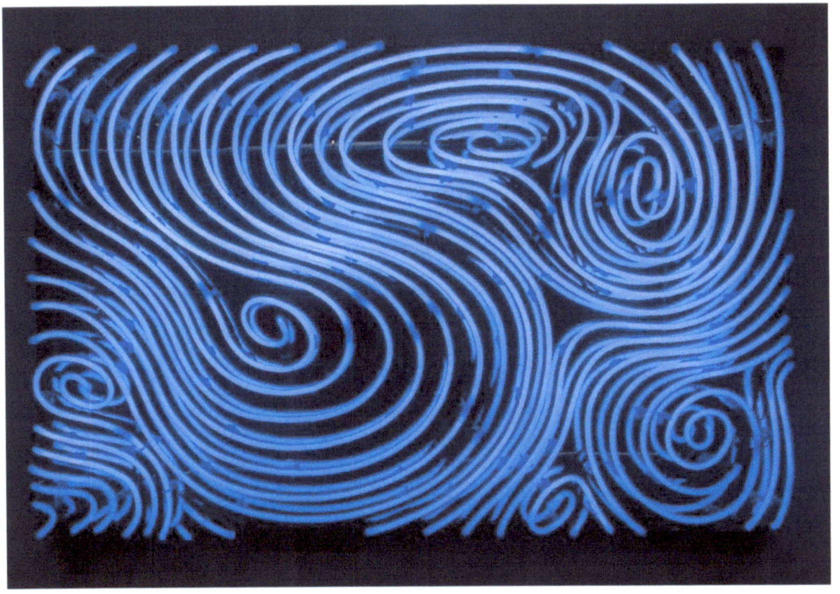

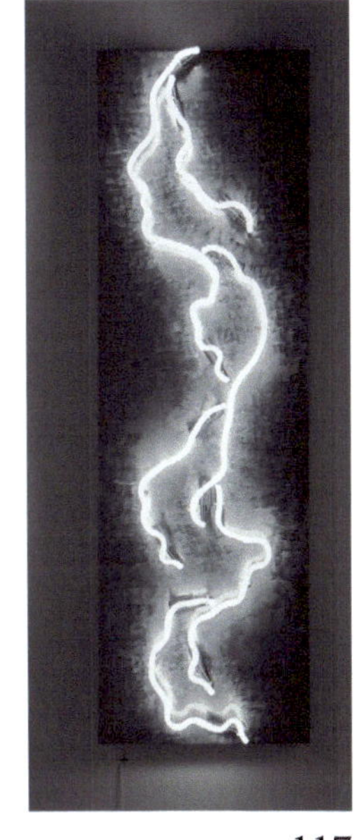

Neon: Japanese Style

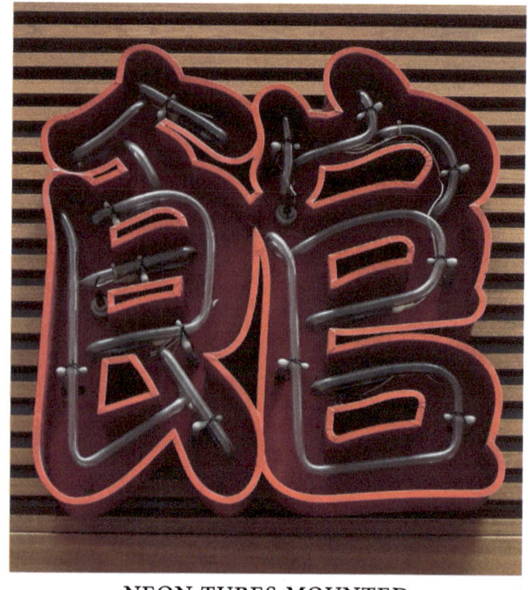

NEON TUBES MOUNTED INTO A STEEL CHANNEL LETTER

The Japanese style of neon making is a hybrid of European and American styles, with its own sprout of developments in materials and methods. Most of the early pioneers in the Japanese neon industry were electric lighting product traders, whom originally focused on light bulbs and illuminated signs. They had stumbled upon the developing Moore and Claude lights when traveling to the United States and Europe.

Methods of neon tube production often vary by country and region. Neon makers may use different types of burners, processing styles, installation methods, and materials. For example, some European countries mainly use borosilicate glass, coat the tubes after bending, and utilize large ovens for processing. Whereas many countries across America and Asia, use soft glass, bend pre-coated tubing, and utilize a high voltage bombarding transformer for processing.

The traditional neon benders in Japan have developed certain practices due to their experience working during the peak time of the industry. Tube production is usually preformed in batches for each step, and all at once. For example; bend all tubes, make all cuts, splice all electrodes, and finally process tubes. One is less likely to make mistakes by preforming one task at a time.

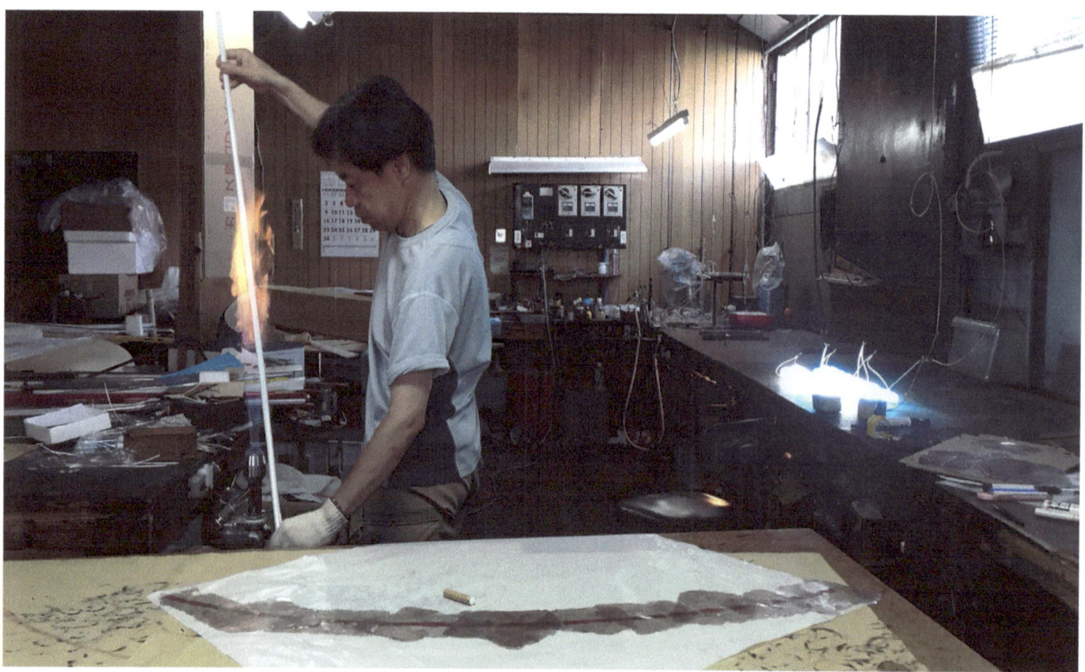

Sign Construction

In the early days, there were not many construction rules, therefor most decisions were formed from opinions. Staff from neon companies would have to visit various regional power companies first in order to settle construction details. Practices differed between Tokyo and Osaka, leading to confusion as rules mostly depended on the thoughts of the supervising official of the area.

During the early Showa Era, a popular style that emerged was steel border signs with neon attached to glass tube framing. This was a simple, safe, and lightweight option that allowed the neon to be viewed from both directions. Neon signs evolved into large-scale advertising towers and signboards, which often use similar geometry, though some advertisers opted for novel shapes. Originally, many signs used an L-type electrode, with wiring performed inside the signboard body through bushings. However, the number of double-backed electrodes gradually increased, significantly simplifying the work.

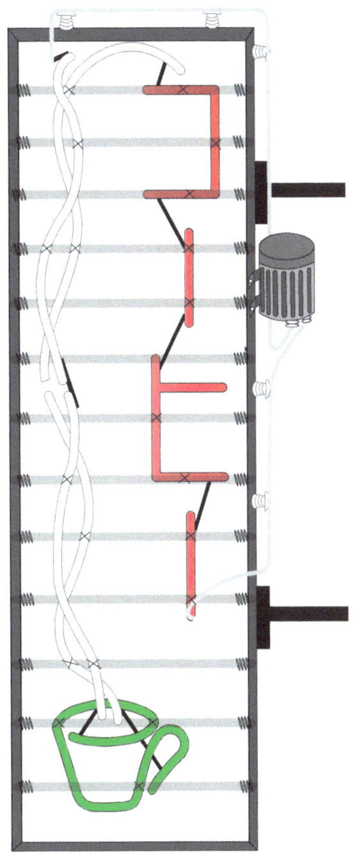

NEON UNITS ATTACHED TO GLASS TUBES PERMIT DOUBLE-SIDED VISIBILITY

Most neon signs consist of structure material (usually steel), glass lamps, channel letters, tube supports, wiring, transformers, porcelain bushings and standoffs. Some signs use animator/flashers, rotating motors, incandescent bulbs, plastic faces, etc. Neon lights in Japan are often mounted onto steel frames, towers, parapets, facades, blade signs, or sprawled across billboards. While they are designed to garner attention, signs are constructed to abide by regulations to prevent accidents. Signs should be designed to withstand the winds of typhoons that hit Japan every year. In addition, signs must be reasonably maintainable.

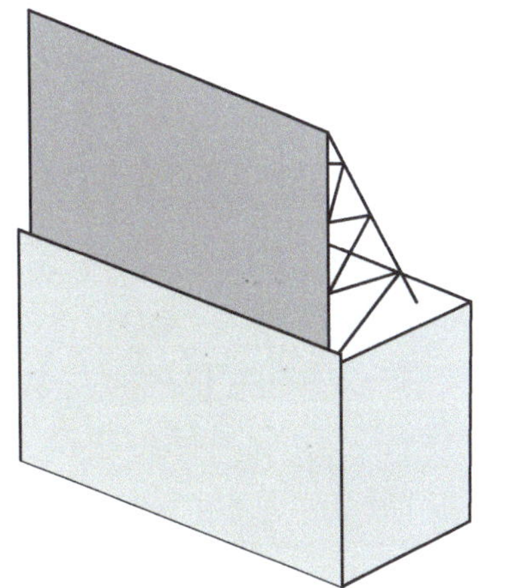
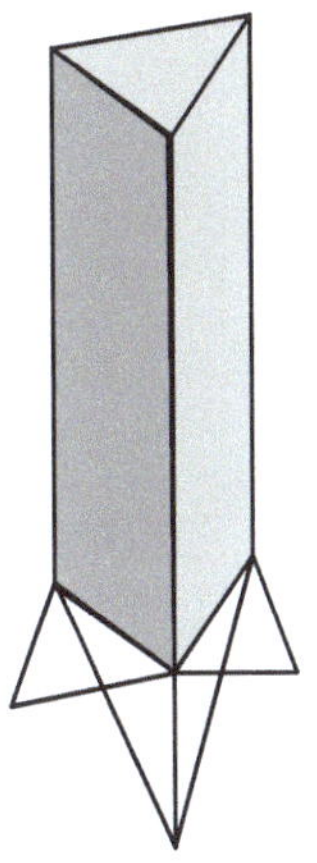
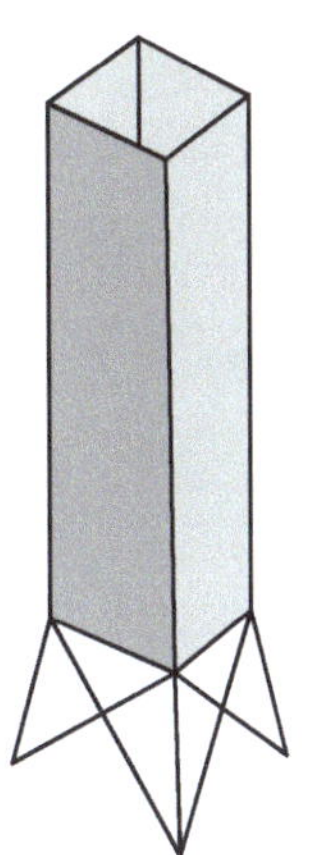
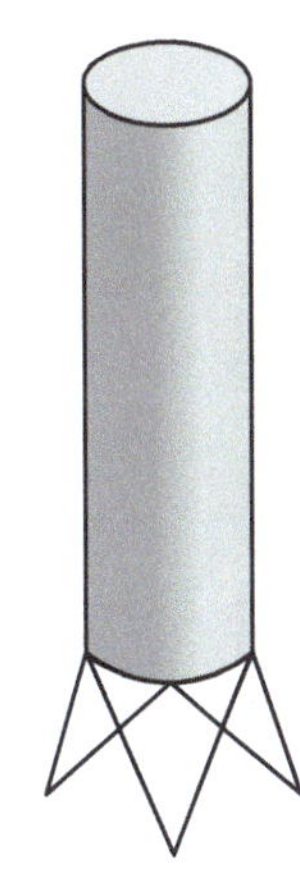

STANDARD ADVERTISING TOWERS

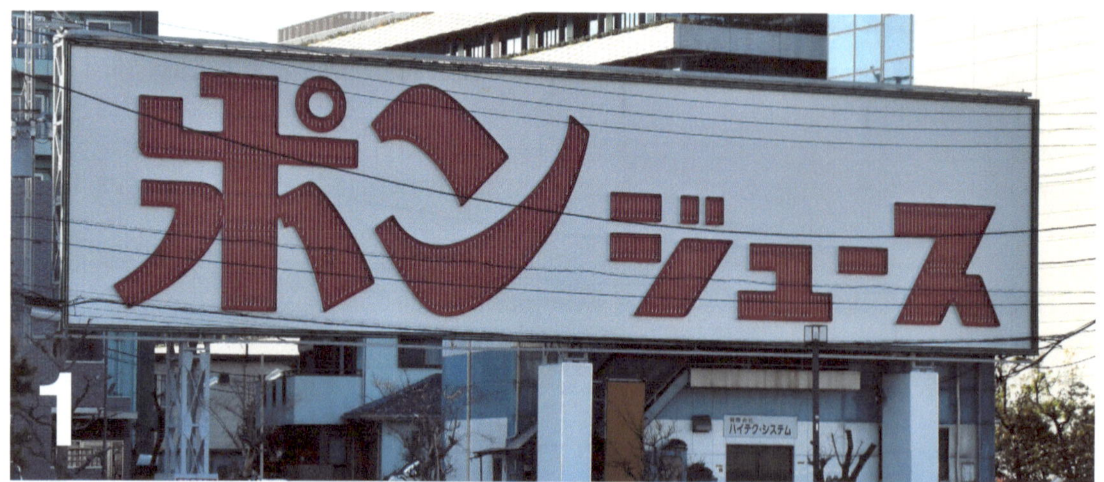
1
ポンジュース
ハイテク・システム

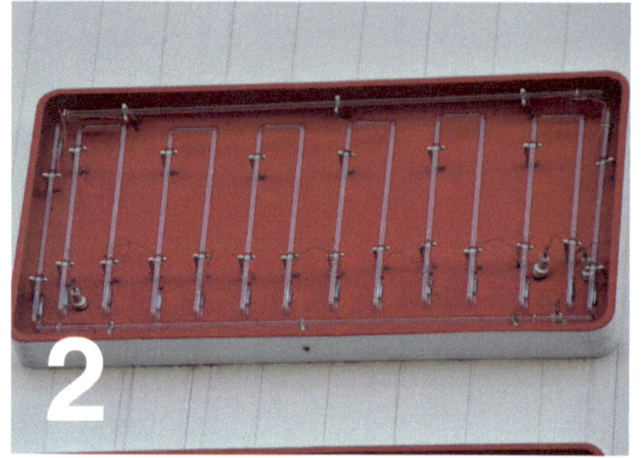
2

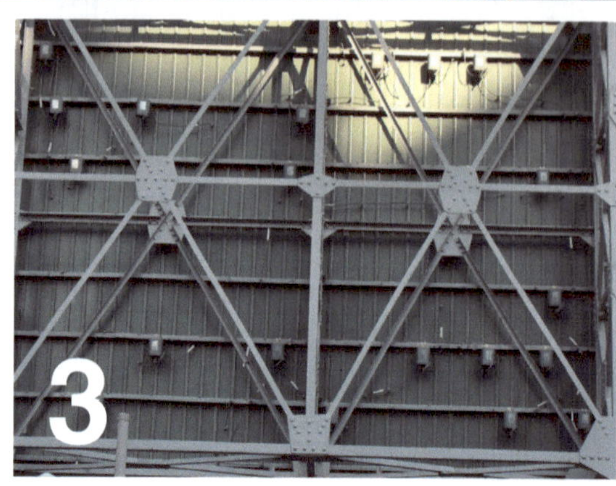
3

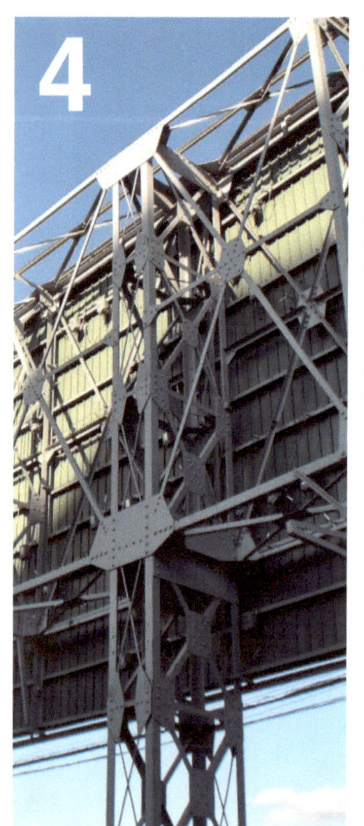
4

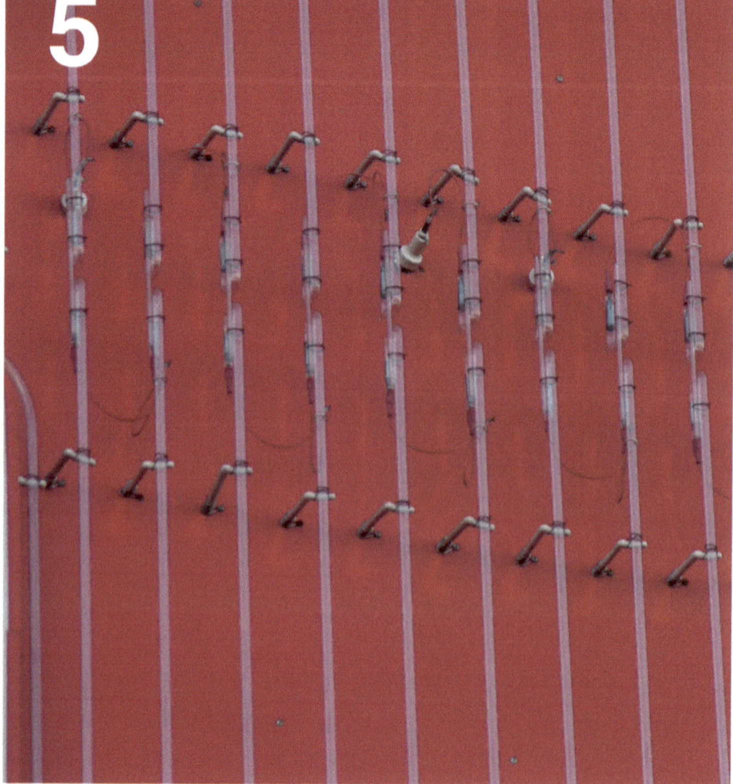
5

Example: Pom Juice Signboard, Tokyo

1. The beverage company, Pom Juice, has a large neon signboard just outside of Tokyo's Haneda Airport. The sign is mostly visible to the monorail passengers, though it can also be seen while airborne. The sign is about 25 meters long and has roughly 1000 meters of neon tubing.

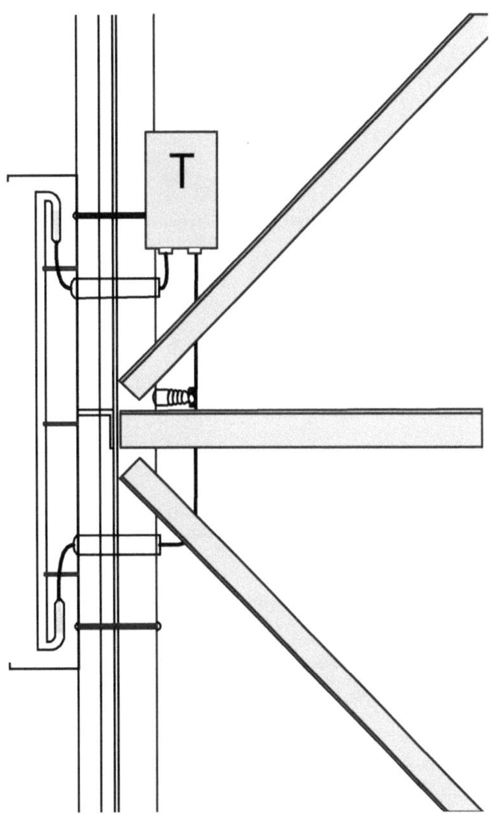

2. Channel letters are typically made out of steel. Each letter consists of vertical rows of neon tubes and an outline. Channel letters have "weep holes" drilled in the bottom to prevent water from collecting within the letter. Water will corrode the letter over time.

3. Transformers are hung along the backside of the steel structure. High voltage wires pass though the sign within porcelain bushings. If there is no barrier between the high voltage wires and the metal sign, the electrical current will slowly work its way through the insulation, eventually grounding out, leading to failure.

4. Heavy steel frames are engineered to survive strong winds from typhoons. They are often reused due to the high cost of the structure. They are routinely painted to prevent corrosion.

5. Glass sleeve tubing is often connected between straight tubes to keep them aligned. Tube supports should be placed about 15cm from the electrode.

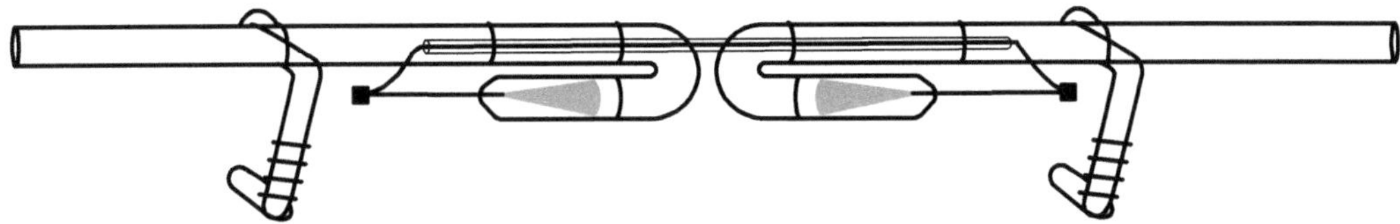

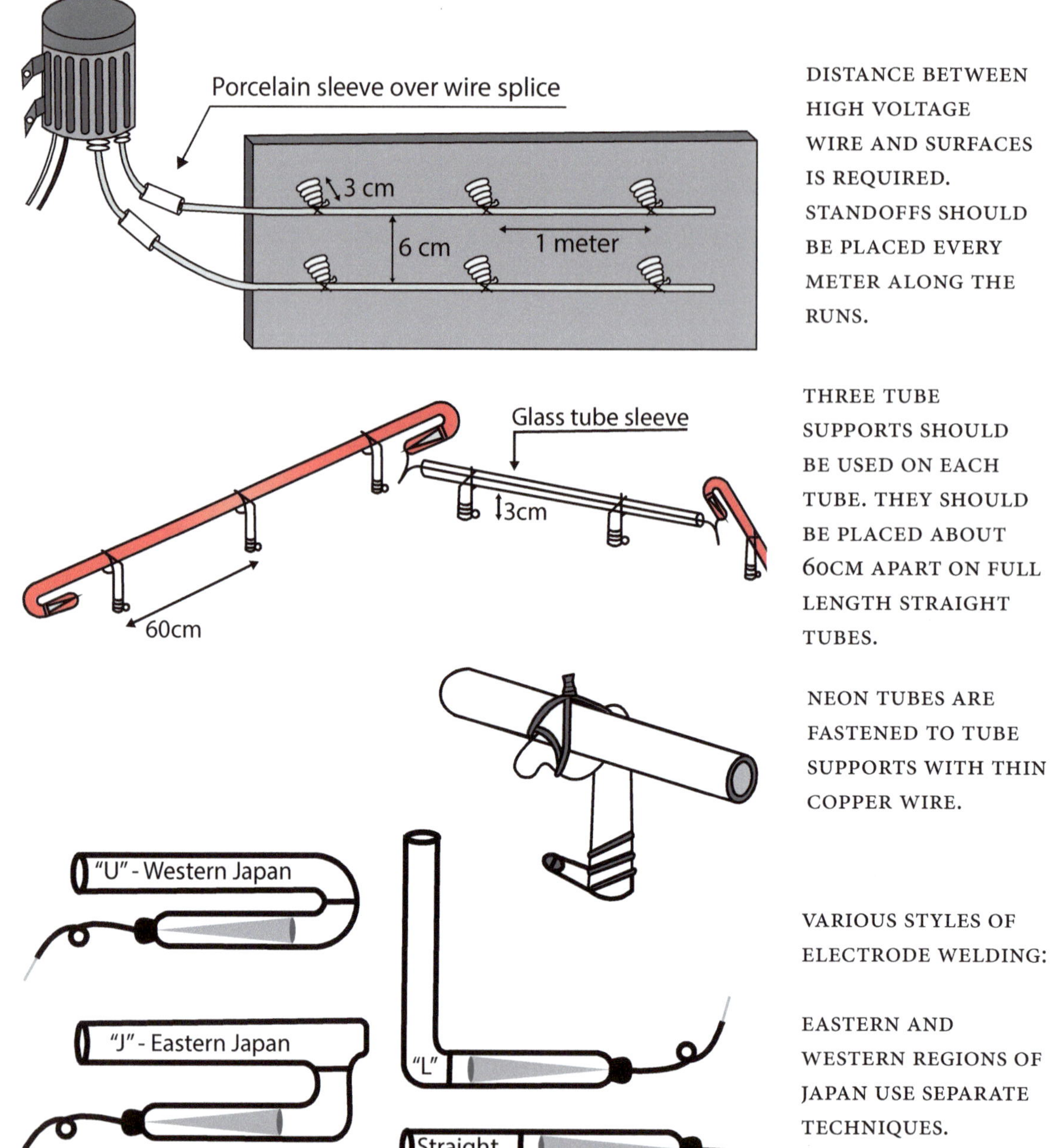

DISTANCE BETWEEN HIGH VOLTAGE WIRE AND SURFACES IS REQUIRED. STANDOFFS SHOULD BE PLACED EVERY METER ALONG THE RUNS.

THREE TUBE SUPPORTS SHOULD BE USED ON EACH TUBE. THEY SHOULD BE PLACED ABOUT 60CM APART ON FULL LENGTH STRAIGHT TUBES.

NEON TUBES ARE FASTENED TO TUBE SUPPORTS WITH THIN COPPER WIRE.

VARIOUS STYLES OF ELECTRODE WELDING:

EASTERN AND WESTERN REGIONS OF JAPAN USE SEPARATE TECHNIQUES.

RIGHT:
CHANNEL LETTERS ARE SHAPED METAL FABRICATIONS THAT "CHANNEL" LIGHT. THEY OFTEN ADD A SENSE OF DIMENSION TO SIGNS.

Channel Letter Styles

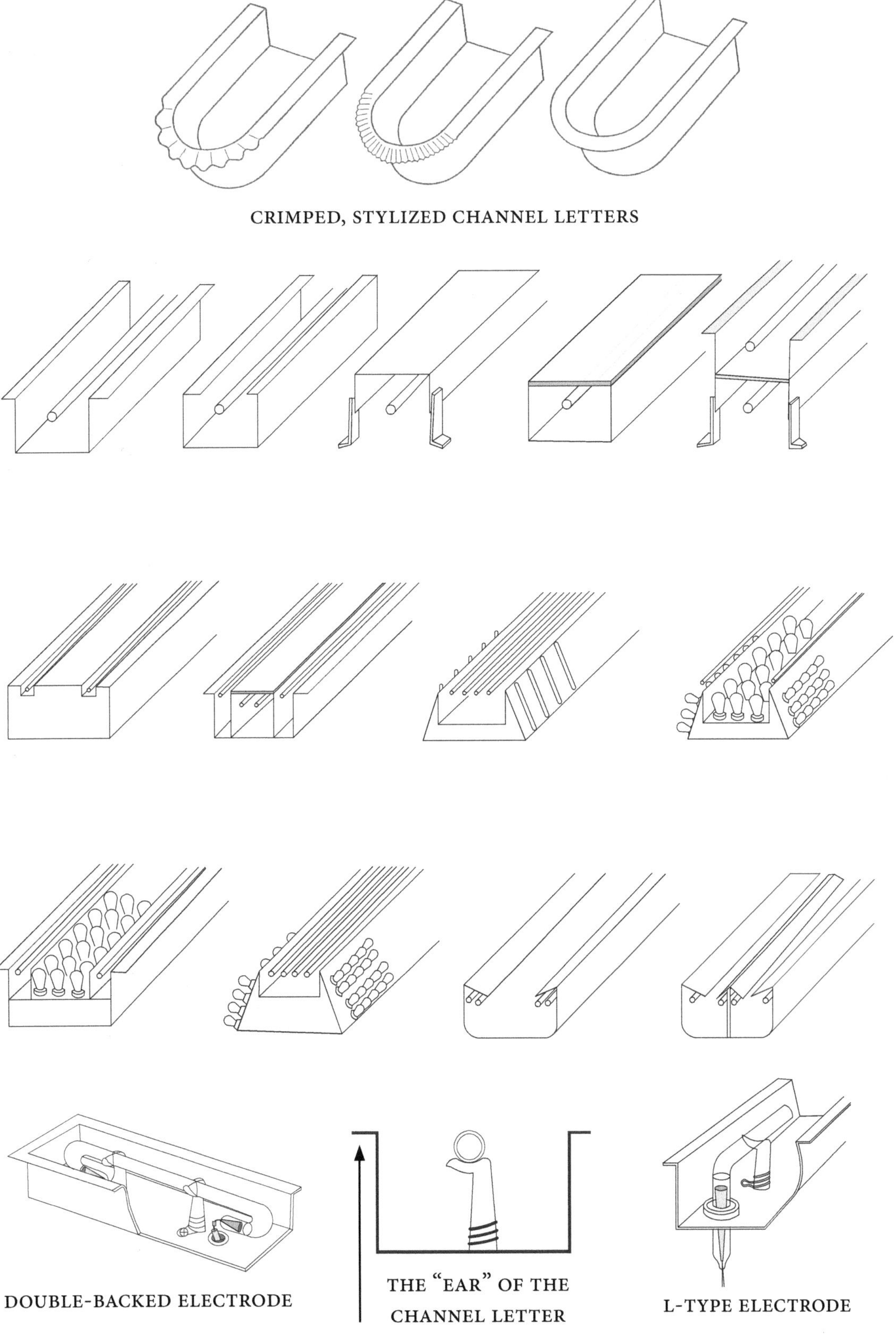

Installation & Maintenance

The biggest concern for neon workers is the danger of working at heights. Large signboards are often high off the ground, requiring the use of scaffolding. Most signs are equipped with built-in ladders, foot pegs, or safety rails for access. It wasn't uncommon that companies would suffer some casualties. The use of pipe scaffolding and crane vehicles has decreased the dangers, though no matter how much care is taken, there is still a risk. There was consensus for enacting more safety procedures among the parties concerned.

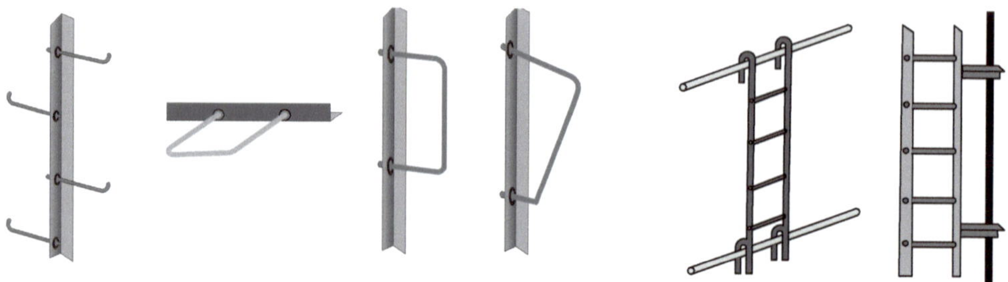

Some of the precautions that have been enacted include:

- Neon workers should hold an official certification from the All Japan Neon Sign Association for installations and maintenance
- Those who work on scaffolding must wear a helmet, long sleeves, safety shoes, and a harness
- Safety nets should be installed within scaffolding

Scaffolding workers are referred to as "Tobishoku", and often wear special clothing and shoes to allow for optimum movement along scaffolding and ladders. They often work in teams, and can been seen working at heroic heights.

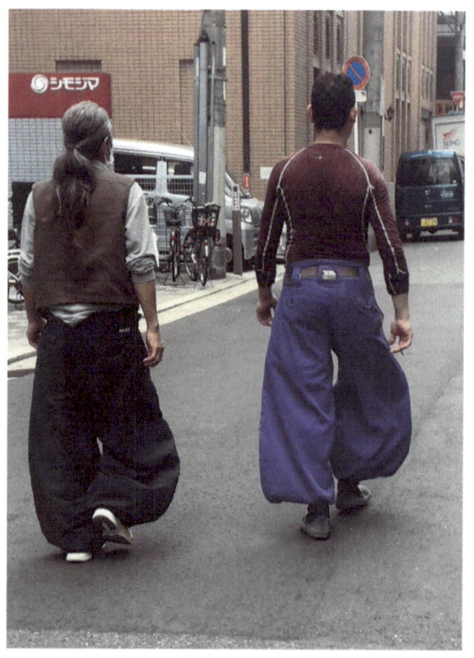

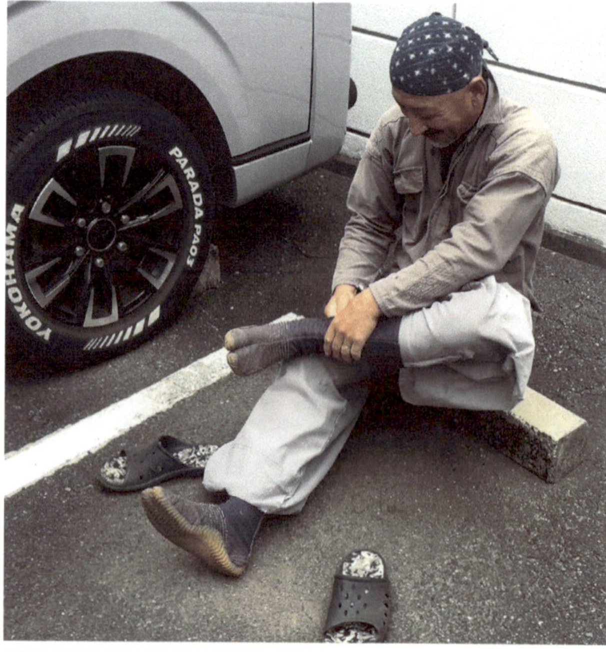

SPECIAL CLOTHING WORN BY TOBISHOKU

Installation takes place in stages for large signboards. Significant planning for compliance precedes the installation. First, a site must be prepped for the structural attachments. A template is used to place precise drilling locations and important markings on the building. Steel frames are generally attached to buildings using long bolts, anchors, and an epoxy resin. Some frames are directly welded or bolted onto existing structural members of the building. At the same time, electricity should be provided to the sign location and tested for adequacy. Eventually sign components will be installed in steps, with positions pre-marked for assembly. Finally, the sign will be tested for faults before the scaffolding is removed.

Signs should be regularly maintained to preserve aesthetics and structural integrity. Steel structures should be painted every few years to prevent corrosion. Procedures for repairing neon signs have been developed to minimize costs and downtime. The procedure starts with troubleshooting to determine the cause of the outage. The worker can usually find the issue by visually inspecting the sign for broken tubes or checking breakers, fuses, and transformers. Transformers can be replaced immediately, but neon tubes take time to fabricate. Tubes are usually marked with a number to allow for identification, as bending patterns and diagrams are often kept on file in the neon shop. Other issues may involve more complex electrical issues that can be time consuming to find and fix. High voltage electricity can easily short-out over time by eating through wire insulation and making contact with metal. The expected lifetime of an outdoor sign is about 5-8 years, as signs over 10 years old often require extensive maintenance.

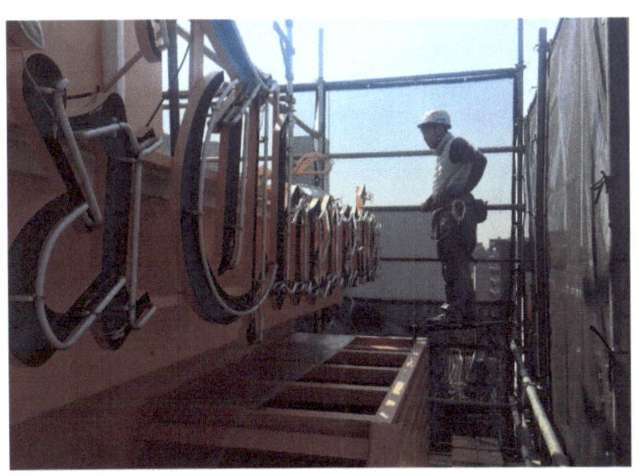

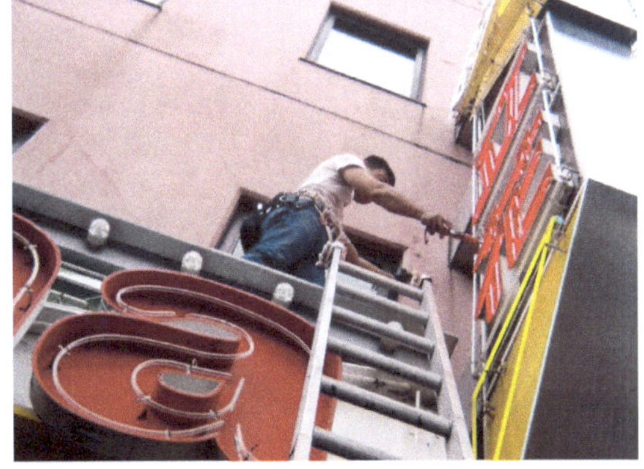

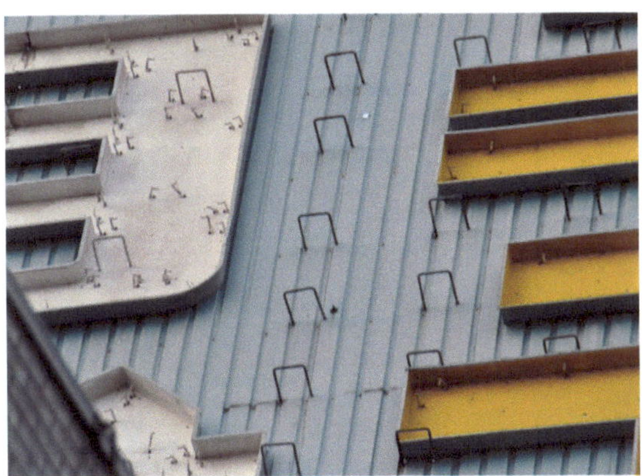

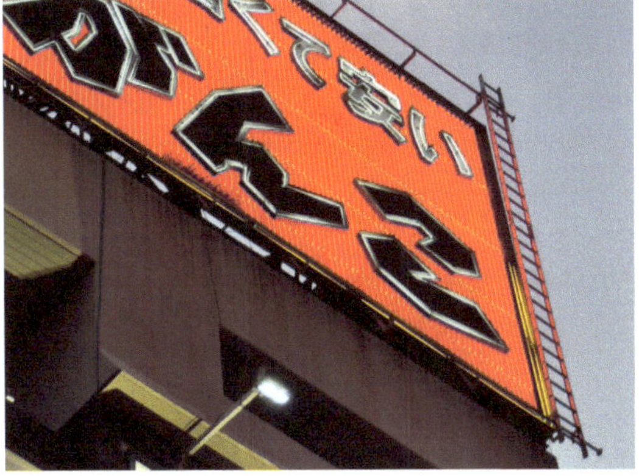

A History of Materials

Japan has developed and manufactured their own glass tubes, electrodes, porcelain bushings, transformers, and other neon-related equipment throughout the years. They initially relied on foreign imports, but were quick to make imitations though trail & error reproductions. Due to the current state of the industry, finding materials has become more difficult. The number of suppliers has dwindled and prices have risen significantly. This forces many neon makers to rely on foreign made materials.

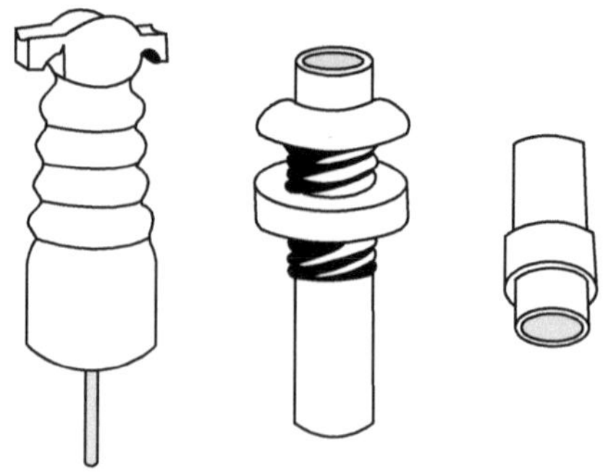

PORCELAIN PRODUCTS PRODUCED FOR HIGH-VOLTAGE INSULATION

Mr. Kenichiro Mochizuki, of Nippon Light Bulb, was dealing with imported goods before the neon era. He took action when he saw the commercialization of neon lighting, and was the first person to import neon gas. At the same time, he dealt with various materials, including machinery and equipment for neon tube production. Nippon Light Bulb became known as the "neon department store" and was a great resource to the early neon companies in Japan, and throughout the world. By 1933, Nippon Light Bulb exported 300,000 American-style glass tube supports to Knoxville, Tennessee. There is also record of the export of about 10 tons of neon tubing.

Neon gas was imported from the United States and Germany. A few domestic companies attempted to produce neon gas, though the quality didn't meet the purity standards. In addition to neon, other gases such as argon, helium, krypton, and xenon were imported. The use of helium gas required special electrodes, as the life span was only about 7 to 8 months.

In 1932, Claude Neon and Tokyo Neon commissioned Uematsu Electric to make insulators for neon purposes. The designs mostly derived from foreign imitations, though they did produce a number of unique products. Due to the large demand, a separate business was formed to supply the various insulators for use in neon signs, such as bobbins and bushings for neon transformers. Uematsu Electric also produced the animation machine supplied to the neon industry. Japan was never dependent on imports for blinkers/chasers, as these were developed in Japan during the earlier years of incandescent bulb signs.

Seidensha Manufacturing Works produced transformers, small motors for flashers and supplies for the production of neon tubes such as bombarders, vacuum pumps, and Tesla coils. They also exported their products around Asia. The Japanese method for processing neon uses a large "bombarding" transformer, adopted from America. Claude Neon, originating in Europe, used an oven pumping system.

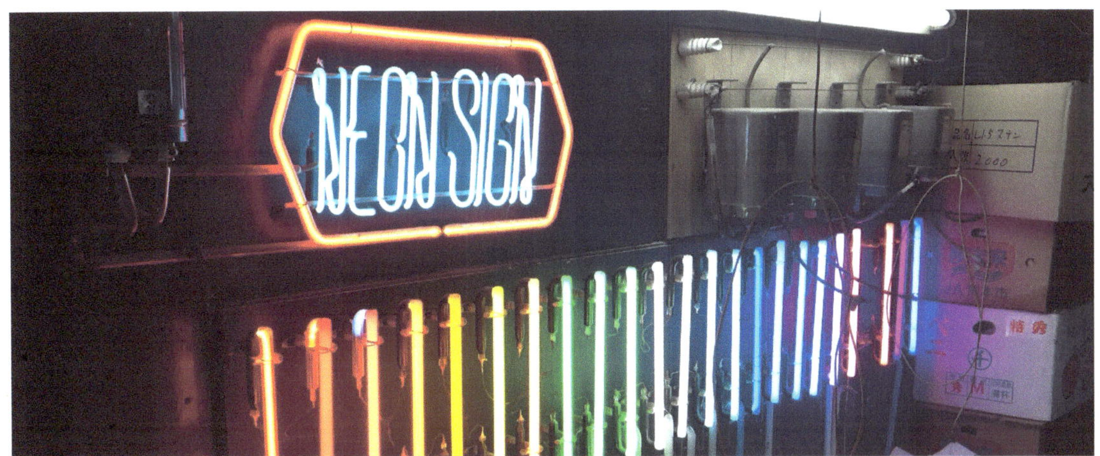

Glass

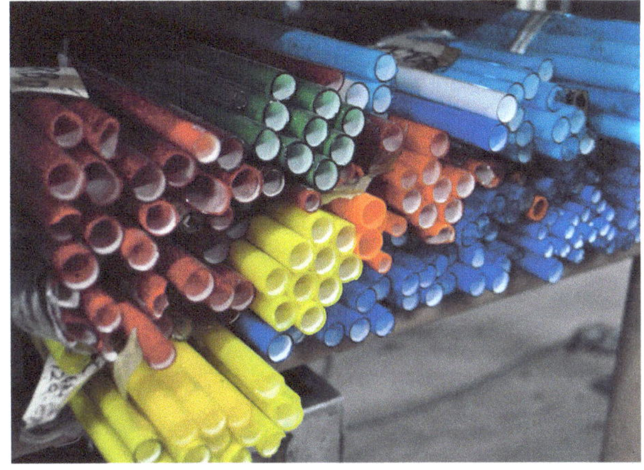

The most notable difference between standard neon tubes and Japanese neon tubes is the wall thickness. Japanese tubes are considerably thinner. Neon makers must consider this during design and production, as tubes are more brittle and difficult to weld together.

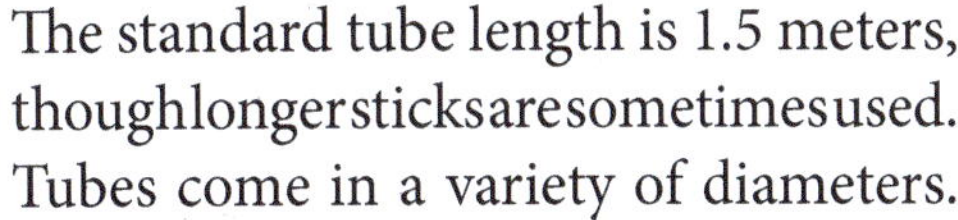

The standard tube length is 1.5 meters, though longer sticks are sometimes used. Tubes come in a variety of diameters. 14mm is the standard for outdoor signs. 12mm, 10mm, and 8mm are the other available sizes available. Japanese neon tubes come pre-coated, and have their own color standards.

Neon tubes used to be made out of lead glass, but have recently been switched to Soda-lime glass. Lead glass contains lead monoxide, has a high refractive index of light, and a low melting temperature, so it was easy to form a tube without cracking. Soda-lime has a higher melting temperature, is more temperamental, and prone to cracking but is now used because of health and environmental regulations.

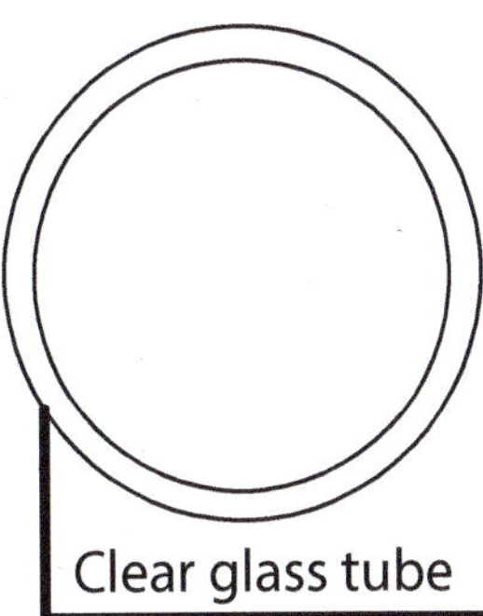

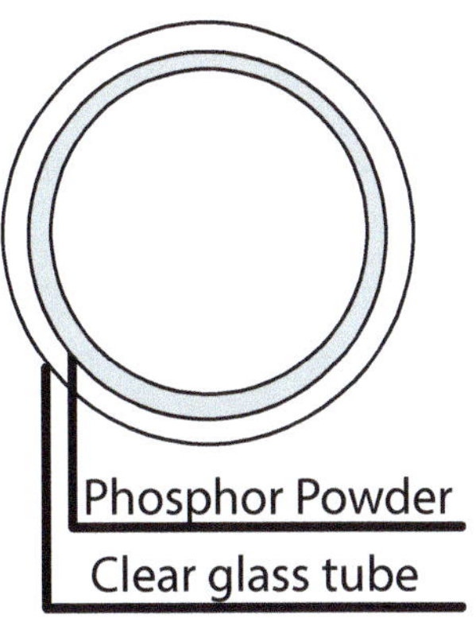

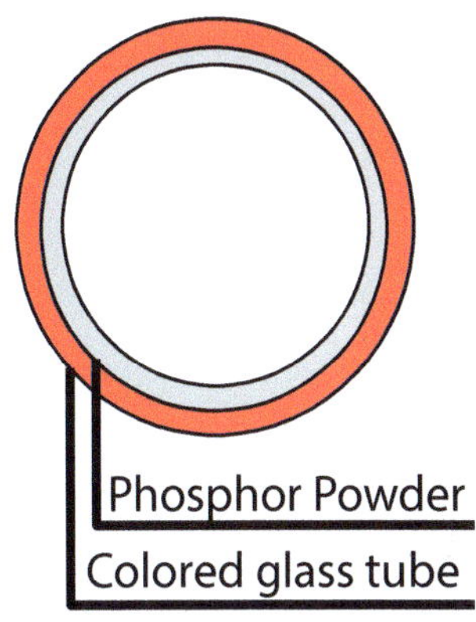

Standard Neon Tube Colors of Japan

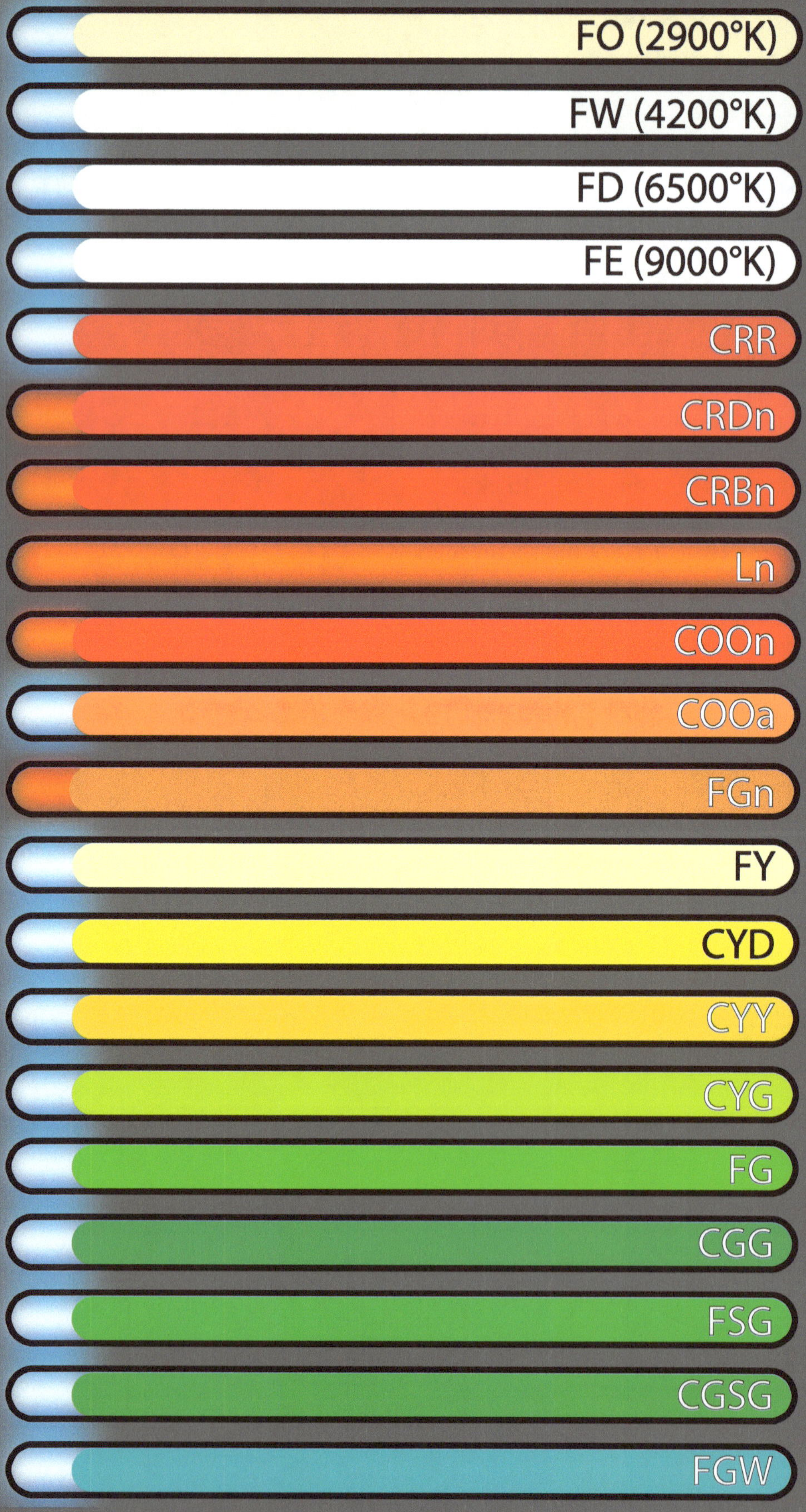

FO (2900°K)
FW (4200°K)
FD (6500°K)
FE (9000°K)
CRR
CRDn
CRBn
Ln
COOn
COOa
FGn
FY
CYD
CYY
CYG
FG
CGG
FSG
CGSG
FGW

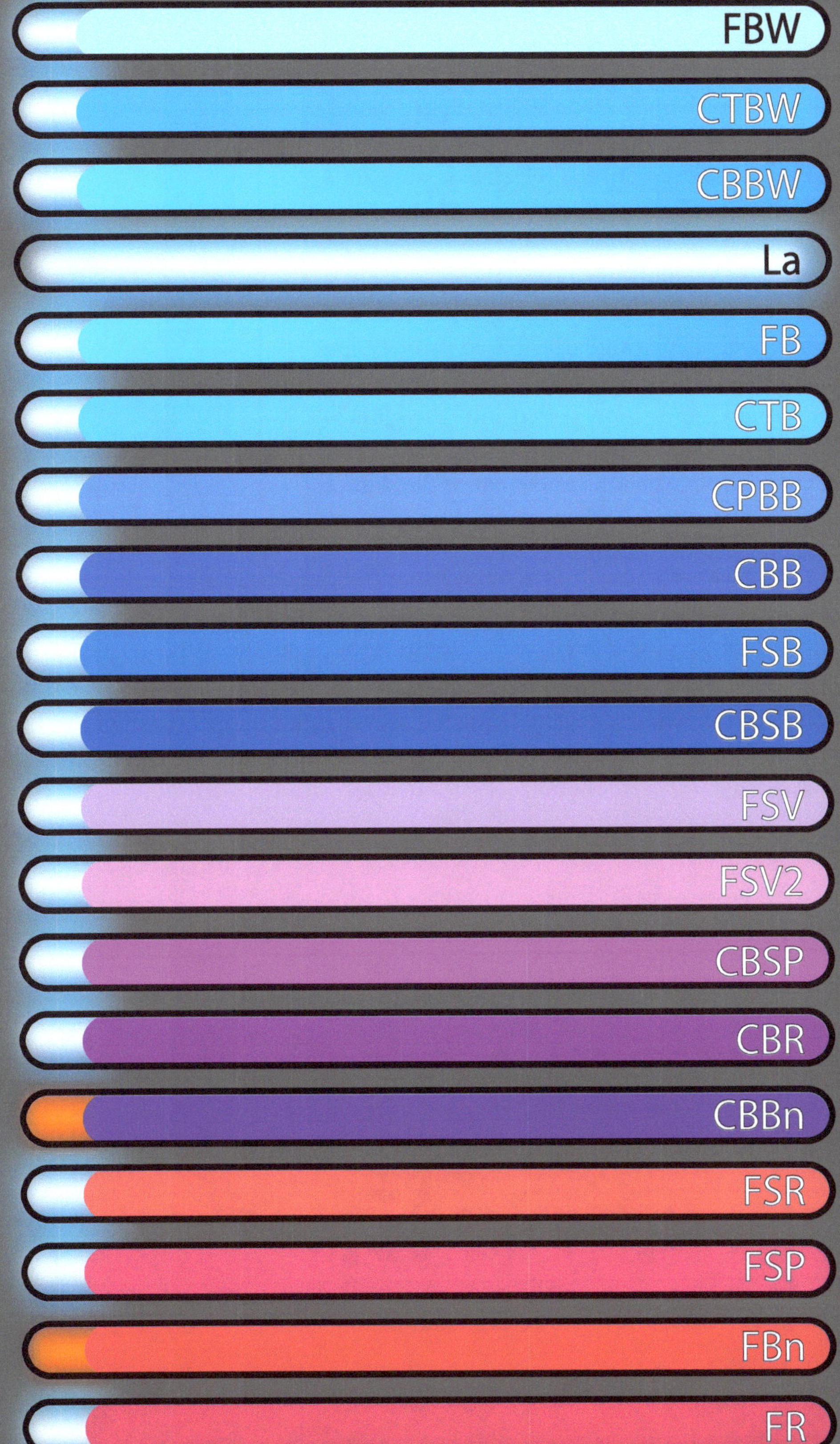

L= CLEAR GLASS TUBING

C= COLORED GLASS TUBING

F=FLUORESCENT GLASS TUBING

N=NEON GAS

Electrodes

An electrode's purpose is to act as a terminal for the high-voltage electricity from the neon transformer. This allows for the ionization to take place within the tube. As electrical polarity changes 50 or 60 times per second, charged particles race towards the oppositely charged electrode. The collision between electrons and ions results in the output of light.

The neon electrode is a high-purity metal shell, within a glass tube with wires sealed through the glass. Electrodes come in a variety of shapes and sizes based on the type of tube. Shells are commonly coated with chemicals to prevent sputtering. The portion sealed into the glass is called a dumet wire, which is made up of a copper-coated nickel-iron alloy. The expansion coefficient of the dumet wire is approximately equal to the expansion coefficient of glass, which makes for a compatible seal.

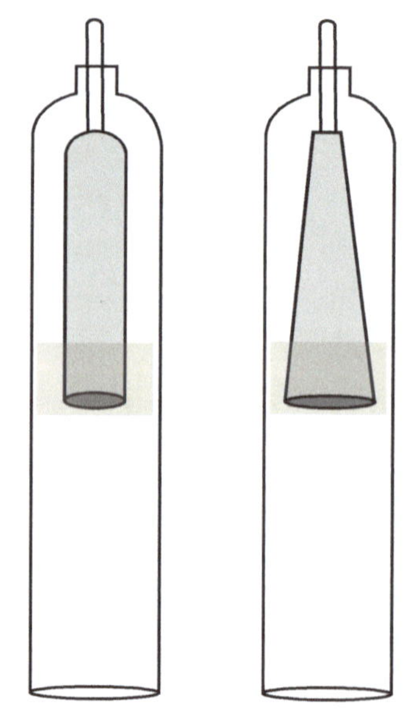

JAPANESE STYLE ELECTRODES

Japanese electrodes are similar to old-style western electrodes. Japanese electrode shells are typically shaped in a conical form, as opposed to a cylindrical form. A thin mica film is placed around the shell to protect the electrode from continuous deterioration. In addition, the lead in wire is usually insulated and shrink-wrapped to the head of the electrode. Lastly, Japanese electrodes do not come with tubulation, so each tube must be manually tubulated.

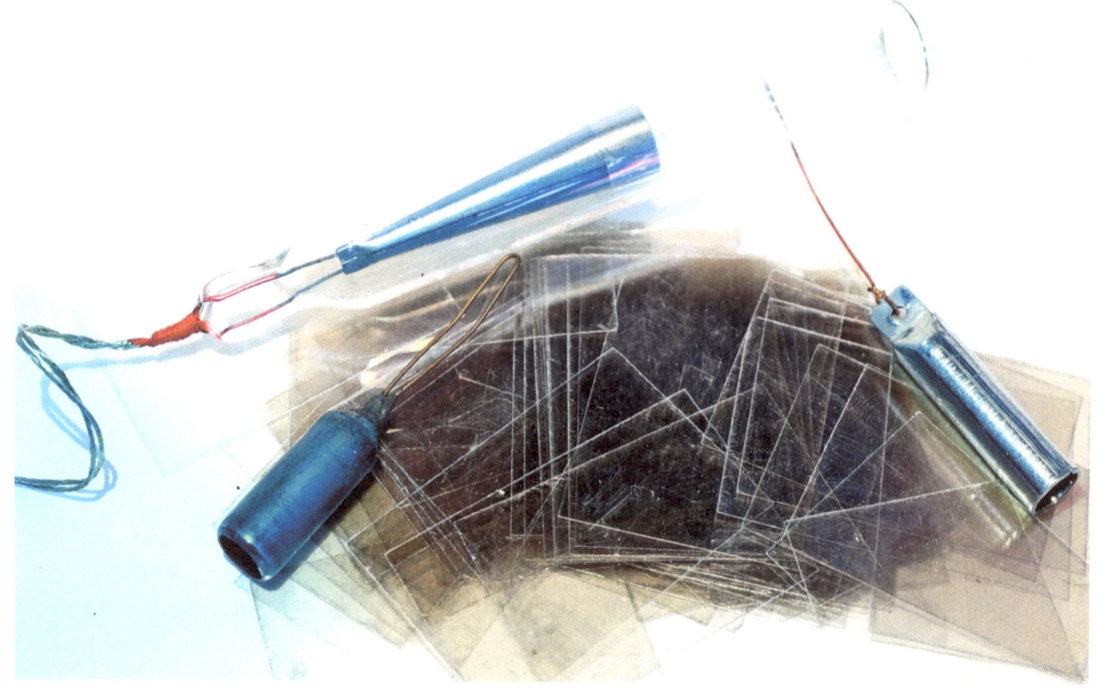

AN IN-SHOP MADE ELECTRODE, MICA SHEETS, AND SPARE ELECTRODE SHELLS

Sign Animation

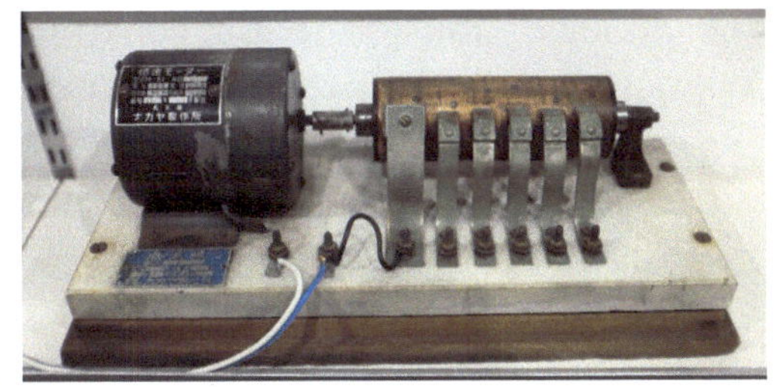

ROLLER-TYPE ANIMATOR

Sign animation was used in Japan before neon was adopted. The neon flashing device used the same principle as light bulb flashers. The original machines were low speed, motor-driven cylindrical drums that used a series of cams to complete electrical circuits in sequence. As neon signs grew in size, the flasher was further developed into a larger machine that turned large drums by gear reduction. Entire rooms would be dedicated to house sign controllers.

One of the original makers of the motors was Seidensha Manufacturing. They produced a 1/5th horsepower motor with a diameter of about 80 millimeters. It was said to have been durable enough to be left on a rooftop for continuous use.

The drums were eventually replaced by rudimentary electronic animators in the 1970s, finally evolving into the use of micro-controllers. The electronic systems do not require much space, as they are much smaller than conventional roller animators. In addition, then can achieve advanced pattern conversion such as flashing at high speed and dimming that cannot be achieved with roller animators. Electronic systems have dramatically enhanced the design potential of neon spectaculars.

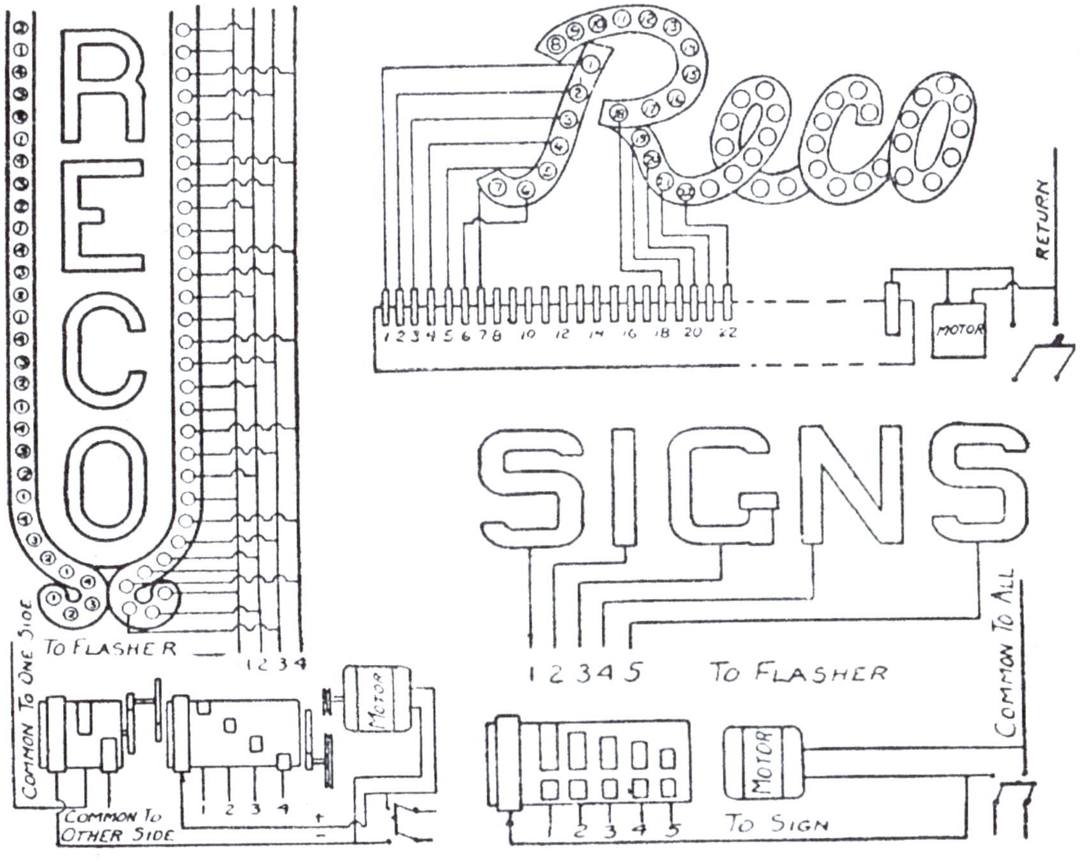

RECO
TO FLASHER
1 2 3 4
COMMON TO ONE SIDE
COMMON TO OTHER SIDE
MOTOR
Reco
RETURN
MOTOR
SIGNS
1 2 3 4 5 TO FLASHER
COMMON TO ALL
MOTOR
TO SIGN

Transformers

Conventional transformers consist of wound copper wire in stages across an iron core, and use the principle of magnetic induction to increase voltage. Conventional transformers are known to be very reliable, but are heavy and bulky. A more recent innovation is the electronic transformer, which operates using a series of electronic components, including rectifiers, transistors, and inverters to create a high frequency charge. They are much lighter and inconspicuous.

Transformers are chosen based on their application with a consideration of various factors. Length of tubing and tube diameter dictate the required voltage to keep a steady discharge. High voltage electricity is known to "leak", so secondary wires must be kept short. Transformers are usually mounted behind the signs, within or behind channel letters, or along the building's roof or facade.

The standard operating current for neon transformers in Japan is 20 milliampere. Most signs use the conventional 15,000-volt transformer or 9000-volt electronic transformers. In addition, lower voltage 1000-volt electronic transformers are often used for animation sequencing, dimming, and various other special uses.

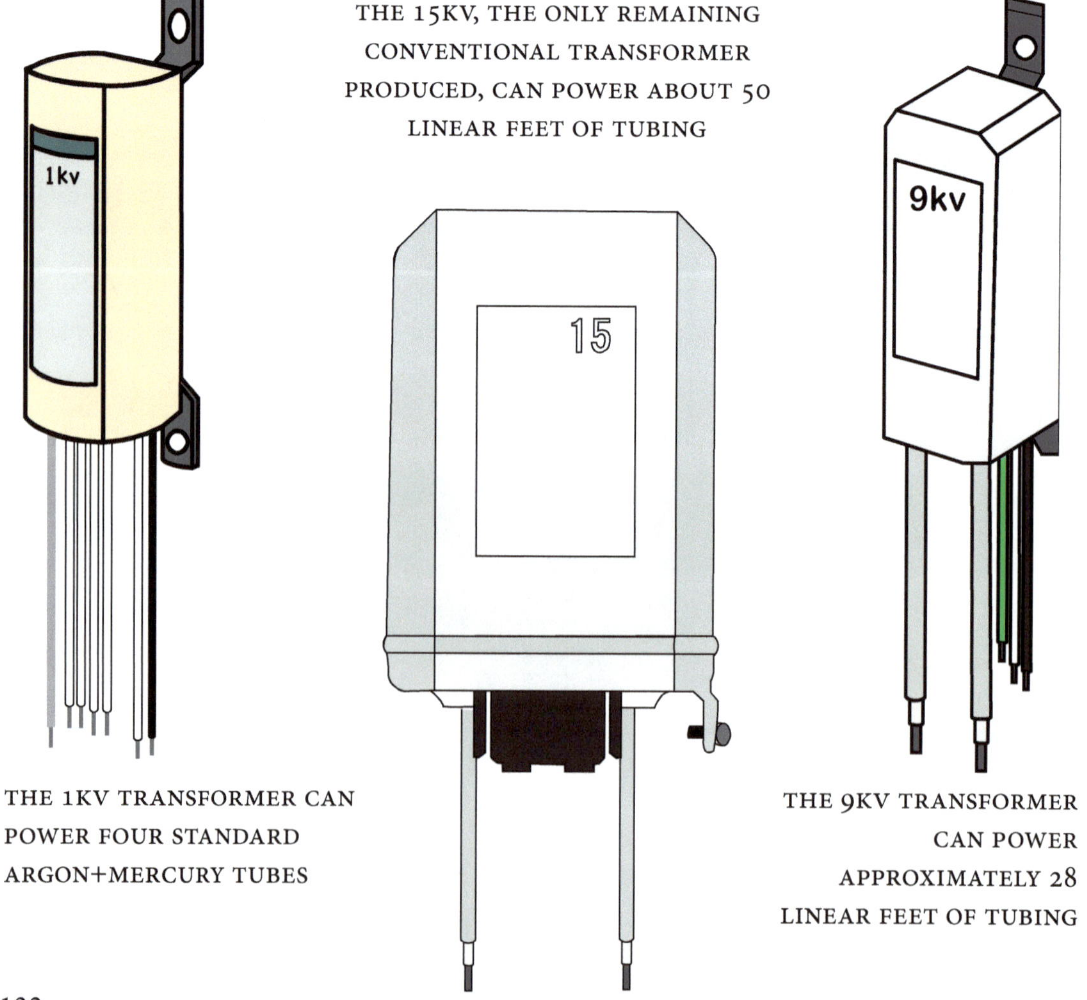

THE 15KV, THE ONLY REMAINING CONVENTIONAL TRANSFORMER PRODUCED, CAN POWER ABOUT 50 LINEAR FEET OF TUBING

THE 1KV TRANSFORMER CAN POWER FOUR STANDARD ARGON+MERCURY TUBES

THE 9KV TRANSFORMER CAN POWER APPROXIMATELY 28 LINEAR FEET OF TUBING

カットアウトはついています
配線が簡単な
エスライトネオントランス
スーパーコンパクト形

〈スーパーコンパクト形の特長〉

■ケースを深絞りとしましたので、上蓋がなくなりスマートになり、併せて雨水が浸入しなくなりました。

■縦、横、斜めのいずれの方向にお取り付けいただいても性能は安定しています。ただし、ブッシング及びカットアウトスイッチ部分に、雨水が直接かかるような取り付け方はおさけ下さい。

■ネオン管の破損などで長時間にわたり二次側が無負荷になっても、トランスはこわれません。

■従来のコンパウンドより放熱性がよく、そのうえ高温度においても溶融しない樹脂系のコンパウンドに変更しました。そのため、コイルの温度上昇が低くなり、充塡物が外部に流れ出ることがなくなり、寿命が長くなりました。

■カットアウトスイッチを用いた完全な保護機構付きです。一次配線は端子にビス止めするだけでよいので、極めて簡単です。カットアウトスイッチを開けば確実に電流を遮断しますので、サインの保守、点検が安全に行えます。

■ハンガーによる吊り下げ取付方式ですから、取付工事が簡単です。

エスライト　ネオントランス　定価表

機種	一次電圧	
	100V用	200V用
15,000V	8,500円	9,000円
12,000	8,000	8,500
9,000	7,400	7,900
6,000	6,800	7,300
3,000	6,200	6,700

上記は高力率形屋外用ネオントランスの価格でございます。

S-Light　株式会社　三陽電機製作所

総発売元　三陽商事株式会社

本社・工場：岐阜市上土居字狭間81番地
電話〈0582〉31－6311（代）

事務所：札幌事務所＜0122＞82－0838　仙台事務所＜0222＞56－7418　東京事務所＜03＞971－0106代　金沢事務所＜0762＞52－9474
大阪事務所＜06＞621－2155代　広島事務所＜0822＞32－4645　九州事務所＜092＞29－5824

Torches

Burners for bending neon glass typically use propane or natural gas, mixed with a steady flow of low-pressure air. Gas and air settings are adjustable to suit the type of glass being used. Dedicated air supplies for are often utilized to keep the flame consistent. The fire produced should be hot enough to heat the glass to a workable temperature.

The most common torch used in Japan is the vertical canon fire. The torch is versatile, as the flame is adjustable from large and bushy, to small and pinpointed. It can be used for curves, tight bends, and welds. The burner can be comfortably positioned for the glass bender to sit down while welding pieces of glass together.

Another commonly used torch is the ribbon burner, which is found in neon shops around the world. Over a foot of glass can be evenly heated at one time, which is why they are favored for making large sweeping bends such as curves.

Neon benders also use a series of hand torches for precise work. The tipping torch is used for welding units onto the processing manifold, and for sealing off tubulation after pumping. A small flame that is easily controlled is used to prevent cracking of the electrode.

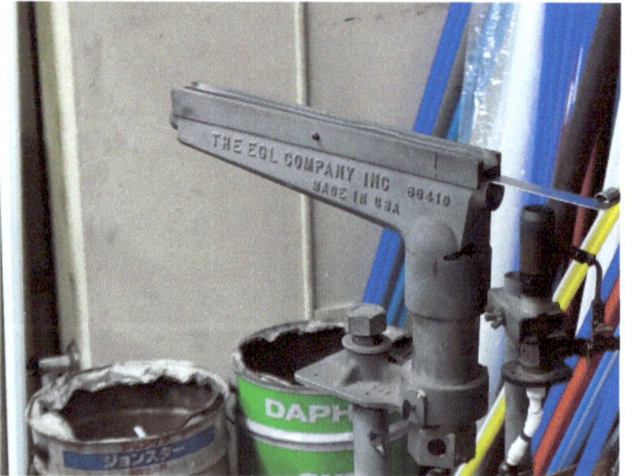

RIBBON BURNER

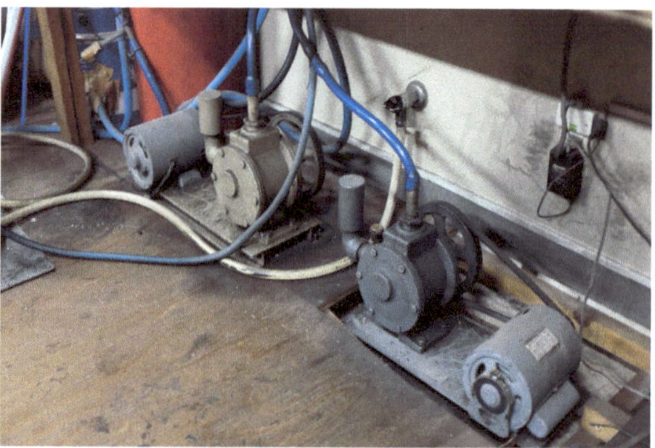
DEDICATED AIR BLOWERS

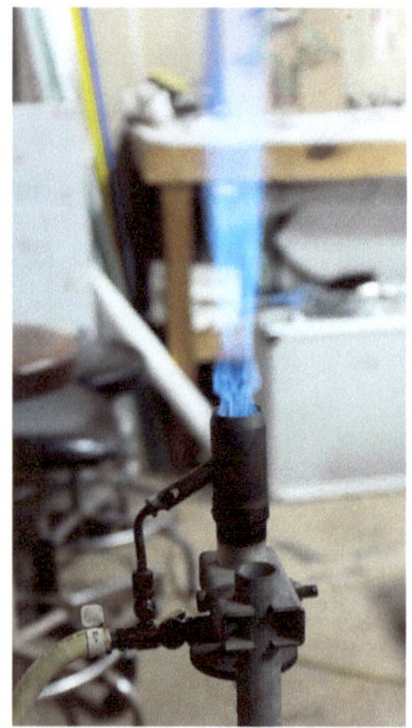
SET FOR BENDING

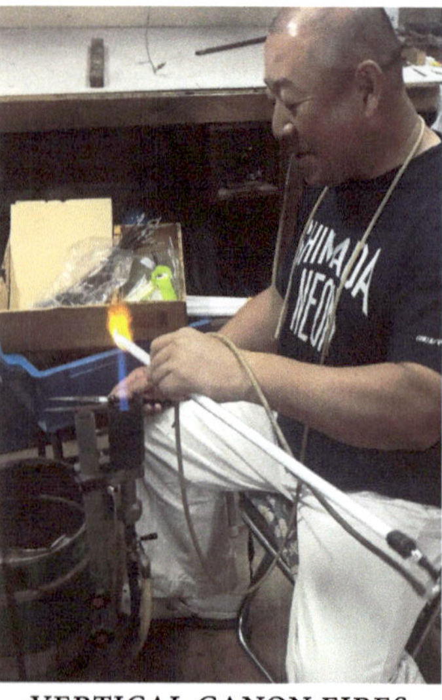
-VERTICAL CANON FIRES-

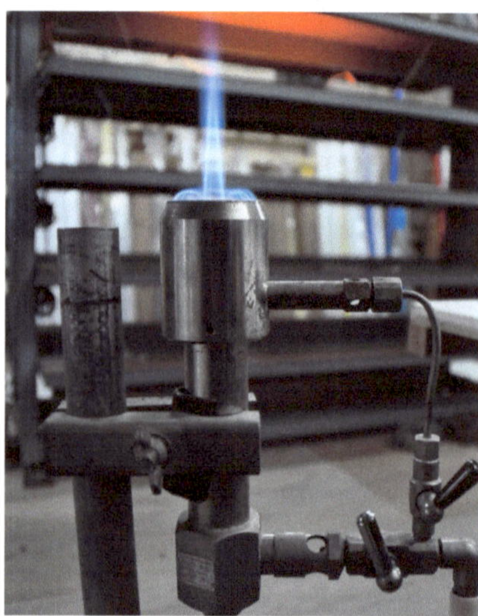
SET FOR WELDS & TIGHT BENDS

Tools

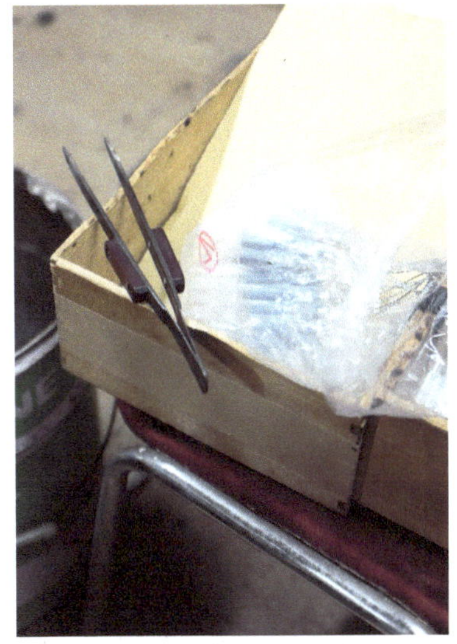

LARGE TWEEZERS

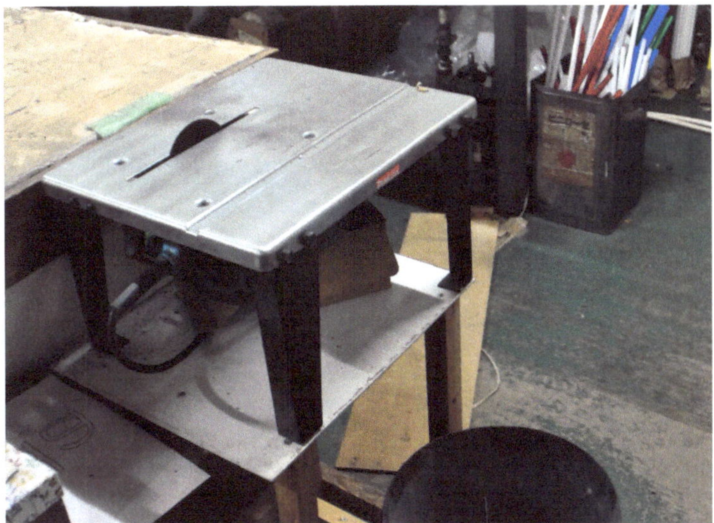

CUTOFF WHEEL FOR CUTTING GLASS TUBING

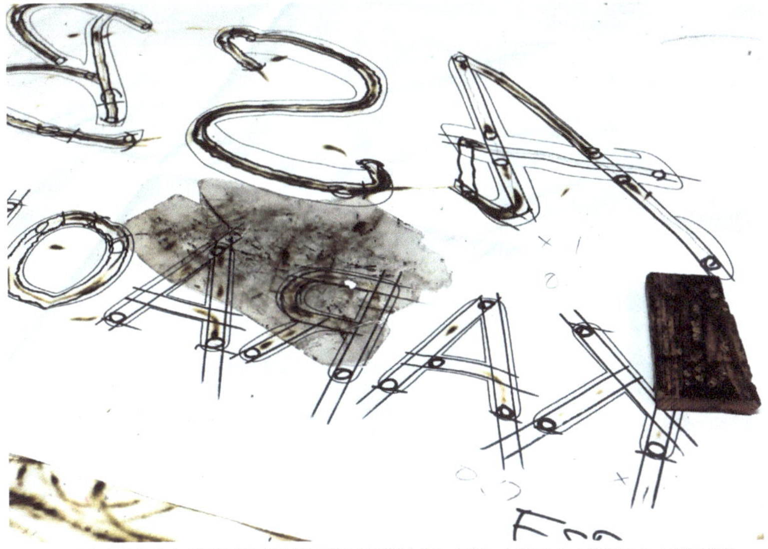

MICA IS PLACED BETWEEN HOT GLASS AND PAPER LAYOUT

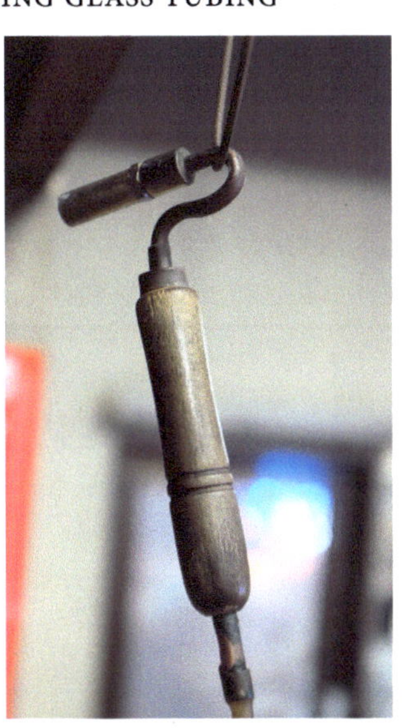

TIPPING TORCH

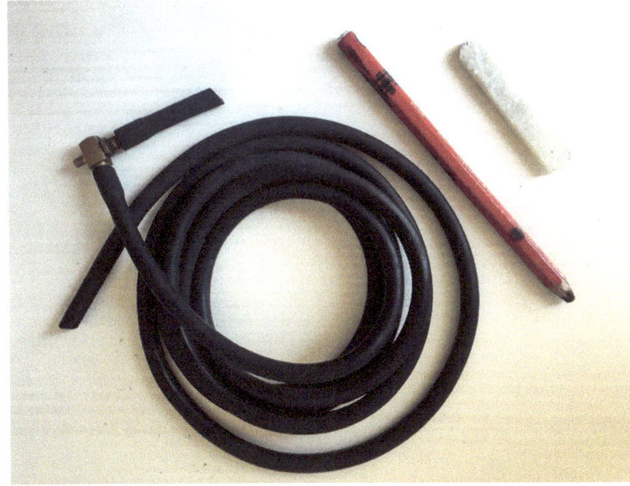

BLOW-HOSE, MARKING PENCIL AND SOAPSTONE

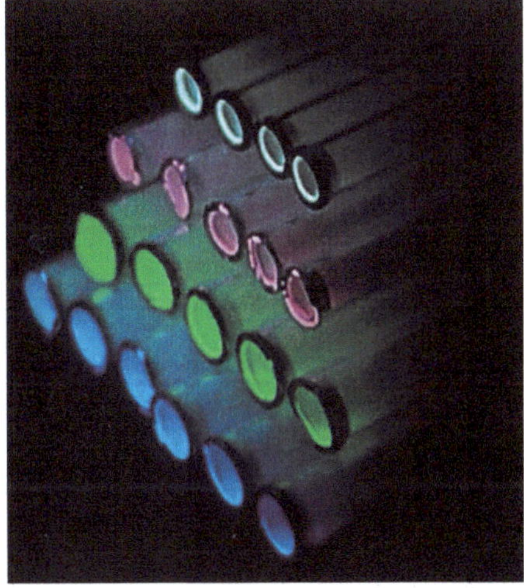

UV LAMPS SHOW TUBE COLORS

Processing Equipment

Bombarding Transformer

The bombarding transformer is used to create a high-voltage arc through the neon tube after removing air with the vacuum pump. The arc heats up the tube to approximately 250° Celsius and thoroughly bakes the electrodes until they glow red.

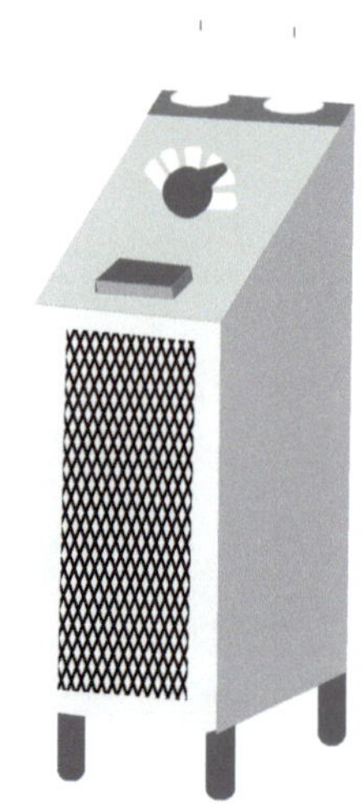

Comparable to a residential transformer on a utility pole, bombarding transformers put out anywhere from 10,000-25,000 volts. They are paired with a choke to control the secondary current within an approximate range of 100 to 800 milliampere.

The bombarding transformer is arguably the most dangerous piece of equipment in the neon shop, and many precautions should be taken to protect against electrocution.

Vacuum Pumps

Commonly used in scientific laboratories, motor driven vacuum pumps evacuate molecules of gas from within a sealed system. They are connected to the main stopcock on the processing manifold.

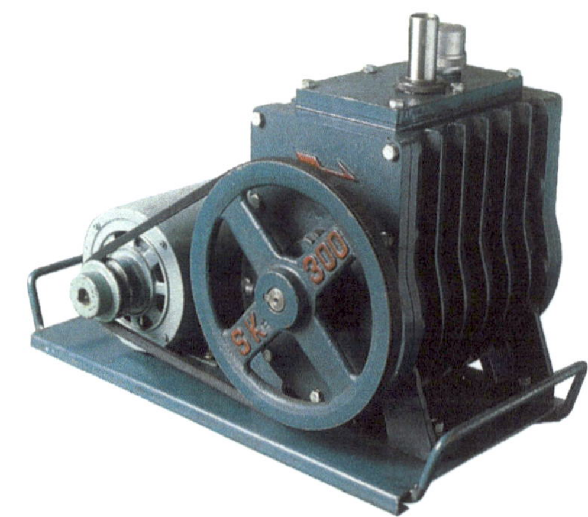

BELT DRIVE ROTARY VANE VACUUM PUMP

Secondary pumps are often utilized in line with the primary pump to achieve high vacuum at a fast rate. The most common secondary pump for neon processing systems are diffusion pumps. They operate by evaporating a high velocity silicone oil that transfers momentum to the evacuated gas molecules, thus significantly speeding up the evacuation.

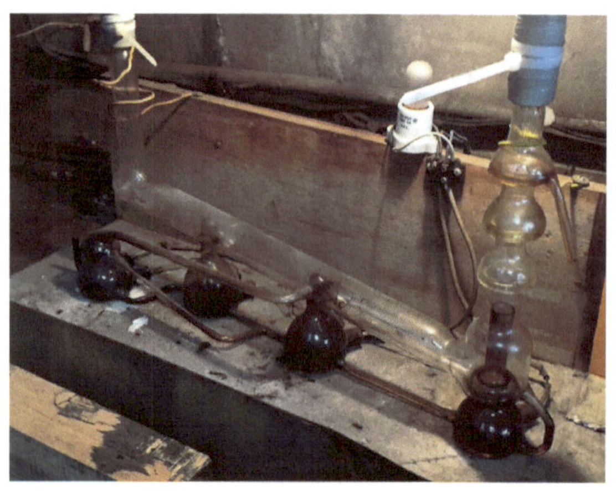

GLASS DIFFUSION PUMP

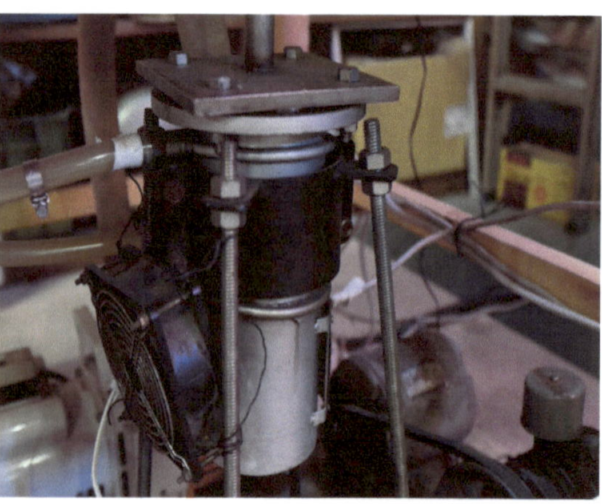

WATER-COOLED METAL DIFFUSION PUMP

The Manifold

Neon processing manifolds are typically glass or metal apparatuses that serve as the control center for processing neon tubes. Tubes are connected to the manifold via tubulation (a small glass tube welded to the neon tube). On conventional systems, stopcocks separate the multiple chambers within the manifold, allowing the operator to evacuate and administer gas to the tube with precision. Manifolds must be vacuum tight to prevent air from contaminating tubes.

Some manifolds in Japan have been optimized for mass production, allowing the operator to process up to eight tubes at the same time. Some of these systems are computerized, with automated steps such as mercury injection that help to limit human exposure. These systems are expensive and difficult to maintain, so they have become less prevalent.

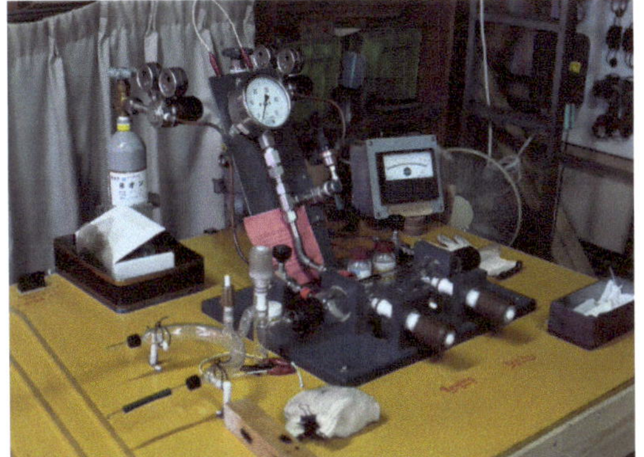

STANDARD MANIFOLD

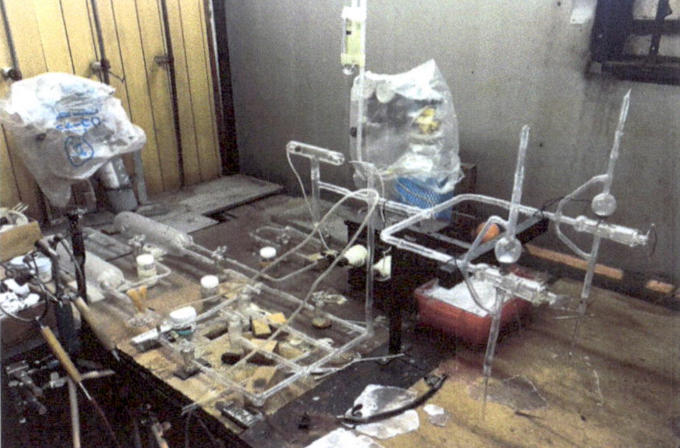

OLD-STYLE MANIFOLD

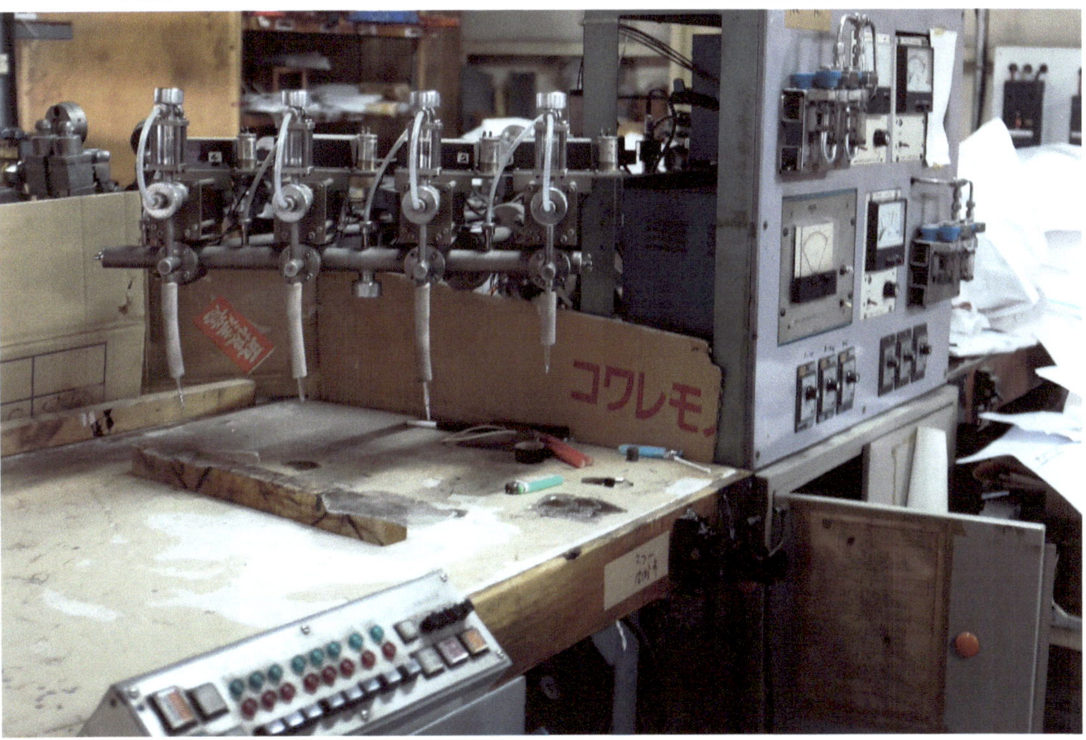

COMPUTERIZED MANIFOLD SYSTEM

Gallery: Neon in Japan 2020

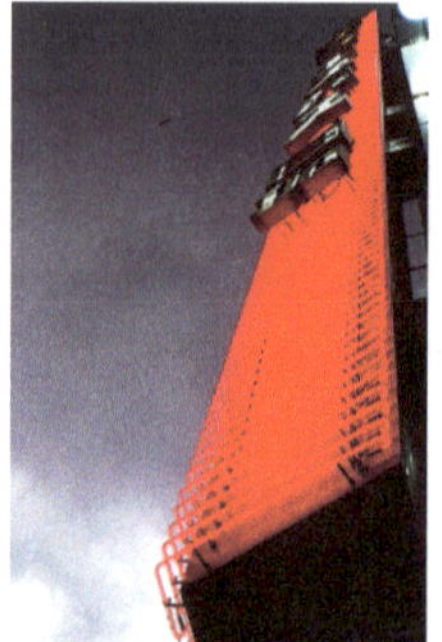
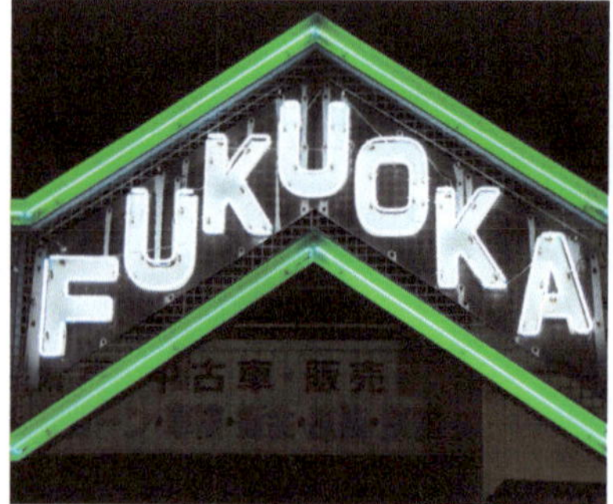

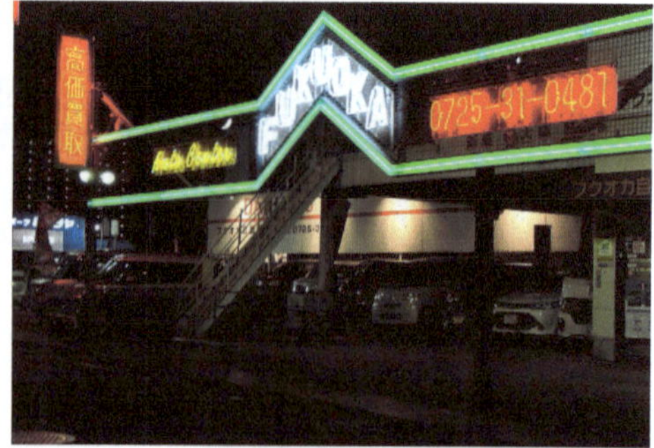

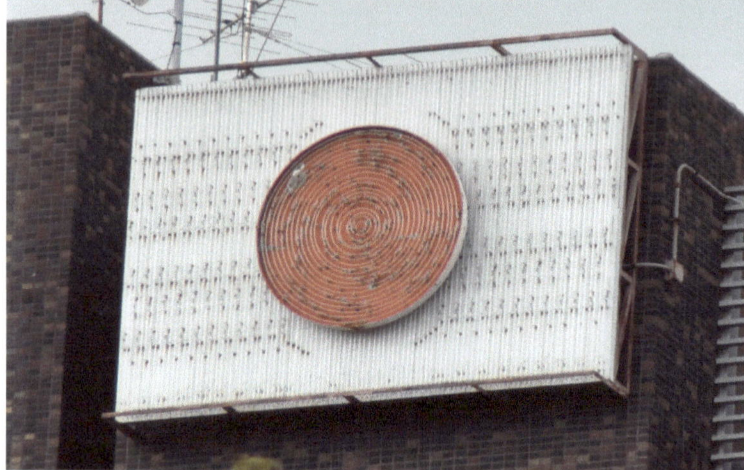
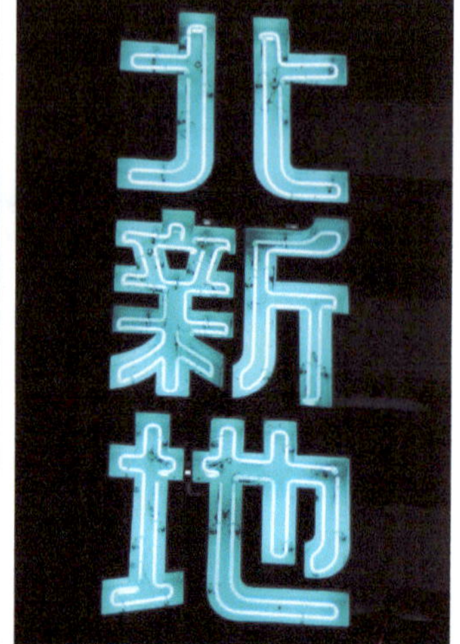

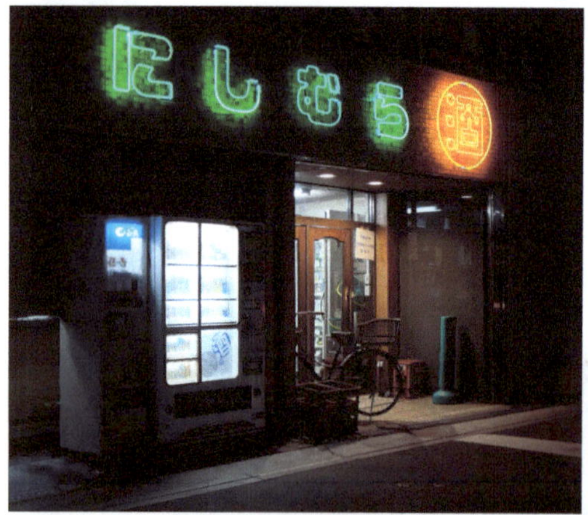

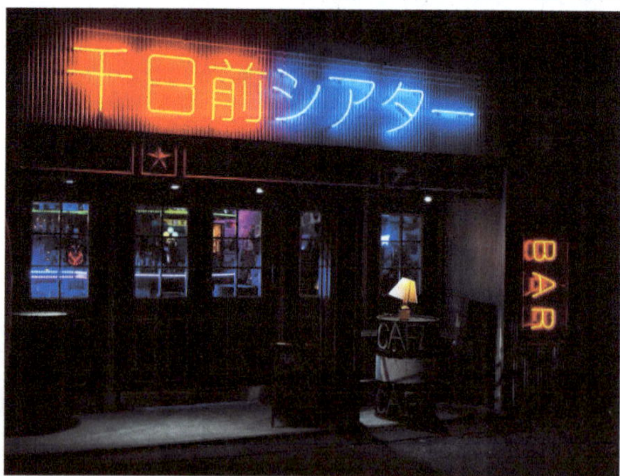

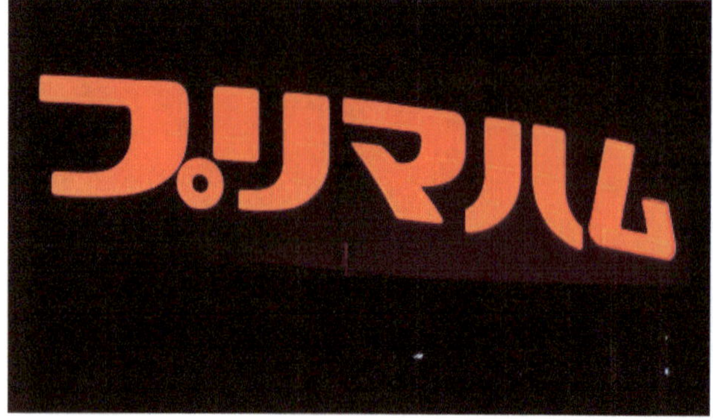

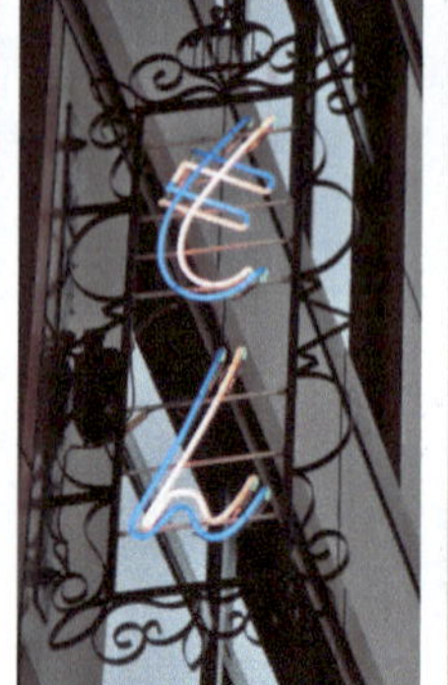
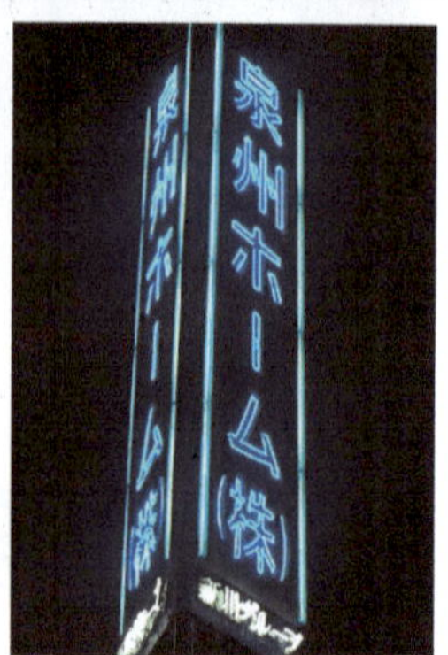

Super Tamade Grocery Store

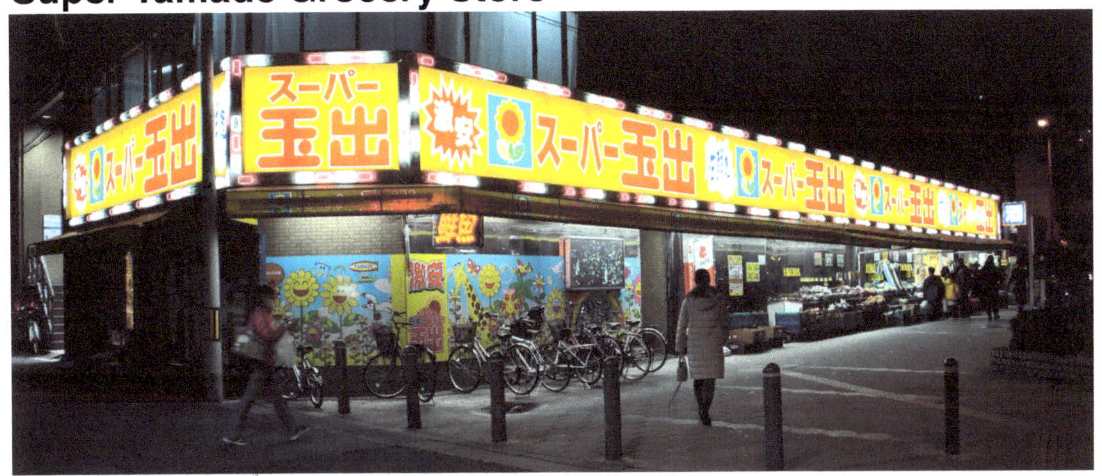

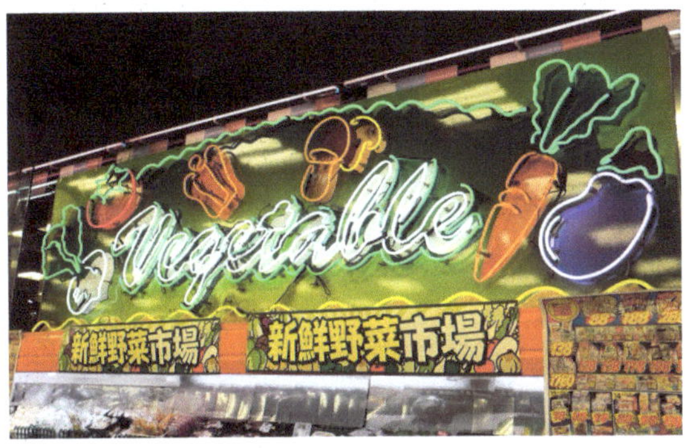

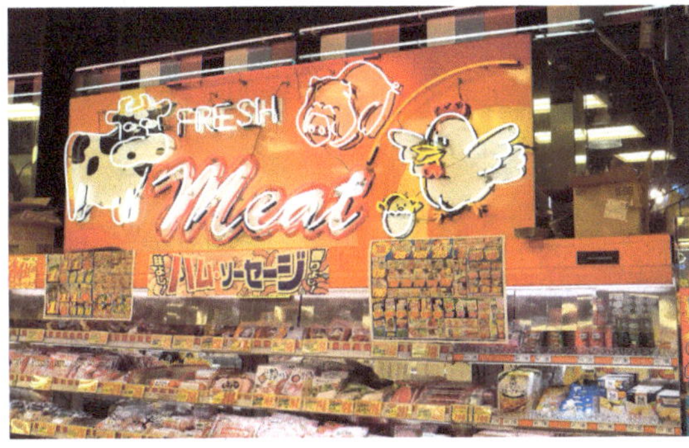

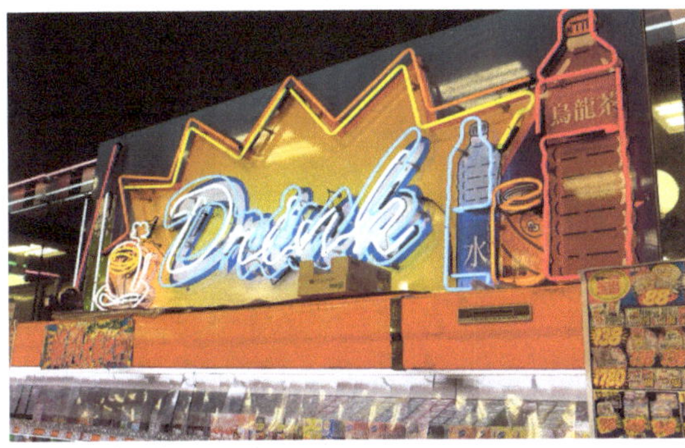

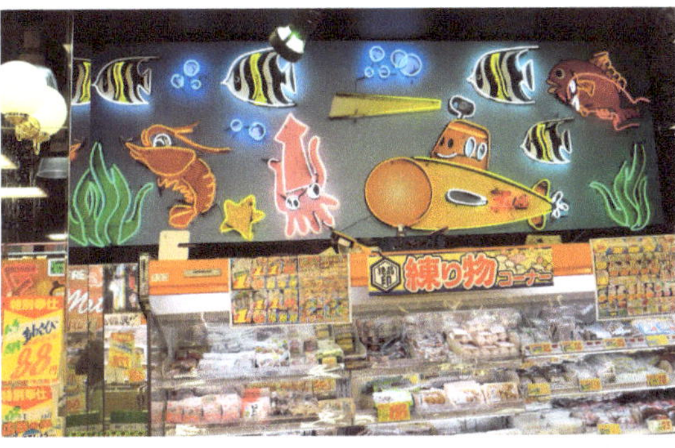

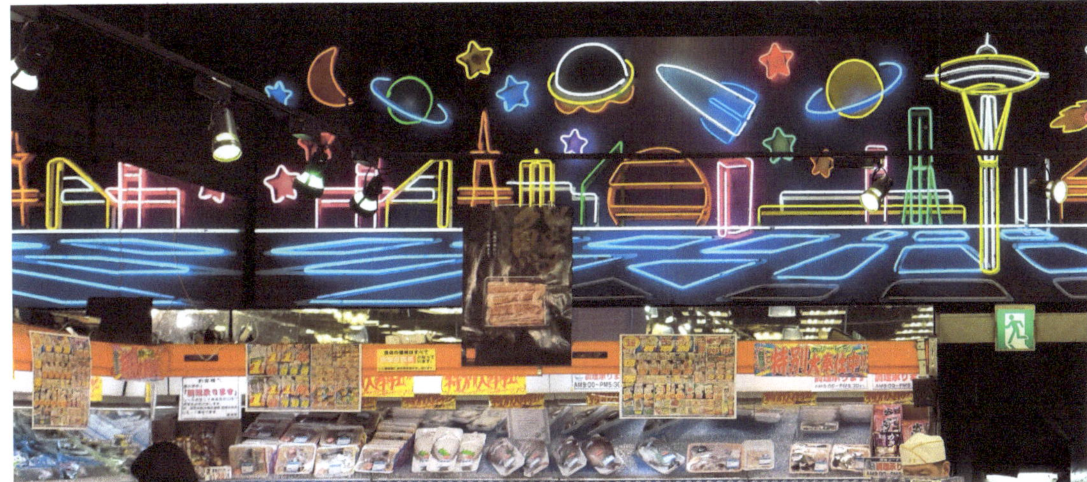

Restaurants

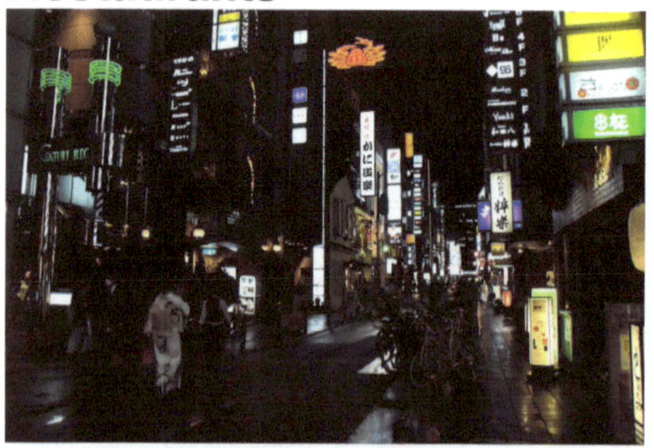

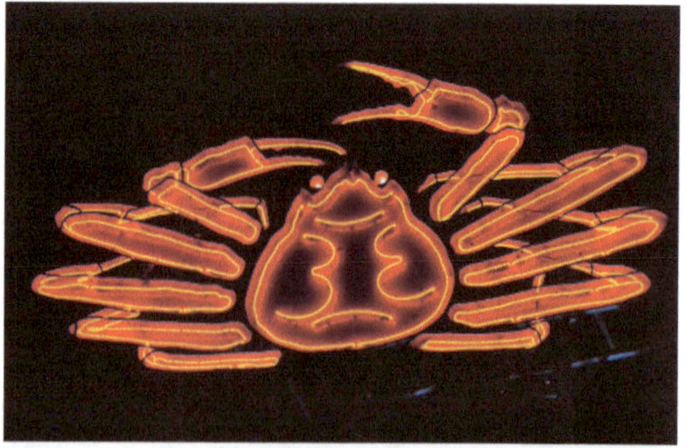

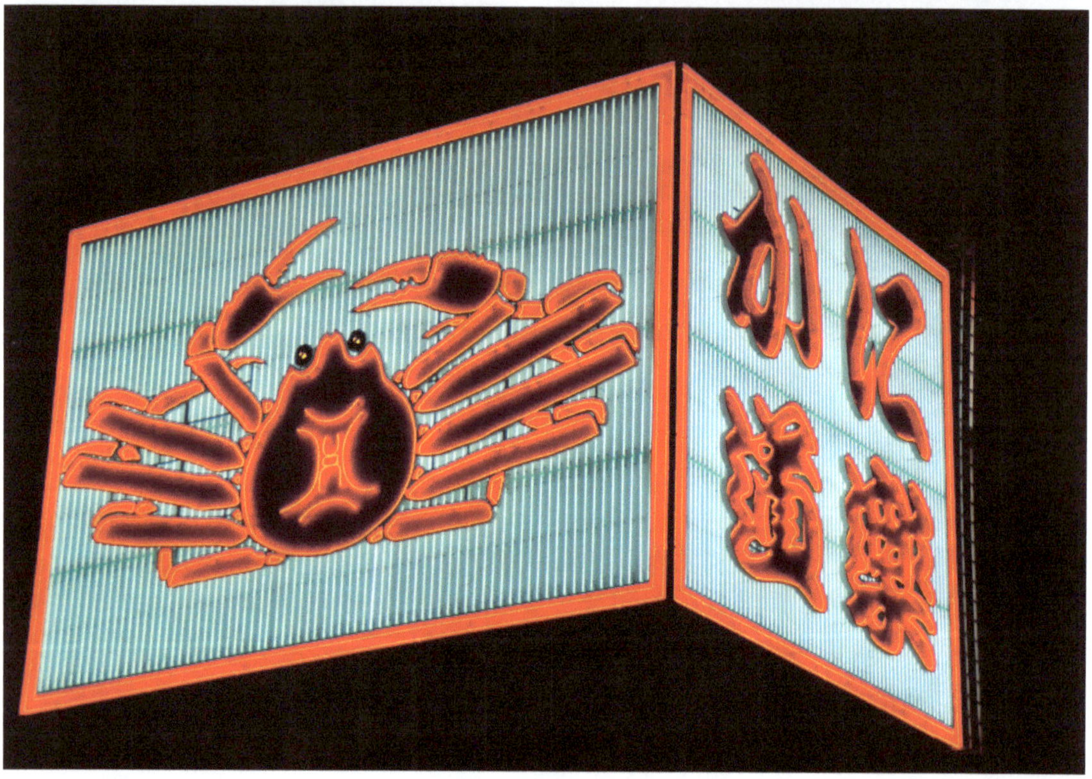

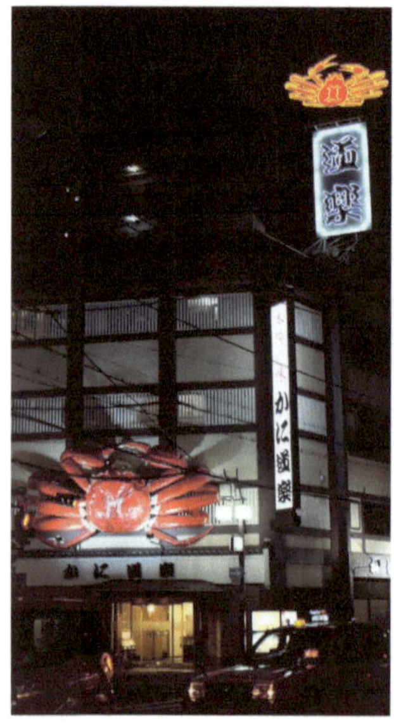

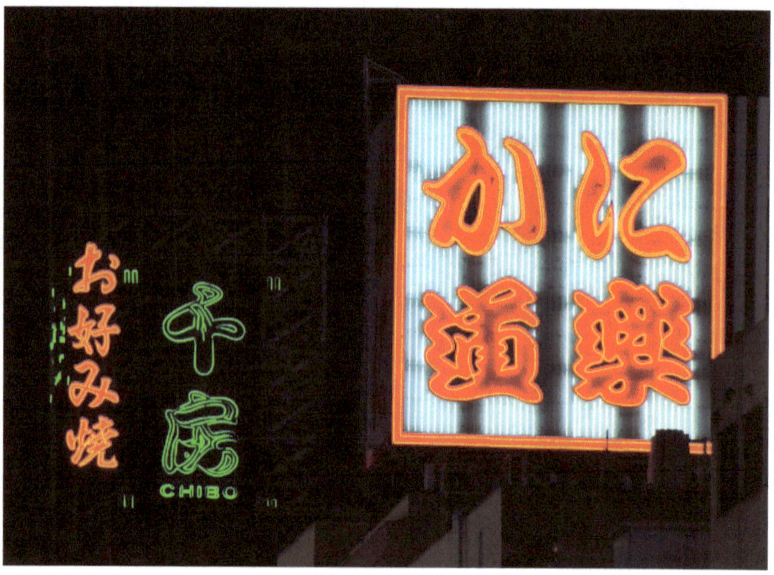

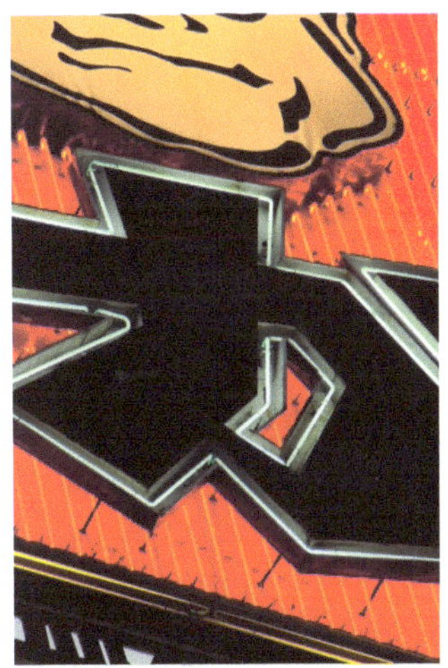

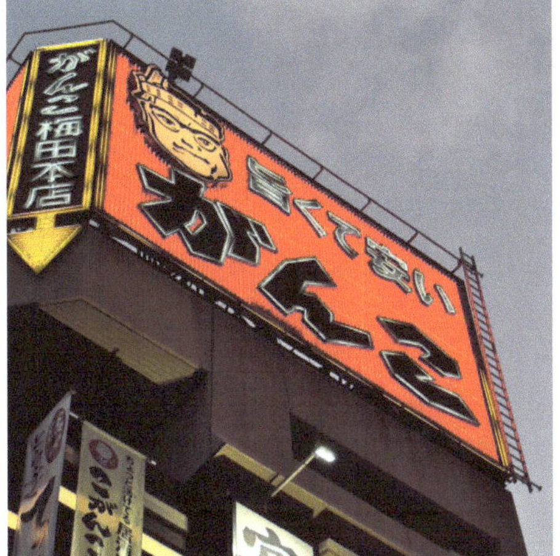
がんこ梅田本店
旨くて安い
がんこ

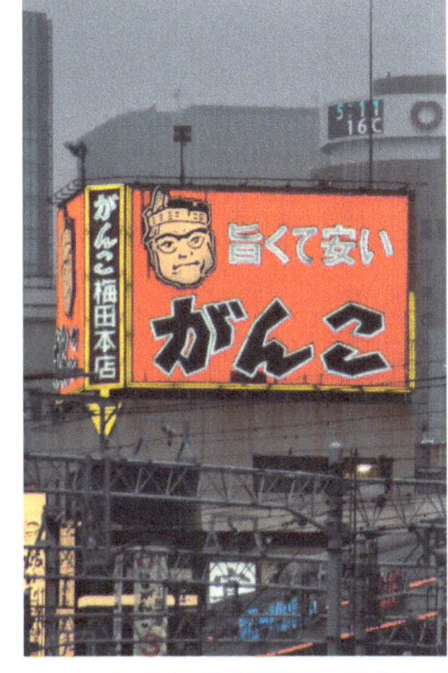
がんこ梅田本店
旨くて安い
がんこ

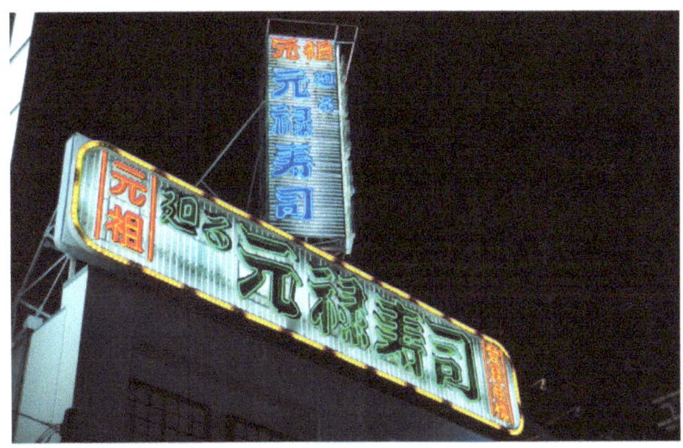
元祖
元禄寿司
元祖
元禄寿司

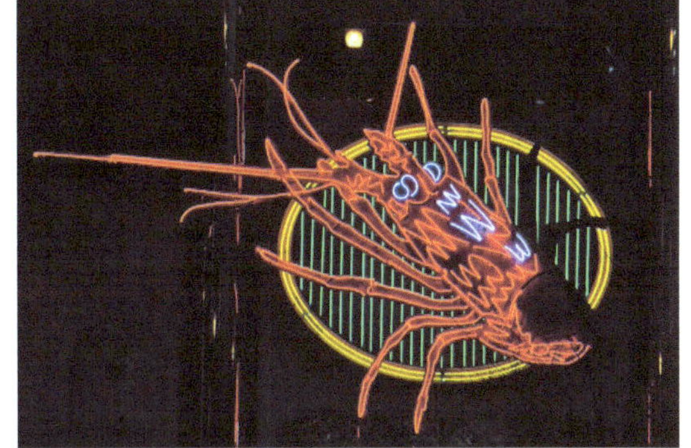

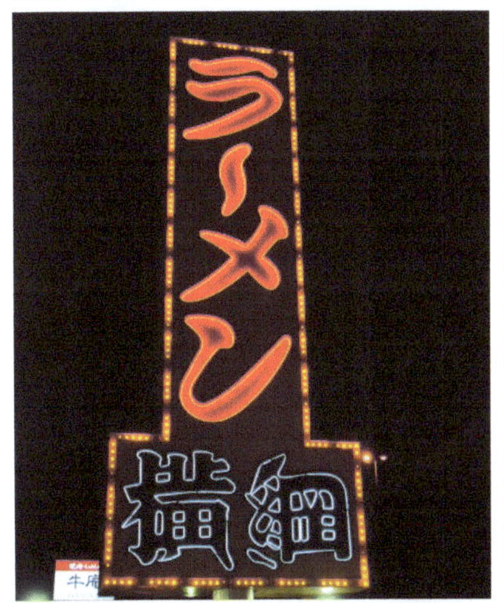
ラーメン
横綱

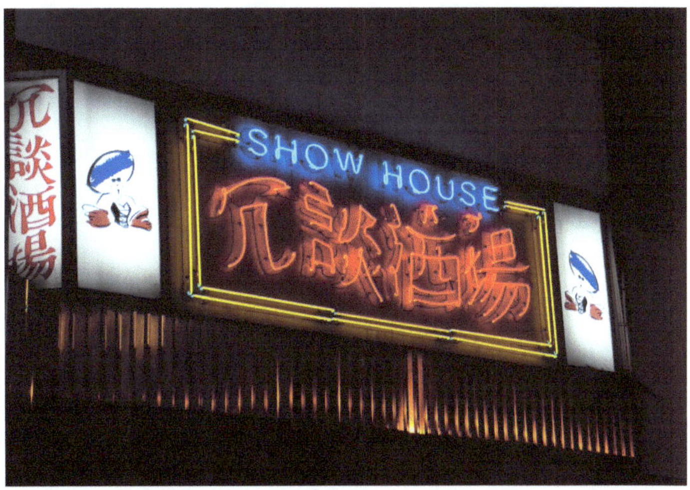
冗談酒場
SHOW HOUSE
冗談酒場

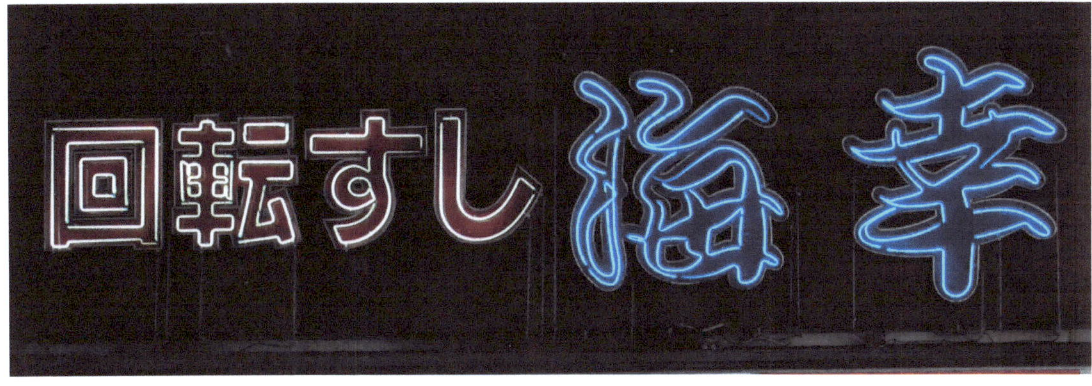
回転すし
海幸

Entertainment: Karaoke and Pachinko

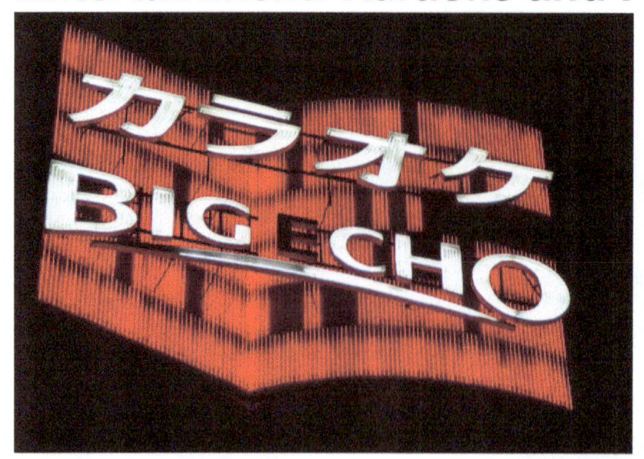

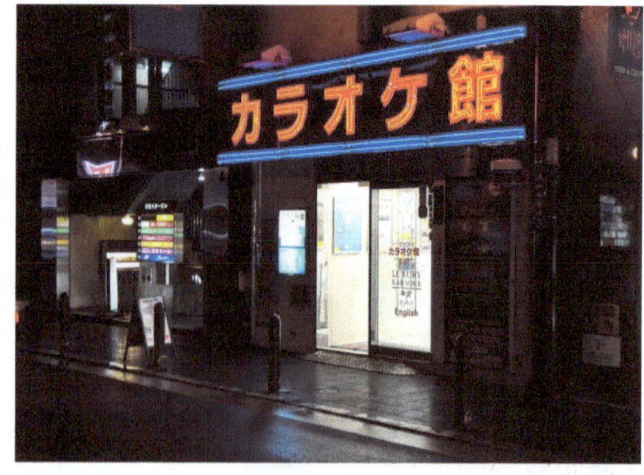

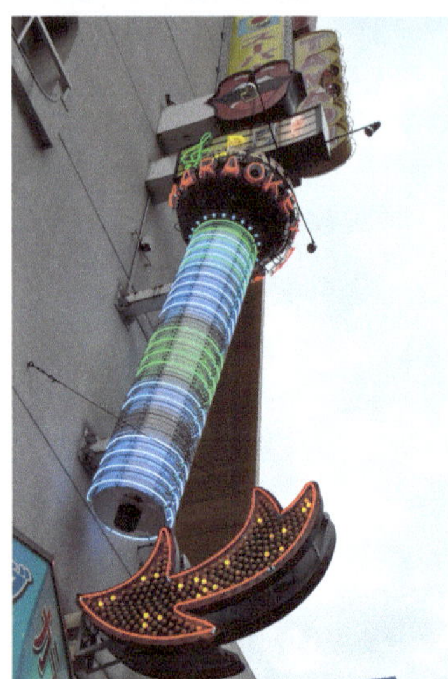

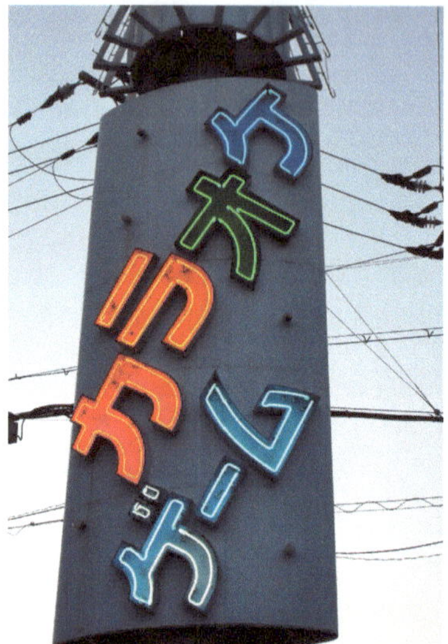

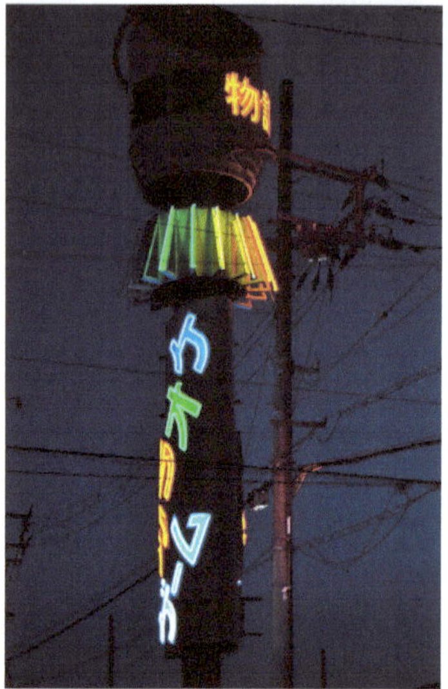

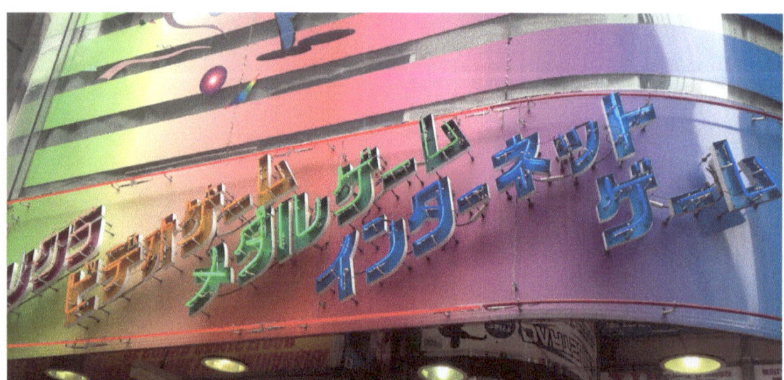

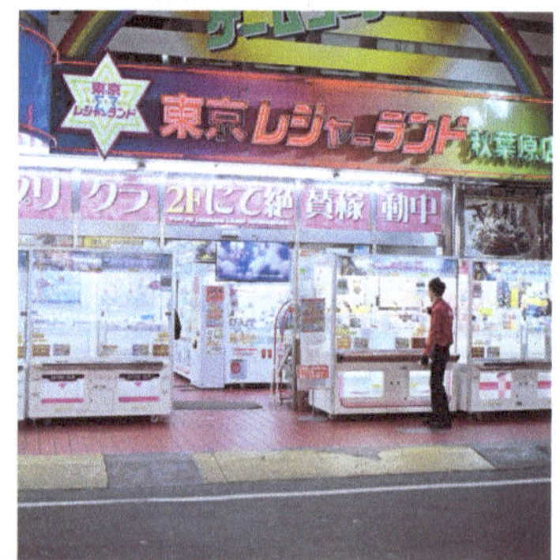

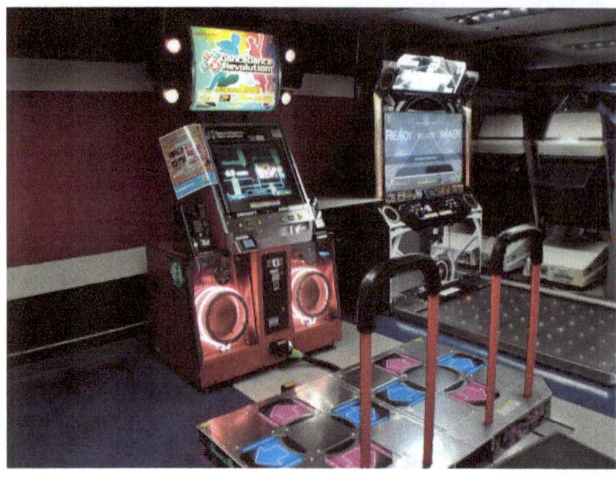

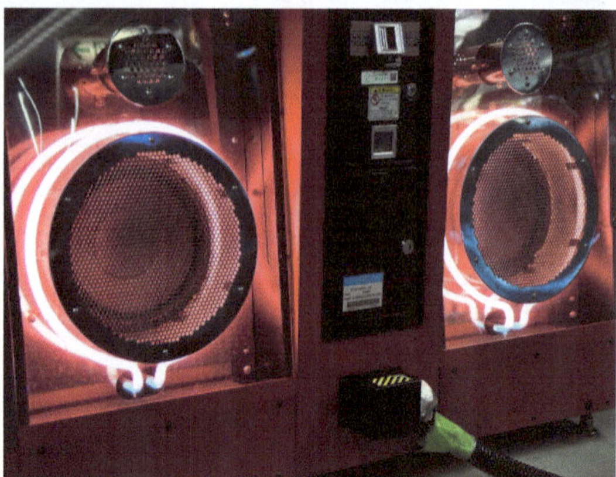

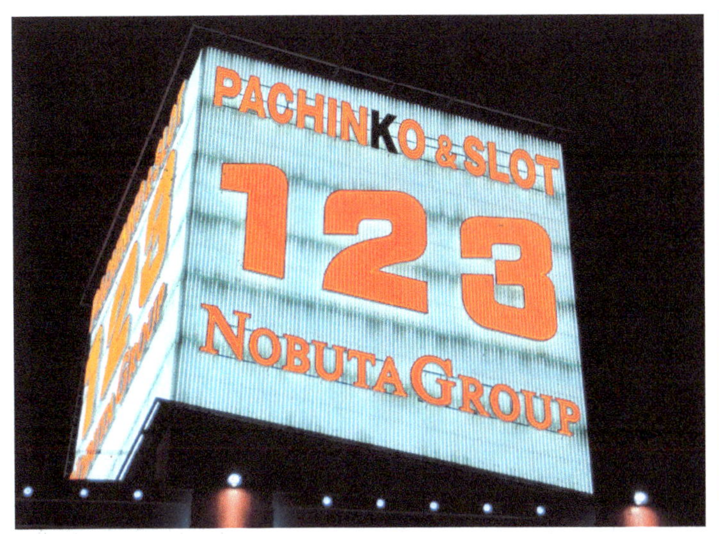
PACHINKO & SLOT
123
NOBUTA GROUP

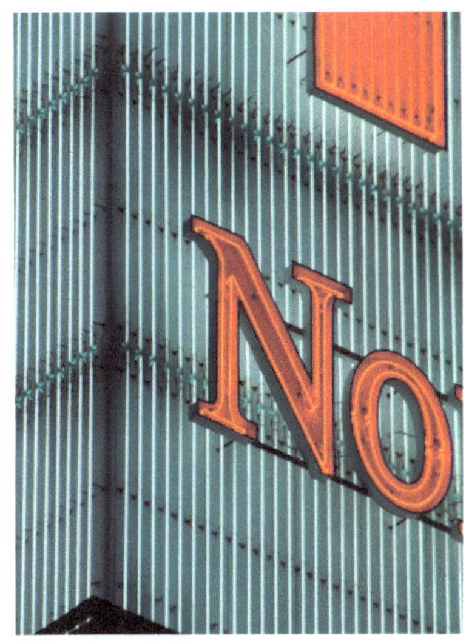

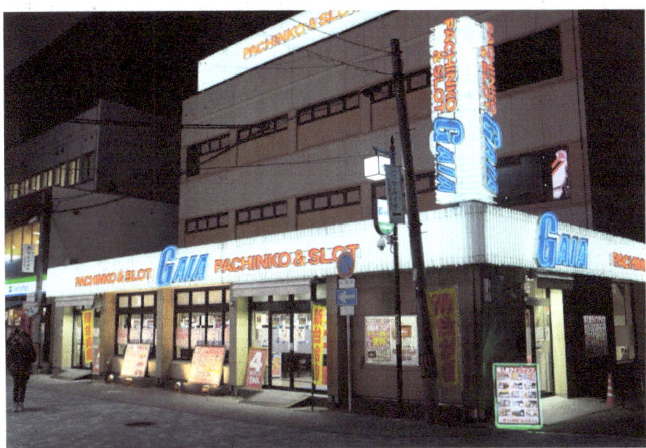
PACHINKO & SLOT
GAIA
PACHINKO & SLOT
GAIA
PACHINKO & SLOT
GAIA

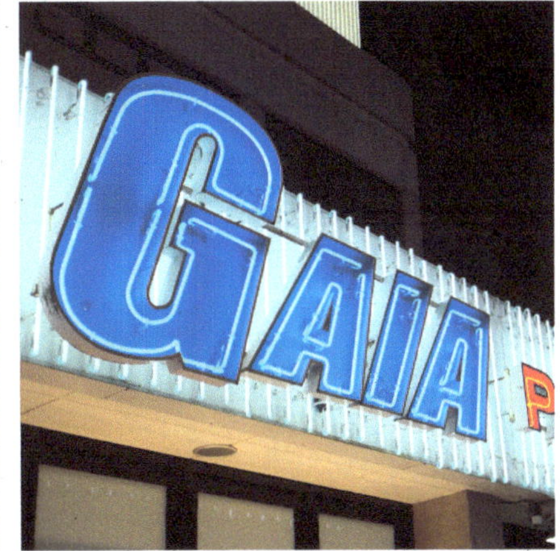
GAIA

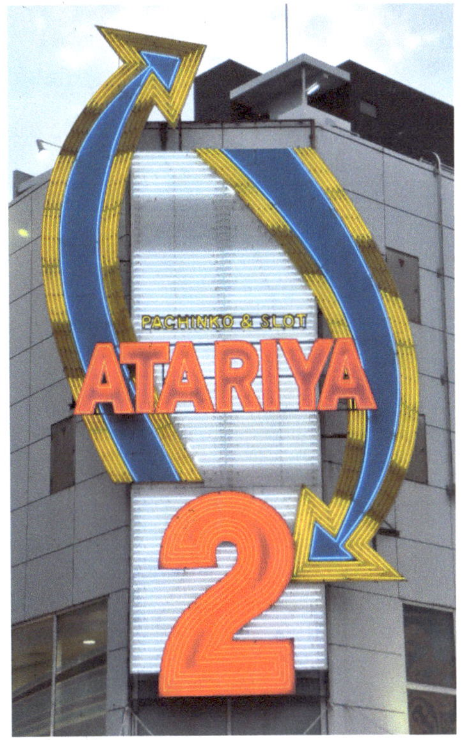
PACHINKO & SLOT
ATARIYA
2

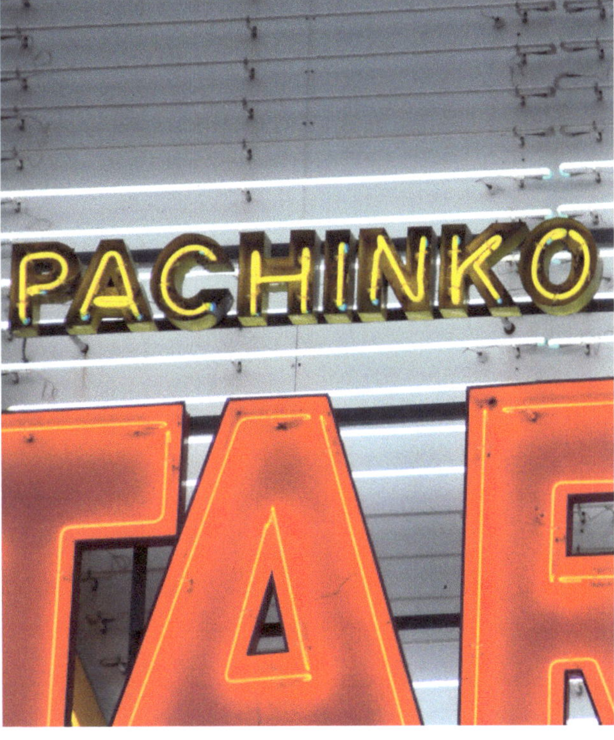
PACHINKO

Various Corporations

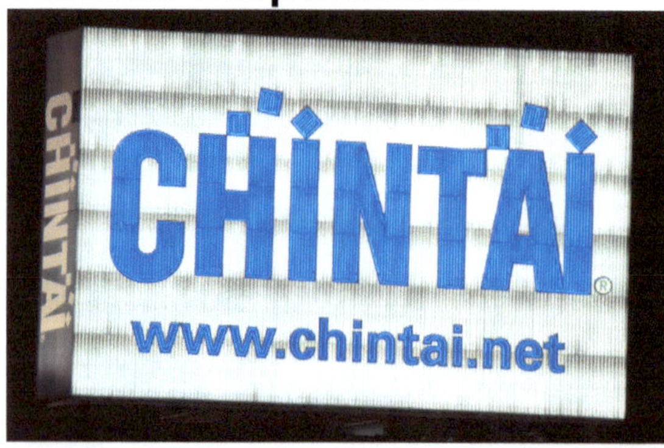

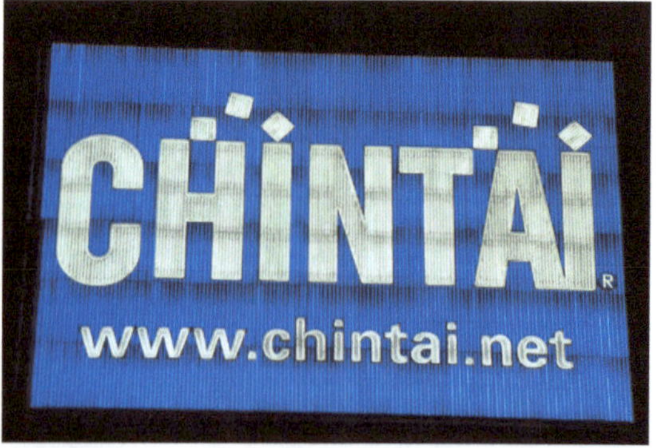

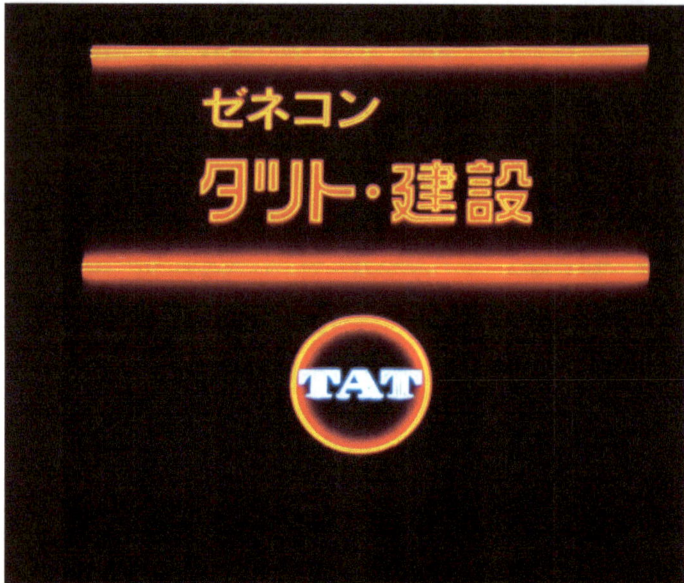

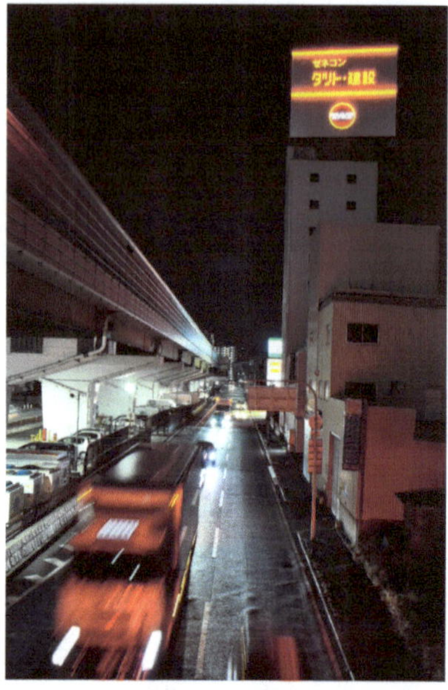

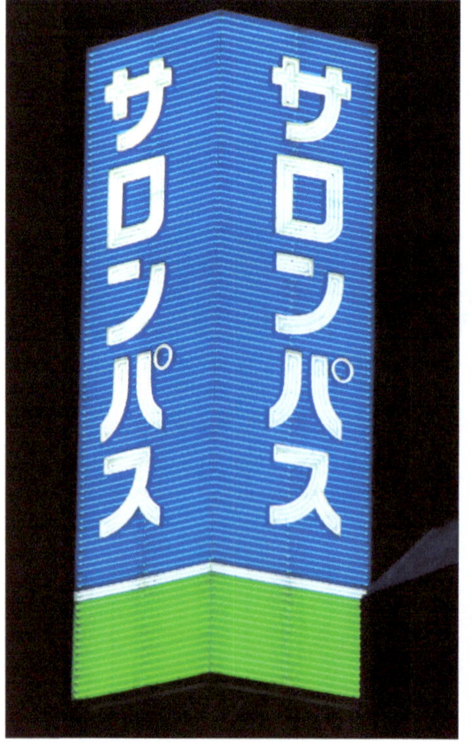

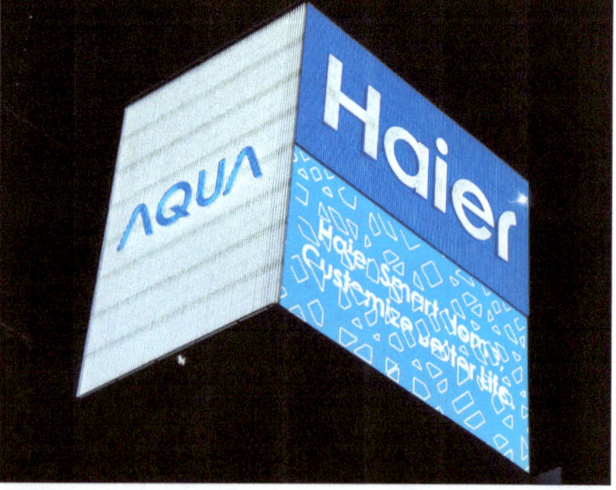

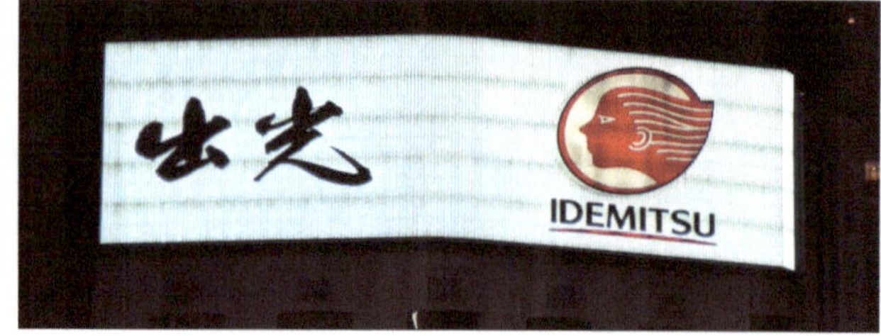

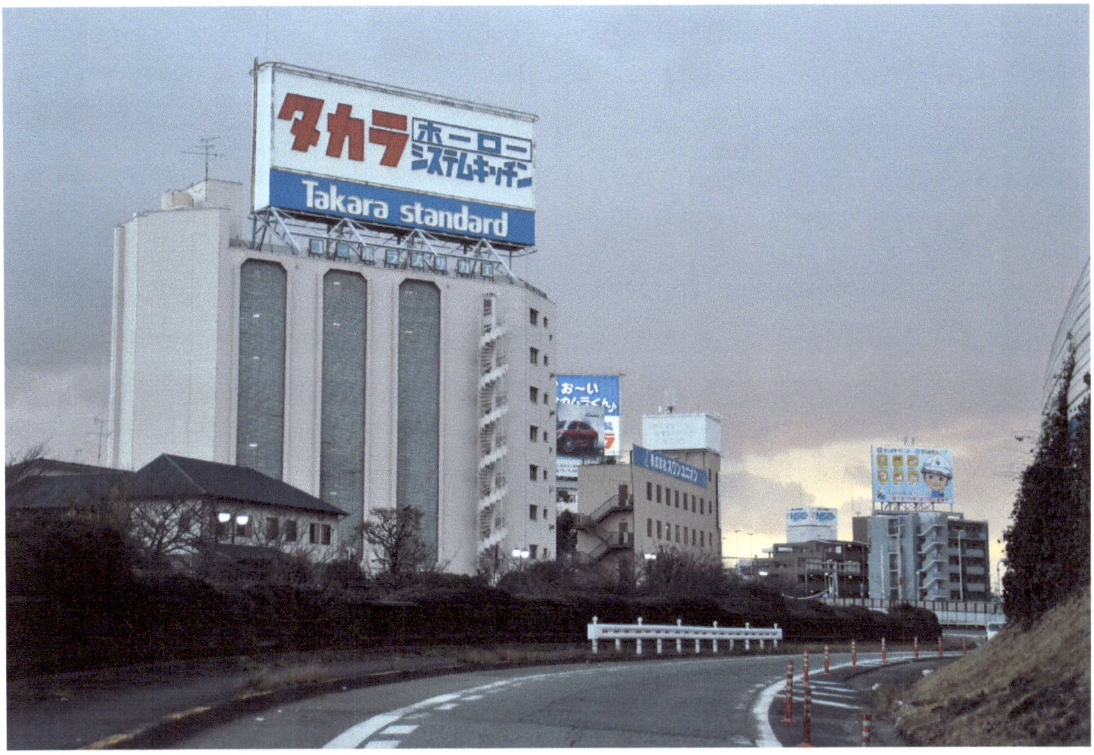

タカラ
ホーロー
システムキッチン
Takara standard
お〜い
オカムラくん♪

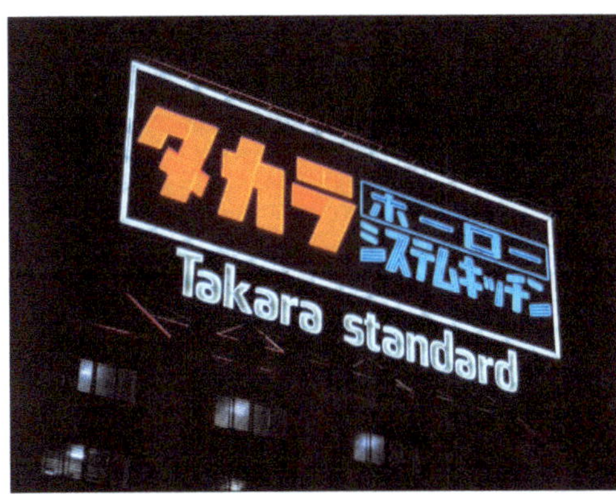
タカラ
ホーロー
システムキッチン
Takara standard

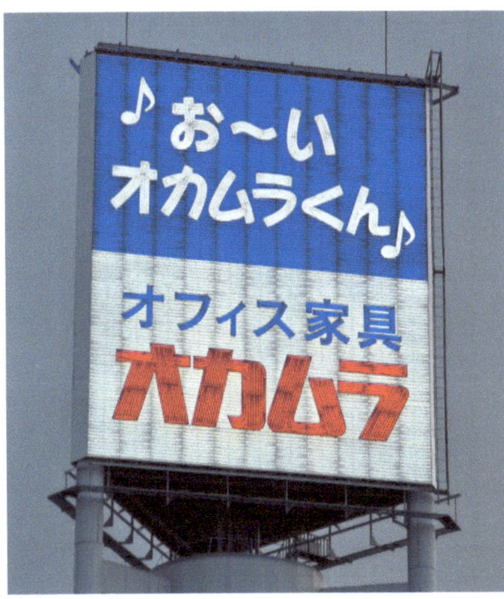
♪お〜い
オカムラくん♪
オフィス家具
オカムラ

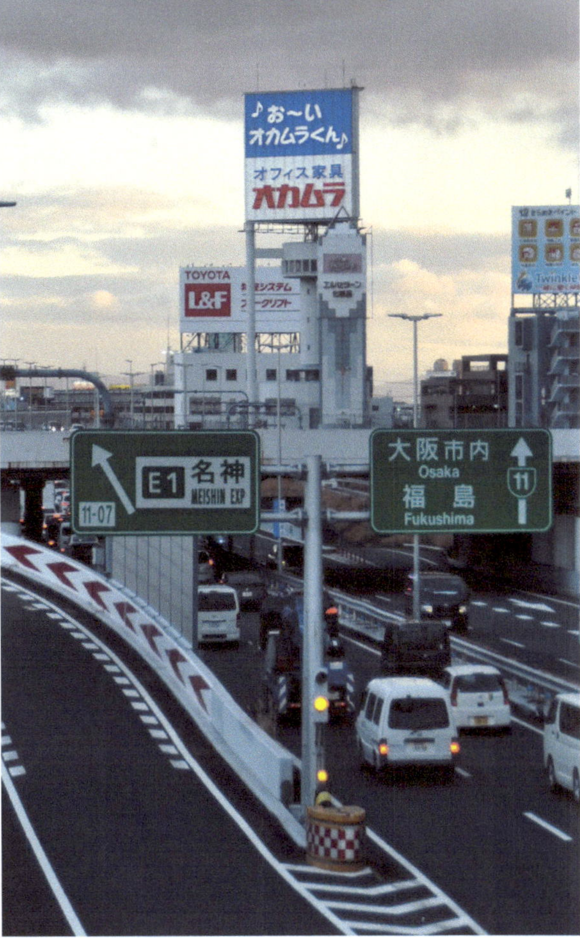
♪お〜い
オカムラくん♪
オフィス家具
オカムラ
TOYOTA
L&F
E1 名神
MEISHIN EXP
11-07
大阪市内
Osaka
福島
Fukushima
11

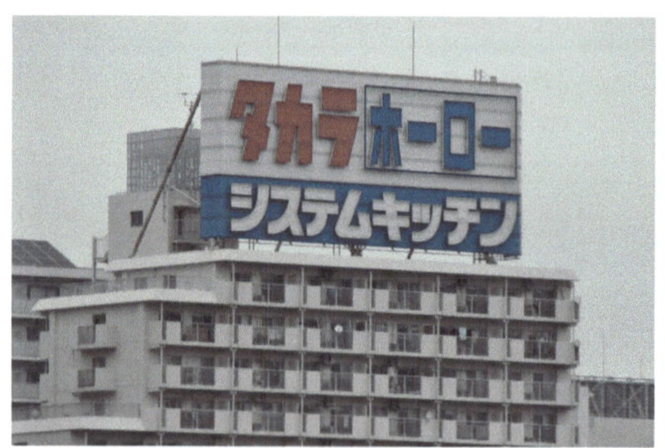
タカラ ホーロー
システムキッチン

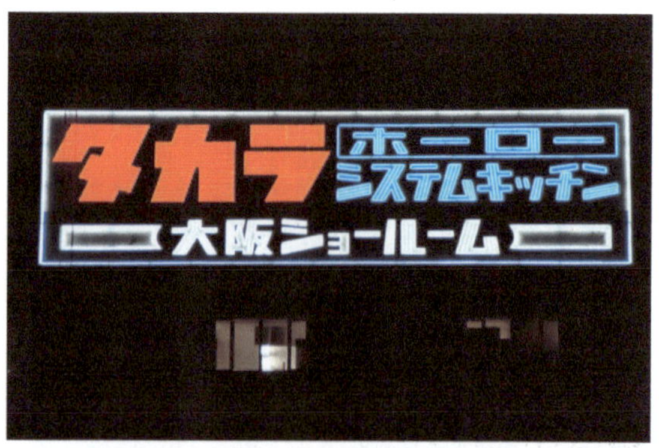
タカラ ホーロー
システムキッチン
大阪ショールーム

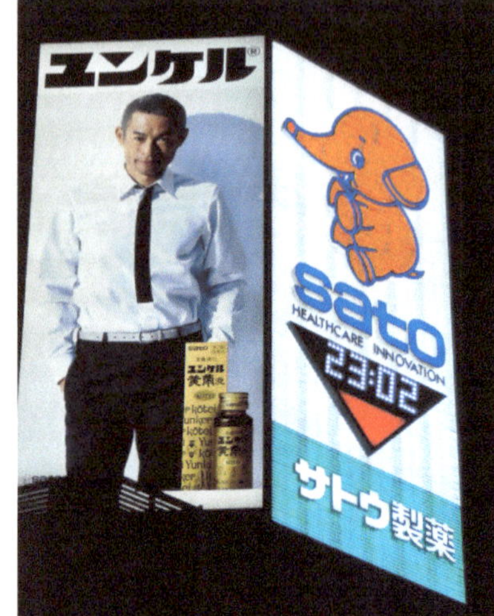
ユンケル
sato
HEALTHCARE INNOVATION
23:02
サトウ製薬

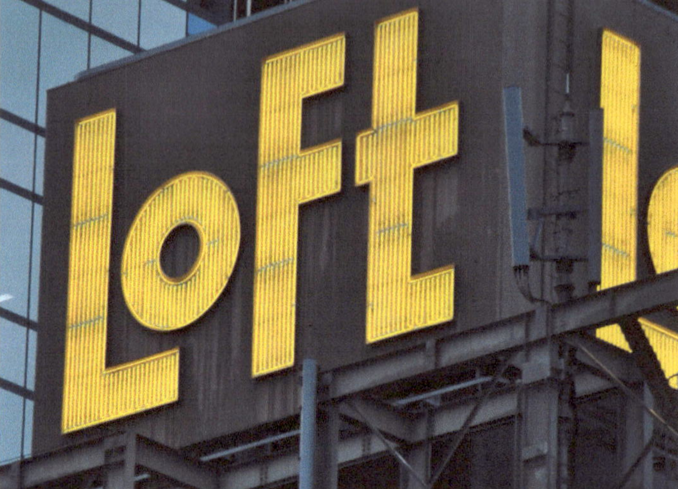
LoFt

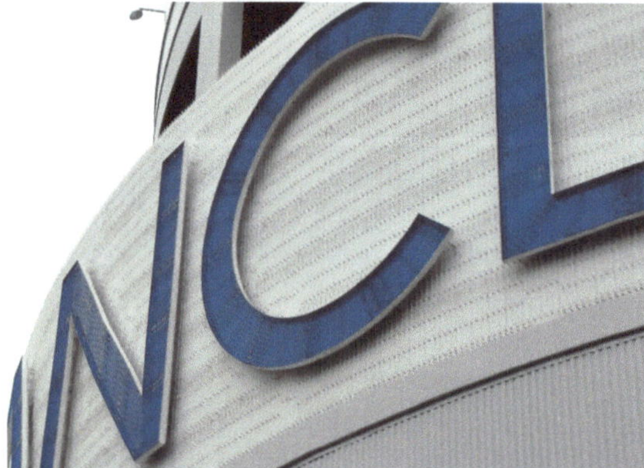
NCL

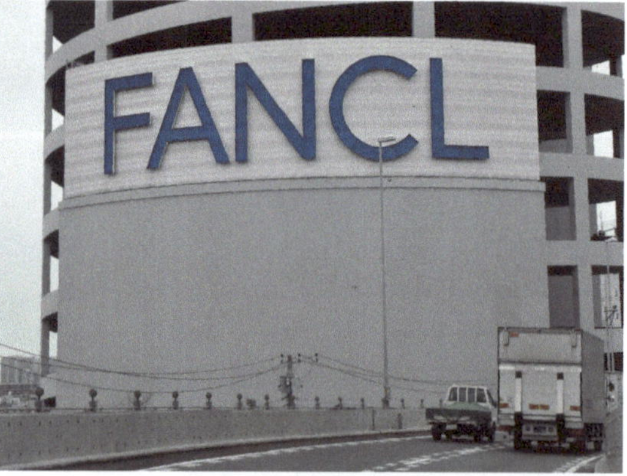
FANCL

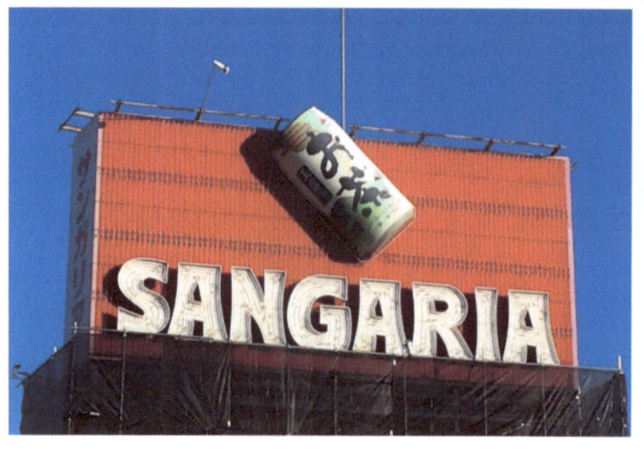
SANGARIA

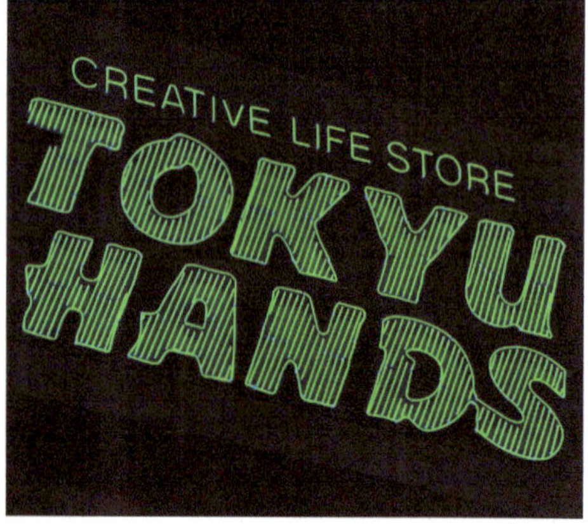
CREATIVE LIFE STORE
TOKYU
HANDS

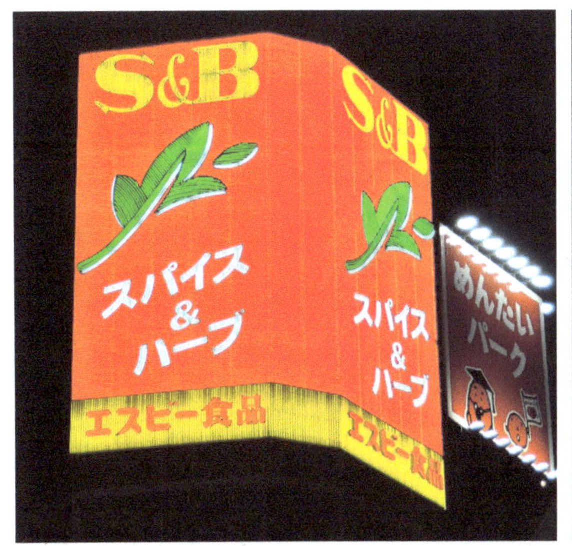
S&B
スパイス
&
ハーブ
エスビー食品
S&B
スパイス
&
ハーブ
エスビー食品
めんたい
パーク

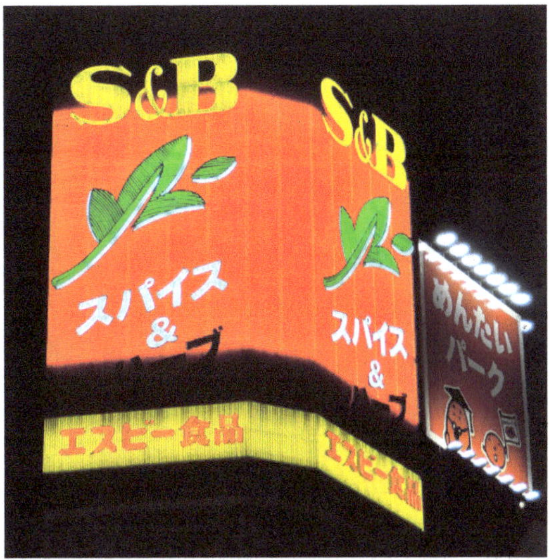
S&B
スパイス
&
エスビー食品
S&B
スパイス
&
エスビー食品
めんたい
パーク

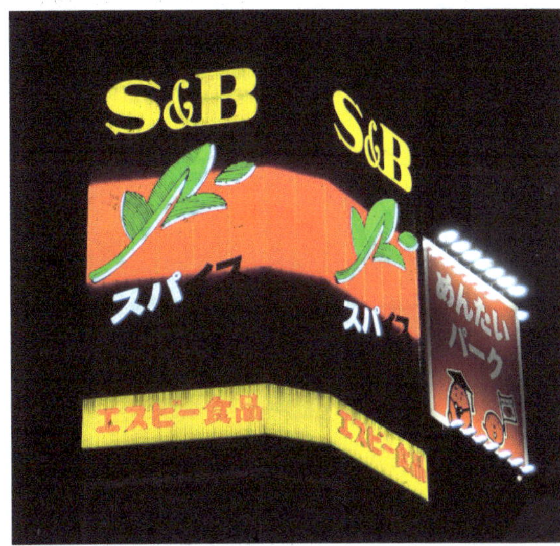
S&B
S&B
エスビー食品
エスビー食品
めんたい
パーク

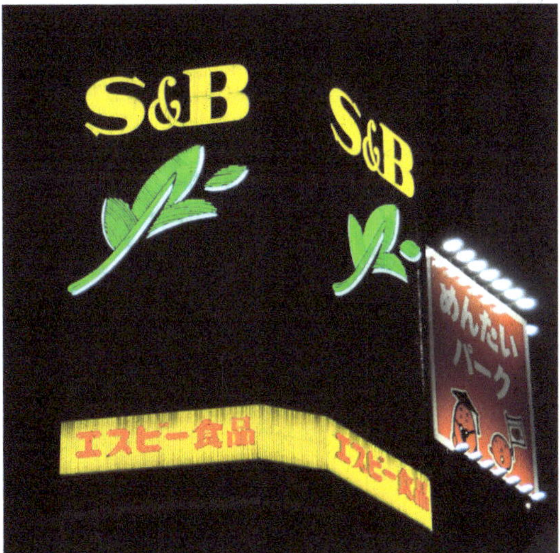
S&B
S&B
エスビー食品
エスビー食品
めんたい
パーク

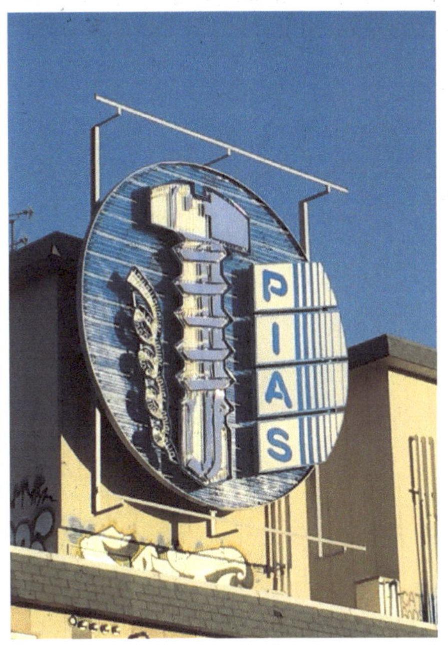
PIAS

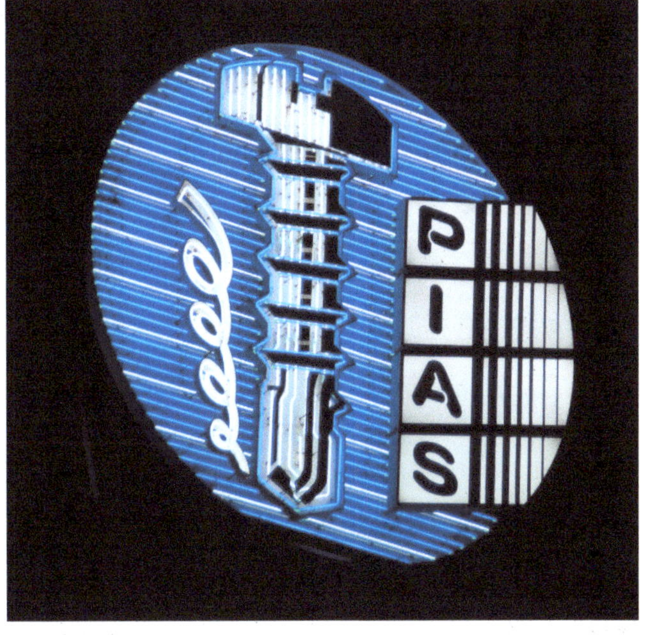
PIAS

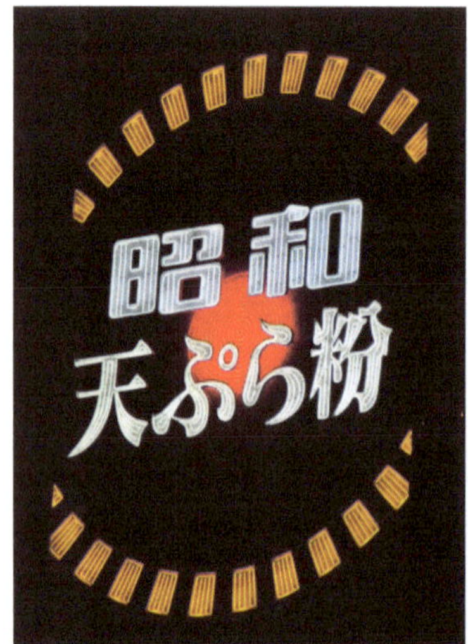
昭和
天ぷら粉
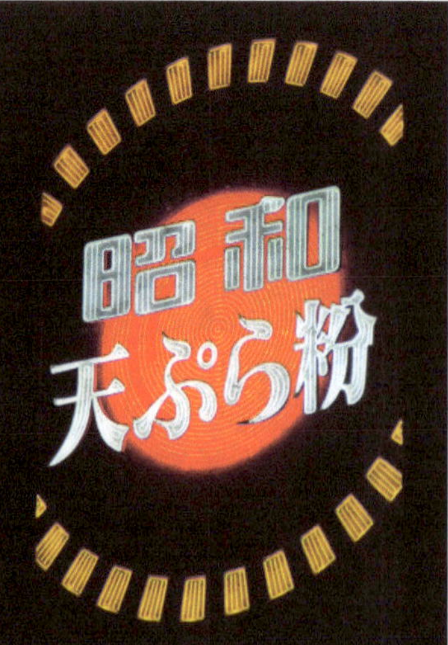
昭和
天ぷら粉
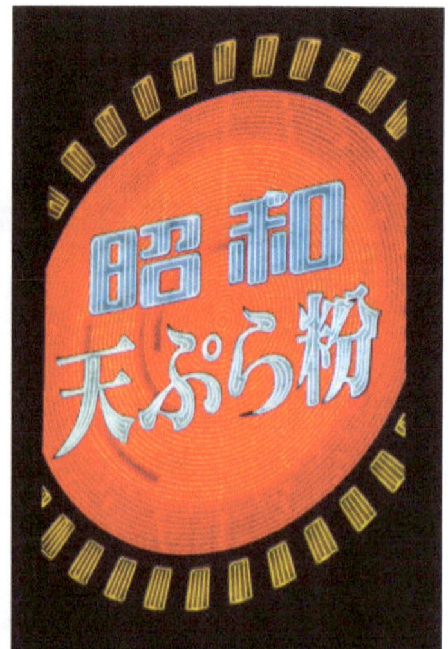
昭和
天ぷら粉
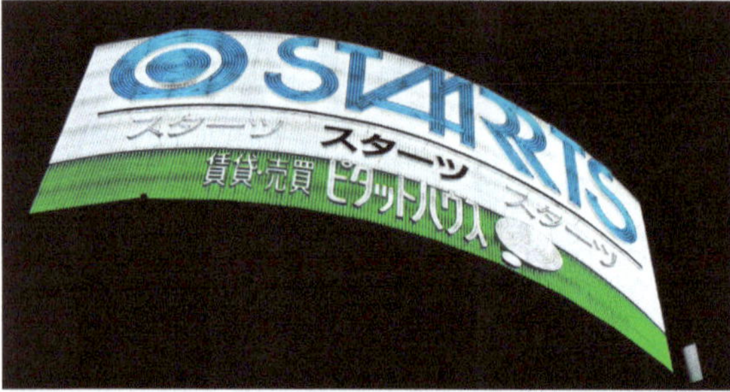
STARTS
スターツ
スターツ
賃貸・売買 ピタットハウス
スターツ
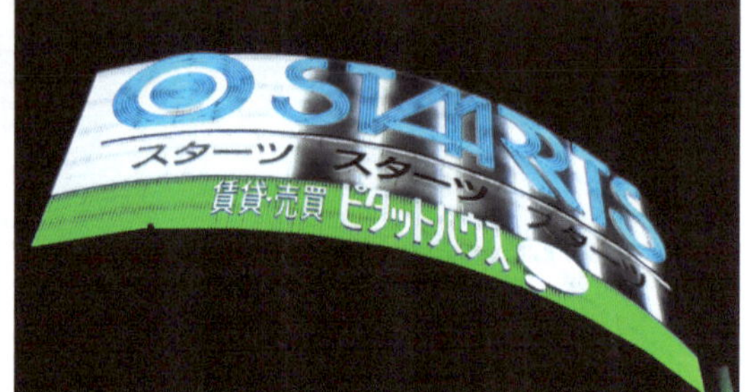
STARTS
スターツ
スターツ
賃貸・売買 ピタットハウス
スターツ
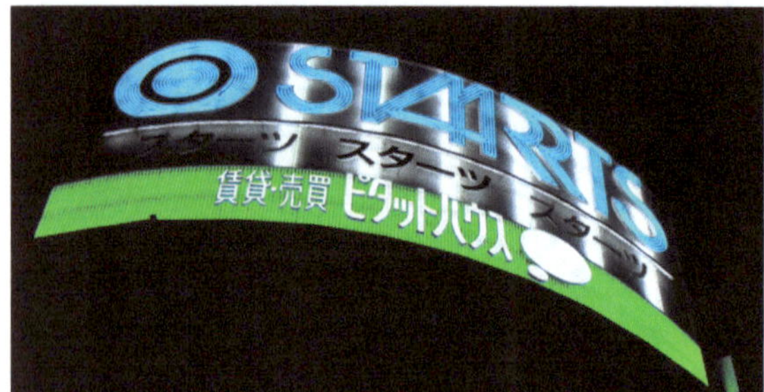
STARTS
スターツ
スターツ
賃貸・売買 ピタットハウス
スターツ
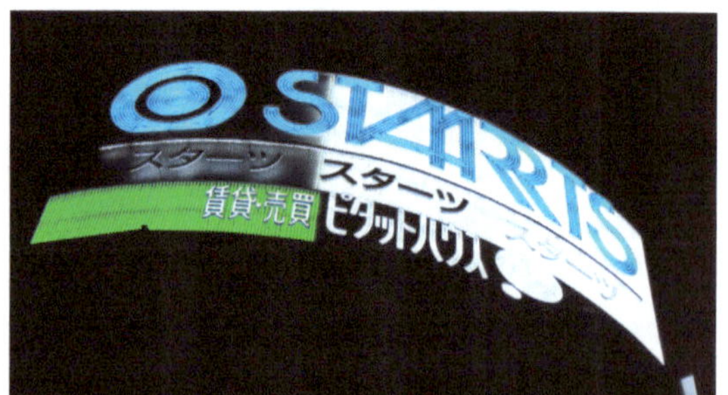
STARTS
スターツ
スターツ
賃貸・売買 ピタットハウス
スターツ
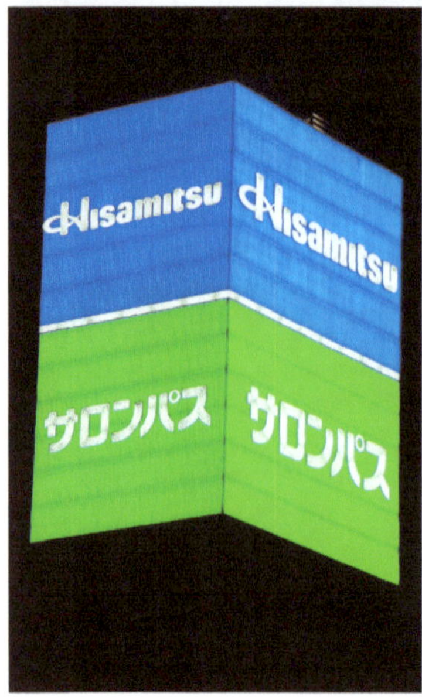
Hisamitsu
Hisamitsu
サロンパス
サロンパス
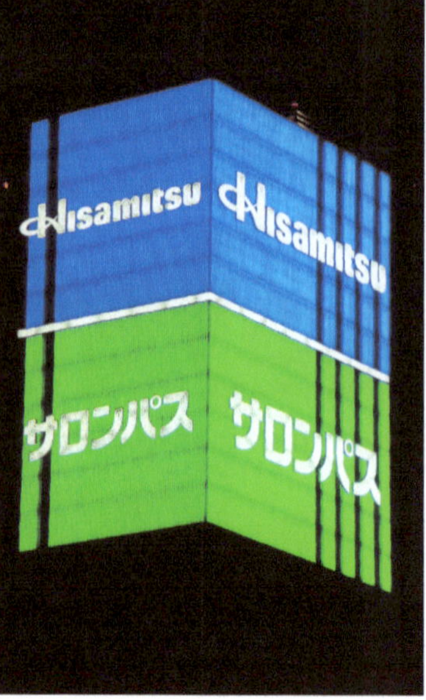
Hisamitsu
Hisamitsu
サロンパス
サロンパス
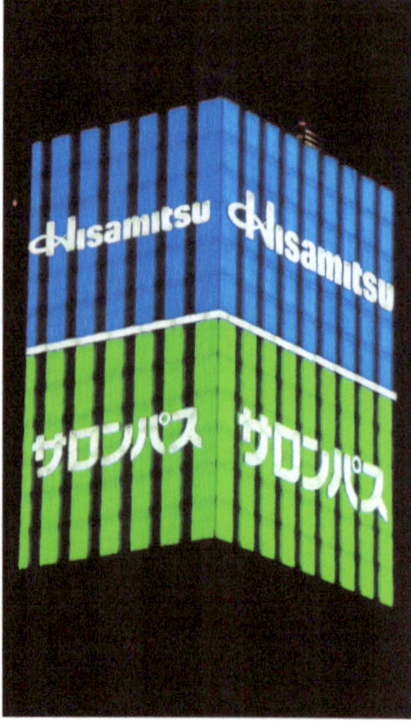
Hisamitsu
Hisamitsu
サロンパス
サロンパス

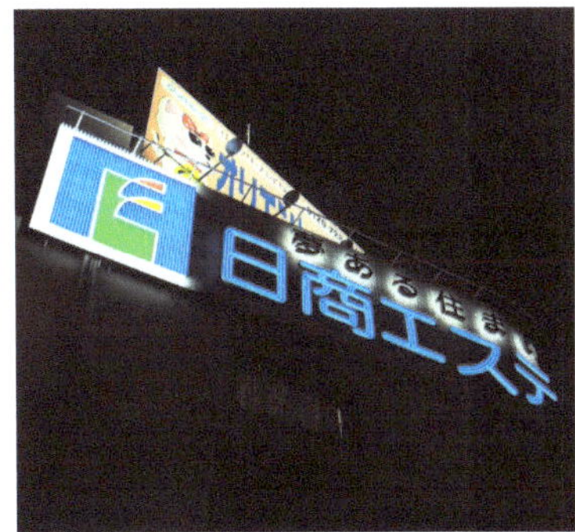
日商エステ

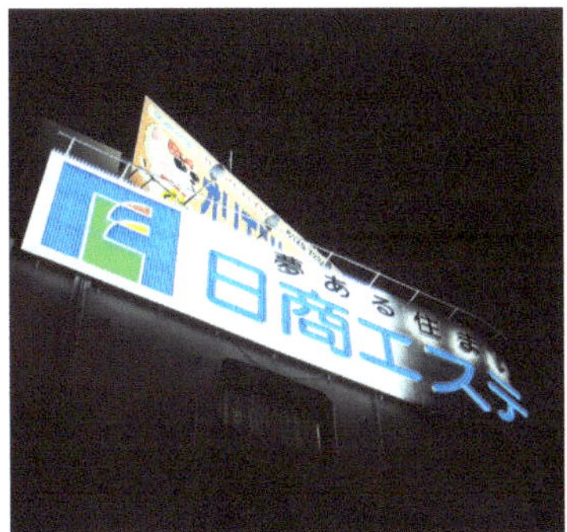
日商エステ

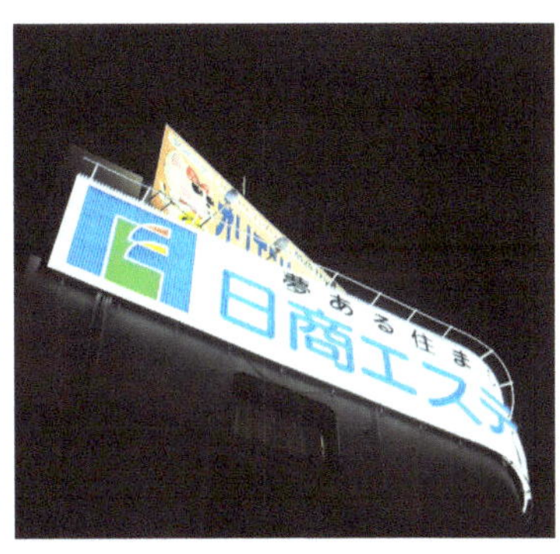
夢ある住ま
日商エステ

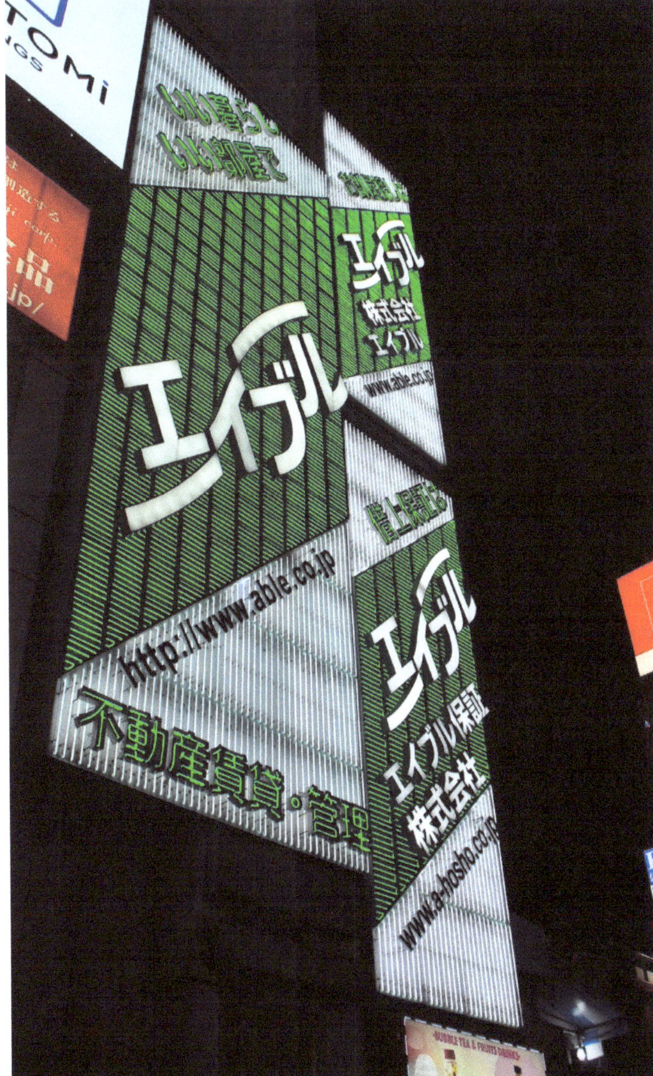
エイブル
株式会社
エイブル
www.able.co.jp
エイブル
http://www.able.co.jp
不動産賃貸・管理
エイブル
エイブル保証
株式会社
www.a-hosho.co.jp

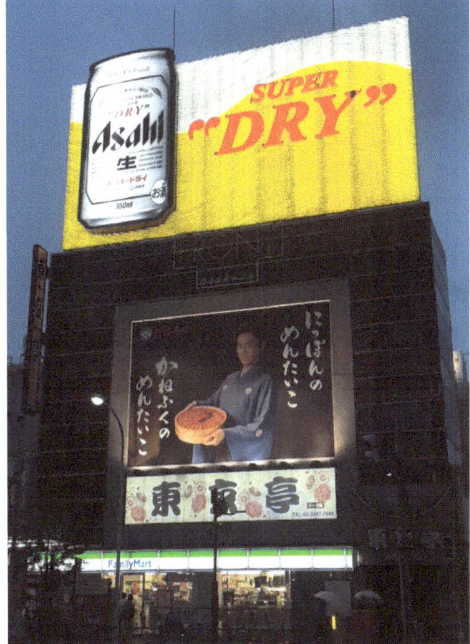
Asahi
生
SUPER
"DRY"
にっぽんのめんたいこ
かねふくのめんたいこ

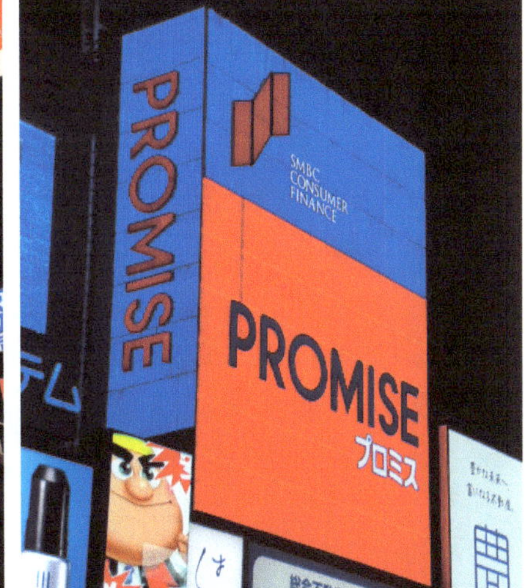
PROMISE
SMBC
CONSUMER
FINANCE
PROMISE
プロミス

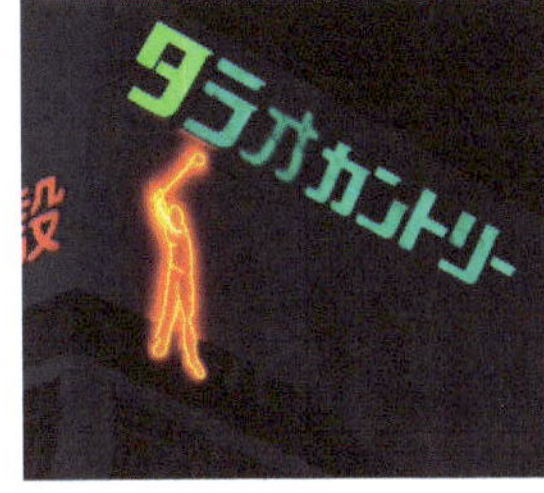
タラオカントリー

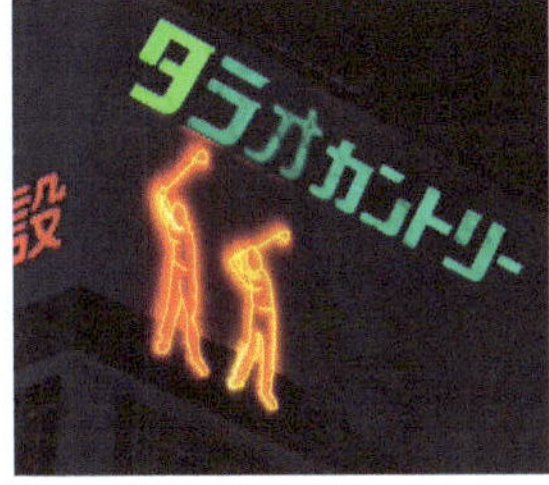
タラオカントリー

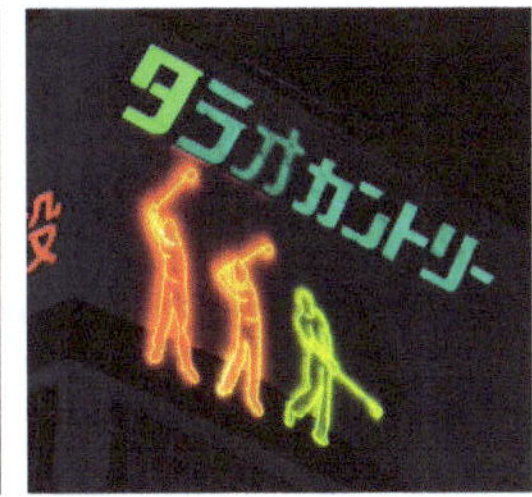
タラオカントリー

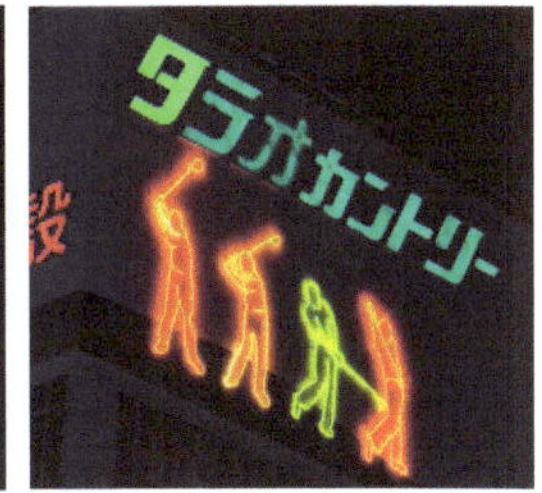
タラオカントリー

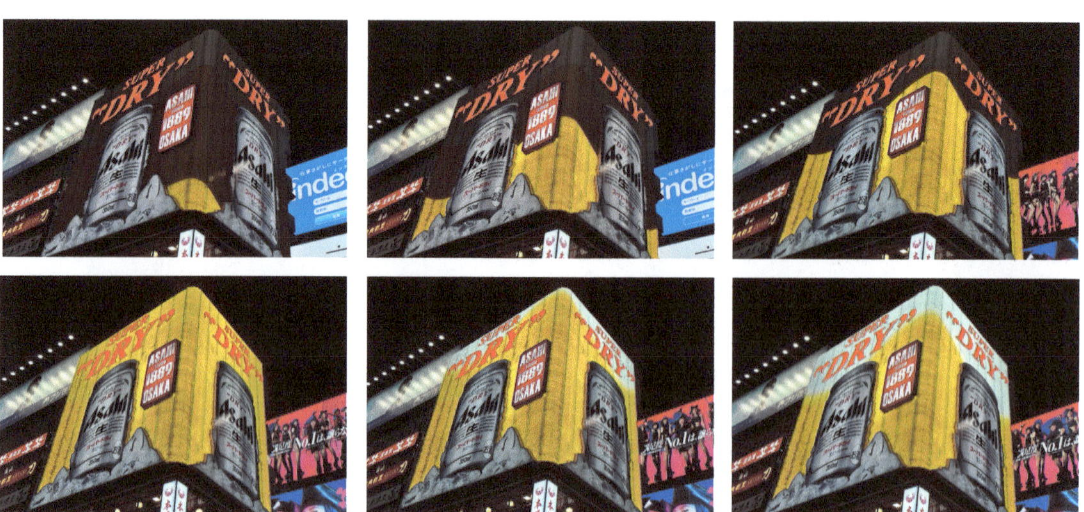

THE ASAHI SUPER DRY NEON SPECTACULAR OF DOTONBORI HAS ABOUT 10,000 NEON TUBES, AND IS ANIMATED TO SIMULATE THE POURING OF A FOAMING BEER

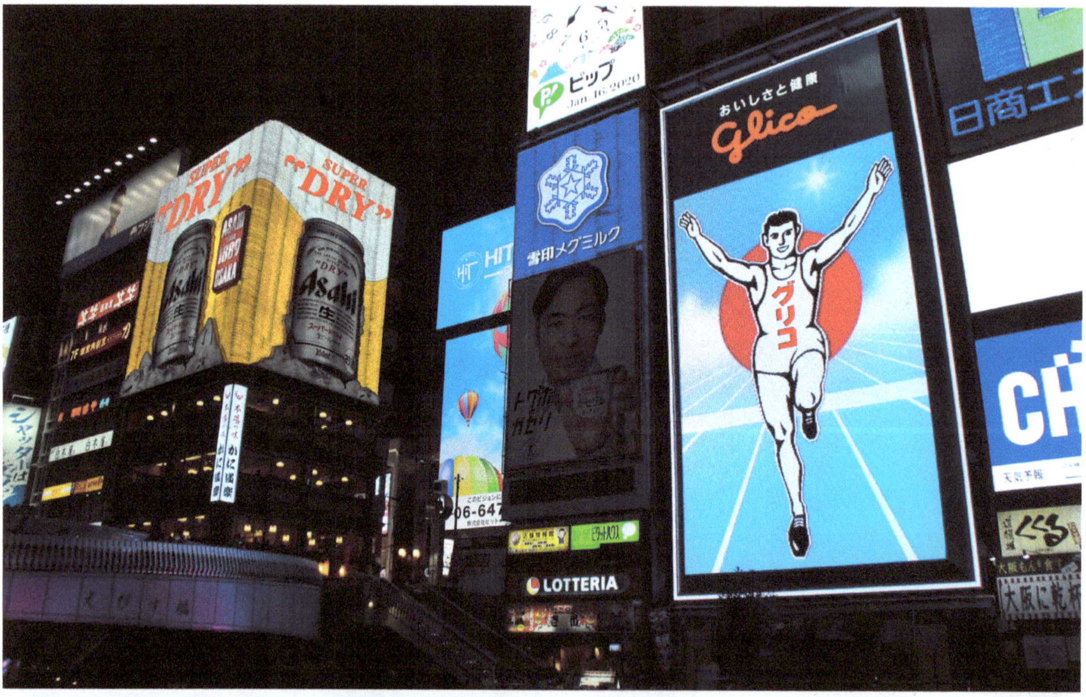

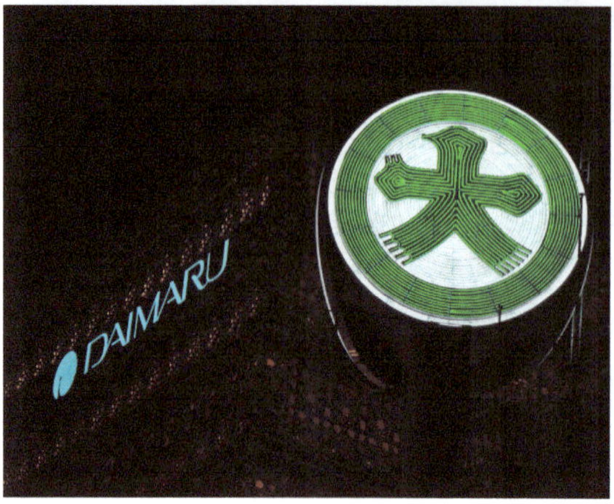

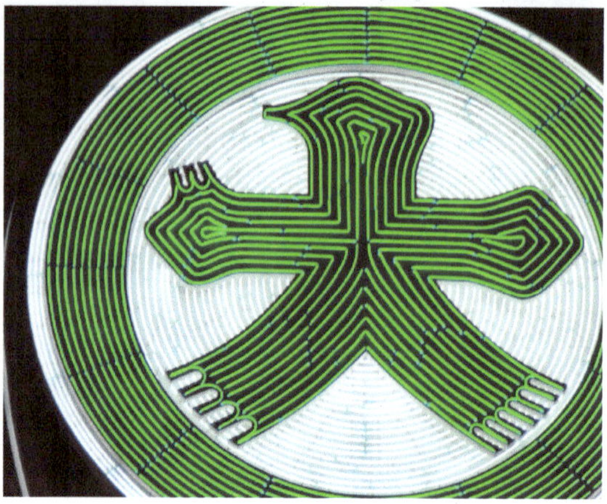

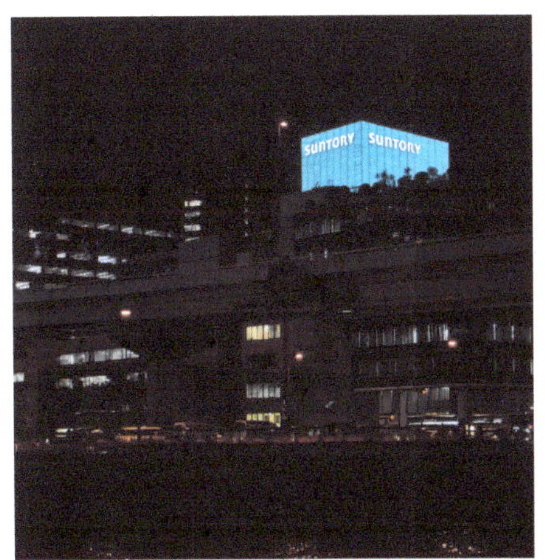
SUNTORY SUNTORY

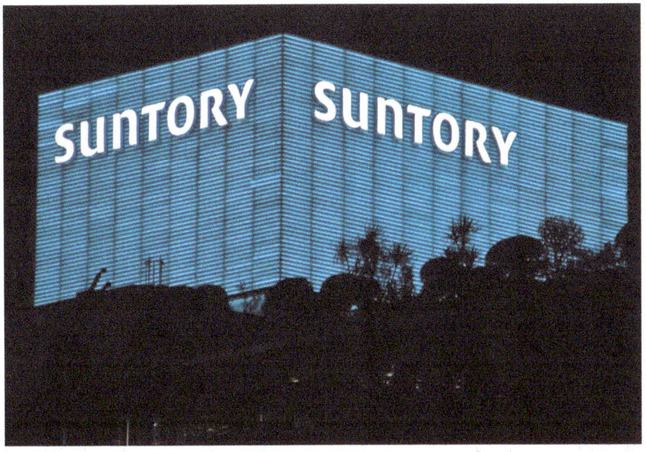
SUNTORY
SUNTORY

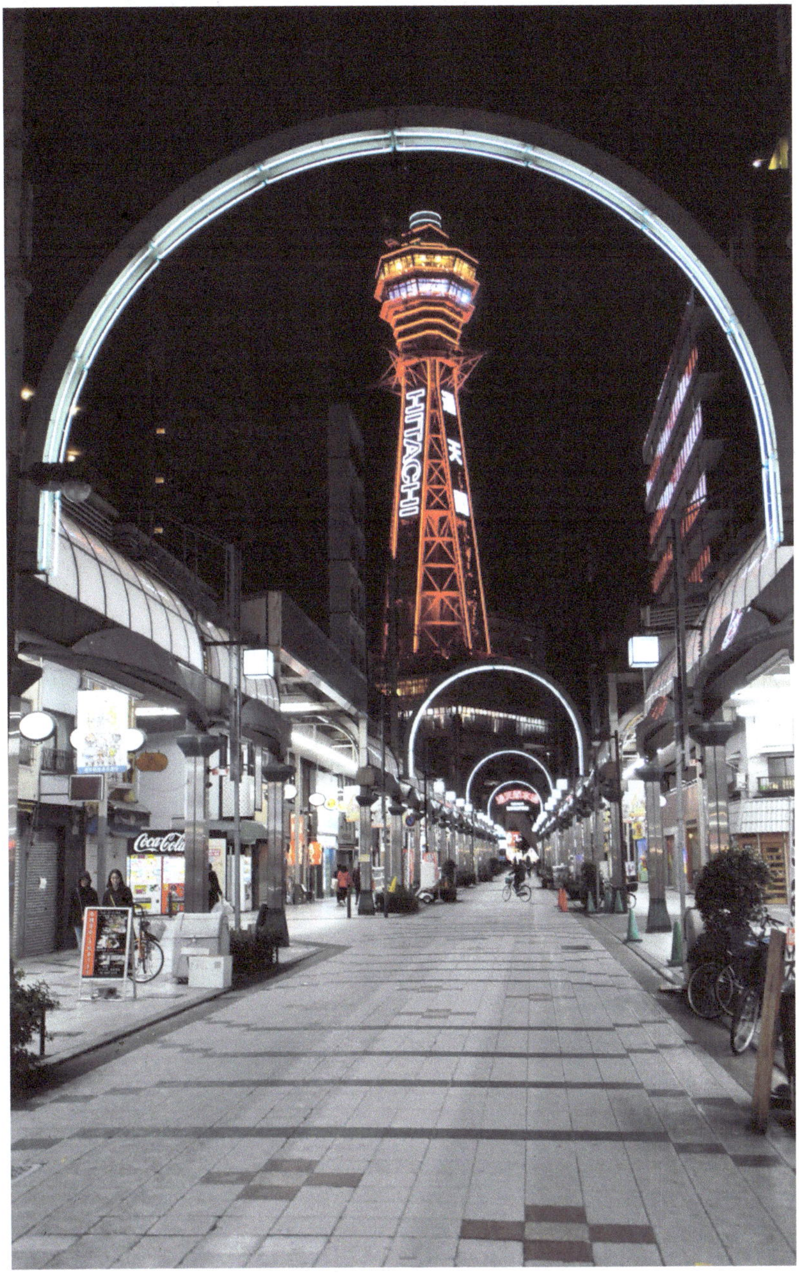

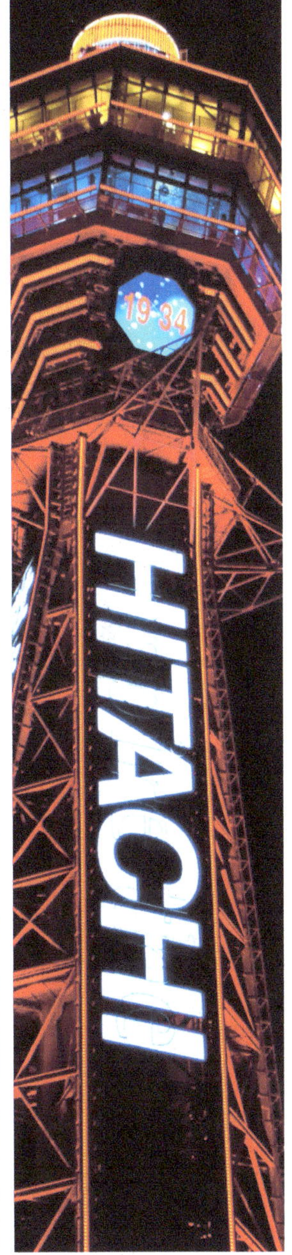
19 34
HITACHI

Hourly Rate Hotels

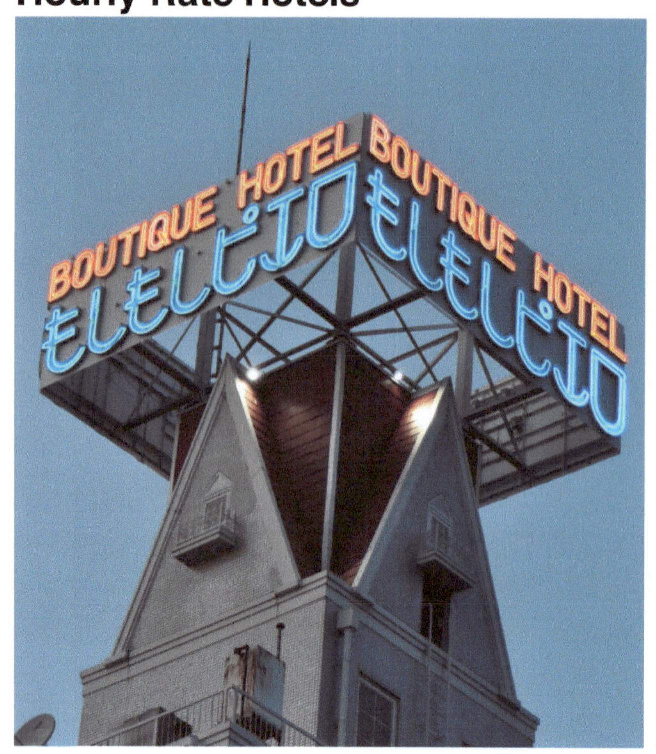

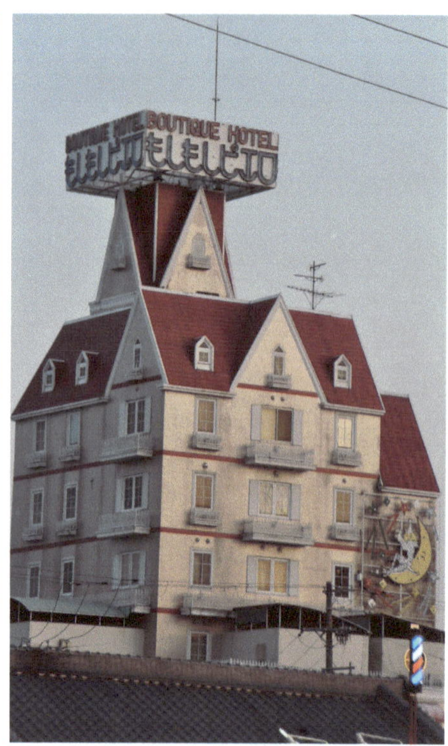

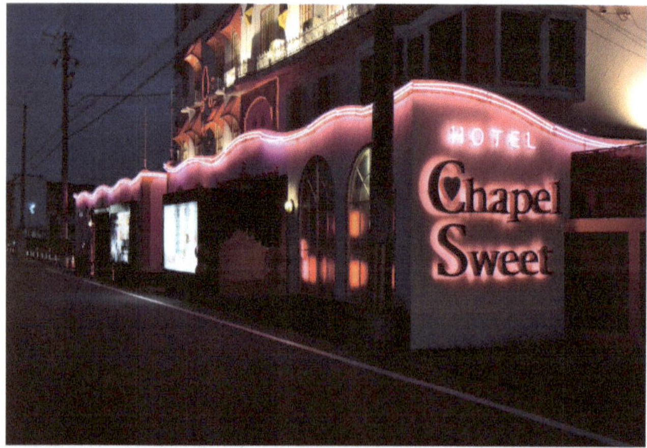

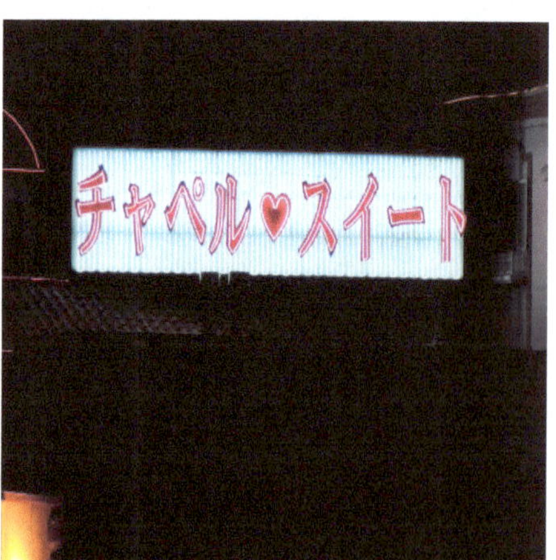

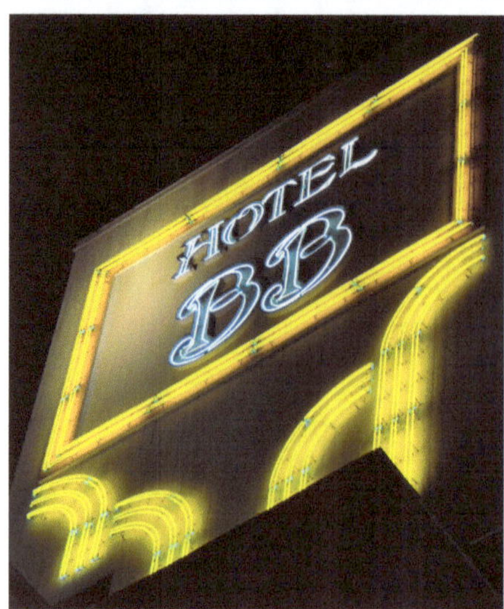

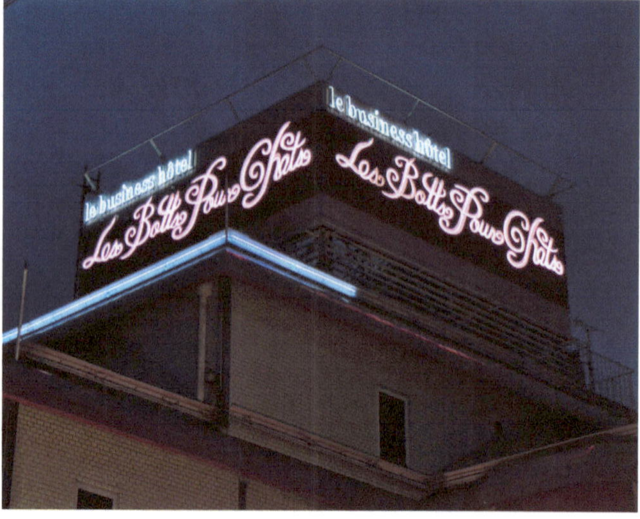

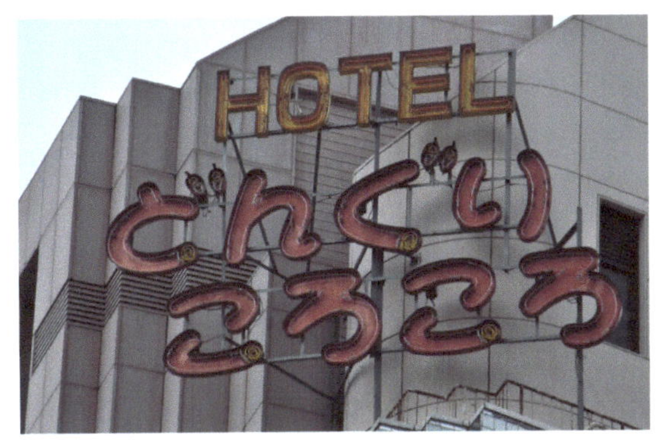
HOTEL
どんぐり
ころころ

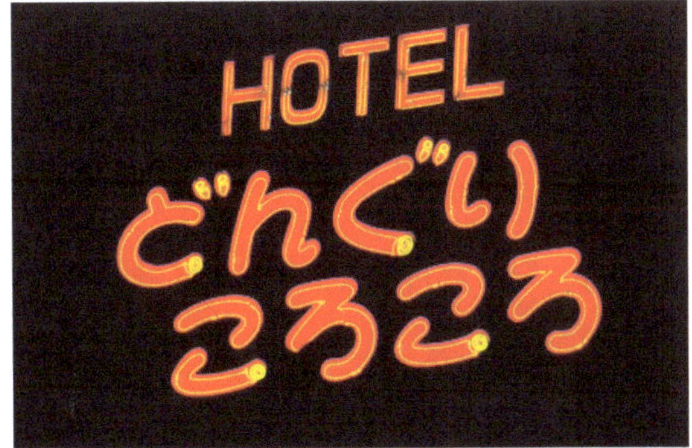
HOTEL
どんぐり
ころころ

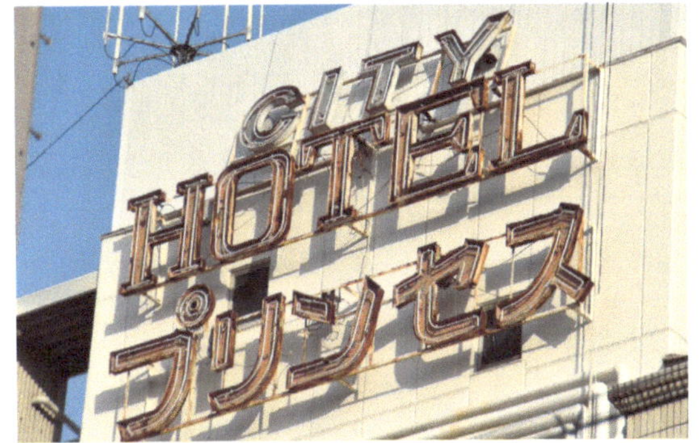
CITY
HOTEL
プリンセス

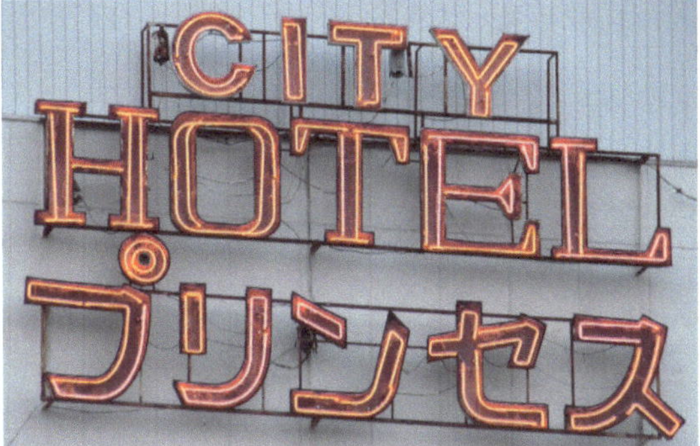
CITY
HOTEL
プリンセス

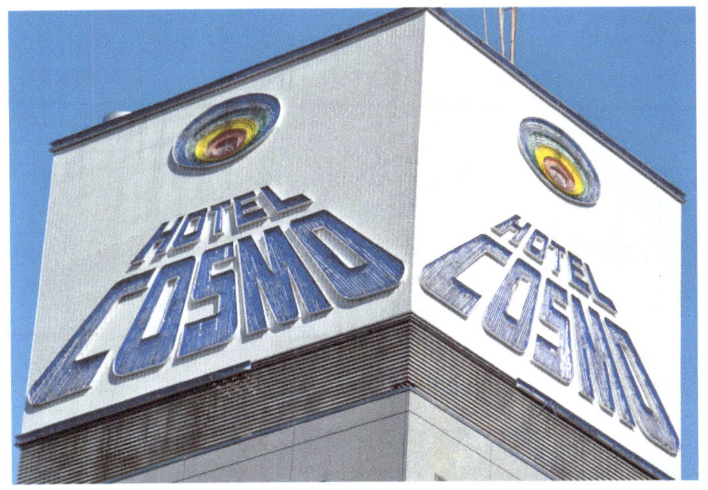
HOTEL
COSMO
HOTEL
COSMO

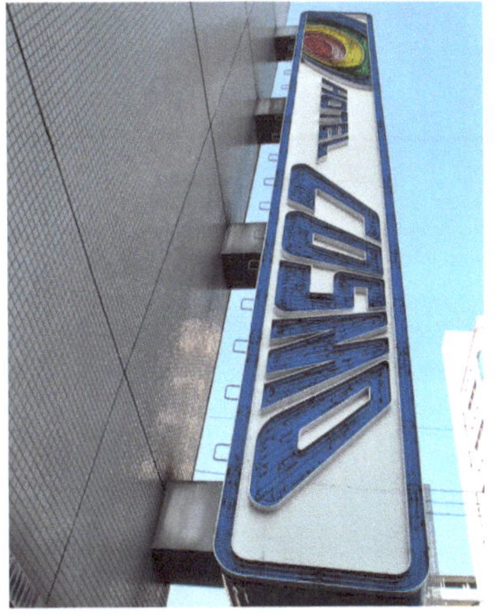
HOTEL
COSMO

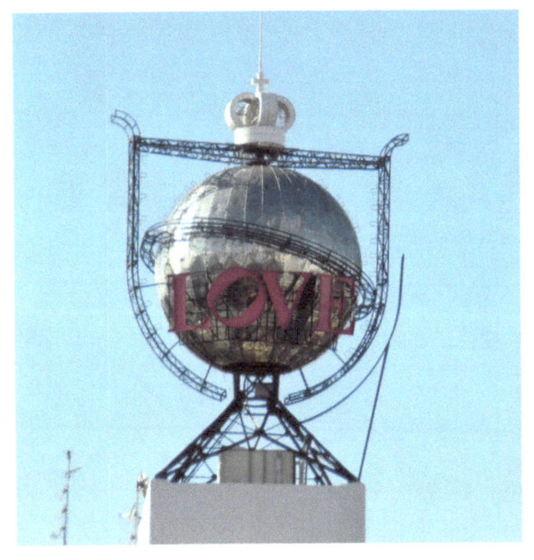
LOVE

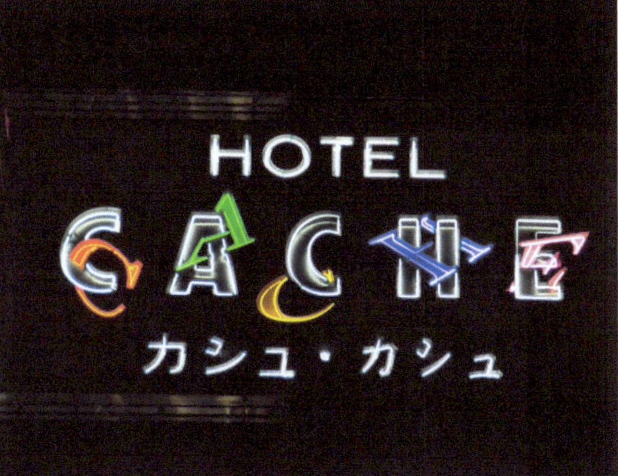
HOTEL
CACHE
カシュ・カシュ

Small Clubs & Cabaret Buildings

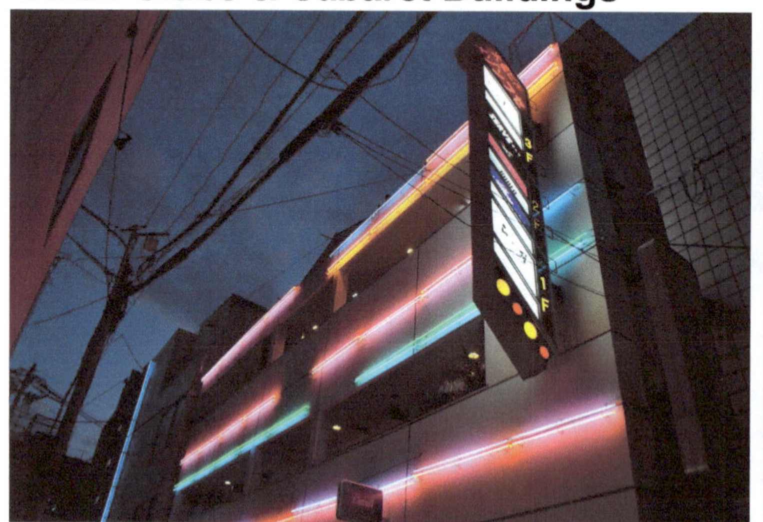

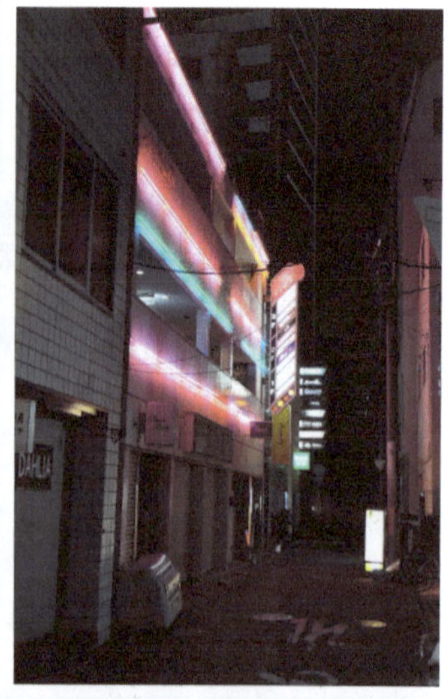

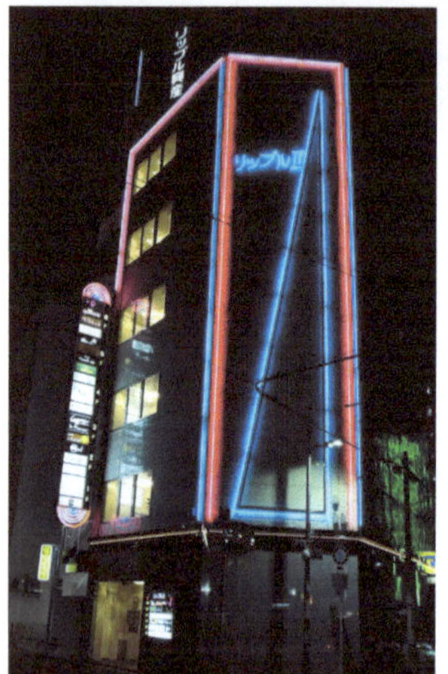

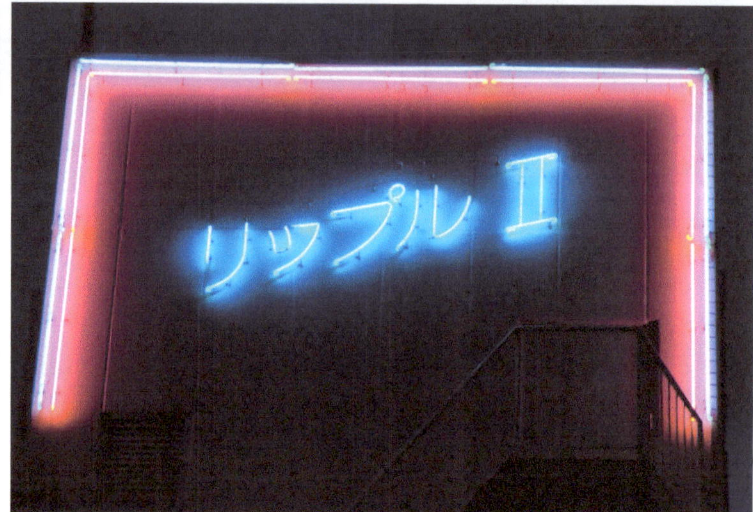

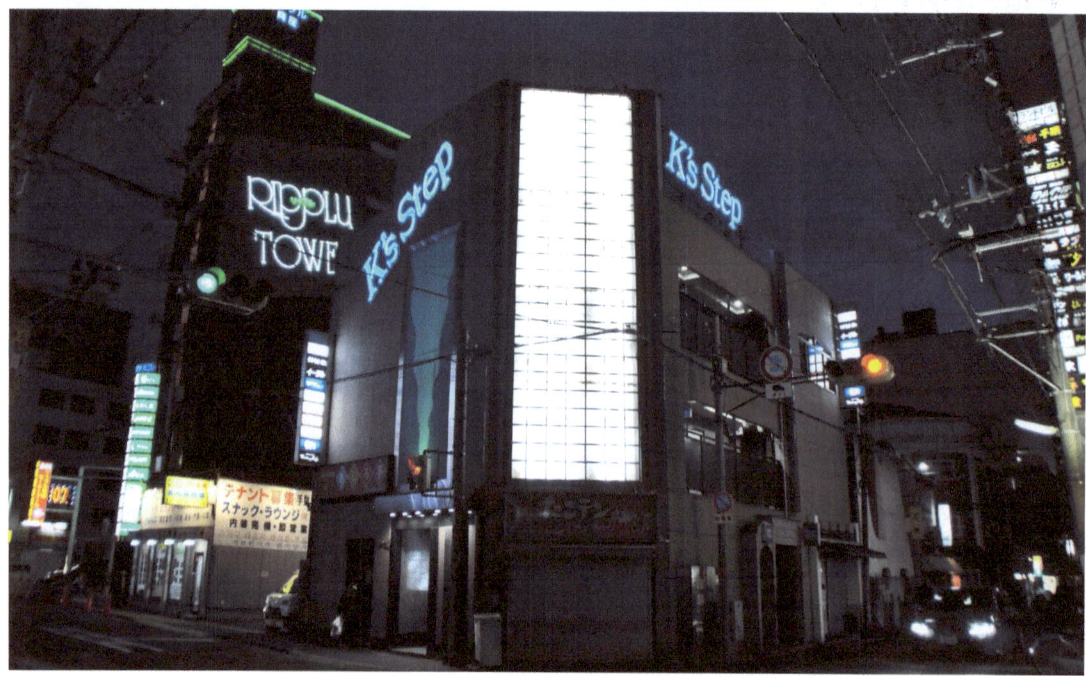

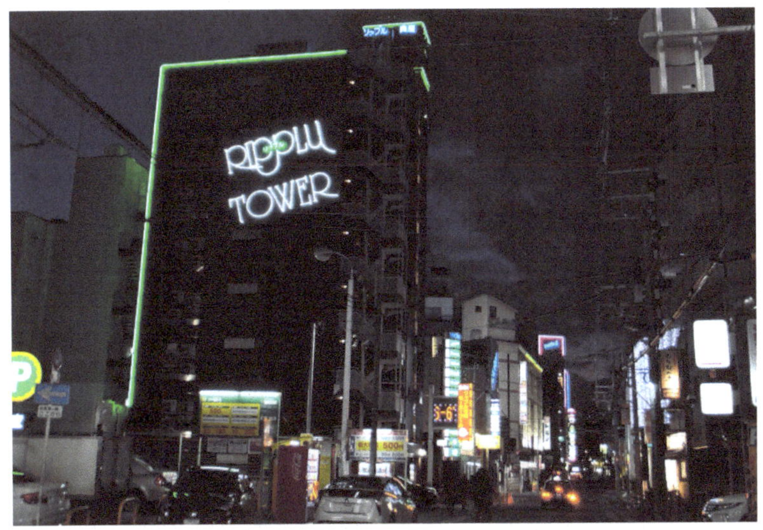
RIPPLY
TOWER

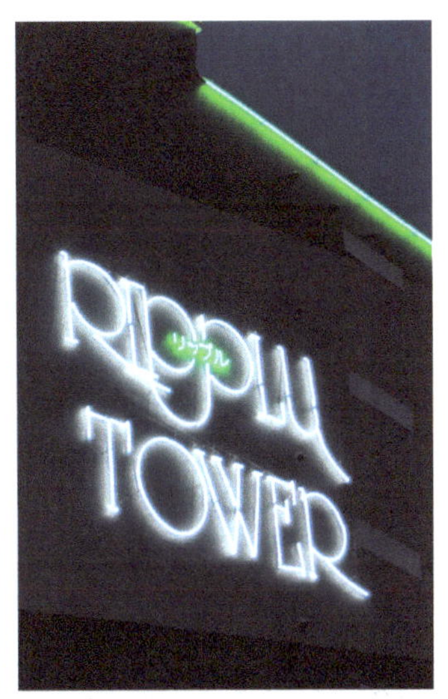
RIPPLY
TOWER

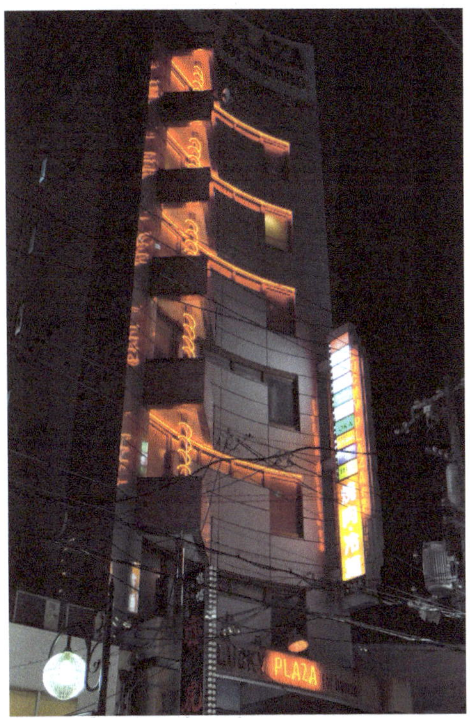
PLAZA

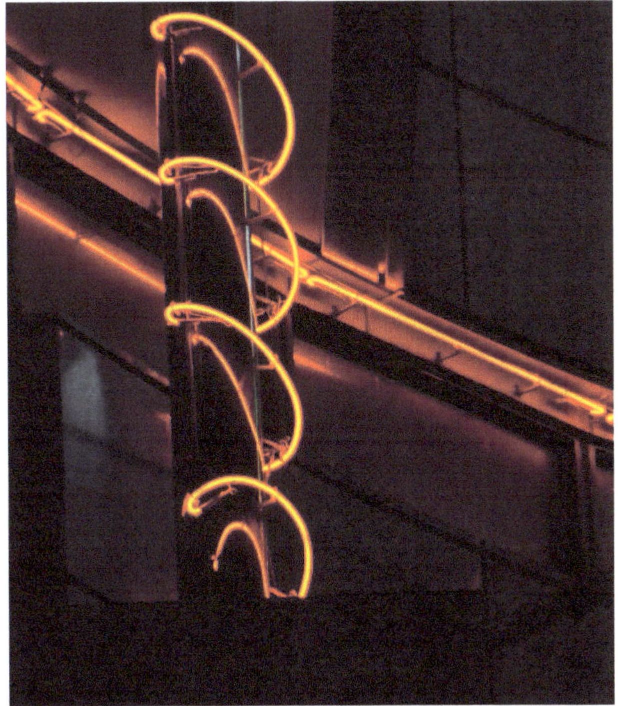

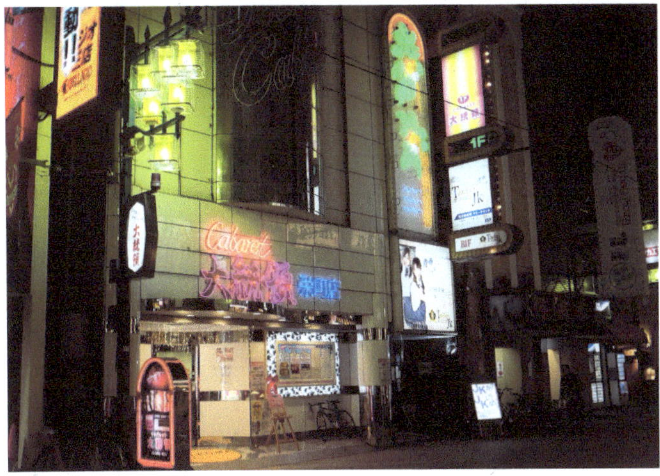
Cabaret

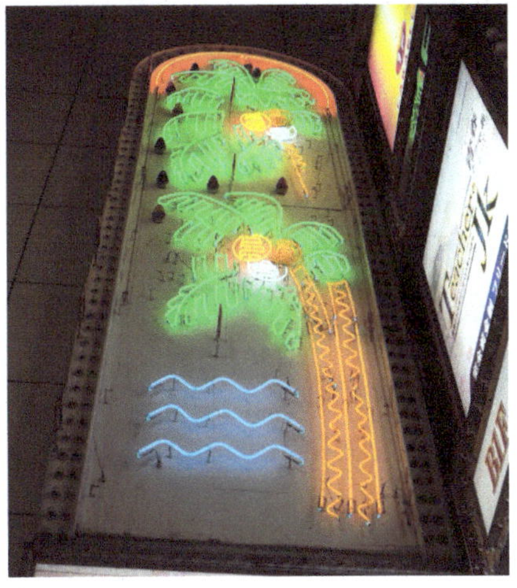

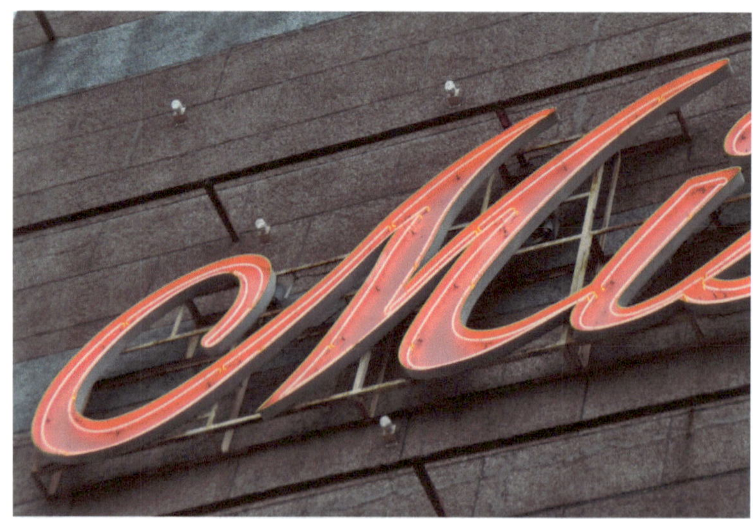
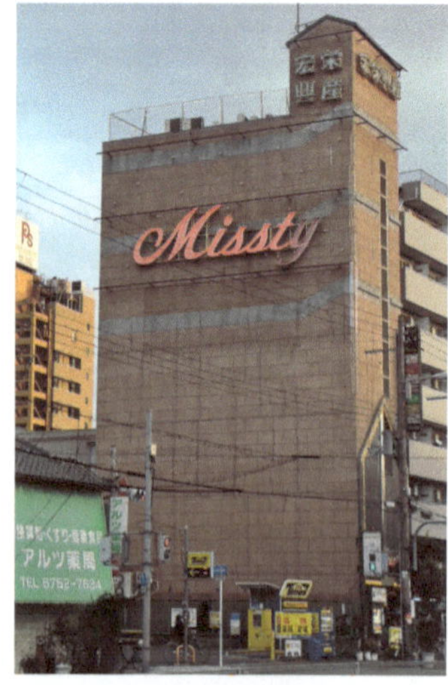
Missty
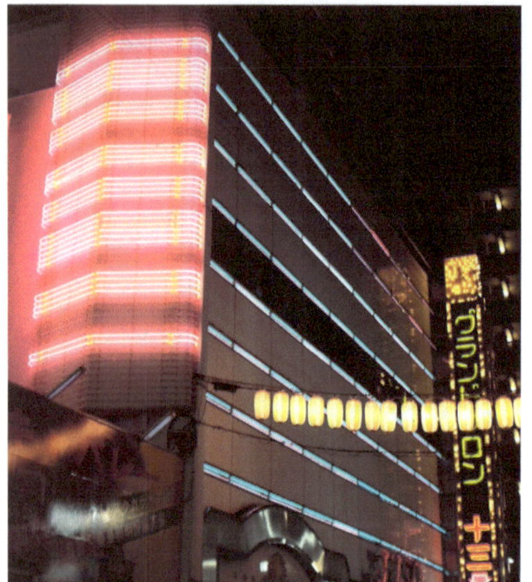
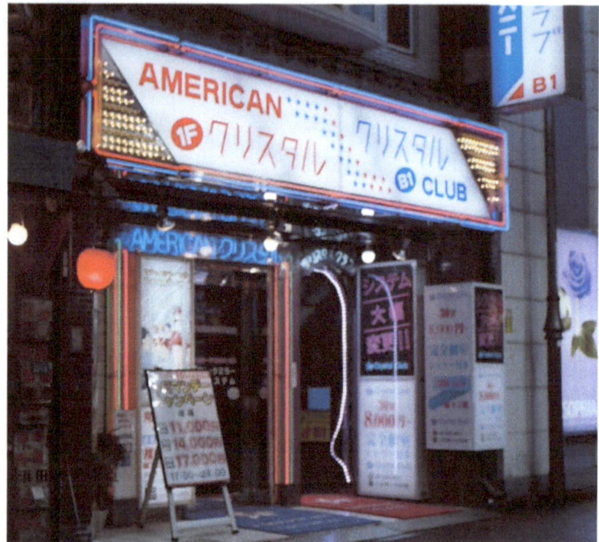
AMERICAN
1F クリスタル
クリスタル
B1 CLUB
B1
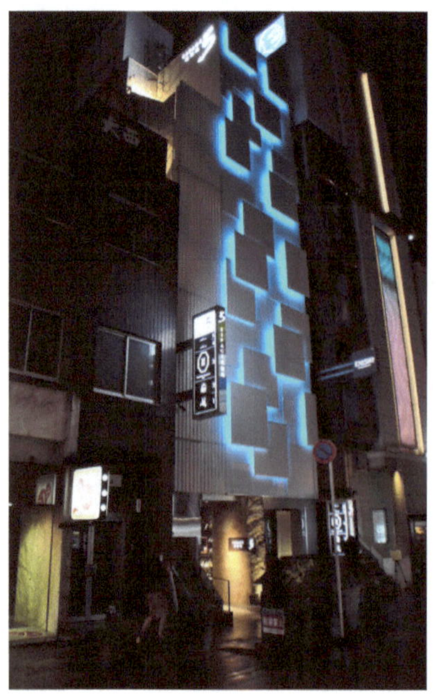
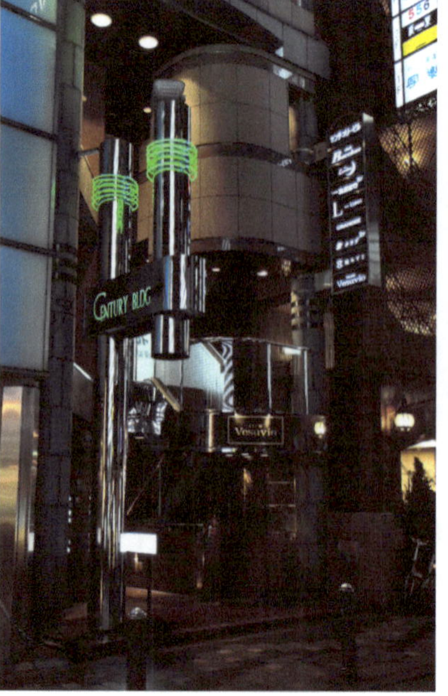
CENTURY BLDG
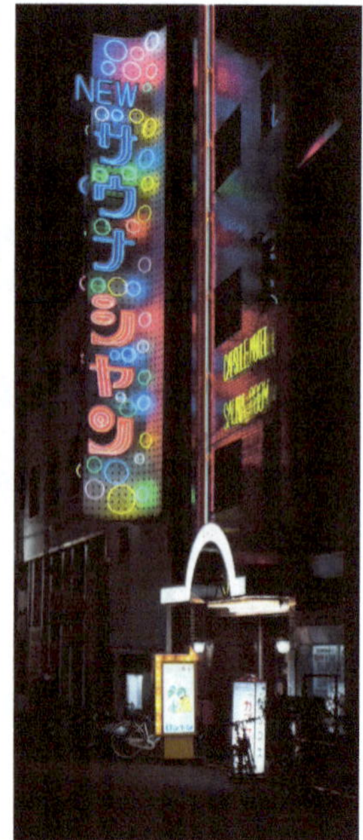
NEW

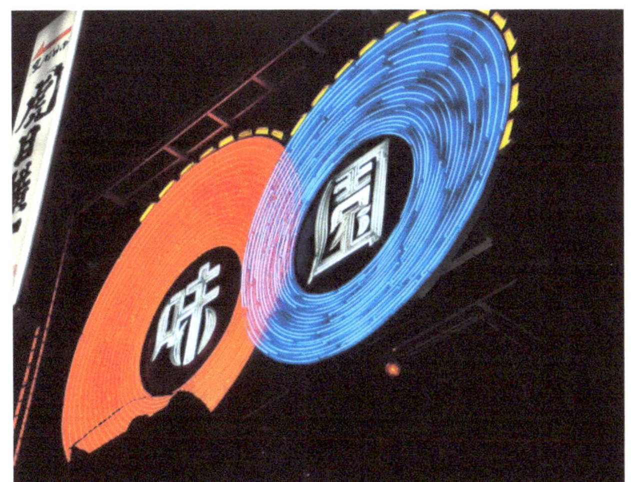
味
園

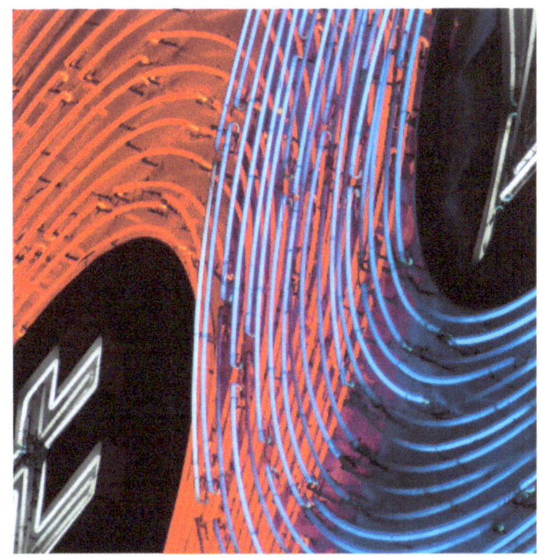

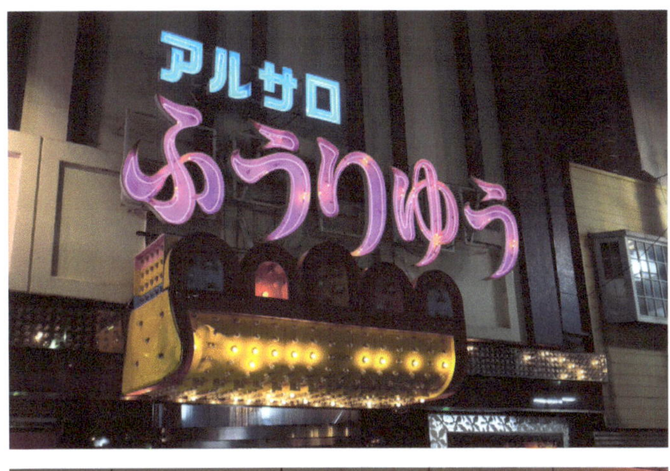
アルサロ
ふうりゅう

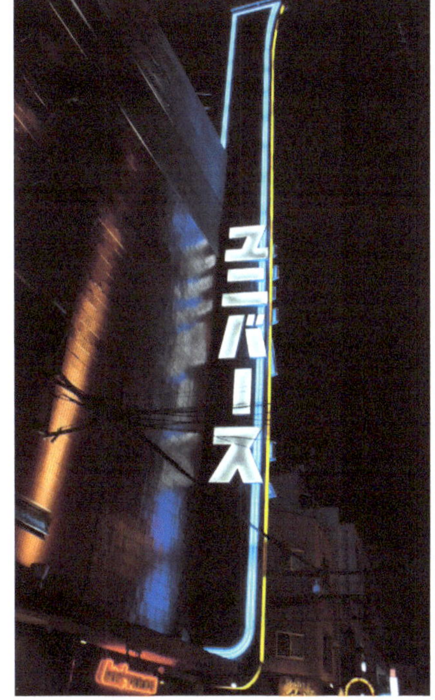
ユニバース

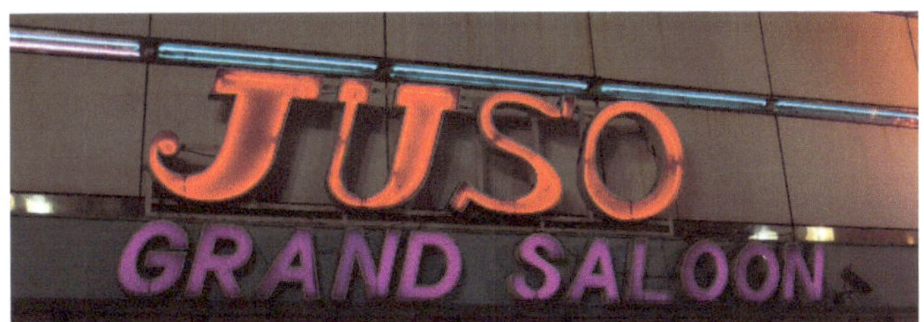
JUSO
GRAND SALOON

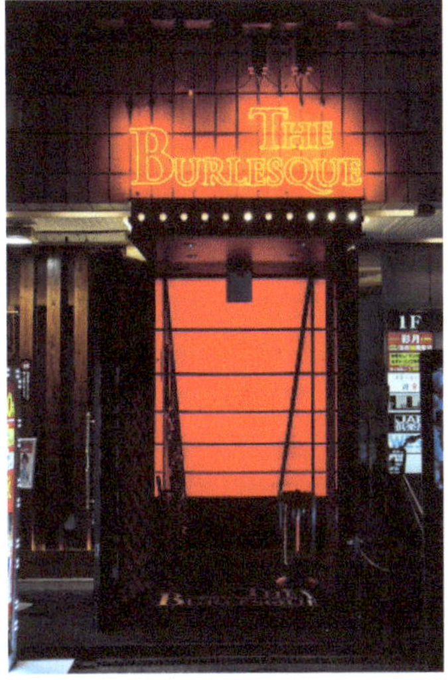
THE
BURLESQUE
1F

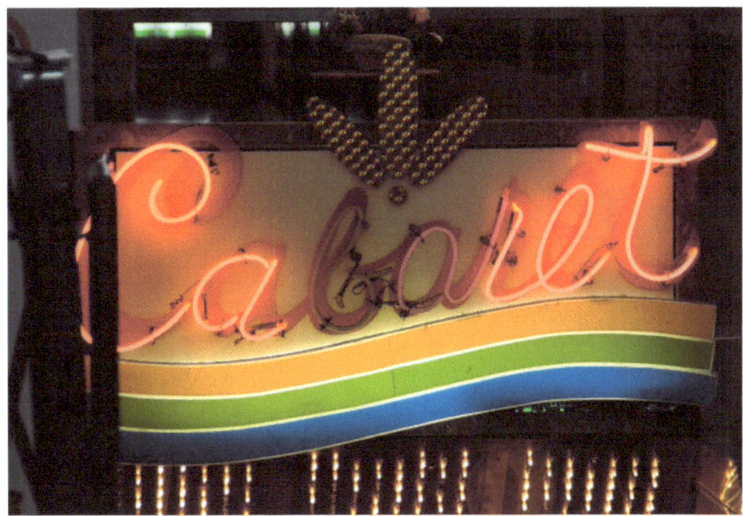
Cabaret

Works Cited

Text References

日本のネオン (Neon of Japan). All Japan Neon-sign Association. , 1977.

"銀座名物だった森永の地球儀ネオン塔." Internet NEOS, All Japan Neon Association, 1 Apr. 2013, www.sign-jp.org/98/neos137/museum.html.

"Dotonbori Glico Neon Tower History and Overview." Internet NEOS, All Japan Neon Association, 5 June 2013, www.sign-jp.org/98/neos76/glico.html.

"Association Member Survey Results 2019 Member Survey Results." Internet NEOS, All Japan Neon Association, Jan. 2020, www.sign-jp.org/98/whatshot/enquete/index.html.

"Chapter7;Is 'Pocketable' Japanese-English" SONY, www.sony.net/SonyInfo/CorporateInfo/History/SonyHistory/1-07.html.

Caba, Randall L. "Finding the Neon Light, Part Three - The Father of Neon." SignIndustry.com - The Online Magazine for the Sign Trade., 1 Jan. 2004, www.signindustry.com/neon/articles/2004-01-14-RC-FindingPt3.php3.

Hatanaka, Bukichi. Hōden dentō To Neonsain. Yodoya Shoten Shuppanbu, 1933.

"History of Japan's Electric Power Industry." History of Japan's Electric Power Industry - The Federation of Electric Power Companies of Japan(FEPC), The Federation of Electric Power Companies of Japan, www.fepc.or.jp/english/energy_electricity/history/.

Larsen, Brooke. "The History Behind Tsutenkaku, One of Osaka's Most Beloved Landmarks." Culture Trip, The Culture Trip, 18 Mar. 2018, theculturetrip.com/asia/japan/articles/the-history-behind-tsutenkaku-one-of-osakas-most-beloved-landmarks/.

Miller, Samuel C., and Donald G. Fink. Neon Signs. McGraw-Hill Book Co., 1935.

Strattman, Wayne. Neon Techniques: Handbook of Neon Sign and Cold Cathode Lighting. ST Media Group, 2015.

Ōhira Keiichi. Neon Sain: Dezain Kara sekō Made. Ōmusha, 1964.

Seki, Shigehiro. Neon Sain to Denki Kanban. Denki Shoin, 1954.

M. Igari, Beginning of Neon Sign in Japan, Journal of the Illuminating Engineering Institute of Japan, 1933, Volume 17, Issue 8, Pages a1-a2, Released March 02, 2011, Online ISSN 2185-1506, Print ISSN 0019-2341, https://doi.org/10.2150/jieij1917.17.8_a1, https://www.jstage.jst.go.jp/article/jieij1917/17/8/17_8_a1/_article/-char/en

[in Japanese], Design for Neon-Sign, Journal of the Illuminating Engineering Institute of Japan, 1957, Volume 41, Issue 10, Pages 441-447, Released July 19, 2011, Online ISSN 2185-1506, Print ISSN 0019-2341, https://doi.org/10.2150/jieij1917.41.10_441, https://www.jstage.jst.go.jp/article/jieij1917/41/10/41_10_441/_article/-char/en

Hiroyuki Yoshino, Neon-sign Luminescence Principles and Their Tools and Materials, JOURNAL OF THE ILLUMINATING ENGINEERING INSTITUTE OF JAPAN, 2002, Volume 86, Issue 4, Pages 235-238, Released July 19, 2011, Online ISSN 1349-838X, Print ISSN 0019-2341, https://doi.org/10.2150/jieij1980.86.4_235, https://www.jstage.jst.go.jp/article/jieij1980/86/4/86_4_235/_article/-char/en

Hiroyuki Ono, History of Neon-Sign Illumination, JOURNAL OF THE ILLUMINATING ENGINEERING INSTITUTE OF JAPAN, 2002, Volume 86, Issue 4, Pages 227-232, Released July 19, 2011, Online ISSN 1349-838X, Print ISSN 0019-2341, https://doi.org/10.2150/jieij1980.86.4_227, https://www.jstage.jst.go.jp/article/jieij1980/86/4/86_4_227/_article/-char/en

[in Japanese], [title in Japanese], Journal of the Illuminating Engineering Institute of Japan, 1956, Volume 40, Issue 9, Pages 355-357, Released July 19, 2011, Online ISSN 2185-1506, Print ISSN 0019-2341, https://doi.org/10.2150/jieij1917.40.9_355, https://www.jstage.jst.go.jp/article/jieij1917/40/9/40_9_355/_article/-char/en

"Short Biography of Johann Heinrich Wilhelm Geissler." Heinrich Geissler, The Cathode Ray Tube Site, www.crtsite.com/Heinrich-Geissler.html.

Henshall, Kenneth G. A History of Japan: From Stone Age to Superpower. Palgrave Macmillan, 2012.

Photography

Asahi Denso 50th History. Asahi Denso , 2000.

Wada, Hirofumi, and Masahiro Nishimura. Korekushon Modan Toshi Bunka. Yumani Shobō, 2006.

"過去文献・資料一覧." Tlt.co.jp, Toshiba Lighting and Technology Corp., www.tlt.co.jp/tlt/corporate/company/akari_story/bunken.htm.

東京の夜. 角川書店, 1957.

"File:Reclamebord met echte rook voor sigarettenmerk Camel op Times Square, Bestanddeelnr 191-0803.jpg." Wikimedia Commons, the free media repository. 14 Sep 2019, 08:36 UTC. <https://commons.wikimedia.org/w/index.php?title=File:Reclamebord_met_echte_rook_voor_sigarettenmerk_Camel_op_Times_Square,_Bestanddeelnr_191-0803.jpg&oldid=365750360>.

"File:Heinrich Geissler.jpg." Wikimedia Commons, the free media repository. 13 Mar 2015, 13:53 UTC. , <https://commons.wikimedia.org/w/index.php?title=File:Heinrich_Geissler.jpg&oldid=153013908>.

"File:Faraday-Millikan-Gale-1913.jpg." Wikimedia Commons, the free media repository. 7 Jan 2016, 19:16 UTC. <https://commons.wikimedia.org/w/index.php?title=File:Faraday-Millikan-Gale-1913.jpg&oldid=184042147>.

"File:Geissler tubes.jpg." Wikimedia Commons, the free media repository. 23 Oct 2018, 01:20 UTC. <https://commons.wikimedia.org/w/index.php?title=File:Geissler_tubes.jpg&oldid=325055538>.

"File:William Ramsay LCCN90708729.jpg." Wikimedia Commons, the free media repository. 8 Jan 2019, 01:50 UTC. <https://commons.wikimedia.org/w/index.php?title=File:William_Ramsay_LCCN90708729.jpg&oldid=333944752>.

"File:Sir William Crookes 1902.jpg." Wikimedia Commons, the free media repository. 23 Dec 2014, 13:14 UTC. <https://commons.wikimedia.org/w/index.php?title=File:Sir_William_Crookes_1902.jpg&oldid=143782427>.

"File:Tess at Sukiyabashi Clossing.jpg." Wikimedia Commons, the free media repository. 3 Jul 2018, 07:50 UTC. 5 May 2020, 05:45 <https://commons.wikimedia.org/w/index.php?title=File:Tess_at_Sukiyabashi_Clossing.jpg&oldid=309305922>.

Works Cited - Photography (continued)

"File:Cosser Crookes xray tube.jpg." Wikimedia Commons, the free media repository. 28 Dec 2017, 18:37 UTC. <https://commons.wikimedia.org/w/index.php?title=File:Cosser_Crookes_xray_tube.jpg&oldid=274827582>.

"File:MooreTubes Newark1904.jpg." Wikimedia Commons, the free media repository. 11 Jan 2015, 09:22 UTC. <https://commons.wikimedia.org/w/index.php?title=File:MooreTubes_Newark1904.jpg&oldid=146115621>.

"File:DMcFarlanMoore06.jpg." Wikimedia Commons, the free media repository. 28 Sep 2019, 16:38 UTC. 30 Apr 2020, 13:18 <https://commons.wikimedia.org/w/index.php?title=File:DMcFarlanMoore06.jpg&oldid=368534340>.

"File:Georges Claude à l'Institut 1926.jpg." Wikimedia Commons, the free media repository. 2 Sep 2017, 08:39 UTC. 30 Apr 2020, 13:19 <https://commons.wikimedia.org/w/index.php?title=File:Georges_Claude_%C3%A0_l%27Institut_1926.jpg&oldid=257195900>.

"File:Nikola Tesla holding bulb.jpg." Wikimedia Commons, the free media repository. 10 Jan 2017, 18:09 UTC. 30 Apr 2020, 13:18 <https://commons.wikimedia.org/w/index.php?title=File:Nikola_Tesla_holding_bulb.jpg&oldid=229311848>.

"File:Colored fluorescent lamps.jpg." Wikimedia Commons, the free media repository. 26 Jun 2018, 23:30 UTC. 30 Apr 2020, 13:21 <https://commons.wikimedia.org/w/index.php?title=File:Colored_fluorescent_lamps.jpg&oldid=308241506>.

"File:Coating CRTs at Research Enterprises.jpg." Wikimedia Commons, the free media repository. 2 Oct 2017, 11:44 UTC. 30 Apr 2020, 13:21 <https://commons.wikimedia.org/w/index.php?title=File:Coating_CRTs_at_Research_Enterprises.jpg&oldid=260915323>.

"File:Gasshukoku suishi teitoku kōjōgaki (Oral statement by the American Navy admiral).png." Wikimedia Commons, the free media repository. 30 Jul 2017, 01:14 UTC. 30 Apr 2020, 13:23 <https://commons.wikimedia.org/w/index.php?title=File:Gasshukoku_suishi_teitoku_k%C5%8Dj%C5%8Dgaki_(Oral_statement_by_the_American_Navy_admiral).png&oldid=253557444>.

"File:Shirokiya Fire.JPG." Wikimedia Commons, the free media repository. 16 Mar 2018, 19:43 UTC. 30 Apr 2020, 13:24 <https://commons.wikimedia.org/w/index.php?title=File:Shirokiya_Fire.JPG&oldid=292427501>.

"File:ISHIMOTO-Shirokiya-3.jpg." Wikimedia Commons, the free media repository. 17 Jun 2018, 20:16 UTC. 30 Apr 2020, 13:24 <https://commons.wikimedia.org/w/index.php?title=File:ISHIMOTO-Shirokiya-3.jpg&oldid=306834545>.

"Expositions, Where the Modern Technology of the Times Was Exhibited." 国立国会図書館—National Diet Library, www.ndl.go.jp/exposition/e/index.html.

"File:Seizure of the Zaibatsu families assets.JPG." Wikimedia Commons, the free media repository. 16 Nov 2019, 07:47 UTC. 5 May 2020, 05:44 <https://commons.wikimedia.org/w/index.php?title=File:Seizure_of_the_Zaibatsu_families_assets.JPG&oldid=375692205>.

"File:JapaneseSurrender.jpg." Wikimedia Commons, the free media repository. 17 Jul 2019, 18:08 UTC. 5 May 2020, 05:43 <https://commons.wikimedia.org/w/index.php?title=File:JapaneseSurrender.jpg&oldid=358468143>.

www.ingramcontent.com/pod-product-compliance
Lightning Source LLC
LaVergne TN
LVHW070122110826
845147LV00002B/169

* 9 7 8 0 5 7 8 6 8 9 9 7 5 *